THE TIMES | Mapping History

Medieval World

Incipit epistola sancti iheronimi ad
paulinum presbiterum de omnibus
diuine historie libris capitulū pmū.

Rater ambrosius
tua michi munus-
cula pferens detulit
sist et suauissimas
lras q a principio
amiciciaz fidei pba-
te iam fidei et veteris amicicie noua
pferebant. Uera eni illa necessitudo e
et xpi glutino copulata. quin non vtili-
tas rei familiaris. non pncia tantum
corpoz. non sbdola et palpās adulaco.
sed dei timoz. et diuinaz scripturarū
studia conciliant. legim̄ in veteribz
historijs quosdā lustrasse puincias.
nouos adijsse pplos. maria trāsisse.
ut eos quos ex libris nouerant. corā
qz viderēt. Sicut pitagoras memphi-
ticos vares. sic plato egiptū et architā
tarentinū. eandemqz oram ytalie. que
quondā magna grecia dicebaz. labo-
riosissime peragrauit. et ut qui athenis
mgr̄ erat. et potens. cuiusqz doctrinas
achademie gignasia plonabāt. fieret
pegrinus atqz discipulus. malēs aliena
verecude discere. quin sua ipudenē ingere.
Denicqz cū lras quasi toto orbe fugien-
tes psequiz. captus a piratis et venūda-
tus. tyrāno crudelissimo paruit. ductus
captiuus vinctus et seruus. Tamē quia
pphus maior emente se fuit. ad tytum
tiuiū. lacteo eloquēcie fonte manantē.
de vltimis hispanie galliarūqz finibz.
quosdam venisse nobiles legimus. et
quos ad contemplacionē sui roma nō
traxerat. unius hois fama pduxit. Ha-
buit illa etas inauditū ōnibz seculis.
celebrandūqz miraclm. ut urbē tantā

ingressi: aliud extra urbem quererent.
Apolloniꝰ siue ille magꝰ ut vulgus
loquitur. siue phus. ut pitagorici tra-
dunt. intrauit psas. ptāsiuit caucasū.
albanos. scithas. massagetas. opule-
tissima indie regna penetrauit. et ad
extremum latissimo physon ampne
trāsmisso puenit ad bragmanas. ut
hyarcam in throno sedentē aureo et de
tantali fonte potantem. inter paucos
discipulos: de natura. de moribz. ac de
cursu diez et sidez audiret docentem.
Inde p elamitas. babilonios. chalde-
os. medos. assyrios. parthos. syros.
phenices. arabes. palestinos. ruisus
ad allexandriā: perrexit ad ethiopiā.
ut gignosophistas et famosissimam
solis mensam videret in sabulo. Jn-
uenit ille vir vbiqz qꝙ disceret. et semp
profichēs. semp se melior fieret. Scrip-
sit super hoc plenissime octo volumi-
nibus: phylostratus.

Quid loquar de seculi hominibz.
cū apostolus paulus: vas eleccōis.
et magister gencū. qui de consciencia
tāti ī se hospitis loquebaz. dicēs. An
experimentū queritis eius qui in me
loquif xpc. Post damascū arabiāqz
lustratā: ascēdit iherosolimā ut vider
petrū et māsit apud eū diebz quindeci.
Hoc eni mistio ebdomadis et ogdo
adis: futurꝰ gencū pdicator instruen-
dus erat. Rursūqz post ānos ꝗtuor-
decim assumpto barnaba et tyto: expo-
suit cū apostolis euāgeliū. ne forte in vacuum curreret aut cucurrisset. Habet
nescio ꝙd latentis energie: viue vocꝭ
actus. et in aures discipli de auctoris
ore transfusa: forcius sonāt. Unde et
eschineus cū rodi exularet. et legeretur

THE TIMES | Mapping History

Medieval World

Rosamond McKitterick

Times Books

First published in 2003 by
TIMES BOOKS,
HarperCollins*Publishers*
77–85 Fulham Palace Road
Hammersmith, London W6 8JB

The HarperCollins website address is
www.harpercollins.co.uk

British Library Cataloguing in Publication Data:
A catalogue record is available from the British Library

Printed and bound in Italy by Editoriale Johnson

ISBN 0 0071 4195 5

THE TIMES MEDIEVAL WORLD
EDITED BY ROSAMOND MCKITTERICK

HARPERCOLLINS*PUBLISHERS*:

EDITORIAL DIRECTION: Philip Parker

EDITORIAL AND PICTURE RESEARCH: Céire Clark, Terry Moore

D&N PUBLISHING

EDITORIAL AND DESIGN DIRECTION: David Goodfellow

EDITORIAL: Elizabeth Mallard-Shaw

DESIGN: Shane O'Dwyer

PROOF-READING: Michael Jones

CARTOGRAPHIC AND DESIGN DIRECTION: Martin Brown

INDEX: Hilary Bird

ADDITIONAL PROOF-READING: Margaret Gilbey

ADDITIONAL CARTOGRAPHY:
Cosmographics, Watford, England

The publishers would also like to thank Martin Allen,
Department of Coins and Medals, Fitzwilliam Museum,
Cambridge; Alex Barrett, akg-images; Robert D. Fiala;
Daniel J. Gritten; Kevin Kosbab; the Master and Fellows of
Trinity College, Cambridge; Julia Szcuka

Contributors

ROSAMOND MCKITTERICK, Professor of Medieval History, University of Cambridge
10-27, 32-53, 56-67, 94-121, 152-155, 166-167, 194-197, 206-207, 270-273, 280-287

DAVID ABULAFIA, Professor of Mediterranean History, University of Cambridge
54-55, 220-221, 232-233, 238-239, 246-247, 278-279

DAUD ALI, Lecturer in the Early History of South Asia, School of Oriental and African Studies, University of London
86-89, 184-187

NORA BEREND, Lecturer in Medieval History, University of Cambridge
126-137, 148-151, 198-201

MARK CHINCA, Senior Lecturer in German, University of Cambridge
244-245

KATE FLEET, Curator, Skilliter Centre for Ottoman Studies, Newnham College, Cambridge
252-255

TIMOTHY N. HARPER, Lecturer in Imperial and Extra-European History, University of Cambridge
90-91, 188-189, 266-267

JOHN HENDERSON, Wellcome Trust Reader in Renaissance Medicine, School of History, Classics and Archaeology, Birkbeck College, London
212-215

CATHERINE HOLMES, Fellow and Praelector in History, University College, Oxford
138-141, 248-251

TIMOTHY INSOLL, Lecturer in Archaeology, School of Art History and Archaeology, University of Manchester
192-193, 268-269

PETER JACKSON, Professor of Medieval History, University of Keele
172-183

PETER F. KORNICKI, Professor of Japanese History and Bibliography, University of Cambridge
258-265

BEAT KÜMIN, Lecturer in Early Modern European History, University of Warwick
208-211

NIELS LUND, Professor of History, University of Copenhagen
196-197

JULIAN MARCUS LUXFORD, Lecturer in the History of Art, University of St Andrews
156-159, 240-243

JOSEPH P. MCDERMOTT, University Lecturer in Chinese History, Faculty of Oriental Studies, and Fellow of St John's College, Cambridge
92-93, 190-191, 256-257

DAVID MCKITTERICK, Fellow and Librarian, Trinity College, Cambridge
274-277

JAMES E. MONTGOMERY, Reader in Classical Arabic, University of Cambridge
78-85, 142-145, 170-171, 228-231

HELEN J. NICHOLSON, Senior Lecturer in Medieval History, University of Cardiff
146-147

DAVID PALLISER, Professor of Medieval History, University of Leeds
160-165, 234-237

DANIEL POWER, Lecturer in Medieval History, University of Sheffield
122-125

STEPHEN ROWELL, Professor of History, Lithuanian Institute of History (Liutuvos Istorijos Institutos) Vilnius, Lithuania
202-207

PETER SARRIS, University Lecturer in Early Medieval History, Trinity College, Cambridge
28-31, 72-77

PAUL STEPHENSON, John W. and Jeanne M. Rowe Professor of Byzantine History, University of Wisconsin - Madison and Dumbarton Oaks
68-71, 168-169, 222-223

ROBERT N. SWANSON, Professor of Medieval Ecclesiastical History, University of Birmingham
224-227

JOHN L. WATTS, Fellow and Tutor in Modern History, Corpus Christi College, Oxford
216-129

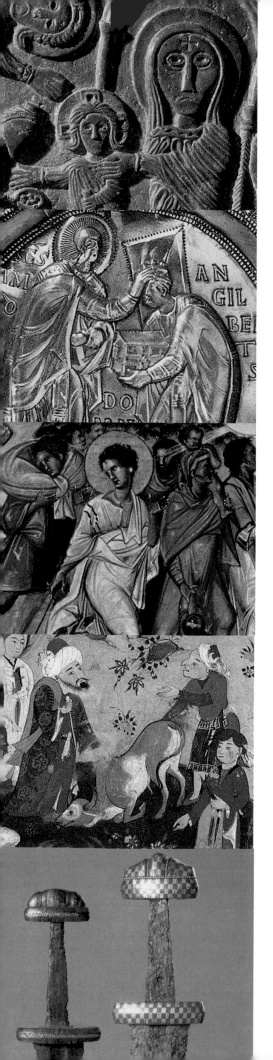

CONTENTS

Contents

PREFACE

The Times Medieval World embraces a period of remarkable cultural vibrancy and political diversity. From the Frankish expansion within western Europe and the creation of the Islamic empire in the Middle East, north Africa and the western Mediterranean to the European colonization of the Americas, the medieval world was a dynamic complex of contrasting and often competing cultures, which together established, over the thousand years between *c.* 500 and *c.* 1500, the foundations of modern societies.

The cartographic history offered in this book is designed to provide a spatial and visual interpretation of the remarkable developments of medieval society. The primary focus of this book is on medieval Europe in the widest possible sense of that elastic term, for the concept itself was coined by European Renaissance scholars. But comparison is made, whether in separate maps or in some of the thematic spreads, with other parts of the rest of the world. In Europe, the book covers the emergence of the Germanic successor states to the Roman empire, the expansion of Islam across the Mediterranean, the dominance of the Frankish empire within western Europe in the earlier Middle Ages (and its interrelations with its neighbours, such as the English, the Danes, the Slavs, Arabs, Croats, Bulgars and Greeks), the formation of centralized states and Christian monarchies in western central and eastern Europe (culminating in the conversion from paganism of the Grand Duchy of Lithuania in the 14th century), the formation of Russia, the retraction of the Byzantine empire in the Balkans, and the emergence of new Slav and Bulgar polities. Political and cultural developments elsewhere in the world, however, provide many interesting parallels and contrasts, from the empires of Ghana, Mali and Songhay in Africa, the Sultanate of Delhi and its successor states, the kings of Cambodia with power centred on Angkor, the end of the Tang dynasty in China and the fragmentation of east Asia to the conquests of Chingghis Khan and his successors and the Malaysian thalassocracy.

Trading links, uncovered in recent years as a result of new work on inscription evidence and marine and field archaeology, are not to be underestimated. They reveal a great amount of information about cross-cultural influences in this period. The work of early missionaries of the different religions, such as the Christians who travelled to Scandinavia and the Slav regions, or the Buddhists who journeyed from India to Japan, also provided connecting threads that bound the world together.

The Christian religion, despite the differences between the Catholic and the Orthodox churches and the presence of Muslims, Jews and many different groups of pagans, created, together with the inheritance of the Roman past, elements of a common culture in Europe as a whole. This acted as a strong magnetic field. It is these elements, of as great an influence on European society as the political developments, which this book will also chart. Further, economic growth and the stimulation of trade in the North Sea, Baltic and Mediterranean regions fostered the establishment of new settlements. In due course, the venturing of merchants and travellers ever further afield, overland to the east as well as out into the Atlantic and down the African coast, brought Africa, Asia and in due course the Americas into contact with Europe. Leif Ericsson's discovery of Newfoundland *c.* 1000, Marco Polo's famous travels to China in the 13th century, the Arab voyages to India and southeast Asia or the Portuguese navigators' explorations to Africa in the 15th century, provide only a few examples from the period. Only the Americas have largely been omitted from this book, for the simple reason that they have already been allocated space in the companion *Times Ancient Civilizations*. Chronologically, however, the Maya, Aztecs and Toltecs, Tiwanako, Chimu and Inca in Central and southern America, and the indigenous peoples of North America also have a place in the histories charted in this volume. It has also not been possible to do more than provide brief indications of developments in the Pacific regions and Australasia.

The book falls into three sections after a three-part introduction, namely, I, *c.* 700–*c.* 1000; II, 1000–1300; III, 1300–1500. Each section includes maps charting political developments in particular regions as well as thematic spreads. Some themes taken up in one section will sometimes cover much of the period of another. A composite Bibliography provides suggestions for further reading and a Glossary amplifies information on particular individuals and topics.

It remains for me as Editor to thank the consultant editors who have enriched this book with their expertise on such a diversity of topics and the designer Shane O'Dwyer and cartographer Martin Brown, who have so ably given shape to our ideas. I am grateful to the staff of the Map Room in Cambridge University Library for all their help. Above all, I am indebted to Philip Parker of HarperCollins, whose profound knowledge, enthusiasm, precision and hard work on the book have been a constant inspiration.

Rosamond McKitterick

August 2003

INTRODUCTION

The medieval world is part of our modern culture. For one thing, it is visible. There are many surviving buildings (churches and cathedrals, castles), town walls, earthworks and street plans, some standing as ruins, others integrated into the fabric of our own daily life but all contributing substantially to the shaping of the physical landscape. There is a wealth of objects from the most humble cooking pot or spade to the spectacular works of art for the ruling elites. There are vast archives of text, with inscriptions and documents relating to every aspect of daily life – letters, laws, legal and governmental records and books on every imaginable subject. Yet the less obvious contribution of the Middle Ages to the modern world is the institutional and cultural legacy, which is one of the themes of this book.

A symbol of this legacy, at least for Europe, is Jerome's Latin Vulgate translation of the Bible. As the book of the Christian faith, it was also the most central and influential text in western medieval culture as a whole. Quite apart from the Jewish and Christian traditions expressed in the Old and New Testaments, the Bible acted as a focus for political ideology, examples, prophetic inspiration, historical knowledge, good stories, scholarly exegesis and theology. Now in Paris at the Bibliothèque National, this particular copy of the Bible was also known as the Vivian Bible or First Bible of Charles the Bald (840–877). It is one of the many Bibles mass-produced in enormous single volumes at Tours in the ninth century, with the text edited, corrected and tidied up by Alcuin of York. Its lavish decoration, in purple and gold and rich ornament made it a gift fit for the King of the Franks to whom it was presented in c. 846. Its many scripts, including Roman capitals, uncial script used for prefaces and headings, half-uncial for introductions and the new script, caroline minuscule, for the main text, comprise both sets of letter forms from the old Roman script system and a newly evolved book hand. These together symbolize the reception by the Franks in the eighth and ninth centuries of Roman culture and their creative departure from it. The initial "D" with its depiction of Sol and the signs of the zodiac indicates that the classical, and especially Roman, inheritance was as important as the Christian faith in the forming of medieval culture. But that classical inheritance played a crucial role in the Middle East as well, and networks of communication ensured that there was interchange at one level or another throughout the world.

The First Bible of Charles the Bald

Continuities and Discontinuities

The notions of continuity and discontinuity imply the recognition of a divide or great contrasts of some kind between the ancient and medieval worlds. The reality is far more complex, for the classical world was also one of enormous diversity. On the other hand, the great religions, especially Christianity and Islam, lent a strong coherence to vast tracts of the medieval world. In Europe there was a particularly strong blend of elements of classical, Christian and non-Roman culture. Violent and sudden physical upheaval was rare; instead there was steady transformation of the societies of the ancient world in the period covered in this volume.

Between the fifth and the eighth centuries, many things undoubtedly changed, most obviously in the forms of economic and social organization, the emergence of Germanic political and military elites in Europe and the steady consolidation of the Christian church. An early medieval traveller to Rome in the late eighth century would have found a city full of Roman buildings, walls, triumphal arches, columns and a multitude of magnificent churches erected from the fourth century onwards, mostly under the auspices of the popes. Such a visual experience of the Roman

past could be replicated in most of the many cities of the former empire which remained in continuous occupation. Not only did travellers reach them by means of the old Roman road network but they would be confronted on all sides by buildings that had existed there hundreds of years before their own time.

Both spaces and buildings, however, could be and were converted to other uses. The great imperial reception hall in Trier, for example, became a Christian church, and so also many pagan temples were consecrated to Christian and ecclesiastical use. Other municipal buildings, notably theatres and amphitheatres went out of use and were pillaged for building materials, or were occupied. At Arles, for instance, private houses began to encroach upon the amphitheatre as early as the sixth century. The theatre at Orange was used for courts of love and mystery plays in the Middle Ages. Not until the 16th century were small houses crowded in behind its great wall and on the tiers, only to be cleared again in the 19th century; the magnificent ruins have been used ever since as a theatre and opera auditorium once more. *Spolia*, in the form of gems, sculpture and building

Charlemagne's sarcophagus, Aachen Cathedral Schatzkammer

Charlemagne's (supposed) sarcophagus is made of Carrara marble and was carved – probably in Italy – in bas-relief sculpture depicting the Rape of Proserpina by the King of the Underworld. Dating from the third century and, therefore, reused, the identification of this sarcophagus as Charlemagne's is not completely secure, but it has been regarded as such from at least the late tenth century. Charlemagne was certainly buried at Aachen. During the Napoleonic wars, Bonaparte took the sarcophagus to Paris, for he regarded Charlemagne as his most illustrious predecessor. The sarcophagus was returned to Aachen in 1815 (remaining invisible to the public between 1843 and 1979) and was restored to its original glory for the Paderborn exhibition on Carolingian art and culture in 1999. That a Roman pagan sarcophagus should be regarded as a fitting tomb for a Christian emperor suggests a very complex attitude towards the Roman past on the part of the Franks.

Hagia Sophia, Istanbul
Visitors throughout the Middle Ages exclaimed at the wonder of this building. Built during the reign of the Byzantine emperor Justinian in the sixth century, this magnificent church cost 23 million gold solidi. It was a radical creation of vast spaces surmounted by a flattish dome 100 feet across and with half-domes and pendentives resting on massive piers and columns cased in coloured marble. All originally glittered with rich mosaics. It was designed by the mathematicians and engineers Anthemius of Tralles and Isidore of Miletus. It was stripped of most of its decoration after the fall of Constantinople to the Turks in 1453 but has remained, with added minarets, in use as a mosque since then.

Umayyad Mosque at Damascus
As the capital of the Umayyad Empire, the mosque at Damascus (constructed between 706 and 714/15 under al-Walid I) was a dramatic celebration of the power of the caliphs and of Islam. Yet it drew its inspiration, both in the arcading and in the interior embellishment with coloured marble and rich mosaics, from late antique Christian churches. Most of the Corinthian columns, moreover, were taken from older buildings in an apparently deliberate attempt to associate the caliphs with another imperial past.

material of all kinds can be found in many medieval artefacts, such as the antique engraved gems included as part of the decoration of the late ninth- to late tenth-century gold reliquary statue of Sainte Foy at Conques. Many physical elements of older cultures were no doubt reused by artisans for their aesthetic value, but their symbolic resonances for the contemporary viewer are not to be underestimated. Similarly, the invocation of Biblical or classical inspiration in art and literature, in law-making and political ideologies sprang from an understanding of the ways in which they could enhance the meaning and significance of words and objects.

Equally, emulation could reflect an appreciation and adoption of a different set of values, as in the case of the eighth-century bathhouse at Qasr al-Amrah east of Amman. This neat little structure is thought to witness to the Islamic elite's acceptance of the classical tradition of bathing as a social and cultural institution and to symbolize the continuity of urban civilization. What then are we to make

of Charlemagne bathing with his courtiers in the hot springs at Aachen? What might seem to be continuity could equally be conscious re-creation or creative introduction. In assessing the medieval world, it is necessary to be alert to unconscious emulation and assimilation, selection and rejection and new influences as well as continuities and discontinuities.

"Furthermore, beloved brother, you profess to be astonished that we call ourselves emperors, not of the Franks, but of the Romans; but you ought to know that we could not be emperors of the Franks without being emperors of the Romans. We took over this title and dignity from the Romans, for it is certain that this supreme and lofty title first shone forth among them; and we received from heaven this people and city to guide and the mother of all the churches of god to defend and exalt…

The Greeks for their 'cacodoxy', that is, wrong thinking, have ceased to be emperors of the Romans. Not only have they deserted the city and the capital of the empire, but they have also abandoned Roman nationality and even the Latin language. They have migrated to another capital city and taken up a completely different nationality and language."

Emperor Louis II, letter to the Byzantine Emperor Basil I, 871

Medieval Perceptions of the World

In the medieval west, geography was not a separate or defined discipline. Directed at a fuller understanding of the Bible, it concerned knowledge of nature and therefore of God. Because places from the historical past and from the afterlife were also included on many medieval maps, the dimension of time as well as of space is crucial to an understanding of medieval perceptions of the world.

Early medieval maps confound modern expectations. Few appear to have been used primarily to tell the viewer where something was. Rather, they expressed a world-view and a total understanding of the earth and man's place in it. Maps often included images from the Christian faith, from mythology, from the past, wonderful creatures and symbolic outer rings of water to represent oceans.

Nevertheless, surviving maps simultaneously reflect two practical developments in geography and mapping. The first is the attempt to represent the land masses, seas and human places on the earth's sphere.

There was no doubt throughout the Middle Ages that the earth was indeed a sphere. Only the question of whether or not the fourth continent posited in the antipodes was actually inhabited was disputed. Pythagoras surmised that the earth was a sphere and Aristotle confirmed his theory by means of observation of such phenomena as the horizon and the shadow of the earth. It was Aristotle's view – augmented by Eratosthenes' remarkably accurate calculation of the circumference of the earth (by spherical geometry) and Hipparchus' use of Babylonian mathematics to divide the globe into 360 degrees – which prevailed throughout the early Middle Ages. The great wars of conquest in the ancient world, not least those of Alexander the Great, did much to extend the knowledge of the world. Greek theory and ancient knowledge were preserved in the writings of a number of Roman geographers, such as Strabo, Pliny and Pomponius Mela, as well as encyclopaedists and geographers of the earlier Middle Ages such as Isidore of Seville and Dicuil in the seventh and ninth centuries respectively. Dicuil in particular only rarely departed from ancient sources to record new knowledge, such as his comments on the islands to the north of Britain and the extraordinary length of the night there during the winter.

The second development is shown in Roman land surveys preserved in texts known collectively as the *Corpus Agrimensores*, which provide precise indications for the geometrical survey and division of land and thus a very different visualization of space for practical purposes, including road building and military campaigns. There are indications that local and regional charts of routes and

(Right) *A copy of Martianus Capella,* On the Marriage of Mercury and Phililogy, *Book VI, showing the three continents surrounded by ocean with information about the dimensions of the world and the boundaries dividing the continents. These are the river Tanais, the Riphean mountains and Lake Meotis between Asia and Europe, Gades between Europe and Africa and the Nile between Asia and Africa.*

The earth is divided into three sections named Europe, Asia and Libya (Africa) and the deified Augustus was first to exhibit this by means of his world map. All my work takes its beginning then from the strait of Europe, which place the Greeks name the columns of Hercules... Priscian in his Periegesis says the following of the same island of Ceylon (Sri Lanka) and of two other islands: from here turning your ship's prow to the warm south winds you will come to Ceylon, the great island which produces elephants at the border of Asia. It lies under the Crab. About its shores leap numerous whales as large as mountains, fed by the vast Red Sea.

DICUIL, LIBER DE MENSURA ORBIS TERRAE, I,2 AND VII.31, C. 825.

a gaditano ostio ingressū interioris (mediterranei) maris p longitudinē cursus uix quindecim passuū milia numerant. Latitudo uero. ubi angustior quinq.; ubi diffusa septem. ubi aplior decē milib; expliat. Hinc defluere p diuersos sinus (s. a gaditano freto). subsidentes (i. iacentes) q. cāpos tot maria. tot fragores. & quantū p diuersa equora tumescit. Undarum ū illa ꝑruptio interfluentis oceani. leua europā facit. libiaq. dextra. & montib; utriq. concluditur. Nā europa calpe. africa abethna (l. auenna) monte despicitur. Qui utriq. ꝑminentes dici columne herculis meruerunt. qd testimonio uetustatis laboris herculei limes nullis sit consecutus. siquidē ultra (i. postes s. herculis) eū ꝑgredi consūpte telluris inuia ꝑhibebant. Denīq. etiā hoc de ei sacre uirtutis possibilitate psuasū. qd cū antea natura terris maria dispararet. ac tanto cingi circuitu firmaret oceani. montiū predictorū effossis radicib; diuulsoq. confinio camporū. deuexis (i. declinatis) lacunisq. terrarū. inprouisum pelagus in usu (i. in honore herculis) impigre mortalitatis admisit. ꝑmutans orbis faciē natureq. discrimina. Hoc igitur freto leuor sū europa distenditur. usq. in tanais fluminis gurgitē. a quo inchoans asia. nili eidem alueo limitat. Qui quidē nilus eandē africaq. dirumpens. telluris complexū intersecans multitudine fluuiorū. europā tamen interminari ꝑpontidis faucib; dicere quā plurimi. que ꝑpontidis p angustā descendens. ad meotidē quoq. perfertur.

Abethna uel auen[na] mons est in gadibu[s] iuxta calpen. qui p[a]riter dicuntur col[um]ne herculis. Ethna uero mons sicilie.

ASIA SCDA PARS MUNDI.
HABET IN LONGITUDINE M SEXAGIES TER. DCCL. Latitudine ab ethiopico mari ad alexandriā iuxta nilū sitā p meroen & sienen decies octies XXV.
NILUS.
tanais.
Meotides paludes.
Ryphei montes
EUROPA
habet in longū & latū octogies bis XC IIII.
AFRICA
que & Libia ultima pars longa tricies septies XC IIII. lata uersus cirenen DCCCC & X.
Gaditanū ostium

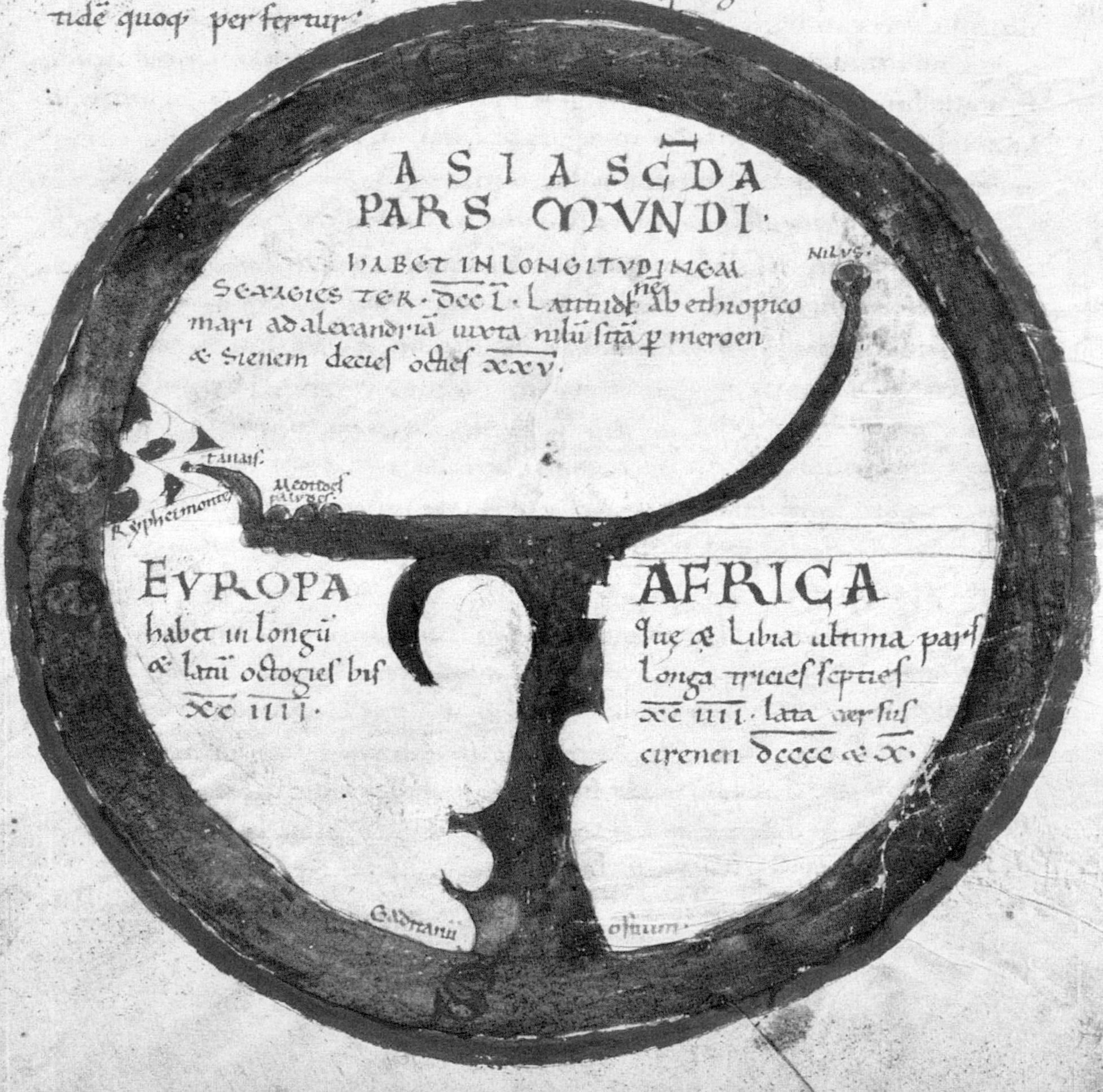

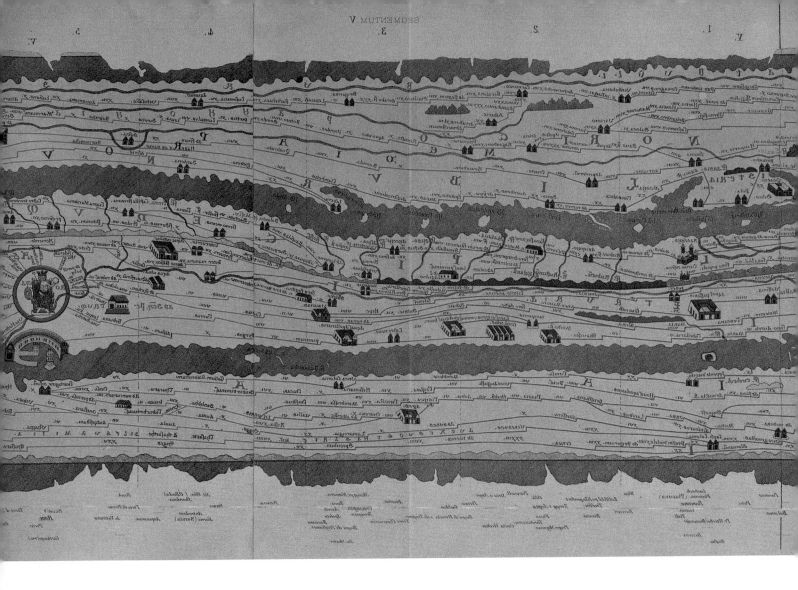

The Peutinger Map (above), a Roman road map with the physical features marked was found by Konrad Celtes (1459–1508) in Augsburg and acquired by Konrad Peutinger (1465–1547) and then Mark Welse who had it published by Aldus Manutius of Venice in 1591. Abraham Ortelius had new copies made of it and published them in engraved form in 1598. Ortelius' copy is in fact now the most reliable representation of it, given the deterioration of the original manuscript.

particular areas were created, of which the Peutinger Map is one of the few surviving remnants. Herodotus had referred to the world as divided into Europe, Asia and Libya (Africa). Many subsequent authors discussed the division of the world. In ninth-century representations of the world, often incorporated into the popular and widely-available encyclopaedic work of Isidore of Seville known as the Etymologiae, this three-fold division of the sphere of the

---

In reply to your query about the sphere for demonstrating the celestial circle and constellations, my brother, it is made completely round, divided equally through the middle by the circumference, which has been divided into sixty parts. Therefore, having placed the hemisphere in the aforementioned manner so that it is immovable, you will be able to determine the North Pole through the upper and lower first tube, the Arctic circle through the second, the summer through the third, the equinoctial through the fourth, the winter through the fifth, the Antarctic Circle through the sixth. As for the south Polestar, because it is under the land, no sky but earth appears to anyone trying to view it through both tubes.

GERBERT OF RHEIMS, LETTER TO CONSTANTINE OF FLEURY, *c.* 978, ON THE CONSTRUCTION OF A HEMISPHERE FOR MAKING ASTRONOMICAL OBSERVATIONS.

earth is represented in a graphically simple way in the form known as the T-O map. Other schemes divided the world into five climatic zones. Another approach can be seen in the maps illustrating Beatus of Liebana's commentary on the Apocalypse. The medieval circular or oval *mappae mundi* such as the famous Evesham map of 1390 and the Hereford map are particularly associated with England between *c.* 1200 and *c.* 1400. Most focus on France and England and their own locality, with the rest of the world clustered schematically around them, though the Hereford map is in effect a detailed T-O map, and attempts to chart cities in accurate relationship with each other. Thus medieval maps reflect the coming together of two different practical traditions and a particular religious perspective.

1456 Arab Map al-Idrisi (c. 1100–c. 1140) from a 12th-century original with south at the top. It records Arab knowledge of ancient geographers such as Ptolemy. Arabia is placed at the centre and many rivers and mountains are marked. That the Indian Ocean is left open reflects influences from Persia, China and India. The map was originally one of many included in The Book of Pleasant Journeys written for Roger II, King of Sicily.

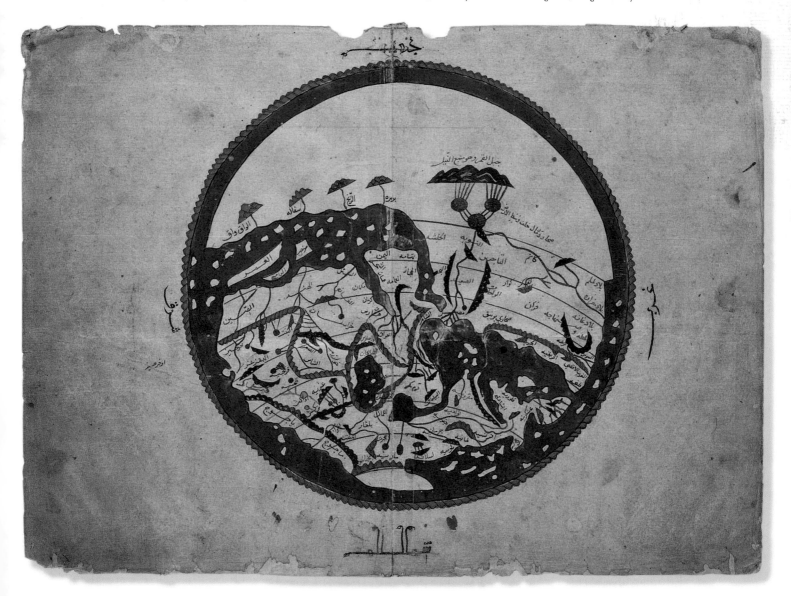

The Six Queens or saints, from the stucco relief sculpture in the church of Santa Maria in Valle, Cividale

The World In 700

By 700 the new political formations emerging from the Roman empire had achieved considerable definition, and the locations of power thereafter were to remain remarkably consistent in both Europe and further to the east and south. Despite fluctuations at the peripheries and volatile internal politics, political structures endured and lasting institutions were established.

A number of individuals undoubtedly possessed knowledge of the different regions of the world by this period, with the probable exception of the Americas. References in European texts preserve ancient, especially Greek, awareness of the lands to the east and south, such as central Asia, India and Africa, even if much may have been regarded as marvellous rather than real. Nonetheless, embassies, missionaries and others ventured far afield even if large movements of peoples were less common in the seventh and eighth centuries than they had been in the fourth, fifth and sixth. Thus Theodore (602–90), a Greek-speaking native of Tarsus in Asia Minor, ended his career as archbishop of Canterbury; Willibald of England (700–87) was imprisoned in Palestine charged with being a spy; and Arculf, a bishop from Frankish Gaul, was marooned on Iona for the winter and related his travels (c. 680) to the holy land to Abbot Adomnan. Moreover, the story is told in a seventh-century Frankish source of how, in the sixth century, a Christian wife of the Persian ruler had sought baptism in Constantinople. In the same text there is an account of a Frankish merchant named Samo who ruled as king of the Slavic Wends in central Europe in the early seventh century. Archaeological finds in eastern and western Europe, the Baltic and the Mediterranean, such as Arabic coins in Scandinavia and Chinese objects in the Danube, corroborate the existence of an extensive network of communications and dissemination of knowledge. Although surviving evidence from the various kingdoms of Europe, Asia, Africa and India shows that strong polities

This mosaic, dated 542–65, is preserved in the church of Madaba in Jordan. Places are indicated in Greek with notes that relate to why the place was important in Biblical history. They appear to have been located in relation to a road map as well as to the Onomasticon of Eusebius of Caesarea (260–340), a text describing the main sites of the Holy Land. The architectural depiction of churches and other structures in the places marked is sufficiently accurate for them to be identified. The portion illustrated here shows Jerusalem with its walls, the Damascus Gate, the central street and the church of the Holy Sepulchre, which are very prominent and enlarged on the map itself. The map's location in a Christian church indicates that this representation of Palestine and lower Egypt with Jerusalem at the centre was of religious significance and positioned so that the lay congregation would see it and be instructed by it. The whole map as preserved is 5×10.5 metres.

POLITIES OF THE MEDIEVAL WORLD C. 700

had been established all over the world, none was completely self contained. None, moreover, ignored its political inheritance in terms of both ideologies and practical institutions. And none displays a culture free from outside influences.

The world in 700 was certainly one for which the memory of the Roman empire remained strong. Each of the various successor states of western Europe was influenced to a greater or lesser degree by Roman institutions. Thus the Visigoths in Gaul and Spain, the Ostrogoths and Lombards in Italy, the Burgundians and Alemans in Gaul, Provence and Southern Germany, the Franks in Gaul and Germany, the Vandals in North Africa,

and even the polities of the English in Britain, the Arabs in Spain and the popes in Rome, all formed between the fifth and eighth centuries, owe something to a Roman past. Yet throughout the world, a striking feature of all these political systems was the great strength of the religious dimension within political ideology. Political leaders of great neighbouring polities also wished to establish or maintain diplomatic relations. Some, most notably Emperor Louis the Pious of the Franks (814–40) in the west, the Byzantine emperors in the East and the emperors of China, were able to sustain a remarkable network of diplomatic contacts and treaties with the peoples ringing their empires.

For the site of Jerusalem itself is so arranged by God, its founder, on a gentle incline, falling away from the northern summit of mount Sion to the low-lying regions at the northern and eastern walls, that this great flood of rain cannot by any means lie stagnant in the streets, but flows like torrents from the higher regions to the low-lying. The flood of heavenly waters, then, pouring through the eastern gates, and bearing all the filth and nuisance with it, enters the valley of Josaphat, swells the torrent of Cedron, and after such a baptism of Jerusalem straightway the copious flood ceases.

FROM ADAMNAN'S *DE LOCIS SANCTIS*

The Successor States To Rome

With the weakening of Roman imperial authority in the west during the fifth century, independent kingdoms were established in all the former provinces of the western Roman empire, usually with the romanized military leaders of the "barbarian" groups ruling over the civilian population. They maintained many of the elements of Roman provincial organization and government.

Relations with the Germanic peoples on the peripheries of the Roman empire are documented in the written and archaeological records from the first century AD. From the fourth century onwards groups identified by the Romans as Vandals, Sueves, Alans, Franks, Burgundians, Alemans, Goths and others advanced into Roman territory. Many had the status of federates, that is, supporting and defensive troops for the Romans. Others served as mercenaries or in the regular Roman army. Daily contact in the frontier regions undoubtedly contributed to the growing familiarity between the barbarians (or non-Romans) and Romans.

The eastern (Greek) and western (Latin) portions of the empire became increasingly distinct in the fifth century. The central control of the western emperor, in particular, steadily declined, with a reduction of interest and contact maintained between the emperor in Italy and the other western provinces in Spain, Gaul, Germany, the Danube region and Britain. Even in Italy, the commanders-in-chief of the army were the effective rulers. Finally, one of them, Odoacer, deposed the young western emperor Romulus Augustulus and assumed control, only to be replaced in his turn by a newcomer from the east, Theodoric the Ostrogoth. Although Theodoric appears to have invaded Italy at the request of the eastern emperor Zeno, he assumed independent command as king in the Italian peninsular.

Romulus's removal inaugurated the mostly peaceful creation of independent polities in all the other former western provinces. Local office-holders and powerful landowners – whether germanic warriors who had hitherto been part of the Roman military regime, long-romanized native and Roman aristocracy (many of whom were Christian bishops), or a coalition of all these elements – took over. The Franks in Gaul, the Visigoths in southern Gaul and subsequently Spain, the Vandals in Africa and the Burgundians in Provence were notably successful in this respect. In Britain, the Romano-Britons appear to have given way before the Angles and Saxons, though the early developments of the English kingdoms remain extremely uncertain in the light of the ambiguous evidence. It is not until the seventh century that the configurations described by Bede in his *Ecclesiastical History of the English People* begin to emerge. There

The silver gilt hen and chicks, practically life size, now in the Cathedral Treasury in Monza, are thought to be a gift from Pope Gregory I (590–604) to the Catholic Queen Theodelinda of the Lombards, though some suggest a later date and non-Roman origin for the workmanship.

378	451	476	481	507	511
The Goths defeat the Emperor Valentinian and his army at the Battle of Adrianople	The Huns led by Attila are defeated by Romans in alliance with Burgundians and Franks at the Battle of the Catalaunian fields	Deposition of Romulus Augustulus by Odoacer, the Skyrian commander in chief of the Roman army	Clovis becomes king of the Franks in northern Gaul	Battle of Vouillé and Clovis drives the Visigoths from Gaul	Clovis divides the kingdom among his sons

THE SUCCESSOR STATES TO ROME 418–568

Despite the new political configurations in the aftermath of the deposition of the last Roman emperor in the west, much of the old Roman way of life survived. The Vandal and Ostrogothic kingdoms were briefly reconquered by Byzantine troops from the east in the sixth century though the Byzantines gave way before the Arabs and Lombards respectively.

The Visigoths
- approximate extent of the Visigothic kingdom, 418
- added by, 475
- lost in 507
- Visigothic Kingdom, 555

The Ostrogoths
- Ostrogothic kingdom, 453–74
- approximate extent of the Ostrogothic kingdom, 474–88
- Ostrogothic kingdom, 493
- under loose Ostrogothic control
- added, 508

The Vandals
- secured by the Vandals, 431
- added in 439
- added by c.460

- Frankish kingdom, 511
- conquered by Byzantine empire, 532–65
- Lombard kingdom, 732

533–534	534	536	536–561	561, 567	568
Byzantine reconquest of North Africa	Conquest of Burgundian kingdom by Franks	Provence ceded to the Franks by Theodoric the Ostrogoth	Ostrogothic wars in Italy	Partitions of the Frankish kingdoms. The latter forms Neustria, Austrasia and Burgundy, which remain important political divisions in France subsequently	Establishment of Lombard kingdom in Italy and Byzantine exarchate based on Ravenna.

were attempts on the part of the eastern emperor Justinian in the sixth century to reconquer the western empire. These, apart from the exarchate of Ravenna, were short-lived. The Byzantine-Gothic wars in Italy, however, enabled the Lombards to invade northern Italy and establish a new kingdom based on Pavia.

In all these successor states, government was based on the foundations of Roman provincial administration. Any emotional talk of invasion and destruction simply does not accord with the predominant picture we have of steady assimilation and a gradual transformation of society. The successor states had at their head Christian kings who assumed responsibility for leading the army, for dispensing justice and for maintaining peace. In this, they were assisted by a cohort of secular and clerical magnates. Rewards for their services gradually were offered in land rather than money and thus a new pattern of the politics of land emerged that was to dominate the earlier Middle Ages.

The Frankish kingdoms under the Merovingians

The Franks in Gaul established the most successful of all the barbarian states (map right). Clovis, king from 481–511, established the tradition of partition of the kingdom. The partitions of 561 and 567 were crucial for the subsequent political development of the Frankish kingdoms. In England, coherent kingdoms had begun to emerge by the seventh century, though they were far less Roman in character than their counterparts on the Continent.

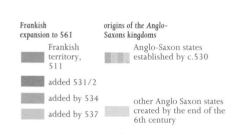

Frankish expansion to 561	origins of the Anglo-Saxons kingdoms
Frankish territory, 511	Anglo-Saxon states established by c.530
added 531/2	
added by 534	other Anglo Saxon states created by the end of the 6th century
added by 537	

<table>
<tr><td>589
Conversion of Visigoths in Spain from Catholicism to Arianism</td><td>614
Chlotar II sole king of the Franks; death of Brunhild. The Edict of Paris articulates a role for both king and aristocracy in the maintenance of law and order</td><td>629–638
Dagobert sole king of the Franks</td><td>657–664/5
Regency of Queen Balthild in Neustria</td><td>687
Battle of Tertry and Pippin I, mayor of the palace in Austrasia assumes control of the Merovingian kingdom</td><td>711
Arabs take over Visigothic Spain</td><td>714
Death of Pippin II, Carolingian mayor of the palace.</td></tr>
</table>

The jewelled ceremonial votive crown of the Visigothic King Recceswinth (649–672), now in the Museo Arqueologico in Madrid, expresses his Christian kingship. The workmanship is influenced by Italian metalwork techniques and design and the letters spell out his name.

"It is the practice of the princely clemency to consider with prudent care what the provincials and all people subject to him require and to draw up a constitution arranged in titles whatever must justly be attended to for their contentment."

Edict of Paris, 14th October, 614

The Arab Conquests of the Middle East, Eastern and Western Mediterranean

Between 632 and 651 the East Roman and Persian empires were overwhelmed by armies of Arabs united by the new religion of Islam. For the first time since the conquests of Alexander the Great a thousand years earlier, the lands of Egypt, the Fertile Crescent, and Persia were united into a political, administrative and economic whole, thus allowing a new civilization to take shape.

In much of western Europe the fifth century had seen the fading away of the structures of the Roman state. In the eastern Mediterranean, however, the Roman empire had survived. The Balkans, Asia Minor, Anatolia, Syria, Palestine and Egypt remained part of a Roman world focused politically and administratively on the city of Constantinople. During the reign of Emperor Justinian (527–65) direct imperial control was reasserted over north Africa, Italy and part of Spain. To the east, however, Roman power faced a belligerent foe in the form of the Sassanid Empire of Persia, with which warfare escalated in the course of the sixth century. This culminated in the Persian conquests of Syria, Palestine and Egypt between 603 and 620. The Roman emperor Heraclius later reversed these losses. By the early 630s, both empires were militarily and financially exhausted.

The rivalry between the two great powers involved them in military and diplomatic dealings with the Arabian tribes to their south. This appears to have sparked-off a "nativist revolt" amongst elements within Arabian society. By the 620s, the tribes of Arabia had come to be united under the leadership of a religious leader originating from Mecca, known as the Prophet Mohammed. Mohammed preached a rigorously monotheist doctrine, strongly influenced by apocalyptic trends within contemporary Christianity, and by Messianic fervour amongst the Jews of the region. Divine judgement was imminent, and all were to submit themselves to the will of the one God. In particular, all Arabs were to set aside their former

The Ka'ba in the Majid al-Haram, Mecca: the principal shrine of Islam (right).

Until c. 622 Mohammed's followers prayed in the direction of Jerusalem. Thereafter they were instructed to pray towards the Black Stone contained in the shrine. This had been a long-standing focus of cultic devotion, drawing on Pre-Islamic Arabian traditions of "litholatry" or "stone worship".

"What do you say, Rabbi, about the prophet who has appeared amongst the Saracens?" And he groaned loudly and said "He is false, for surely the prophets do not come with sword and chariot ... I fear lest the Christ who came first, whom the Christians worship, was himself he that was sent by God" ... And I Abraham made enquiry and learned from those that had met him, that you find nothing true in the so-called prophet, save shedding the blood of men; for he claims to hold the keys to paradise, which is untrue."

FROM *THE DOCTRINES OF JACOB THE RECENTLY BAPTIZED JEW* – A PROPAGANDISTIC BYZANTINE SOURCE OF THE 630S. THE RAPID EXPANSION OF ISLAM INSTILLED TERROR THROUGHOUT THE CHRISTIAN WORLD.

c. 610	622	630	632	636	638
Mohammed, a merchant from the Arabian city of Mecca, begins to receive visions of the Archangel Gabriel revealing to him the will of the one true God, on the basis of which Mohammed begins to preach his new religion. These visions will later be collected together in the form of the Qu'ran	In response to a plot to murder him, Mohammed and his followers flee from Mecca to the town of Medina. This migration, known as the Hijra or "flight", is taken as marking year one of the Muslim calendar	After a protracted period of warfare between his followers in Medina and his Meccan opponents, Mecca capitulates to Mohammed. Most of the Arabian peninsula would appear to have been subject to his rule	Approximate date of Mohammed's death. A number of Arab tribes revolt against Islam in the so-called Riddah or wars of "apostasy". Under the rule of Abu Bakr (632–34) these revolts are crushed. Incursions into Byzantine territory then begin	The Byzantine field army is decisively beaten at the battle of Yarmuk. Imperial forces are evacuated from Syria	Victorious Arab forces enter Jerusalem: the relic of the "True Cross" falls into Muslim hands and is probably destroyed

traditions and embrace the new faith. In return, Mohammed declared that God would grant the Arabs (as descendants of Abraham's first-born son, Ishmael) mastery over the Holy Land that He had promised to Abraham and his seed forever. This return to the Holy Land was to be achieved by means of holy war.

Mohammed died around 632, but his creed lived on. From 633/4, Roman Palestine suffered savage Arab incursions that combined the terrorizing and massacring of the rural population with assaults on towns and cities. Although the size of the Arab armies would appear to have been relatively small, the imperial authorities were in little position to offer effective resistance. Faced with such a situation, a number of cities in Palestine and Syria simply capitulated. The city of Damascus was taken in 635, whilst in 636 a large Roman army was decisively defeated near the river Yarmuk in northern Jordan. Thereafter, conquest was swift. Jerusalem fell in 638. The following year retreating Roman forces were pursued into Egypt. Only as they found themselves forced back into Anatolia and Asia Minor were the Roman commanders able to begin to stem the enemy advance. The capital of the Sassanid empire at Ctesiphon fell to the forces of Islam in the same year as Jerusalem. Soon Persia was subjected in its entirety. Conquest continued apace: by 705 North Africa had been overrun, and in 711 victorious Arab armies entered Spain. From their capital at Damascus, the early Islamic Caliphs ruled over an empire of enormous extent within which the Muslims remained a small and vulnerable governmental elite. Pre-existing Roman and Persian administrative structures were maintained until c. 700, when Arabic finally became the official language of state and a new Islamic governmental system began to emerge.

(Above) *An Islamic gold coin minted in Syria in 696–97 under the Caliph 'Abd al-Malik. The coin would appear to depict a representation of the Caliph holding a sword. Until the late seventh century the caliphal authorities issued mock Byzantine coins in the former Roman territories, and mock Sassanid coins in the Persian domains. At the end of the century a uniform Islamic coinage was introduced from which all figural images were removed.*

The Arab Conquests to 750

- growth under Mohammed
- growth under first four caliphs (632-661)
- expansion of Umayyad Caliphate (661–750)
- routes of advance
- **638** date of Muslim conquest

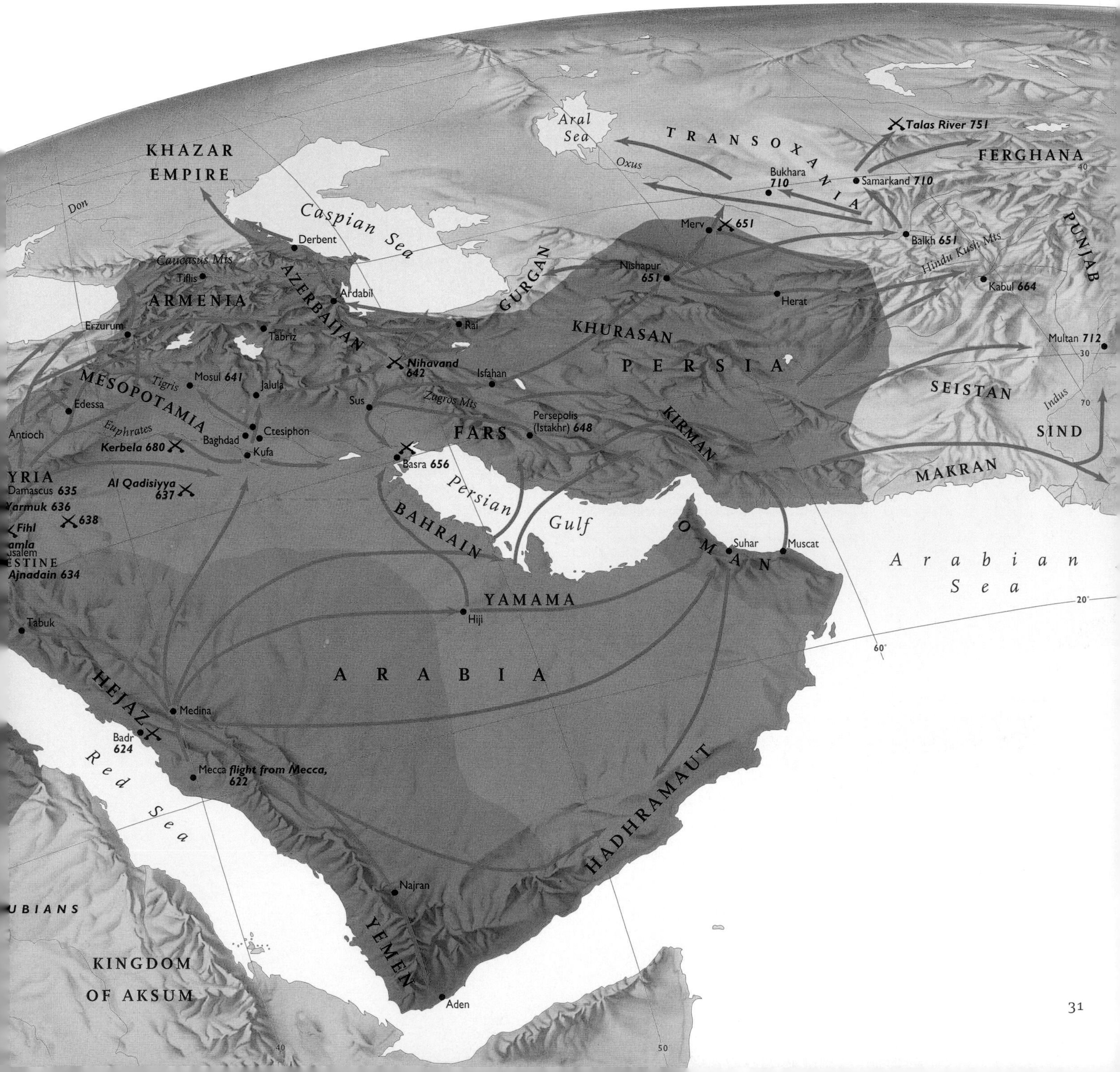

KHAZAR EMPIRE
Don
Caspian Sea
Aral Sea
Oxus
TRANSOXANIA
Talas River 751
FERGHANA
Bukhara 710
Samarkand 710
Merv 651
Balkh 651
Hindu Kush Mts
PUNJAB
Kabul 664
Nishapur 651
Herat
GURGAN
Derbent
Caucasus Mts
Tiflis
ARMENIA
AZERBAIJAN
Ardabil
Rai
KHURASAN
Erzurum
Tabriz
Multan 712
Nihavand 642
Isfahan
PERSIA
MESOPOTAMIA
Mosul 641
Jalula
Tigris
Edessa
Sus
Zagros Mts
Persepolis (Istakhr) 648
KIRMAN
SEISTAN
Indus
SIND
Antioch
Euphrates
Baghdad
Ctesiphon
Kufa
Kerbela 680
FARS
Basra 656
MAKRAN
YRIA
Damascus 635
Yarmuk 636
Fihl
638
Al Qadisiyya 637
Persian Gulf
BAHRAIN
OMAN
Suhar
Muscat
Arabian Sea
amla
usalem
ESTINE
Ajnadain 634
YAMAMA
Hiji
Tabuk
ARABIA
HEJAZ
Medina
Badr 624
Red Sea
Mecca flight from Mecca, 622
HADHRAMAUT
Najran
UBIANS
YEMEN
KINGDOM OF AKSUM
Aden

The Rise of the Carolingians
in the Merovingian Kingdoms

Many leading families contended for power within the later Merovingian kingdom, but it was the Carolingians who emerged triumphant in the early decades of the eighth century. Their control was established by means of an extraordinarily effective combination of military and administrative genius and strong ideological underpinning as a result of ecclesiastical support.

The Merovingian rulers of the seventh century presided over a peaceful kingdom. It was also a period of ecclesiastical consolidation, with some missionary work in the north and east of the kingdom, many church councils convened, and much creative work in the spheres of canon law and liturgical composition achieved. The lives of many politically active bishops, subsequently regarded as saints, such as Eligius of Noyon (c. 590–660),

Audoin of Rouen (d. 639/643) and Leudegar of Autun (662–676), provide rich, if sometimes oblique, evidence for the politics and culture of the period.

The areas south of the Loire and east of the Rhine became increasingly independent of Merovingian dominance, though diplomatic relations with Spain and Italy continued to be of importance. Factions (in which the higher clergy were as much involved as the secular aristocracy) were a constant element in court-centred politics. One of these factions formed around the Arnulfing and Pippinid families led by Pippin I and his colleague Arnulf, subsequently bishop of Metz. Pippin and Arnulf are first mentioned in early medieval Frankish narrative histories as loyal supporters of the Merovingian king Chlothar II (584-629). It was from Pippin II, son of a union between Pippin's daughter and Arnulf's son, that the Carolingian family descended. Their descendants married into wealthy families and thereby enhanced their personal wealth and network of connections.

In 623, Chlothar II created the west Frankish subkingdom of Neustria for his son Dagobert I. This kingdom combined with Burgundy and the east Frankish kingdom of Austrasia to form the entire Frankish kingdom of the time. By the end of the seventh century the leading males of the Carolingian family had secured a firm monopoly of the senior political office of "mayor of the palace" in Austrasia, that is, the eastern part of the Merovingian kingdom, and extended their influence over Neustria and Burgundy as well. Pippin II's victory over the forces of the Neustrian mayor of the palace at the Battle of Tertry in 687 was decisive in this respect. On Pippin II's death in 714, however, the family fortunes foundered for a time. By 718, however, Pippin's bastard son Charles Martel had emerged triumphant in the face of Neustrian and Frisian opposition. Thereafter, he proceeded systematically to reconstitute the Merovingian kingdom as it had been at its height.

The book is a Gelasian Sacramentary, containing the texts of the masses and prayers for the liturgical year. In addition to the characteristically Merovingian fancy capitals it is written in a confident uncial script, though other parts of the manuscript are written in a distinctive "b-minuscule". Rome, Biblioteca apostolica Vaticana, reg. 316.

613	687	714–18	732–34	741	743
Chlothar II reunites the Merovingian kingdom with the assistance of Arnulf of Metz and Pippin I	Battle of Tertry. Pippin II, mayor of the palace in Neustria, assumes control of the Merovingian kingdom and the Merovingian ruler Theudebert III	Death of Pippin II. Charles Martel contends for power against Ragamfred of Neustria and Radbod, king of the Frisians	Battle of Poitiers. Charles Martel defeats the Arabs	Death of Charles Martel. His sons Pippin III and Carloman succeed him as mayors of the palace in Neustria and Austrasia	Carloman elevates the last Merovingian king, Chilperic III, to the throne

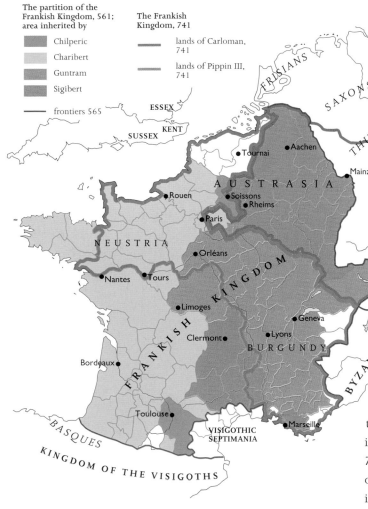

The rise of the Carolingians in the Merovingian Kingdom

The partition of the Frankish Kingdom, 561; area inherited by

- Chilperic
- Charibert
- Guntram
- Sigibert

— frontiers 565

The Frankish Kingdom, 741

— lands of Carloman, 741

— lands of Pippin III, 741

FRISIANS
SAXONS
THURINGIANS
ESSEX
KENT
SUSSEX

●Tournai
●Aachen
Mainz
●Würzburg

AUSTRASIA

●Rouen
●Soissons
●Rheims
●Paris

●Augsburg

NEUSTRIA

●Orléans

F R A N K I S H   K I N G D O M

●Nantes ●Tours

●Limoges

●Geneva

Clermont●
●Lyons

BURGUNDY

Bordeaux●

BYZANTINE EMPIRE

●Marseille

Toulouse●

VISIGOTHIC
SEPTIMANIA

BASQUES

KINGDOM OF THE VISIGOTHS

The Frankish kingdom, showing the Partition of 561 and the division of the Kingdom between Carloman and Pippin III in 741.

For [Pippin III's] father Charles Martel had brilliantly discharged the same civil office [of mayor of the palace], which had been laid down for him by his father Pippin II. This Charles overthrew those oppressors who claimed personal control over all of Francia and he so completely defeated the Saracens, who were attempting to conquer Gaul, in two great battles... that he forced them to fall back into Spain.

EINHARD, *VITA CAROLI*

All this time these powerful mayors of the palace had maintained Merovingian kings on the throne. Charles Martel's son, Pippin III, who succeeded his father in 741, after a period of co-rule with his brother Carloman, then took the revolutionary step of usurping the kingship itself in 751. The Royal Frankish annals (first written c. 783) assure us that this was with the advice and consent of all the Franks. The succession was also marked by the inauguration by the Frankish bishops of a new liturgical ritual of anointing the king. Pippin III thereupon embarked on a process of territorial expansion, ecclesiastical reform and administrative consolidation, including the assumption of control of the production of coinage. In 754 the pope crossed the Alps for the first time and consecrated Pippin, his wife and two sons as the new ruling family of Francia. Thereafter the Frankish kings' relationship with the pope and involvement in Italy was of major practical and theoretical importance. The relationship culminated in Pope Leo III consecrating Charlemagne, king of the Franks, as emperor of the Romans, an act that was to have far-reaching ideological repercussions in the succeeding centuries.

751	754	755	768	771
Pippin III deposes King Chilperic III and makes himself king of the Franks	Pippin III, his wife Bertrada and sons Charles and Carloman anointed by Pope Stephen II (III) in Francia	Capitulary of Herstal and reform of the Frankish coinage	Death of Pippin III. Conquest of Aquitaine completed. He is succeeded by his two sons who divide the kingdom between them	Charlemagne left as sole ruler of the Franks

Italy and the Lombards

Lombard Italy had developed a sophisticated political culture by the eighth century. Cities were important concentrations of local power, but the king and a network of dukes and public officials (gastalds and judges), who held local power, administered the fiscal property and the law. Despite its conquest by Charlemagne in 774, Italy retained its separate identity, though the emphasis in political life became increasingly that of city-centred politics.

The Lombards settled in northern and central Italy in the aftermath of the Gothic wars. They established dukedoms governing many of the major cities and formed, among others, the "duchies" of Spoleto, Friuli, and Benevento. The Lombard kings were elected from among the dukes.

Lombard monarchy was strong and perpetuated many Roman methods of government, with a written law code, coinage, production of legal documents, and law courts with specific personnel, the judges. A high level of Latin culture was maintained, mostly centred on the courts of the Lombard kings and the dukes of Benevento. Many of the Lombard kings attempted to expand the kingdom, most notably into the Byzantine territory of the exarchate of Ravenna and the papal states. The former comprised a territory affiliated to the Byzantine empire but peopled by a local military aristocracy. It was conquered by the Lombards in the middle of the eighth century. Although within the Byzantine orbit, Venice (under the doges from

The Altar of King Ratchis, c. 737
Depicting the adoration of the Magi, with an abstract presentation of the figures, in the chapter house of San Martino, Cividale, a church built by King Ratchis.

	secured from Byzantine Empire by Lombards by 590
	Byzantine territory conquered by Lombards and ceded to the Franks, 575
	Lombard conquests under King Agilulf, 590 – 615
	other 7th century Lombard conquests from the Byzantines (with dates)
	Papal State and Duchy of Rome
	8th century Lombard conquests from the Byzantines (with dates)
	Frankish territory conquered by Lombards (with dates)
	under Byzantine rule, c. 750
	recovered by Byzantines, c. 876 – 885
	conquered by Charlemagne, 774
	Duchy of Benevento, brought into dependency by Charlemagne, 787/9
	granted to Papal State by Charlemagne, 781–7

Trent

Como
Castelseprio
Brescia
Milan
Verona
Ivrea
Susa
Pavia
Po
Cremona
Mantua
Turin
Padua
Treviso *(c.644)*
Aquileia
Grado
Trieste
Torcello
Venice

ISTRIA

Tortona
Parma
Reggio
Ferrara
Bobbio
Bologna
Comacchio
Ravenna
(c.716)

Genoa
Imola
Rimini
(c.684)
(727- 43)
(730)
Pesaro
Fano
Senigallia
Ancona

(680)
Lucca
Arno
Urbino
PENTAPOLIS

TUSCANY
Volterra
Sienna
Gubbio
(727)

Perugia

Orvieto
Todi
Spoleto
SPOLETO
Rieti

Corsica
(c.725)
Ajaccio

Civitavecchia
Tiber
Rome
ROME
(c.702)
Isenia
(c.670)

BENEVENTO
GAETA
Gaeta
Benevento
Bari
Capua
Naples
CAPUA
(c.645)
APULIA
(c.670)
NAPLES
Amalfi
CALABRIA
AMALFI
SALERNO

Sardinia

Cagliari

Adriatic Sea

Tyrrhenian

Sea

Otranto

Crotone

BRUTTIUM

Squillace

Mediterranean

Messina
Reggio

Palermo

Taormina

Marsala

Sea

SICILY
Catania

Sicily
Syracuse

LOMBARD AND
CAROLINGIAN ITALY

Italy was essentially divided between three powers in the aftermath of the Ostrogothic wars, namely
the Lombard kingdom, the exarchate of Ravenna and the papal state. Southern Italy remained
to a considerable degree within the Byzantine orbit for much of the early middle ages.

But Liutprand indeed after he had held the sovereignty thirty one years and seven months, already mature in age, completed the course of this life, and his body was buried in the church of the blessed martyr Adrian, where his father also reposes. He was indeed a man of much wisdom, very religious and a lover of peace, shrewd in counsel, powerful in war, merciful to offenders, chaste, modest, prayerful in the night watches, generous in charities, ignorant of letters indeed yet worthy to be likened to philosophers, a supporter of his people, an increaser of the law.

FROM PAUL THE DEACON, *HISTORY OF THE LOMBARDS*

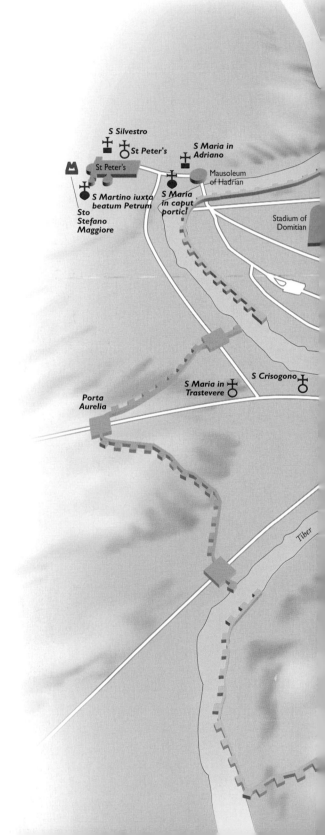

the ninth century onwards), on the other hand, remained independent and emerged as economically important, with many commercial links across the Adriatic and eastern Mediterranean.

Although the popes had consolidated their own secular power within the papal states (the Republic of St Peter), fear of Lombard aggression was a major factor in their seeking the support and protection of the Franks in the middle of the eighth century – first from Pippin III and subsequently from Charlemagne. The popes extended their spiritual influence even further with the missionary enterprises in northern and central Europe and the reforms of the Frankish church. Political influence from north of the Alps thereafter was a constant factor in papal domestic and foreign policy. Byzantium remained a focus of conflict over papal jurisdictions (secular and ecclesiastical) in southern Italy and Illyricum well into the tenth century.

When Charlemagne seized the Lombard kingship in 774, he established Carolingian rule, basing Franks in many of the duchies, bishoprics and abbacies of the kingdom. He installed his young son Pippin as subking of Italy, based at Pavia, preserving the identity of the kingdom of Italy as a separate entity. Nonetheless, between 774 and 840 Italy mostly had absentee or youthful kings. The emperor Lothar (817–55), for example, spent only the decade 831–41 in Italy, used it as a base for political and military forays north of the Alps, and totally subordinated the kingdom to Frankish interests. Subsequent Carolingian rulers, however, most notably Louis II, fiercely defended Italy's territory against outside encroachment or attack, especially from the Byzantines. The Carolingians largely maintained the administrative system established by the Lombards, with its public hierarchy of officials and a strong emphasis on legal documentation at all levels. To a considerable degree, the coherence of the Italian kingdom broke down after Louis II's death in 875. The kings, especially Berengar, relinquished royal control over too much land and too many rights to the church and the aristocracy, so that their power rarely extended much beyond their own areas of family land and lordship. Ottonian and German interest in Italy after 951 provided a semblance of coherence, but there was a marked shift from comital or marchesal to urban politics at the local level in the course of the tenth century.

CHRISTIAN ROME

Rome's topography was transformed in the early Middle Ages, with the focus of the city moving away from the forum to concentrations of the many new churches founded by successive popes to honour the saints and martyrs of early Christian Rome.

Legend:
- Aurelian walls
- Christian churches c. AD 500
- churches c. AD 500–600
- churches c. AD 600–750
- churches founded after AD 750
- major Latin monasteries to AD 700
- major Eastern monasteries to AD 700

Map labels:

Porta Flaminea
Porta Salaria
Porta Nomentana
Quirinal Hill
Baths of Diocletian
S Lorenzo in Lucina
S Vitale
S Andrea Catabarbara
S Maria in Aquiro
Viminal Hill
S Agata de Caballis
S Maris Maggiore
Pantheon
S Pude ziana
Esquiline Hill
Porta Tiburtina
stachio
S Maria inVia Lata
S Marcello
S Vito
S Bibiana
S Marco
S Agata dei Goti
SS Silvestro e Martino
Capitoline Hill
S Adriano
S Lucia in Selcis
S Martino ai Monti
Porta Praenestina
S Angelo Pescheria
SS Sergio e Bacco
SS Cosma e Damiano
S Pietro in Vincoli
Oppian Hill
S Giorgio in Velabro
S Teodoro
S Maria Antiqua
Palatine Hill
Colosseum
S Croce in Gerusalemme
S Anastasia
S Clemente
Imperial Forum
Circus Maximus
S Maria in Cosmedin
S Lucia in Septem Via
SS Giovanni e Paolo
Caelian Hill
S Greforio in Clivo Scauro
Lateran Basilica
S Erasmo
S Maria in Domnica
Porta Asinaria
S Sabina
Bonifazio Alessio
Aventine Hill
Sto Stefano Rotondo
Little Aventine Hill
SS Nereo ed Achilleo
S Sisto Vecchio
S Saba
Baths of Caracalla
Porta Ostiensis
Porta Latina
Porta Appia

37

The Empire Of Charlemagne And His Successors

The empire created by Charlemagne extended over most of what is now regarded as western Europe. For most of the ninth and tenth centuries this empire, or smaller kingdoms within it, were ruled by members of the Carolingian family. The separate kingdoms and territorial principalities which formed in the course of the tenth and eleventh centuries also had many political and legal institutions, and Christian and cultural traditions in common.

Pippin III's territorial expansion was triumphantly extended by his son Charlemagne with the conclusion of the conquest of Aquitaine (768), the conquests of the Lombard kingdom (774) and of the Saxons (completed by 797 after protracted campaigns), the annexation of Bavaria in 788, the submission of the Avars in 796, and the establishment of the Breton and Spanish marches between 800 and 813. Major expansion effectively ceased from about 803. Thereafter more military effort was expended on defence, such as the efforts to fight off Viking attacks, and occasional campaigns. Many of the latter were to support contenders for local power in peripheral territories, such as Ceadrag of the Obodrites in northern Germany and the Croatian prince Ljudovit in Dalmatia. Charlemagne's coronation in 800 recognized the territorial extent of his dominance over many regions, though the title made little practical difference to his actual power. In 806, Charlemagne stated his intention to divide his realm among his three sons. By 813, however, all his sons save Louis were dead. Louis inherited the entire empire and the imperial title and was crowned as emperor by his father shortly before Charlemagne's death.

Louis' reign sustained a skilful network of diplomatic relations with Danes, Slavs, the Islamic and Christian polities in Spain, the Croatians, the Byzantines and the papacy. Internally, however, he was increasingly beset by rivalries between his sons, rivalries which became open

768	773–74	778	782	788
Charlemagne succeeds to the Frankish kingship together with his brother Carloman	Lombard kingdom conquered	Defeat of Frankish army at Roncevaux and death of Count Roland (later celebrated in the *Chanson de Roland*)	Execution of 4,000 Saxon prisoners	Annexation of Bavaria by Charlemagne

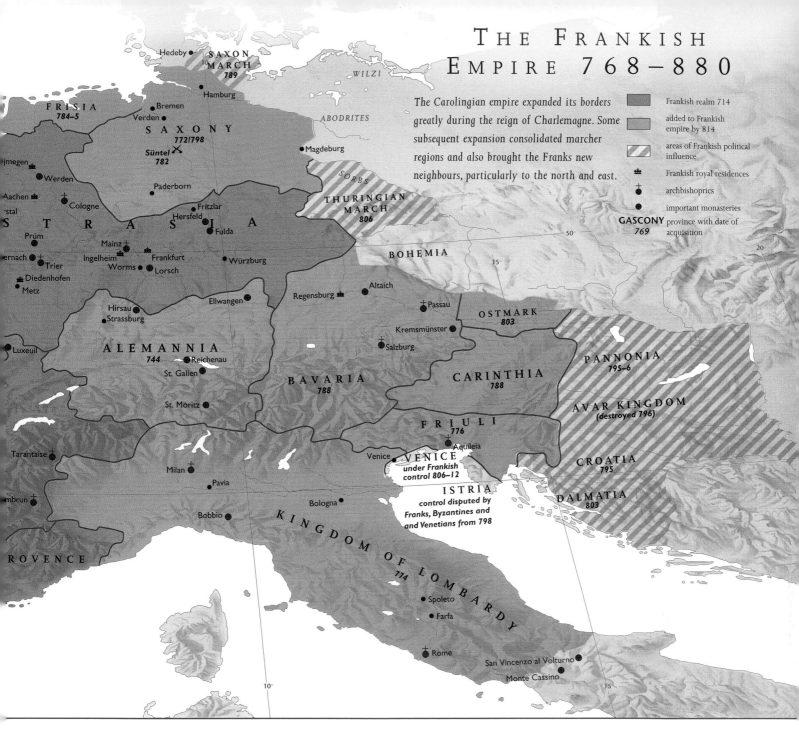

THE FRANKISH EMPIRE 768—880

The Carolingian empire expanded its borders greatly during the reign of Charlemagne. Some subsequent expansion consolidated marcher regions and also brought the Franks new neighbours, particularly to the north and east.

▨	Frankish realm 714
▨	added to Frankish empire by 814
▨	areas of Frankish political influence
⚜	Frankish royal residences
✝	archbishoprics
●	important monasteries
GASCONY *769*	province with date of acquisition

Map labels: Hedeby, SAXON MARCH 789, WILZI, FRISIA 784–5, Hamburg, Bremen, Verden, ABODRITES, SAXONY 772/798, Süntel 782, Magdeburg, jmegen, Werden, Paderborn, SORBS, Aachen, Cologne, stal, Fritzlar, THURINGIAN MARCH 806, AUSTRASIA, Hersfeld, Fulda, BOHEMIA, Prüm, Mainz, Würzburg, ernach, Ingelheim, Frankfurt, Trier, Worms, Lorsch, Diedenhofen, Metz, Hirsau, Regensburg, Altaich, Passau, OSTMARK 803, Strassburg, Ellwangen, Kremsmünster, Luxeuil, ALEMANNIA 744, Reichenau, Salzburg, PANNONIA 795–6, St. Gallen, BAVARIA 788, CARINTHIA 788, AVAR KINGDOM (destroyed 796), St. Moritz, FRIULI 776, Tarantaise, Aquileia, CROATIA 795, Milan, Venice, VENICE under Frankish control 806–12, Pavia, ISTRIA control disputed by Franks, Byzantines and Venetians from 798, DALMATIA 803, mbrun, Bologna, Bobbio, PROVENCE, KINGDOM OF LOMBARDY 774, Spoleto, Farfa, Rome, San Vincenzo al Volturno, Monte Cassino

war after Louis' death in 840. Only in 843 was the conflict resolved with the Treaty of Verdun, which divided the kingdom into East and West Francia and the Middle Kingdom. Subsequent divisions would alter the territorial extent of the Middle Kingdom so that it remained contested ground until 1945. Moreover, the essential partition created between the east and west Frankish kingdoms, and thus between what became France and Germany, has persisted ever since.

Viking attacks on the western kingdom concentrated Frankish efforts on a gradual and ultimately successful effort to integrate the Northmen into the politics of the kingdom, culminating in the establishment in 911 of the region which came to be known as Normandy. In

794	796	798	800
Council of Frankfurt. As well as dealing with religious and doctrinal issues Charlemagne reforms the coinage and regulates weights and measures	Destruction of Avar Ring and capture of the Avar treasure by the Franks	Subjugation of the Saxons by the Franks after 30 years of military campaigning	Charlemagne crowned by Pope Leo III as Emperor of the Romans in St Peter's church, Rome

Portrait of Charles the Bald enthroned, from the Codex Aureus of St Emmeram. The king is flanked by two armed men who will "serve Christ against his enemies", and personifications of Gotia and Francia. The hand of God appears above the king signifying God's protection and the king's source of authority.

812	813	814	843	875
Byzantium recognized Charlemagne as basileus	Charlemagne crowns his son Louis as emperor	Death of Charlemagne	Treaty of Verdun and tripartite division of the Carolingian empire	Charles the Bald, king of the west Franks (840–877), crowned emperor by Pope John VIII

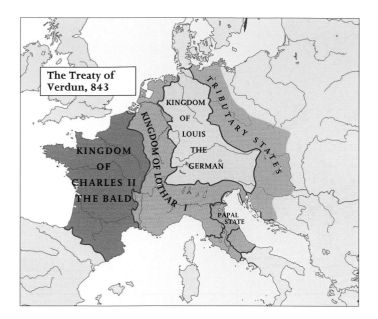

The division of the Carolingian empire at the Treaty of Verdun in 843, between the surviving sons of Louis the Pious: Lothar, Charles the Bald and Louis the German.

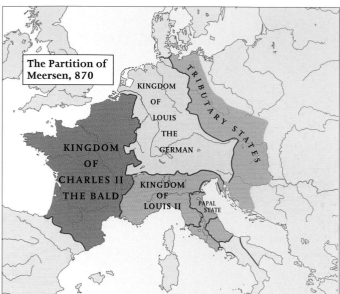

With the Treaty of Meersen in 870, Charles the Bald and Louis the German had divided Lotharingia between them. In 880 Carloman, king of the east Franks and heir of Louis the German, died and his territory was acquired by his brother Louis the Younger. Louis invaded the west Frankish kingdom and won more territory with the Treaty of Ribemont.

In the times of Charles the Great of good memory, who died almost thirty years ago, peace and concord ruled everywhere because our people were treading the one proper way, the way of the common welfare, and thus the way of God. But now each goes his separate way, dissension and struggle abound.

NITHARD, GRANDSON OF CHARLEMAGNE, WRITING IN 843, *HISTORIES OF THE SONS OF LOUIS THE PIOUS*, IV.7

---

the east Frankish kingdom, however, there was still room for expansion. Under special military organization, the marcher or frontier regions regulated Frankish relations with the neighbouring Slavic peoples, including the Ododrites, Linones, Sorbs and Daleminzi to the north and the Moravians, Bulgars, Bohemians and Slovenes to the south. As with the earlier conquests of the Frisians and Saxons by Pippin II, Charles Martel, Pippin III and Charlemagne, so later military action was often preceded or accompanied by missionary work. The consolidation of ecclesiastical organization proved an effective long-term means for cultural imperialism and the spread of Frankish influence and Latin Christianity over much of western Europe.

The Carolingian imperial ideal, with its connotations of Roman and Christian imperial rule in emulation of Constantine and Theodosius, played a powerful role in European political ideology. Although the Carolingian empire in due course separated out into many smaller kingdoms and duchies, common institutional, ideological and cultural elements nevertheless bound it together. The new Capetian dynasty in France, which replaced the Carolingian family in 987, ruled over a disparate group of semi-autonomous territorial principalities. The Ottonian rulers in Germany for their part built a new empire on the east Frankish foundations established by the Carolingians.

885–86	936	962	955	987
Viking siege of Paris	Otto I is crowned king at Aachen	Otto I crowned emperor by Pope John XVI	Otto defeats the Magyars at the Battle of the Lech	Hugh Capet succeeds the last Carolingian Louis V as king of the west Franks

Carolingian Administration

Frankish expansion entailed not only Charlemagne's consolidation of the empire in terms of political structures but also the extension of the effective administration established by his grandfather and father, Charles Martel and Pippin. They, in their turn, had drawn on existing models within Frankish Gaul in which much of the late Roman system was preserved. The achievement of the Carolingians to a very considerable degree determined the forms of government in Europe for the rest of the Middle Ages as well as providing an enduring model of kingship.

The comprehensive and ambitious scheme of Carolingian administration extended the ruler's power and authority, in principle, to every corner of the empire. The king's authority, as many ninth-century treatises on kingship insisted, ultimately derived from God and imposed specific obligations on a Christian ruler. He was war leader, guardian of justice and peace, and legislator. He worked with the support and advice of his leading men, both clerics and laymen, many of whom represented royal power at a local level and who gathered together in regular assemblies. The Carolingian kings required an oath of fidelity from all their *fideles* (faithful men). His sons were recruited, as subkings of designated territories, to assist in the government of the realm and they too had royal courts. With a system of partible inheritance rather than primogeniture, moreover, it was not generally expected that complete unity of the whole empire exclusively under one emperor would be maintained. The empire was divided into counties presided over by counts. These in their turn were gathered together into larger districts called *missatica* which would be investigated on the king's behalf by a pair of *missi dominici*, one bishop and one count. In the second half of the ninth century the king, at least in the west Frankish kingdom, appears to have ventured on a degree of organized devolution of power, with a number of countries being assigned to one individual appointed by the king. In due

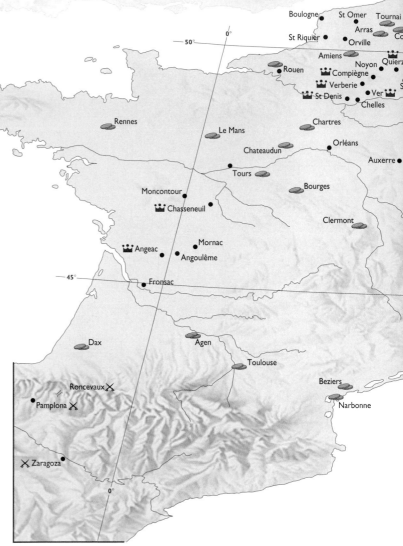

Seal of Lothar, king of the
West Franks.
King Lothar of the West Franks (954–66) continued the administrative traditions of his ninth-century predecessors in the format of his royal charters and the use of a royal seal (right) with a bust portrait of the king as part of the authentification of the charter .

781	789	794	802	805
Charlemagne creates subkingdoms for his sons Charles, Pippin (in Italy) and Louis (in Aquitaine)	*Admonitio generalis* on the general reform of the church	Assembly at Frankfurt discusses matters of Christian doctrine as well as the reform of weights and measures	General capitulary for the missi; the *missatica* system is reorganized, and many other decrees concerning administration and justice are issued	capitulary of Thionville on the control of feuds, obligations of justice and the control of trade, especially in arms

CAROLINGIAN ADMINISTRATION

The Carolingian empire, showing the itinerary of Charlemagne and other residences used by Charlemagne's successors on their itineraries, and the places where the most important assemblies of the Carolingian period were convened. The king's movements can be reconstructed from their capitularies, the charters they issued (mostly at the request of individuals or to settle judicial disputes) and the narrative evidence.

- • places on the itinerary of Charlemagne
- royal residence or palace
- mint ✕ battle

Map labels:

Dorestad · Nijmegen · Bocholt · Lippeham · Alisni · Hollenstedt · Bardowiek · Lüne · Verden · Petershagen · Minden · Suntel · Ohrum · Steinfurt · Ohremündung · Lübbecke · Rehme · Uffeln · Schöningen · Detmold · Lügde · Brunsburg · Maastricht · Aachen · Cologne · Lippspringe · Paderborn · Herstelle · Ghent · Düren · Syburg · Eresburg · Bonn · Hersfeld · Fulda · Herstal · Liege · Seilles · enciennes · Godinne · Dinant · Mainz · Kostheim · Salz · ussy · Longlier · Trier · Ingelheim · Frankfurt · Würzburg · eny · Douzy · Worms · Lorsch · ims · Attigny · Thionville · Speyer · am Karlsgraben · Regensburg · Verdun · Blanzée · Metz · Schweigen · Langres · Gondreville · Brumath · Strassburg · Lechfeld · an der Enns · Raabmün · Champ-le-Duc · Schlettstadt · Salzburg · Steinamanger · Remiremont · oyes · Besançon · Geneva · Great St Bernard Pass · Cividale · Bergamo · Treviso · Ivrea · Milan · Verona · Mt Cenis Pass · Pavia · Mantua · Avignon · Parma · Bologna · les · Ravenna · Lucca · Florence · San Mezzano · Ancona · Pisa · Marseilles · Spoleto · San Andrea al Mt Soratte · Rome · Monte Cassino · Capua

Our most serene and most Christian lord and emperor, Charles, has selected the most prudent and wise from among his leading men, archbishops and bishops, together with venerable abbots and devout laymen, and has sent them out into all his kingdom, and bestowed through them on all his subjects the right to live in accordance with a right rule of law.

GENERAL CAPITULARY FOR THE MISSI, 802, C. 1

806	813	816/817	817	825 and 853	864
Divisio regnorum provides for the succession	Reform councils deal with ecclesiastcal issues	Louis legislates for monastic reform.	*Ordinatio imperii* provides for the succession and the continuation of the imperial title	Further regulation of missatica	Charles the Bald issues the edict of Pitres, another major reform of the coinage

course these developed into the territorial principalities of the tenth and eleventh centuries.

Within the royal household, the chamberlain, count of the stable, treasurer and many lesser officials ensured the smooth running of the palace, probably under the supervision of the queen. The Carolingians maintained a royal chapel at the head of which was the archchaplain, usually a bishop seconded, with papal permission, from his diocese. Often the archchaplain and chaplains would combine the duties of service in the chapel and advice on ecclesiastical affairs with those of chancellor and notaries respectively. In the royal writing office, they recorded the king's legal transactions, grants of land and privileges in the diplomas and legal and administrative enactments in the form of the capitularies, letters, memoranda, records of assemblies, legal judgements and the like. These documents reflect the complicated network of political

The Carolingian empire, showing the missatica for 802 (below).

and kinship alliances which the Carolingians forged across the empire and which did much to hold the realm together in the process of the gradual reconfiguration of the Frankish realms in the aftermath of 843.

Income was from the royal estates, tributes from peripheral peoples, war booty and plunder, judicial and military fines, seigneurage from coinage, tolls (on bridges, roads etc.), annual and compulsory "gifts" and no doubt revenues from trade and merchants' activity. Charlemagne's reform of the coinage in 794 built on the control his father Pippin III had already established over mint production and money and was emulated by his successors throughout most of the ninth century to such good effect that the Carolingians achieved what was effectively a single European currency.

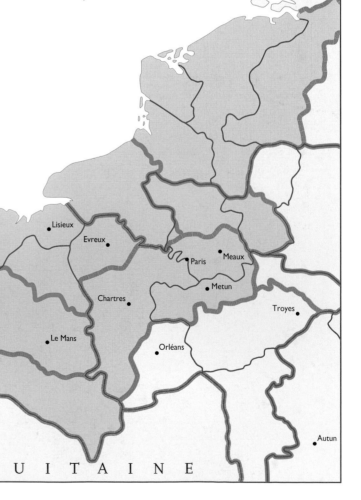

The Missatica

boundaries of Missatica,

— 802

— 825–7

— 853

traditional extent of Neustria

BRITTANY

Bayeux
Coutances
Avranches
Lisieux
Evreux
Paris
Meaux
Metun
Chartres
Troyes
Le Mans
Orléans
Autun

AQUITAINE

St Paul in Lavanthal (Kärnten), Stiftsbibliothek MS 411, early ninth-century from North Italy, possibly Aquileia, a book containing Lex Salica, Lex Ribuaria, Lex Baiuuariorum, Lex Alamannorum, Lex Burgundionum and an epitome of Roman law as well as Carolingian royal capitularies. It is apparently a local count or judge's law book. Although the figures in this picture have been variously interpreted as a king and ecclesia (the church personified) it seems most likely that the picture is intended to represent a secular count, acting as a judge, with a plaintiff.

The Church in Europe

The Christian church within Europe expanded rapidly from its late antique foundations in the course of the early Middle Ages, with the consolidation of the Christian faith, the establishment of new bishoprics and the foundation of many monasteries. Gradually the pope emerged as the spiritual leader of a church, This Christian church in the west had a profound impact on the landscape and the economy and depended heavily on the laity for its support.

The Plan of St Gall
Now in the Stiftsbibliothek Sankt Gallen, is a blueprint for an ideal monastery devised c. 825–35 at Reichenau and sent to the abbot of St Gall. Its dimensions are architecturally accurate and it provides a comprehensive impression of all the activities and needs of a monastery, including the cellar, school, scriptorium and library, the altars for the saints in the church, the guest house for visiting dignitaries and the latrines.

The organization of the church in early medieval Europe was both a direct extension of the administrative divisions of the Roman empire and a continuation of ecclesiastical structures developed in the fourth and fifth centuries. Dioceses headed by bishops were grouped into provinces, with a metropolitan or archbishop at the head. Each bishop had his *familia* within his cathedral and a cohort of priests working in the towns and countryside of the diocese. Churches were usually in the charge of a priest, sometimes with deacons and those holding lower clerical grades, such as subdeacon and lector, assisting them to care pastorally for the laity and to conduct all the church services and rites. The church was funded by endowment and by tithe. Lay devotion was above all manifest in the laity's support of the church, the foundation of many monasteries and the numbers of their sons and daughters who entered the religious life. Monasteries, all with their own chosen patron saints, became veritable powerhouses of prayer. Many bishops became substantial landowners and landlords, and made important contributions to the economy and to trading networks with the produce from their estates. Monasteries were also important in this respect, despite being founded on aspirations for poverty and the ascetic life.

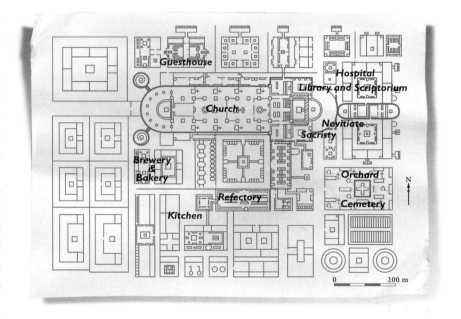

Early medieval monasticism derived much of its inspiration from the Egyptian desert fathers. John Cassian in Marseilles, for example, promoted their ascetic ideals, but other responses to the religious life, such as those of Martin of Tours, the holy men of Lérins, Benedict (author of the famous Rule) and the Irishman Columbanus, whose asceticism inspired many in Frankish Gaul, were also influential. Very many monasteries were founded in Britain and on the Continent in the early Middle Ages. By 700, the practice of monasticism was so diverse that this period is known as that of the *regula mixta* or mixed rule. The Carolingians' attempts to impose uniform observance

589	590	664
Conversion of the Visigoths in Spain from Arianism to Catholicism	Columbanus leaves Ireland for Gaul	The synod of Whitby adopts the Roman calculation of the date of Easter

"It was ruled by our lord the King and by the holy synod that a bishop should not move from one city to another, but should stay and take care of his church;' likewise a priest or a deacon should stay in his church according to the canons. ...That the Catholic faith of the holy Trinity, the Lord's Prayer and the creed should be preached and handed on to all men."

Synod of Frankfurt (794) cc.7 and 33

The magnificent Milan altar frontal in the church of San Ambrogio, dated c. 840, is the work of the goldsmith Volvinus. It depicts the life of St Ambrose as well as many scenes from the life of Christ in twenty panels on the front and back. On the back there is the portrait of Angilbert, archbishop of Milan (824–59) and of Volvinus the artisan being blessed by St Ambrose.

of the Rule of Benedict met with considerable success, but it was not until the Cluniac movement of the later tenth and eleventh century that Benedictine monasticism became really predominant throughout Europe.

Carolingian ecclesiastical reforms (recorded in conciliar decrees and royal legislation) also focused on organization, clerical behaviour, Christian morality, canon law, liturgy and ritual, and the correct form of the texts, which expressed and regulated all these things. Christian education was the primary responsibility of the monastic schools (*see* map p. 51) and there was also a great emphasis on orthodoxy. Theological debate continued to focus on Christology and predestination, but a new concern, brought to a head at the Second Council of Nicaea in 787, was the role of images of God and the saints. The decrees of 787 were misunderstood in the west, where both iconoclasm and the Greek definitions of the veneration to be accorded images were condemned.

The pope, whose spiritual authority was in the process of being established in this period, played a relatively ineffective role in these disputes. In the course of the eighth century the popes turned for political protection away from Byzantium towards the Franks. With his new role in the consecration of emperors, the pope became an important figure in the formulation of political ideology. Moreover, the pope was also an independent ruler of the papal territories, and Rome – his see – became the Christian centre of the west. Dramatic phases of city planning and church building by the popes from 380 to 440 and again from 760 to 860 transformed the city. Roman activity was emulated elsewhere with new churches springing up all over Europe, the sanctity of many enhanced by the presence of saints' relics brought from Rome.

The ciborium of King Arnulf, in the Schatzkammer der Residenz in Munich (right), was given by Odo, king of the west Franks (888–98) to King Arnulf (888–99) of the east Franks in about 896. It is a small travelling altar. The goldsmiths' work is that of the workshop associated with Charles the Bald, king of the west Franks (840–77) and the relief sculptures depict many New Testament scenes.

716	730	742/743	789	794
Duke Theodo of Bavaria asks the pope for help in the reorganization of the church in Bavaria	The Byzantine Emperor Leo III orders the destruction of all icons in the Byzantine empire, allowing only crosses to remain	*Concilium Germanicum*, presided over by Boniface of Mainz and Carloman, Frankish mayor of the palace, with proposals for the reform of the Frankish church	Charlemagne issues the *Admonitio Generalis* for reform of the Frankish church	Synod of Frankfurt condemns Adoptionism and iconoclasm and the Acts of Nicaea II (787)

THE CHURCH IN EUROPE

The organization of the church into dioceses and ecclesiastical provinces provided the essential framework throughout the Middle Ages. Adjustments were made to accommodate the steady expansion of the Christian church into the pagan territories beyond the former Roman empire, which is also reflected in the establishment of monasteries.

approximate extent of Christianity, c.600

approximate division between Catholic (Roman) and Orthodox (Byzantine) spheres of influence, c.1000

approximate extent of Monophysite Christianity to 1000

approximate extent of Nestorian Christianity to 1000

area taken into Catholic (Roman) sphere around 10C

area conquered by Arab Muslim invaders, 622–c.750

patriarchal seats

archbishoprics

important bishoprics

monasteries founded before 590

monasteries founded 590–690

monasteries founded 690–800

816/817	843	860	910	970
Aachen reform decrees on the observance of the Rule of Benedict in the monasteries of the Frankish empire	Restoration of icons in Byzantium	Synod of Tusey Predestination controversy concluded with Gottschalk's condemnation	Foundation of Cluny	*Regularis concordia* compiled in England in response to the tenth-century monastic reforms

Carolingian Culture

The Carolingians laid the foundations for the intellectual and cultural development of medieval Europe. Besides their emulation of Roman culture, they made many remarkable innovations in all aspects of cultural life in centres throughout western Europe.

In the early Middle Ages, education and learning, once concentrated in the secular schools of the Roman empire, became increasingly the prerogative of the monastic and cathedral centres of the successor kingdoms. There was also a gradual shift in emphasis from secular and classical to Christian learning. The curriculum comprised the trivium (grammar, rhetoric and dialectic) and *quadrivium* (arithmetic, geometry, music and astronomy) of the "seven liberal arts" defined by Martianus Capella in the fifth century. This remained the basis of education throughout the Middle Ages. Its goal was Christian knowledge and understanding.

Education, then as much as now, needed funding and long-term planning as well as expert personnel. In the Carolingian world an essential difference from elsewhere was the extent of royal involvement in the support of learning and education. Scholars were encouraged at court and there was a massive endowment of monasteries. Courtiers in due course were granted abbacies and

The Stuttgart Psalter

(Württemburgische Landesbibliothek Biblia folio 23), with the illustration for Psalm 7. The script is caroline minuscule in the style written at St Germain des Prés in Paris, c. 820. This was a type of writing that had evolved during the Merovingian period from the system of scripts in use in the late Roman empire. Other Roman scripts, such as capitals, uncials (seen above the picture) were retained as display scripts. Many scriptoria developed a "house style" of caroline minuscule.

CAROLINGIAN CULTURE

A number of major cultural centres developed in the course of the late eighth and the ninth
centuries, producing their own books, building up comprehensive libraries and attracting pupils
to their schools. Many smaller centres were also noted for particular scholars.

DENMARK

Hamburg
Bremen
Verden
Osnabrück
Münster
Minden
Hildesheim
Corvey
Halberstadt

SLAVS

St Bertin
Gent
Maastricht
Xanten
Essen
Werden
Paderborn
St Riquier
St Amand
Nivelles
St Trond
Aachen
Cologne
Inden
Fritzlar
Ohrdruf
Liège
Hersfeld
Fulda

SORB MARCH

St Pol de Léon
Lehon
Amiens
Jumièges
Arras
Cambrai
Peronne
Echternach
Stablo Malmedy
Prüm
Mainz
Würzburg
Kitzingen
Landevennec
St Wandrille
Noyon
Corbie
Laon
Trier
Worms
Amorbach
Dol
Rouen
Beauvais
Soissons
Verdun
Lorsch
Mont St Michel
Paris
Jouarre
Rheims
Metz
Speyer
Vannes
Rennes
Chartres
Chelles
Meaux
Chalôns sur Marne
Weissenburg
Eichstätt
Regensburg

BRETON MARCH

Noirmoutier
Angers
Orléans
Faremoutier
Toul
Strasbourg
Augsburg
Freising
Passau
Nantes
Ferrières
Sens
Troyes
Montierender
Schüttern
Reichenau
Kremsmünster

Danube

Poitiers
Tours
Fleury
Auxerre
Remiremont
Murbach
Wessobrun
Schaftlärn
Bourges
Flavigny
Langres
Luxeil
Tegernsee
Mondsee
St Maxient
Nevers
Dijon
Basel
Constance
St Gallen
Chiemsee
Salzburg
Autun
Besançon
Pfäfers
Benediktbeuten

FRANKISH EMPIRE

Saintes
Chalon sur Sâone
Disentis
Chur
Angoulême
Menat
Mâcon
Mustair
CARINTHIA
Clermont
Bergamo
Civdale
Aquleia
Bordeaux
Brioude-St Julian
Lyons
Novalesa
Ivrea
Monza
Grado
Vienne
Aosta
Vercelli
Pavia
Brescia
Verona
Le Puy
Tarentaise
Milan
Cremona
Venice
Conques
Grenoble
Bobbio
Parma
Cahors
STURIAS
Eauze-Auch
Albi
Uzés
Digne
Nonantola
Burgos
Liebana
Oloron
Toulouse
Ravenna
Lucca
Rimini
Gellone
Aniane
Nîmes
Aix
Urgel
Narbonne
Arles
Arezzo
PAPAL STATE
Saragossa
FRANKISH MARCH
Marseilles
Perugia
MIRATE OF CORDOBA
Gerona
Lézins
Spoleto St Marco
Barcelona
Monte Soracte
Farfa
Chieti
Tarragona
Rome
Tortosa
San Vincenzo
Monte Cassino

Rhine
Elbe
Seine
Loire

BULGARIA
SLAVS

Corsica

PRINCIPALITY OF BENEVENTO
Naples

BYZANTINE EMPIRE

Baleorics

Sardinia

MEDITERRANEAN SEA

Legend:
- marches
- Papal patrimony
- Kingdom of Italy
- monasteries
- bishoprics
- archbishoprics
- Scriptorium (principal writing centre)

51

bishoprics where they taught the next generation of scholars. Such royal involvement provided an inspiration for ecclesiastical and lay magnates as well. Culture was disseminated out from the court to many centres across the empire. Charlemagne's *Admonitio Generalis* of 789 had insisted that schools be established and he reinforced this in the letter sent in *c.* 800 to all the bishops and abbots of his kingdoms emphasizing the close association of learning and correct observance of the Christian faith.

The extraordinary response to this encouragement by Frankish scholars, artists and artisans is the intensely creative cultural and religious achievement known as the Carolingian Renaissance. The most obvious symbol of cultural continuity with the Roman past was the cultivation of Latin as the language of religion, education and learning; very few scholars in the Latin West could read Greek before the eleventh century. There was a spectacular increase in book production in the Carolingian period, with books produced in scriptoria (writing centres) closely related to the education, religious and administrative requirements of the empire. The need for texts, and communications across the empire between libraries and scholars, prompted the refinement and wide dissemination of caroline minuscule script. Caroline minuscule was also introduced into Italy, Spain and England along with the texts produced by the Carolingian scribes. These comprised copies of classical Latin texts, of which most of the earliest surviving manuscripts are Frankish copies of the ninth century. They also included the voluminous output of Christian "fathers", such as Augustine, Jerome and Origen. There were liturgical books, tracts on spiritual discipline and new works of early medieval writers in all fields: theology, grammar, poetry, encyclopaedias, geography, astronomy, philosophy, mathematics, law, saints' lives, practical manuals and, above all, biblical commentary, history and music. Library catalogues give us clear indications of the contents of many of the great Carolingian libraries of the period, comprising books acquired from elsewhere in the empire as well as England and Ireland, older books preserved from the fifth to the eighth centuries, and many new books produced in-house. A canon of knowledge was defined.

The Carolingian royal court, like many other centres, had groups of scholars, scribes and artists associated with it. They discussed theology, wrote poetry, taught members of the royal family and also assisted in the administration of the palace and the empire. Artists and scribes produced books for the royal library and for use in the palace chapel. Metalworkers, sculptors, ivory carvers and builders produced beautiful book covers, church ornaments, fine tableware, sculpture, jewellery and magnificent stone buildings, among them the great palace chapel at Aachen.

An ivory carving of the Marriage of Cana from the palace workshop of Charles the Bald, King of the West Franks (840–77). This one was probably used to decorate a book cover.

We exhort you not only not to neglect the study of letters but also with most humble and God-pleasing application to learn zealously for a purpose, namely, that you may be able the more easily and the more correctly to penetrate the mysteries of divine scripture.

CHARLEMAGNE TO THE BISHOPS AND ABBOTS OF HIS KINGDOM, *ON THE CULTIVATION OF LETTERS*, C.800

*Charles the Bald's
Second Bible*
Paris, Bibliothèque Nationale de France
lat. 2, produced at St Amand, with the
lavish decoration in Franco-Saxon style
of the E from the beginning of Joshua.

Islamic Spain and the Northern Christian Kingdoms

The invasion of Spain that began in 711 resulted in the immediate extinction of the Visigothic state, whether because of its fragility, or because of the invader's power. The invaders were mainly Berbers of many religions, rather than Islamic holy warriors, though Islam emerged gradually as the dominant faith. Berber pastoralists occupied the high ground, briefly reaching the Atlantic. The rich south also acted as a magnet for settlers and Cordoba (capital of al-Andalus, as Muslim Spain was called) became one of Europe's largest cities, attracting Berbers, Copts, Jews and Arabs. Internal rivalries among the officer class soon tore al-Andalus apart, reflecting wider Muslim rivalries between "Syrians" and "Yemenites".

In the middle of the eighth century, when revolution convulsed the central Islamic world, a prince of the old Umayyad ruling dynasty fled to Spain, seizing power in al-Andalus and separating it from the rest of the Islamic empire. Abd ar-Rahman I brought much of Spain under his control, also addressing the Carolingian threat in the north. His enduring monument is the Umayyad mosque in Cordoba.

The mosque testified to the expansion of Spanish Islam, by conversion and immigration; converted Visigothic nobles achieved great influence as Muslim warlords. However, the majority of inhabitants remained Christian as late as 900. Christians and Jews were employed in high levels of the administration, though subject to disabilities, such as a poll tax. Jewish culture, impregnated with Arabic philosophy, flourished magnificently after a terrible period of Visigothic persecution. Many Christians slipped easily into Islam, after adopting the Arabic language and culture, but a protest movement emerged in ninth-century Cordoba, where at least forty men and women publicly denounced Islam, seeking execution as martyrs. This was a rearguard action, which horrified those who preferred quiet assimilation. The Berbers, despised for their country ways, rapidly became Arabized and fully Islamized.

The only areas where Islam was held at bay lay in the mountains of the far north. In the eighth century the

The Great Mosque at Cordoba
The mosque was begun in the eighth century, but was constantly enlarged as the proportion of Muslims in the population of the greatest city in Spain grew. In the tenth century craftsmen came from Byzantium to decorate the interior with mosaics inspired by those of the ancient mosque in Damascus.

Atlantic coastal strip (Asturias) became the seat of a Christian statelet, claiming the Visigothic heritage, while in the Basque country the seeds of the kingdom of Navarre were laid. Further east, Carolingian penetration south of the Pyrenees was sustained by local counts, notably Wilfred the Hairy, in what came to be known as

711	851	929	1085	1086	1102	1229
Arab-Berber invasion of Spain begins	Execution of Isaac, first of the 'Martyrs of Cordoba'	Abd ar-Rahman III takes the title of Caliph	Conquest of Toledo by Alfonso VI of Castile	Almoravids defeat Alfonso VI of Leon at Sagrajas	Almoravids capture Valencia	Conquest of Majorca by James I of Aragon-Catalonia

FRANCE

NAVARRE
Oviedo
Santander
León
Pamplona
ARAGON
RIBAGORZA
SOBRARBE
SMALL COUNTIES
Burgos
Girona
LEON
CASTILE
Saragossa
Lerida
KINGDOM OF LÉRIDA
BARCELONA
Barcelona
Calatayud
KINGDOM OF SARAGOSSA
Tarragona
KINGDOM OF TORTOSA
Tortosa
ALBARRAZIN
Coria
Palma
Toledo
ALPUENTE
Valencia
KINGDOM OF BADAJOZ
KINGDOM OF VALENCIA
Denia
KINGDOM OF THE BALEARES
Badajoz
Zallaca
Mérida
KINGDOM OF SEVILLE
KINGDOM OF MURCIA
Murcia
Cordoba
KINGDOM OF GRANADA
Granada
KINGDOM OF ALMERÍA
Seville
Málaga
Almería

EMPIRE OF THE ALMORAVIDS

ISLAMIC SPAIN

— Northern limit of Muslim conquest, 732
— Northern limit of Emirate of Cordova, 814
— Caliphate of Cordova, 1010
— Kingdom of Toledo, 1031–85
▪ Areas lost to Christians 1030–85

The Iberian Peninsula in the elventh century, during the age of the taifa or "Party Kingdoms".

Catalonia ("land of the castellans"). Barcelona shook off Islamic rule in 802 and the Muslims concentrated their power in the south, treating the Christian states as subordinates, which could be raided when they needed to chalk up some victories. This was particularly true in the long and glorious reign of Abd ar-Rahman III who had achieved sufficient power by 929 to have himself declared Caliph (the religious and political head of Islam), though his influence extended only to Spain and Morocco. While he ruled embassies were exchanged with the emperors of Byzantium and Germany; under his son, Greek craftsmen arrived to beautify the Great Mosque and international trade flourished.

The caliphate was soon riven apart by factional strife, and the 11th century saw the emergence of dozens of petty statelets (the *taifa* or "party" kingdoms). Granada emerged as a glittering centre of Muslim and Jewish culture under Berber kings with Jewish viziers. However, Christian armies made massive inroads in search of tribute from the once feeble fringe territories of Leon, Castile and Aragon. Toledo fell to Castile in 1085, and the Christian warlord El Cid captured Valencia. The balance in the peninsula appeared to be shifting away from Islam, until new Berber empires in Africa came to the aid of the beleaguered Muslims. With the coming of the Almoravids, al-Andalus became a province of a vast African empire.

Anglo-Saxon Kingdoms to c. 1000

Although England emerged as a unified kingdom by the end of the tenth century, this was more by accident than design. Much of England's political development is better understood in terms of the different regions, especially Mercia, Kent, Wessex and Northumbria, though a greater abundance of evidence from Wessex dominates the historical record. Strong government, wealth (especially in the south) and a vigorous Christian culture characterized all the kingdoms.

By 600, a group of English kingdoms, notably Wessex, East Anglia, Kent, Mercia and Northumbria, had emerged and gradually absorbed their smaller neighbours, such as Sussex, Essex, the Hwicce and the western marches. By 700, all were Christian kingdoms as a result of the consolidation of the conversion to Christianity initiated by Augustine of Canterbury in the south in 597 and by Irish missionaries in the north in the early seventh century. Mercia's rise under King Aethelbald and Beornred was rapid, but it was Offa, based in the Midlands, who expanded his territory to embrace London and whose economic activity and mint in London (attested by surviving coins from his reign) have been confirmed by archaeological excavation since the 1980s. Links with the Frankish kingdoms remained important, however, and a number of political exiles from English kingdoms took refuge at the Frankish court. Offa's own power did not long survive his death and Wessex emerged in the course of the ninth century as the strongest kingdom of England. It was helped in this, paradoxically enough, by the Viking raids on England, for it was the kings of Wessex who fought hard against the rulers of the Scandinavian-controlled Danelaw region. Alfred the Great successfully beat off Viking attacks and consolidated the kingdom of Wessex. He reached an agreement with the Vikings in the Danelaw and reoccupied London in 886. His sons and grandsons Edward the Elder (899–924), Aethelstan (924–39), Edmund (939–46) and Eadred (946–55) extended their power over Mercia, the Danelaw and, ultimately, Northumbria; they also received the submission from time to time of various Welsh and Scottish rulers. The conquest of the Danelaw and the expanding economy paved the way for the unification of England.

Nonetheless, England remained subject to Danish attacks and these culminated in the reign of the Danish king Cnut who ruled Norway and Denmark as well as England and introduced many Danish and "Norman"

The Franks Casket (British Museum, London). Made in northern England in the first half of the eighth century, this carved whalebone casket combines imagery from Roman, Jewish, Christian and Germanic tradition, with scenes from the story of Weland the Smith, Romulus and Remus suckled by the wolf, the destruction of Jerusalem by Titus (on the back panel, illustrated here) and the Adoration of the Magi as well as a cryptic runic inscription and Latin texts describing the pictures.

731	747	786	786	793
Completion of Bede's Ecclesiastical history of the English people	Synod of Cloveshoe many reforms, very similar to the Frankish reforms of the same period, are agreed.	Papal and Frankish legates convene reform synods in Northumbria and the kingdom of Mercia.	Lichfield elevated (temporarily) to an archbishopric	Norse raid on Lindisfarne

EARLY ANGLO-SAXON ENGLAND

The regional divisions of England have their roots in the origins of the Anglo-Saxon kingdoms. The areas occupied by the Danes, moreover, still retain (especially in place names) the marks of that occupation. The unification of England was a long and far from steady or planned process.

Northumbria to c.750

Northumbria under Oswiu, 657

annexed temporarily by Northumbria (with dates)

to Northumbria, 750

Mercia to c.800

sub-kingdoms of Mercia during parts of 7–8th centuries

southern and eastern limit of direct rule by Mercia under Aethelbald, 757

Mercia at the end of Offa's rule, 796

Offa's dyke, completed by c.790's

Wessex to c.850

Wessex, Mercian dependency 789–802; Egbert's kingdom, from 802

added to Wessex by 825

northern and eastern limit of area acquired by Wessex, 829–30

→ Anglo-Saxon campaign, with details

✷ revolt, with details

KINGDOM OF THE PICTS (658-685)

✗ Nechtansmere 685

✷ 676, against Northumbria

DALRIADA

Dumbarton

STRATHCLYDE

• Edinburgh

Eadberth, 756

KYLE

Bamburgh •

NORTHUMBRIA

Whitby •

• York

Winwaed 655 ✗

Aegrifth, 684

IRISH KINGDOMS

Deganway 822 ✗

• Chester

Dore

✗ 678

LINDSEY (674-678)

GWYNEDD

Cenwulf, 816

(655-657)

MERCIA

Lichfield • • Tamworth

✷ 657, against Northumbria; 830, against Wessex

EAST ANGLIA

✷ 825, against Mercia

POWYS

MAGONSAETE

(656-657)

BUELLT

Hereford 760

Offa, 778, 796; Cenwulf, 818

SEISYLLWG

BRYCHEINIOG

HWICCE

GWENT

ESSEX

Disputed area, to Wessex c.757–719 ✗

Bensington 779

London •

Otford 776 ✗

DYFED

GLYWYSING

Ellendun 825 ✗

WESSEX

✗ 752, 802, against Mercia

• Winchester

KENT

• Canterbury

796, against Mercia ✷

Annexed by Wessex 658–c.720

✗ Peonnum 658

Annexed by Wessex 680's

SUSSEX

WEST WALES
Under lordship of Wessex by c.830

• Exeter

Egbert, 815

878	886	937	941	954
Battle of Edington: Alfred defeats the Norse leader Guthrum	Alfred occupied London	Battle of Brunanburgh: Aethelstan defeats a coalition of the kings of Scotland, York and Dublin	Edmund Ironside annexes the Five Boroughs	Defeat of Eric Bloodaxe and Northumbria brought under English control

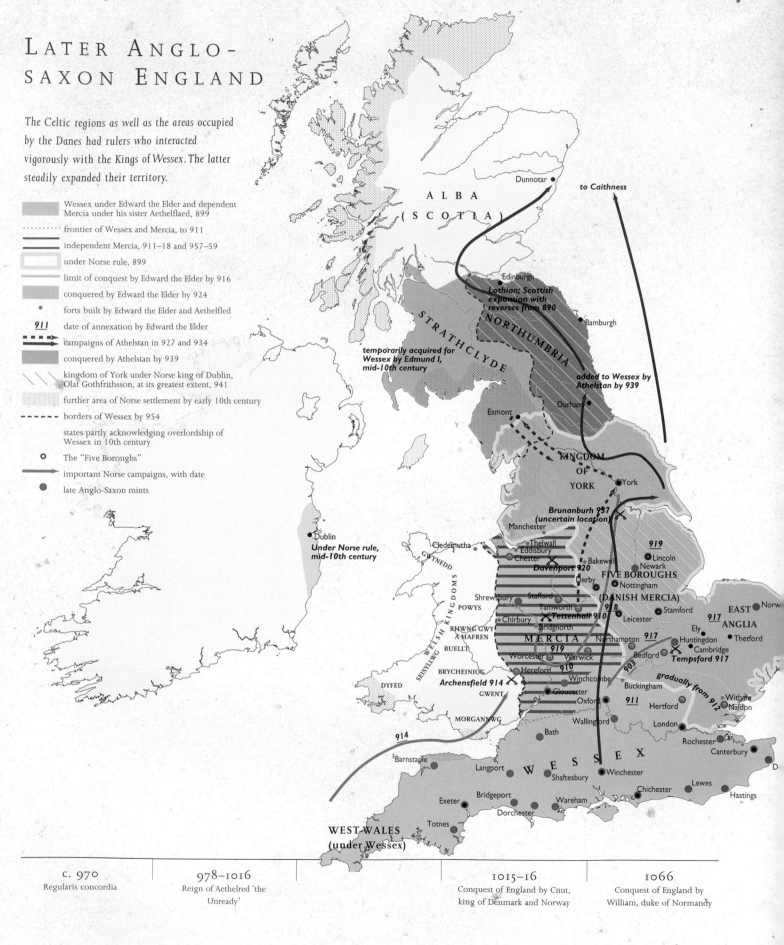

LATER ANGLO-SAXON ENGLAND

The Celtic regions as well as the areas occupied
by the Danes had rulers who interacted
vigorously with the Kings of Wessex. The latter
steadily expanded their territory.

Wessex under Edward the Elder and dependent
Mercia under his sister Aethelflaed, 899

frontier of Wessex and Mercia, to 911

independent Mercia, 911–18 and 957–59

under Norse rule, 899

limit of conquest by Edward the Elder by 916

conquered by Edward the Elder by 924

forts built by Edward the Elder and Aethelfled

911 date of annexation by Edward the Elder

campaigns of Athelstan in 927 and 934

conquered by Athelstan by 939

kingdom of York under Norse king of Dublin,
Olaf Gothfrithsson, at its greatest extent, 941

further area of Norse settlement by early 10th century

borders of Wessex by 954

states partly acknowledging overlordship of
Wessex in 10th century

○ The "Five Boroughs"

→ important Norse campaigns, with date

● late Anglo-Saxon mints

ALBA
(SCOTIA)

Dunnotar

to Caithness

Edinburgh

*Lothian; Scottish
expansion with
reverses from 890*

Bamburgh

STRATHCLYDE

NORTHUMBRIA

*temporarily acquired for
Wessex by Edmund I,
mid-10th century*

*added to Wessex by
Athelstan by 939*

Eamont

Durham

KINGDOM
OF
YORK

York

*Brunanburh 937
(uncertain location)*

Manchester

Dublin

*Under Norse rule,
mid-10th century*

Clederriutha

GWYNEDD

Thelwall
Eddisbury
Chester

Davenport 920

Derby

Bakewell

919
Lincoln
Newark

FIVE BOROUGHS

Nottingham

Shrewsbury

Stafford

(DANISH MERCIA)

POWYS

Tamworth

918

Stamford

EAST
ANGLIA

Norw

Chirbury

Tettenhall 910

Bridgnorth

Leicester

Ely

917

RHWNG GWY
A HAFREN

MERCIA

Northampton

917

Huntingdon

Thetford

Cambridge

BUELLT

919

Worcester

Warwick

903

Bedford

Tempsford 917

BRYCHEINIOG

Hereford

910

gradually from 912

WELSH
KINGDOMS

SEISYLLWG

Archensfield 914

Winchcombe

Buckingham

DYFED

GWENT

Gloucester
Oxford

911

Hertford

Witham

MORGANNWG

Wallingford

London

Maldon

914

Bath

Rochester

Canterbury

Barnstaple

Langport

WESSEX

Shaftesbury

Winchester

Lewes

D

Exeter

Bridgeport

Wareham

Chichester

Hastings

Dorchester

Totnes

WEST WALES
(under Wessex)

c. 970	978–1016	1015–16	1066
Regularis concordia	Reign of Aethelred 'the Unready'	Conquest of England by Cnut, king of Denmark and Norway	Conquest of England by William, duke of Normandy

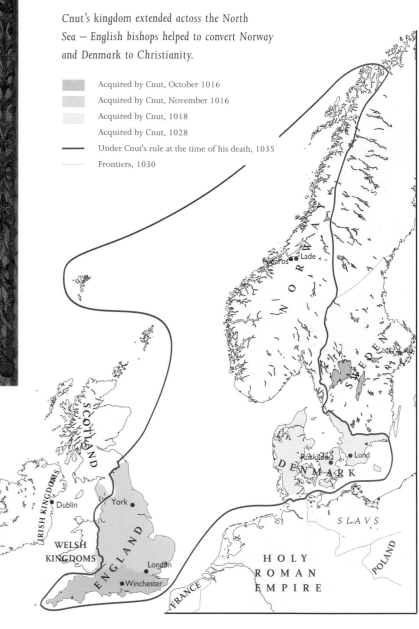

CNUT'S KINGDOM

Cnut's kingdom extended actoss the North Sea — English bishops helped to convert Norway and Denmark to Christianity.

- Acquired by Cnut, October 1016
- Acquired by Cnut, November 1016
- Acquired by Cnut, 1018
- Acquired by Cnut, 1028
- Under Cnut's rule at the time of his death, 1035
- Frontiers, 1030

King Edgar offers the charter of the New Minster Winchester to Christ (above). The illustration represents the earliest example of the Winchester style of manuscript illumination, a vigorous and basically linear style with fluttering drapery and distinctively light clear washes of colour.

connections into English politics. With the Norman conquest, however, England's political and cultural orientation altered once more, and links with Flanders, France and the Mediterranean were strengthened still further at the expense of those with the Scandinavian world.

From their beginnings, English kings had been closely allied with the church. It was a relationship enhanced from c. 900 onwards by the introduction of a religious ceremony to mark the coronation of a new king. Strong government and judicial institutions were developed. Alfred the Great's methods of government, stressing the rule of law and encouraging the use of vernacular English were buttressed by his own remarkable writings in English on kingship and government. His successors, especially

Aethelstan and Edgar (957-975), further elaborated the role of the king, with the exertion of royal control over charter production, extensive legislation which built on the laws issued by kings in England since the seventh century and a state-regulated coinage of remarkable stability. Royal government was supported by a land-owning and office-holding aristocracy of earls and thegns. King Edgar was closely involved in the ecclesiastical and monastic reforms of the late tenth century, which were inspired by religious reforms on the Continent. The tenth and eleventh centuries, moreover, like the seventh and eighth, were periods of rich cultural achievement in both Latin and Old English, book production, painting, building and sculpture.

The Kingdoms of Scotland, Wales and Ireland

The kingdoms of Wales, Scotland and Ireland comprised a complex group of polities alongside a strong Christian church and enjoyed independent political and economic connections with England and the Continent. Norse raiders affected the political development of all three regions to varying degrees, but it was Scotland, with the most diverse population, which emerged in the eleventh century as the most unified and stable.

Only from a modern perspective does the grouping of Ireland, Scotland and Wales have much justification, for in the earlier Middle Ages they were very different and separate groups of polities. Wales and southern Scotland had been within the Roman Empire whereas Ireland and northern Scotland had remained beyond its frontiers. Nevertheless, both the latter regions were influenced by contacts with Rome, evidenced not least in the reception of Christianity in Ireland from western Britain in the fifth century.

The reconstruction of the history of these regions before 900 is dependent on very patchy and often ambiguous sources. From Irish legal texts of the eighth and ninth centuries we learn of the *tuatha* or petty kingdoms of Ireland, ruled by competing dynasties of kings. Among these the Uí Néill were paramount, with their principal seat at Tara. In the twelfth century they were replaced by the Uí Briuín (originally rulers of

(Right) Pictish symbol stone from Hilton of Caboll, dated to the eighth or ninth century, depicting a hunting scene.

678–683	c. 736	840–41	842	848–49	855
Cáin Fhuithirbe earliest datable Irish law code	Brude, king of the Picts, establishes rule over the "Scottish" kingdom of Dál Riata	Norse establish a base at Dublin	Kenneth I, king of the Picts and Dál Riata	Dunkeld becomes the new ecclesiastical centre of Kenneth I's kingdom	Rhodri Mawr, king of Gwynedd defeats the Danish leader Gorm

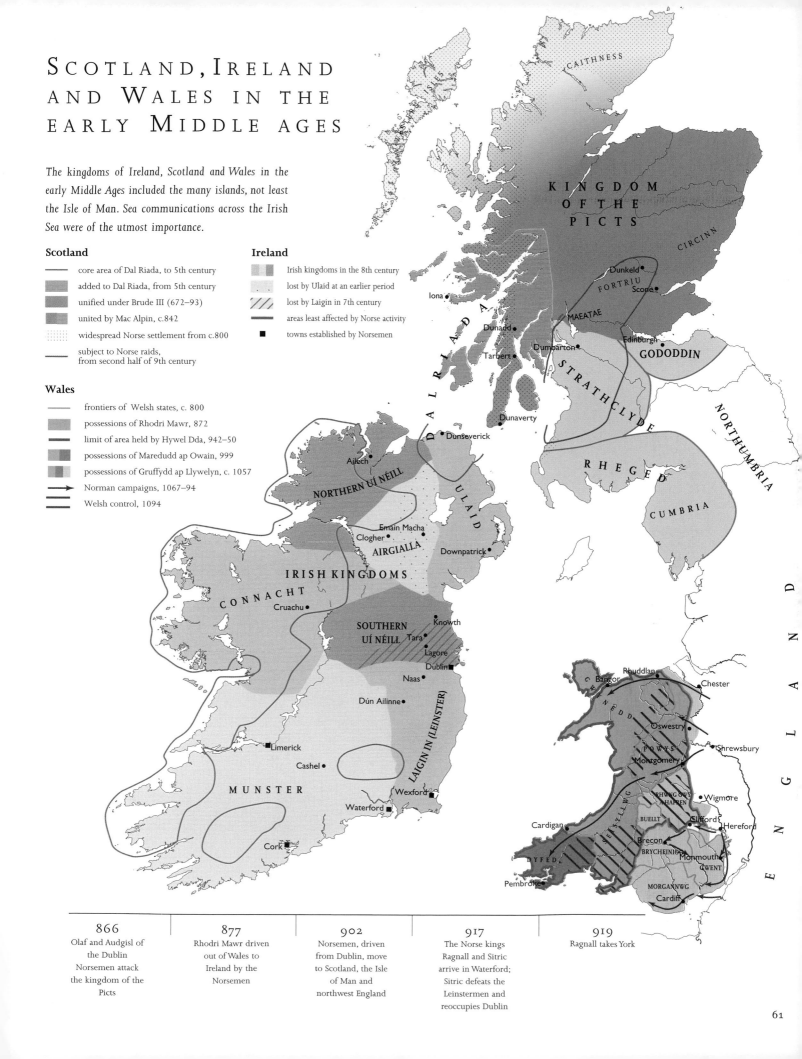

SCOTLAND, IRELAND AND WALES IN THE EARLY MIDDLE AGES

The kingdoms of Ireland, Scotland and Wales in the early Middle Ages included the many islands, not least the Isle of Man. Sea communications across the Irish Sea were of the utmost importance.

Scotland

- core area of Dal Riada, to 5th century
- added to Dal Riada, from 5th century
- unified under Brude III (672–93)
- united by Mac Alpin, c.842
- widespread Norse settlement from c.800
- subject to Norse raids, from second half of 9th century

Wales

- frontiers of Welsh states, c. 800
- possessions of Rhodri Mawr, 872
- limit of area held by Hywel Dda, 942–50
- possessions of Maredudd ap Owain, 999
- possessions of Gruffydd ap Llywelyn, c. 1057
- Norman campaigns, 1067–94
- Welsh control, 1094

Ireland

- Irish kingdoms in the 8th century
- lost by Ulaid at an earlier period
- lost by Laigin in 7th century
- areas least affected by Norse activity
- towns established by Norsemen

CAITHNESS

WESTERN ISLES

KINGDOM OF THE PICTS

CIRCINN

Dunkeld

FORTRIU

Scone

Iona

MAEATAE

Dunadd

Dumbarton

Edinburgh

Tarbert

GODODDIN

STRATHCLYDE

Dunaverty

RHEGED

NORTHUMBRIA

Dunseverick

DAL RIADA

CUMBRIA

Ailech

NORTHERN UÍ NÉILL

ULAID

Emain Macha

Clogher

Downpatrick

AIRGIALLA

IRISH KINGDOMS

CONNACHT

Cruachu

SOUTHERN UÍ NÉILL

Knowth

Tara

Lagore

Dublin

Naas

Dún Ailinne

LAIGIN (IN LEINSTER)

Limerick

Cashel

Wexford

Waterford

MUNSTER

Cork

Rhuddlan

Bangor

Chester

GWYNEDD

Oswestry

POWYS

Shrewsbury

Montgomery

CEREDIGION

Wigmore

RHWNG GWY A HAFREN

BUELLT

Clifford

Hereford

Cardigan

Brecon

BRYCHEINIOG

Monmouth

DYFED

GWENT

Pembroke

MORGANNWG

Cardiff

ENGLAND

866	877	902	917	919
Olaf and Audgisl of the Dublin Norsemen attack the kingdom of the Picts	Rhodri Mawr driven out of Wales to Ireland by the Norsemen	Norsemen, driven from Dublin, move to Scotland, the Isle of Man and northwest England	The Norse kings Ragnall and Sitric arrive in Waterford; Sitric defeats the Leinstermen and reoccupies Dublin	Ragnall takes York

Five young kings lay on that field of battle, slain by the swords, and also seven of Olaf's earls, and a countless host of seamen and Scots. There the prince of the Norsemen was put to flight, driven perforce to the prow of his ship with a small company; the vessel pressed on in the water, the king set out over the fallow flood and saved his life.

ANGLO-SAXON CHRONICLE, 937

Connacht). The kings collaborated closely with the church, which was full of learned men, especially the see of Armagh and the monastery of Kildare. Many bishops and heads of religious houses were themselves members of a royal family. Ecclesiastical office was as much a political as a clerical position and often held in hereditary succession.

Vikings, probably from Norway, first raided Ireland in the late eighth century but from the 840s they overwintered on Lough Neagh (840–41) and at Dublin (841–42) and by about 900 many coastal bases were established, notably at Waterford, Cork, Wexford, Limerick and Dublin as well as the Isle of Man. From there they conducted raids inland as well as a wide-ranging trade across the Irish Sea and beyond. In the early tenth century strong links were formed with the Viking kingdom of York, and in 937 a political alliance between the kings of Dublin, York, Scotland and Strathclyde against the English ruler King Aethelstan was heavily defeated at *Brunanburgh*. Although Dublin became a political and economic focus of disputes between Vikings and Irish rulers, these parties occasionally also formed alliances within Ireland. In 1012–14, for example, Viking Dubliners, Leinstermen, Sigurd, Earl of Orkney and fleets from the Hebrides and the Isle of Man together revolted against the Irish king Brian Boru. Although the alliance was defeated at the Battle of Clontarf, Brian Boru himself was killed.

By contrast, the Vikings at first had little impact on Welsh politics, and for the most part the Welsh rulers successfully beat off raids. Thus Rhodri Mawr drove the Viking leader Gorm from Anglesey (though Rhodri Mawr later had to flee to Ireland) and Hywel Dda held the southwest against sporadic Viking attacks. The kings of Gwynedd claimed precedence over the many kingdoms of Wales and tried to enforce these claims by attacking their Welsh neighbours, but with mixed success. The English kingdom was able to take advantage of the relative political instability within Wales which Scandinavian raids had exacerbated.

The Picts, the Gaelic speaking Dál Riata (the "Scots") from northeast Ireland and the Britons of Strathclyde had earlier combined in the country now known as Scotland to resist the encroachments of the English in Northumbria. The Dál Riata and Picts may have formed an alliance by the late eighth century; Kenneth I certainly emerged as ruler of both Picts and Scots in the middle of the ninth century. Vikings from Norway and Ireland attacked Pictland and Scotland in the ninth century, occupied many of the northern islands of the Orkneys, Hebrides and Faroes, and overwhelmed the Pictish community in northern Caithness. Even with the complications of English involvement in Scottish politics from the early 11th century onwards, and internal feuding, Scotland achieved considerable stability and a degree of unity despite the diversity of its population.

The Book of Durrow (right)

(Trinity College, Dublin). The book was probably produced on Iona in the second half of the seventh century. It is one of the many examples of the intricate cross fertilization of different "celtic", English and Pictish ornament and Christian symbolism in books from the kingdoms of Ireland, Scotland and the Isles, and Wales.

919	920	937	Dublin and Scotland is defeated by Aethelstan of England	987
Ragnall takes York	Hywel Dda beats off Viking attacks in south-west Wales	The "great, lamentable and horrible" battle of Brunanburgh. An alliance of the kings of Strathclyde, York,		Viking victory on the Isle of Man

The Norsemen at Home and Abroad

Communication by sea was a major determinant in the spheres of activity of the Norsemen in the Atlantic, North and Baltic Sea regions. The Norsemen abroad were very active politically and economically wherever they settled. At home, the Scandinavian kingdoms of Denmark, Sweden and Norway, together with the republic of Iceland, had emerged by the early 11th century.

A major problem in reconstructing the internal history of Scandinavia in the eighth, ninth and tenth centuries is that most of the contemporary written sources are English, German or Frankish. Later histories and sagas of Scandinavians (written in the 12th and 13th centuries) give rich but untrustworthy accounts of the earlier period. These late literary texts can be supplemented, however, by the wealth of contemporary archaeological material and runic inscriptions, though this is rarely unambiguous. Denmark, Sweden and Norway, quite apart from the Norse settlements elsewhere in the Atlantic and North Sea regions (Iceland, Greenland, the Scottish Islands, Ireland, England and Francia) had separate developments in this early period. Certainly in the eighth century there was no unity and probably many local leaders or else a few strong kings, especially in Denmark where the landscape was arguably more favourable to the exercise of power. Massive building works such as the Kanhave canal, the Danevirke across the Jutland peninsula and the Fyrkat and Trelleborg fortresses witness to Danish political power as well as extraordinary technical creativity. These are manifest in their shipbuilding and navigation skills, and adaptability to the challenging environments they encountered in new settlements across the Atlantic seaboard.

Conversion to Christianity was a key factor in the formation of all three Scandinavian kingdoms as well as the republic of Iceland by the early 11th century. The new Christian religion with its tradition of Latin learning brought the Scandinavians within the cultural sphere of the rest of western Europe. Legal material, such as the *Landamabok* from Iceland, is also late in composition but

From Denmark, with dramatic decoration depicting the Crucifixion and the "Jelling beast". The elaborate runic inscription reads "King Harald commanded this monument to be made in memory of Gorm his father, and in memory of Thorvi (Thyre) his mother — that Harald who won the whole of Denmark for himself, and Norway, and made the Danes Christian."

A Jelling memorial stone

the rune stones yield information about a very diverse society of farmers, warriors, merchants and artisans of many different degrees of wealth and social status.

Settlements abroad appear to have combined raiding with trading activities. Trading centres discovered in Scandinavia, such as Birka, Kaupang, Ribe and Hedeby, had their counterparts abroad, especially on the Irish coast in the west, and at Staraia Ladoga, Kiev and Novgorod in

726	737	826	c. 840–c. 880	c. 870	c. 878–90	911
Kanhave canal constructed across Samsø in Denmark	Danevirk constructed across the bottom of the Jutland peninsula	Baptism of Harald Klak of Denmark at Ingelheim with Emperor Louis the Pious of the Franks standing godfather	many Viking raids recorded on the continent and in England and Ireland	Iceland settled	Guthrum's treaty with Alfred the Great of Wessex and recognition of the Danelaw region	Charles the Simple cedes the county of Rouen to the Viking leader Rollo. The Norsemen's territory expanded to become Normandy

THE NORSE WORLD

The consolidation of the three kingdoms within
Scandinavia was complemented by the remarkable
spread of Norse settlements, many of them
commercial entrepots, from Kiev to Limerick with
bases established even as far afield as Greenland
and the coast of North America.

→ Norse routes
✴ main Norse raids (with dates)
⬠ site of three or more rune stones
● Icelandic bishopric
✥ site of Althing

GREENLAND

Northern
hunting ground
(to c. 1200)

Western settlement
(to 1341)

Middle settlement
(to 1380)

Eastern settlement
(to 15th century)

60

Gunnbjorn
Skerries

first permanent viking settlement c. 873

982

ICELAND
WESTERN
QUARTER
Reykjavik
Thingvellir
Althing established 930
SOUTHERN
QUARTER

Holar
1106
Skalholt
1056
Grimsvotn

NORTHERN
QUARTER

EASTERN
QUARTER
Western
Horn

Eastern
Horn

c. 870

c. 870

Atlantic
Ocean

60

Faroe Is

Shetland Is

Orkney Is

Hebrides

Iona
795, 802, 806,
807, 825

Kerry
856

Dublin
838

Chester
893

Winchester
860

North
Sea

Lindisfarne
793
Jarrow
794
York
866

Hedeby

Dorestad
834

Quentovic
820

St-Lô
889
St Malo
872
Nantes
799, 842, 897

Rouen
841

Clermont
864

Nijmegen
881

Louvain
884

Paris
845, 885–6

Le Mans
865

Poitiers
864

Noirmoutier
799

Santiago de
Compostela
968

844

Gijón
844, 1013

FRANCIA
(GAUL)

Nîmes
844

Narbonne
844

Arles
844

Luna
844

Pisa
844

CALIPHATE OF
CÓRDOBA

859

Lisbon
844

Algarve
971

Seville
844

859

40

10

Balearic Is

Mediterranean Sea

FROSTA
Stiklestad
Nidaros
Seija
NORWAY TRØNDELAG
Guli
Oppland
Bergen
Viken
HORDALAND
Oslo
Oseberg
Kaupang
Stavanger
ROGALAND
Skara
VÄSTER-
GÖTLAND
Gothenburg
ÖSTER-
GÖTLAND
Viborg
Jelling
Arhus
Roskilde
Lund
Ribe
SMÅLAND
Öland
Schleswig
DENMARK
Trelleborg
Hamburg
845
Wolin

SWEDEN
UPPLAND
Uppsala
Helgö
Aland Is
Götland

FINLAND
Lake
Ladoga
Aldeigjuborg
(Staraya Ladoga)
Holmgard
(Novgorod)
Yaroslavl

Baltic Sea

Truso

Smolensk

Kiev

PECHENEGS

MAGYARS

Preslav

Philippopolis

Adrianopolis

Black Sea

Constantinople
907, 944

BYZANTINE EMPIRE

65

the east. These show great skill in urban planning and the artefacts indicate an extensive trade in local products, such as amber and furs, as well as luxury items. Excavated ships indicate a variety of vessels designed both to serve the needs of fast moving war bands and the shipment of heavy cargoes for trade. In the Atlantic the Scandinavian settlers often moved into uninhabited areas, though there are some indications of other peoples displaced, such as Irish hermits on Iceland and Picts in northern Caithness, quite apart from the intense and complex relations in Ireland and England.

Political relations and economic rivalries with the Franks were increasingly strained once the Franks had conquered Frisia and Saxony. Although it is difficult to determine the extent to which Danish activities abroad were or were not coordinated from Denmark, the frequency and ferocity of Norse raids on the west Frankish kingdom, England and Ireland in particular, increased greatly from the 840s. There was frequent pillaging of commercial

centres such as Dorestad, attacks on wealthy monasteries, and Norsemen acting as mercenaries and allies for different political factions. In Ireland and England the Norsemen formed the independent kingdoms of Dublin and York as well as founding important commercial centres. In England, moreover, the Norsemen were settled in the Danelaw and had a lasting influence on this region, roughly comprising Yorkshire, East Anglia and the central and east Midlands. In Francia the Norsemen were far more integrated into Frankish politics, culminating in their settlement in the early tenth century in the area which became known as Normandy but which remained a principality within the French kingdom as a whole.

On this expedition Godofrid, king of the Danes, had as his allies the Slavs called Wilzi ... before his return he destroyed a trading place on the [Baltic] seashore, in Danish called Reric, which, because of the taxes it paid was of great advantage to his kingdom. Transferring the merchants from Reric he weighed anchor and came with his whole army to the harbour of Schleswig.

ROYAL FRANKISH ANNALS, 808

The Oseberg ship, c. 820
This ornately carved ship (21.58m long, 5.10m broad, 1.58m deep), full of carved wooden gear and domestic utensils needed for the journey in the after life was interred in its burial mound in the summer of 834.

The consolidation of the three kingdoms within Britain (map right) was complemented by the remarkable spread of Viking settlements, many of them commercial entrepots, from Huntingdon to Limerick with bases established even as far afield as John O' Groats and Bognor Regis.

948	958	995	999	1000	1019	1066
Bishops appointed to Ribe, Schleswig and Arhus in Denmark	Death of Gorm, king of Denmark and burial at Jelling where a stone is erected in his memory by Harald Bluetooth	Olaf Tryggvason recognized as king in western Norway	Olaf Tryggvason killed by Sven Forkbeard who restores Danish overlordship of Norway	Leif Ericsson reaches North America, probably Newfoundland, where the early 11th century Norsesettlement of L'Anse aux Meadows has been uncovered.	Cnut rules Denmark and England	Harald Hardrada killed at Stamford Bridge

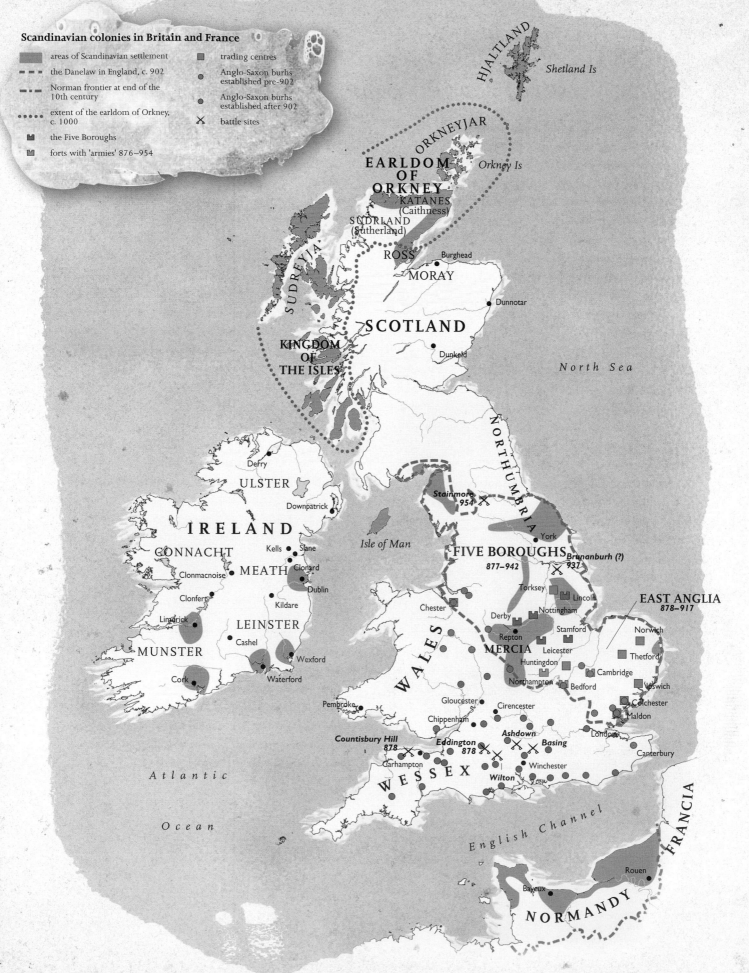

Scandinavian colonies in Britain and France

- areas of Scandinavian settlement
- - - the Danelaw in England, c. 902
- -··- Norman frontier at end of the 10th century
- ···· extent of the earldom of Orkney, c. 1000
- the Five Boroughs
- forts with 'armies' 876–954
- trading centres
- Anglo-Saxon burhs established pre-902
- Anglo-Saxon burhs established after 902
- × battle sites

HJALTLAND
Shetland Is

ORKNEYJAR
EARLDOM OF ORKNEY
Orkney Is
KATANES (Caithness)
SUDRLAND (Sutherland)
ROSS
Burghead
MORAY
Dunnotar
SCOTLAND
Dunkeld

SUDREYJAR

KINGDOM OF THE ISLES

North Sea

Derry
ULSTER
Downpatrick

IRELAND
CONNACHT
Kells   Slane
Clonmacnoise
MEATH   Clonard
Clonfert   Dublin
Kildare
Limerick
LEINSTER
Cashel
MUNSTER   Wexford
Cork   Waterford

Isle of Man

NORTHUMBRIA

Stainmore 954 ×

York

FIVE BOROUGHS
877–942
Brunanburh (?) 937 ×

Torksey
Chester   Lincoln
Derby   Nottingham
Stamford
Repton   **MERCIA**   Leicester
EAST ANGLIA
878–917
Norwich
Huntingdon   Thetford
Northampton   Cambridge
Bedford   Ipswich
Gloucester   Colchester
Cirencester   Maldon
Chippenham
Countisbury Hill 878 ×   Eddington 878 ×   × × Basing   London
Carhampton   Ashdown   Winchester   Canterbury
WESSEX   Wilton

Pembroke
WALES

Atlantic

Ocean

English Channel

Rouen
Bayeux
NORMANDY
FRANCIA

67

Byzantium's Neighbours: Slavs, Bulgars and Magyars; Armenians and Georgians

From the sixth century various peoples migrated across the south Russian steppe to establish themselves in the lands north and south of the River Danube. The Slavic-speaking people, who settled throughout the Balkan peninsula, as far as the southern Peloponnese, were followed by the Turkic Bulgars, who dominated lands north of the Balkan mountains on both sides of the Danube. Two centuries later, the Magyars conquered the Carpathian Basin and ended Bulgar rule north of the river. Each people interacted with the Byzantine empire, hitherto the dominant power in the region. To the east, Armenians and Georgians lived first under Muslim rule, and later under native dynasties, before being annexed by Byzantine expansion.

Slavic peoples began to migrate into the Balkan peninsula from the sixth century, but we first hear of the seven *Sklaviniai* (a Greek term for regions occupied by Slavs) in the *Miracles of St Demetrius*. We must then wait until the arrival of the Turkic Bulgars in 679–80 for more information, and rely on the testimony of the *Chronicle of Theophanes Confessor*, completed 813–14, which relates that a group of Bulgars led by Asperuch settled in the vicinity of Varna. From here they "subjugated the so-called Seven Tribes of the neighbouring Slavic peoples". Legend recounts that Asperuch was one of five sons of Kuvrat who led Bulgars away from their *Urheimat* north of the Black Sea. Kuvrat's

"grave" was discovered in 1912 at Malo Pereschchepino near Poltava in Ukraine. It contained no bones, but twenty kilos of gold and silver goods, including two signet rings bearing the monograms, in Greek characters "of Kuvrat the Patrician". The Byzantine emperor Justinian II confronted the Bulgars in 687–88, and transferred up to 30,000 Slavs to Asia Minor. However, the Balkan Slavs were still sufficiently numerous and troublesome to justify a full-scale Byzantine invasion in 758 by Constantine V, who "conquered the *Sklaviniai* in Macedonia and subjected the rest". Through the two centuries of their recorded existence the *Sklaviniai* did not form a coherent polity. The Turkic Bulgars, in marked contrast, established a powerful empire able to resist Byzantine attempts to recover the northern Balkans.

On 26 July 811, Emperor Nikephoros I was slaughtered with his army in a Bulgarian mountain pass by the troops of Khan Krum. Around 816 a thirty-year peace treaty was negotiated between Byzantines and Bulgars, a summary of which was inscribed on a column found at the Bulgar capital of Pliska. The Bulgars also maintained relations with western powers. In 862 Khan Boris (852–89) approached Louis the German, indicating that he was prepared to accept Christianity. However, following defeat by a Byzantine army in 864, the khan was baptized according to the eastern rite. Byzantine missionaries, including Saints

---

The eldest son [of Kuvrat], called Batbaian, observed his father's command and has remained until this day in his ancestral land. His younger brother, called Kotragos, crossed the river Tanais and dwelt opposite his eldest brother. The fourth and fifth went over the Istros, that is the Danube: the former became the subject of the Khagan of the Avars in Avar Pannonia and remained there with his army, whereas the latter reached Pentapolis, which is near Ravenna, and accepted allegiance to the Christian Empire. Coming after them, the third brother, named Asperuch, crossed the Danapris and Danastris rivers (rivers that are farther north than the Danube) and, on reaching the Oglos, settled between the former and the latter, since he judged that place to be secure and impregnable on both sides.

THEOPHANES THE CONFESSOR, *CHRONICLE*, AM 6171, OR AD 680.

614–18	679–80	811	864–65	888
Slavs attack Thessalonica	Bulgars cross Danube into the Balkans	Khan Krum kills Byzantine emperor Nikephoros I	Khan Boris is baptised as Orthodox Christian	Bagratid dynasty rule Armenia and Georgia

BYZANTIUM AND ITS NEIGHBOURS

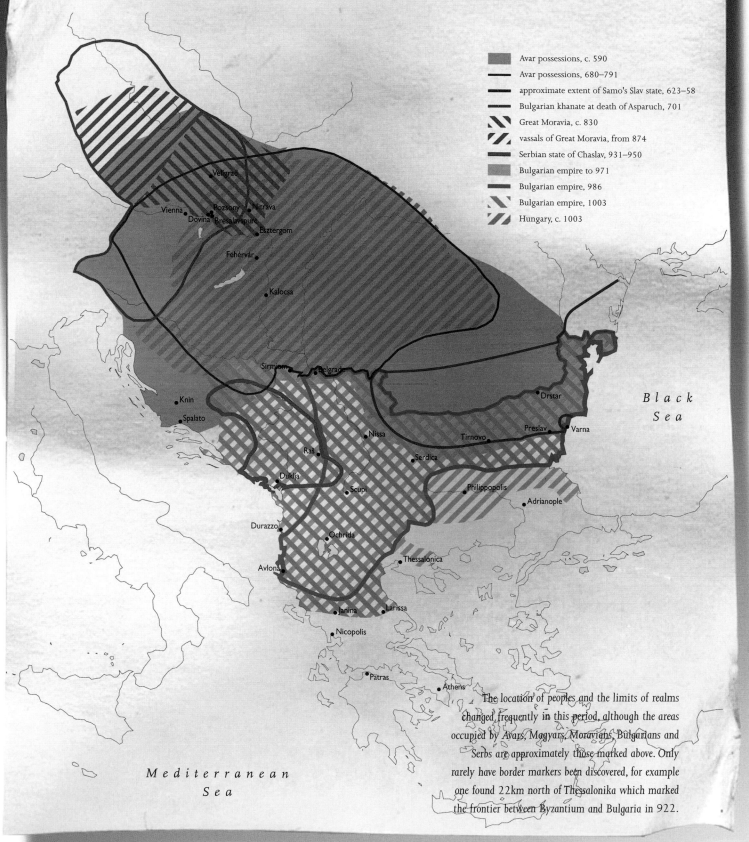

Avar possessions, c. 590

Avar possessions, 680–791

approximate extent of Samo's Slav state, 623–58

Bulgarian khanate at death of Asparuch, 701

Great Moravia, c. 830

vassals of Great Moravia, from 874

Serbian state of Chaslav, 931–950

Bulgarian empire to 971

Bulgarian empire, 986

Bulgarian empire, 1003

Hungary, c. 1003

Veligrad

Vienna · Pozsony · Nitrava
Dovina · Bresalavspurc
Esztergom

Fehérvár

Kalocsa

Sirmium · Belgrade

Knin

Spalato

Nissa

Raš

Drstar

Duklja

Scupi

Preslav · Varna
Tirnovo

Serdica

Durazzo

Ochrida

Philippopolis

Adrianople

Avlona

Thessalonica

Janina · Larissa

Nicopolis

Patras

Athens

Black Sea

Mediterranean Sea

The location of peoples and the limits of realms
changed frequently in this period, although the areas
occupied by Avars, Magyars, Moravians, Bulgarians and
Serbs are approximately those marked above. Only
rarely have border markers been discovered, for example
one found 22km north of Thessalonika which marked
the frontier between Byzantium and Bulgaria in 922.

Treasure from the period
of migrations.
A portion of the treasure discovered at
Nagy-Szent-Miklos, in modern Romania,
now housed in the Kunsthistorisches
Museum in Vienna.

Clement and Naum, were sent to Bulgaria to speed the process of conversion, bringing with them the Glagolitic script devised by Cyril and Methodius. Patriarch Photius of Constantinople (858–67; 877–86) provided Boris with instructions on the principles of Christian rulership. Still, Boris also sent a legation to pose a series of questions to Pope Nicholas I (858–67), including whether Bulgars may bathe on Sundays, and wear trousers. Bulgaria reached its apogee in the reigns of Khan Symeon (c. 894–927) and his son Peter (927–67), who married Maria, the granddaughter of the ruling Byzantine emperor Romanos I.

In 895–6 the Magyars arrived in the Carpathian Basin, and subsequently raided lands to the west until the infamous battle of Lechfeld in 955, and to the south between 934 and 970. The raids were carefully planned and executed either to fulfil paid contracts for, or to extract payments of tribute. While the charisma that was associated with success in battle bolstered the authority of Magyar tribal leaders, the distribution of wealth among followers was as significant. The Magyars also took over established trade routes, developing towns and becoming increasingly sedentary, although nomadism was still common at the time of the conversion of King St Stephen I, c. 1000.

To the east of Byzantium, both Armenians and Georgians were, in 700, subject to the authority of the Caliphate. Their lands, together with Caucasian Albania, comprised the province of Armeniya governed from Tbilisi. Initially, they provided defensive troops and cavalry for the Muslims' wars against the Khazars, beyond the Caucasus, and Byzantium to the west. Later, however, taxation was increased and the native leaders, inspired to rebel, were crushed. The decline of the Abbasid Caliphate in the later ninth century facilitated a native revival. In 884 the Bagratid dynasty claimed the royal title, ruling northern Albania and Georgia. The Artsruni dynasty ruled the southern region of Vaspurkan from 908. This period of political independence was fragile, but saw a flourishing of regional art, architecture and culture, which was brought to an end by the eastwards expansion of Byzantium in the later tenth century.

We consider what you ask about trousers to be irrelevant, for we do not wish the exterior style of your clothes to be changed, but rather the behaviour of the inner person ... But since you ask about these matters in your simplicity, namely because you are afraid lest you have sinned if you diverge in any way from the customs of other Christians in your trouser wearing, we declare that, in our books, trousers are ordered to be made so that men, and not women may wear them ... But do as you please, since whether you or your women wear trousers neither impedes your salvation nor leads to any increase in your virtue. Of course, since we have said that trousers were ordered to be made we must explain that we meant spiritual trousers, by which we restrain the lust of the flesh through abstinence. This is why the first humans, when they felt illicit motions in their parts, grabbed the leaves of a fig tree. These are spiritual trousers...

ONE OF POPE NICHOLAS' RESPONSES TO KHAN BORIS' QUESTIONS ABOUT CORRECT CHRISTIAN PRACTICES.

After 894	895–96	955	c. 1000
Khan Symeon transfers Bulgar capital to Preslav	Magyars arrive in Carpathian Basin	Magyars defeated at Battle of Lechfeld	Magyar ruler Stephen I baptised as Catholic Christian

Byzantium 700–1000

From the late 630s the East Roman or "Byzantine" empire found itself engaged in a struggle for survival against an expansionist Islamic foe which dwarfed it in terms of military and economic resources. The fragmentation of the Islamic world from the 750s onwards, however, permitted the Byzantines the opportunity first to consolidate their position and ultimately to go on the offensive. The emperor in Constantinople, who claimed to be God's representative on earth, saw both his realm extended and his prestige restored.

The Arab conquests of the seventh century reduced the East Roman empire to an Anatolian core, whilst, in the Balkans, Slav incursions left the empire with little more than nominal control beyond the coastlands of the region. From its capital in Constantinople, the imperial authorities were obliged to contend with almost yearly Arab raids into what remained of imperial territory. Beyond Constantinople and Thessalonica, the cities of the empire had been transformed from the bustling urban centres of late antiquity, into more readily defendable military hard-points and fortresses. The Byzantine army, organized into new territorial units called "themes", fought a protracted guerrilla war against the invaders, motivated by the belief that theirs was the empire of Christ, and that with Christ's aid they would be victorious. Control of local government was entrusted to military governors called "strategoi", whose activities were carefully scrutinized by civil servants sent out from the capital. All available resources were harnessed to maximize the military effectiveness of the empire. As the Arab forces advanced, the civilian population of the frontier zone would seek refuge in underground citadels and redoubts, whilst the army would lie in wait in mountain passes and defiles to ambush their numerically-superior foe.

The fragmentation of the Islamic world occasioned by the Abbasid revolution in the mid-eighth century began to alter this military balance and the Byzantine army was able to take on the invaders with increasing success. By the early tenth century, Byzantine armies led by members of the military aristocracy of the eastern marchlands, characterized by their knowledge of the local terrain and with generations of accumulated experience of Byzantine-Arab warfare behind them, began to advance into Arab-held territory. Thus in the 930s the Byzantine general John Curcuas led victorious Byzantine forces into the cities of Melitene and Samosata, and began to strike beyond the Euphrates. The Byzantines were careful to ensure that their military gains were measured and sustainable in character. They avoided striking at prestige targets such as Baghdad or Jerusalem, for fear that in doing so they would unite the Islamic world in a

Tenth-century mosaic from the vestibule of the Cathedral Church of Hagia Sophia or "Holy Wisdom", Constantinople. The greatest monument of the early medieval Christian world. The Virgin Mary or "Theotokos" sits enthroned with Child. To the left, the Emperor Justinian presents the Cathedral, which he had rebuilt in the sixth century: to the right, the Emperor Constantine the Great presents the imperial city, which he had founded in the fourth century. From the fifth century onwards, the Virgin had come to be regarded as the imperial capital's divine patron and supernatural defender.

674
Arab fleet raids up to the walls of Constantinople. The Byzantine navy, armed with "Greek fire" is able to repel the enemy by sea, but by land the Arabs continue to hold the upper hand

717
All remaining Byzantine outposts east of the Euphrates now in Arab hands, whilst Byzantiums' eastern frontier has been pushed back from the Taurus mountain range to the Antitaurus. A full-scale Islamic assault is launched on the empire, with 120,000 men invading Anatolia by land, and a fleet of 1,800 ships advancing along the coast. Aided by a mutiny amongst Christian sailors serving in the Arabic navy, and an outbreak of bubonic plague among the Islamic troops, Constantinople withstands the assault

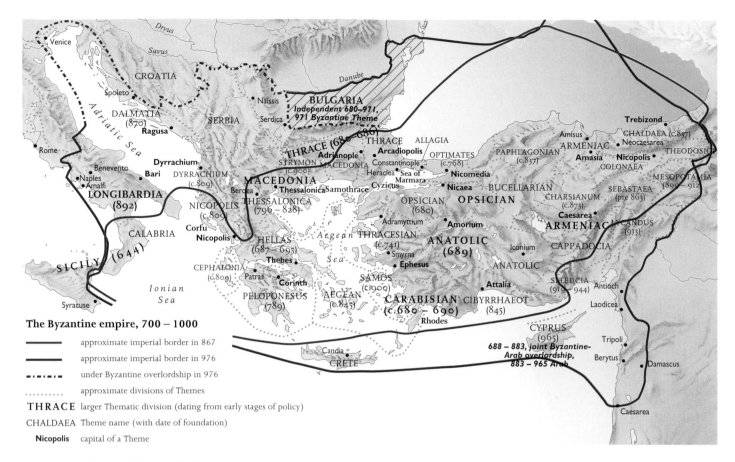

The Byzantine empire, 700 – 1000

Map labels: Venice, Drvus, Savus, CROATIA, Spoleto, Naissis, Danube, BULGARIA Independent 680–971, 971 Byzantine Theme, Serdica, SERBIA, DALMATIA (870), Ragusa, *Adriatic Sea*, Rome, Benevento, Dyrrachium, Bari, DYRRACHIUM (c.809), THRACE (680–686), THRACE, ALLAGIA, Arcadiopolis, Constantinople, OPTIMATES, PAPHLAGONIAN (c.837), Trebizond, Amisus, CHALDAEA (c.837), Neocaesarea, ARMENIAC, Amasia, Nicopolis, THEODOSIO, Naples, Amalfi, LONGIBARDIA (892), Bergea, Adrianople, STRYMON (c.900), MACEDONIA, Heraclea, Sea of Marmara, Cyzicus, Nicomedia, Nicaea, BUCELLARIAN, COLONAEA, MESOPOTAMIA (899–912), SEBASTAEA (pre 863), MACEDONIA, Thessalonica, Samothrace, OPSICIAN, OPSICIAN (680), CHARSIANUM (c.873), CALABRIA, THESSALONICA (796–828), NICOPOLIS (c.809), Corfu, Nicopolis, Adramyttium, THRACESIAN (c.741), Amorium, ANATOLIC (689), Caesarea, ARMENIAC, LYCANDUS (913), SICILY (644), HELLAS (687–695), Thebes, *Aegean Sea*, Smyrna, ANATOLIC, Iconium, CAPPADOCIA, Syracuse, *Ionian Sea*, CEPHALONIA (c.809), Patras, Corinth, Ephesus, SAMOS (c.900), Attalia, SELEUCIA (919–944), Antioch, PELOPONESUS (789), AEGEAN (c.843), CARABISIAN (c.680–690), CIBYRRHAEOT (845), Laodicea, Rhodes, CYPRUS (965), Tripoli, Candia, CRETE, 688–883, joint Byzantine-Arab overlordship, 883–965 Arab, Berytus, Damascus, Caesarea

Legend:
— approximate imperial border in 867
— approximate imperial border in 976
–·–·– under Byzantine overlordship in 976
········· approximate divisions of Themes

THRACE larger Thematic division (dating from early stages of policy)
CHALDAEA Theme name (with date of foundation)
Nicopolis capital of a Theme

concerted holy war for which the Byzantines would be no match. As the empire became increasingly dependent militarily on members of the frontier dynasties, so too did these families come to vie for the imperial crown.

As the military situation stabilized, economic conditions within the empire began to improve. Trade quickened, agriculture became more productive and cities began to recover. The aristocracy of the empire took advantage of these new circumstances, enlarging their estates at the expense of the peasantry. To the west, the Byzantines gradually brought the Slav population of the southern Balkans within the embrace of Orthodox Christianity, and, during the reign of Basil II (976–1025), overcame the rival empire of the Bulgars. In southern Italy, Byzantium yet again became a force to be reckoned with, leading the Christian lords of the region in resistance to Muslim arms. By the 11th century, Constantinople was once more the capital of the greatest power in Christendom.

In Byzantine imperial ideology, there existed only one legitimate emperor on earth – the emperor of Constantinople, whose imperial court was a reflection of the heavenly court, his authority derived from his unique relationship with God. This lofty imperial worldview remained central to Byzantine self-perception, in spite of the enormous territorial contraction the empire had suffered in the seventh century. The extent to which Byzantine society and administration focused on the imperial court meant that, however devastating Islamic raids were, so long as the imperial capital remained unconquered, the empire maintained its cohesion and its potential for recovery, as the imperial reconquests of the tenth century demonstrated. The map shows the military units or "themes" into which the empire was divided during the course of the seventh century. As the military situation changed, the thematic divisions were redrawn and the reconquered territories incorporated.

"God sets Emperors on the throne and gives them lordship over all"
(from the De Administrando Imperio of
Emperor Constantine VII, 913–59)

750
The Abbasid revolution within the Islamic world, centred on eastern Persia, leads to the downfall of the ruling Umayyad dynasty based at Damascus and a relocation of caliphal power to Baghdad. This eases the military pressure on Byzantium's eastern flank.

900
The Byzantine emperor Leo VI sends an army into the Arab emirate of Tarsus and captures its emir. Byzantium's period of expansion to the east begins

975
The Byzantine emperor John Tzimisces brings the coastline of Syria/Lebanon between Antioch and Tripoli under imperial control

Byzantine Culture: Iconoclasm and The Renaissance of the Tenth Century

Persian and Islamic attacks on the Byzantine empire in the seventh century caused large-scale urban destruction, which led to a period of pronounced cultural dislocation in what remained of the East Roman world. An improvement in Byzantium's military fortunes in the late ninth and tenth centuries, however, was associated with a widespread cultural renaissance and the restoration of icons to the Eastern Orthodox Church.

In the late antique East Roman empire, from the fourth century to the seventh, cultural and artistic activity was concentrated in the cities, which were home to its governing elite. Members of this civic elite preserved the literary forms of the ancient Hellenistic world, and competed with one another to adorn their native cities with splendid public monuments and places of worship. By the end of the seventh century, however, chronic insecurity caused by decades of near constant warfare had critically

A 15th-century icon depicting the "Triumph of Orthodoxy", the final defeat of Iconoclasm in 843. To the left of an image of the Virgin and Child stand the Empress Theodora and her young son Michael III.

undermined much of the empire's urban infrastructure. The aristocracy responded to this by retreating to the countryside to live directly off the produce of their estates. They adapted to the prevailing military conditions by adopting an increasingly martial character. As a result, many of the literary and artistic traditions of Greco-Roman antiquity were lost. Neither the imperial authorities nor secular patrons had the resources available to build on the same scale as their late antique predecessors, and, beyond Constantinople and Thessalonica, the public context for such commissions no longer existed. Artisanal skills, such as those associated with the crafting of monumental sculptures, were simply forgotten.

One of the religious traditions that characterized the East Roman world in this period was the use of images of Christ, the Saints, and the Old Testament Prophets in Christian worship. It is a sign of the great cultural chasm that had opened up between Byzantium and its past that in the early eighth century the use of such images or "icons" came to be viewed with increasing suspicion. At the end of the seventh century, the Islamic authorities in Damascus condemned the Christian use of images as idolatrous. This accusation appears to have struck home in imperial circles in Constantinople. Byzantium was suffering terribly at the hands of marauding Muslim armies, a fact that was interpreted as a sign of God's displeasure with the empire. In 726, in an attempt to regain divine favour, the Emperor Leo III publicly declared his opposition to icons. The relative military success that characterized his reign, as well as that of his son Constantine V, appeared to justify the adoption of this policy of "iconoclasm" and, especially in the vicinity of Constantinople, images were either destroyed, whitewashed over, or removed from places of worship.

The correlation between military success and iconoclastic policy eventually broke down, and finally, in 843, the pro-image or "iconophile" faction at court emerged triumphant (they had first tried in 787). The

---

The Ascension, a dome mosaic from Hagia Sophia, Thessalonica. The cathedral of the second greatest city of the empire was rebuilt in the late eighth century. The mosaic was placed in the dome c. 885. To see the mosaic, the viewer was obliged to gaze upwards, just as the New Testament records the Apostles doing as the resurrected Christ was borne towards heaven.

iconoclasts were branded heretics, and religious images were restored to the churches of the empire on an even greater scale than had hitherto been the case. This court-sponsored revival in iconic church decoration went hand in hand with a more general cultural awakening in the Byzantine world. As the military position of the empire first stabilized and, eventually, as the empire began to prosper and expand in the late ninth and early tenth centuries, more resources became available with which to patronise architecture and the arts. Artists began once more to look back to the surviving monuments of late antiquity, and sought to emulate and copy them.

However, the great public setting to late antique art was never quite reconstituted. Rather, images and motifs from late antique public monuments and media were transposed to more private contexts, such as enamels and metalwork, ivory miniatures and illuminated manuscripts. In the latter, whilst individual images were often transferred with great skill and finesse, at times they can be seen to have something of the pastiche about them. Both in relation to manuscript illumination and religious images, the naturalistic style of antiquity was aspired to, but achieved only intermittently. Churches were rebuilt, although typically on a reduced scale according to new architectural principles. Within the shrunken interiors of these Byzantine churches, the devout were free to view the images of the Saints with far greater physical proximity than had been the case in the great basilica churches of late antiquity. This greater intimacy between icon and worshipper reinforced the central role played by the image in the spiritual life of the post-iconoclast Eastern Orthodox Church.

(Above) *Crossing of the Red Sea. Taken from the Paris Psalter, a mid tenth-century illuminated manuscript. Although certain of the individual images, such as that of Moses and the Israelites, are strikingly expressive, others, such as the classical personification of the Red Sea in the bottom right-hand corner, are less successful.*

Middle panel of the cover of a container for a Relic of the True Cross, c. 965 (right). It is made of gold cloisonné and chased silver, and is set with precious and semiprecious stones. In the centre of the sliding cover Christ can be seen enthroned, with Mary and John interceding ("Deesis") on either side of Him. Next to John and Mary stand the Archangels Gabriel and Michael. Above and below, the twelve Apostles are represented. The images are framed with precious stones and enamel busts of Saints.

The Abbasid Caliphate and Subsequent Fragmentation

The Umayyad Caliphs (661–750), with their capital located in Damascus, inherited the religious authority of the Prophet Muhammad (c. 570–632) and the Byzantine administrative and cultural tradition in Syria and the Levant. They were overthrown by the "Sons of al-Abbas" in the third Islamic civil war, the Abbasid Revolution. The Abbasids ruled from 749–1258, founding Baghdad as their capital and ruling over a golden age of political, religious, cultural and intellectual efflorescence, until the Mongols sacked Baghdad in 1258.

The Sons of al-Abbas are the most renowned of Islamic dynasties. They based their right to the Caliphate (the vice-gerency of the Prophet Muhammad) on their descent from al-Abbas, uncle of Muhammad, and their membership of the Prophet's tribe, the Quraysh. They thus argued that they were more rightful heirs to the Prophet than the Umayyad dynasty, who ruled from the death of 'Ali, the cousin of the Prophet (and married to Fatima, one of his daughters). The Abbasid "mission" to overthrow the Umayyads was an astounding success which involved capitalization upon anti-Umayyad resentment among the party (shi'a) of 'Ali, mobilization of the Khurasanians, and appeals to the ambitions and traditions of the recently converted Persian aristocracy.

The history of the Abbasids can be divided into two stages: the theocratic imperium of the first Caliphs (749–847); and the rise of regional dynastic autonomies, together with the emergence of the Turks and the consolidation of the Ulema (847–1055).

The first Abbasid Caliphs considered themselves to be the charismatic inheritors of two traditions: the Arabian-Islamic (bearers of the mantle of the Prophet Muhammad) and the Persian (the successors of the Sassanid monarchs). They thus sought to combine the hegemony of the Arab

Al-Mutawakkil built this Friday Mosque at the new Caliphal Palace complex of Samarra' (which means literally, "Delighted are those who see it") in 848–852. The Minaret, which is 50 metres high, is known as the Malwiya (the "Twisted") and has been much imitated. For many centuries, al-Mutawakkil's Mosque was the biggest in the Islamic world. Samarra' (125 kilometres north of Baghdad) was created by al-Mu'tasim in 836 to house his army and extended for 35 kilometres along the bank of the Tigris and eventually covered 57 square kilometres. It was abandoned in 883, when Caliph al-Mu'tadid returned the capital to Baghdad.

750	762	811–13	821–73	861–945	977
Abbasids defeat the Umayyads at the Battle of the river Zab and al-Saffah is installed as Caliph	Foundation of Baghdad	Civil war breaks out between the Sons of Harun al-Rashid, al-Amin and al-Ma'mun	Tahirids create a quasi-independent kingdom	Emergence of regional autonomies: the Saffarids, the Samanids, the Tulunids and the Buyids	'Adud al-Dawla (949–83) becomes King (malik) of Baghdad and de facto ruler of the Abbasid empire

When al-Mansur, the second Abbasid Caliph constructed the Round City of Baghdad, near Ctesiphon, he named it Madinat al-Salam ("the City of Peace"). It is thought that al-Mansur was following an ancient Iranian design in building Baghdad, such as the round city of Gur (modern day Firuzabad) the capital of Ardashir I in South-western Iran. The Caliph's residence was located at the centre of the circular city, adjacent to the mosque, and there were four Gates: the Khurasan Gate on the northeast, the Kufa gate on the southeast, the Basra Gate on the southwest and the Damascus Gate on the northwest. It was an urban experiment, which could not be sustained, for Baghdad soon became a sprawling urban conglomeration of palaces and residential quarters, trading districts and administrative centres.

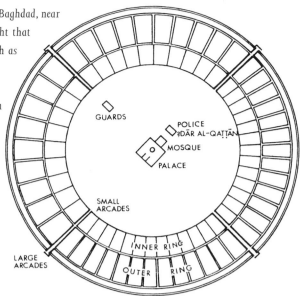

tribes under the ascendancy of the Quraysh with the imperial court ceremonial and administrative structures of the Persians. This is evident in the construction, after Persian models, of the Round City of Baghdad by the second Abbasid Caliph al-Mansur (754–75). Furthermore, Baghdad was built on the Tigris and near Ctesiphon, the imperial seat of the Sassanids. Al-Mansur was also responsible for the commencement of the "Translation Movement", the drive, actuated by religious propaganda and the need to create a representative Arabo-Islamic identity, to translate Hellenistic learning into Arabic, from texts in Greek, Syriac and Pahlavi. This Movement reached its apogee under Caliphal patronage in the reign of al-Ma'mun (814–33). The territorial domains of the Abbasids were at their most extensive under Harun al-Rashid (786–809).

TABLE OF RULERS
(WITH DATES OF ACCESSION)

1.	Al-Saffah, 749.	14.	Al-Muhtadi, 869.
2.	Al-Mansur, 754.	15.	Al-Mu'tamid, 870.
3.	Al-Mahdi, 775.	16.	Al-Mu'tadid, 892.
4.	Al-Hadi, 785.	17.	Al-Muktafi, 902.
5.	Al-Rashid, 786.	18.	Al-Muqtadir, 908.
6.	Al-Amin, 809.	19.	Al-Qahir, 932.
7.	Al-Ma'mun, 813.	20.	Al-Radi, 934.
8.	Al-Mu'tasim, 833.	21.	Al-Muttaqi, 940.
9.	Al-Wathiq, 842.	22.	Al-Mustakfi, 944.
10.	Al-Mutawakkil, 847.	23.	Al-Muti', 946.
11.	Al-Muntasir, 861.	24.	Al-Ta'i', 974.
12.	Al-Musta'in, 862.	25.	Al-Qadir, 991.
13.	Al-Mu'tazz, 866.	26.	Al-Qa'im, 1031.

The reign of al-Ma'mun witnessed the initiation of The Trial (Mihna), an attempt to secure religious authority as vested in the figure of the Caliph, continued by his successors al-Mu'tasim (833–42) and al-Wathiq (842–47). The failure of The Trial led to the emergence, under al-Mutawakkil, of the religious scholars, the Ulema, under the aegis of Ahmad ibn Hanbal (d. 854), founder of the literalist Hanbali law school. Al-Mu'tasim had, in 836, founded a new capital, the vast palace complex of Samarra', which was replaced by Baghdad in 883. His practice of using Turkish slaves as soldiers marks the beginning of the end of Arab hegemony, the demise of the Abbasid theocracy, and political fragmentation in the form of autonomous, regional dynasties.

The Abbasids had lost Islamic Spain to the Umayyads at the onset of rule. They gradually lost control over territories west of Mosul, as the Tulunids and then the Fatimids took control of Egypt and Ifriqiya and the Hamdanids ruled Syria. The eastern empire, however, experienced more extensive fragmentation, with the emergence on the shores of the Caspian Sea of the Daylamites and the Samanids in Transoxania (819–1005), destroyed by the Ghaznavids (977–1186). The Buyids, from Daylam, were effective rulers of the Abbasid empire from 945–1055, having deposed the Caliph al-Mustakfi.

The religious aura of the Abbasid custodianship of the office of the Caliphate was still strong enough, even in 1258, for one of their descendants to be placed on the throne in Cairo by the Mamluk Sultan.

ABBASID CALIPHATE AND FRAGMENTATION

When the Abbasids ousted the Umayyads in 750, they inherited an Islamic empire that stretched from the Pyrenees to Ferghana and the Punjab and comprised Armenia, Transoxania and the supra-Saharan North African littoral. After a century, however, Islamic Spain and North Africa had been lost, and Transoxania was as good as independent. The core of the Abbasid empire now stretched from Egypt to the Black Sea and as far east as Rayy. Most dynasties in the East, however, continued to recognize the overlordship of the Caliph.

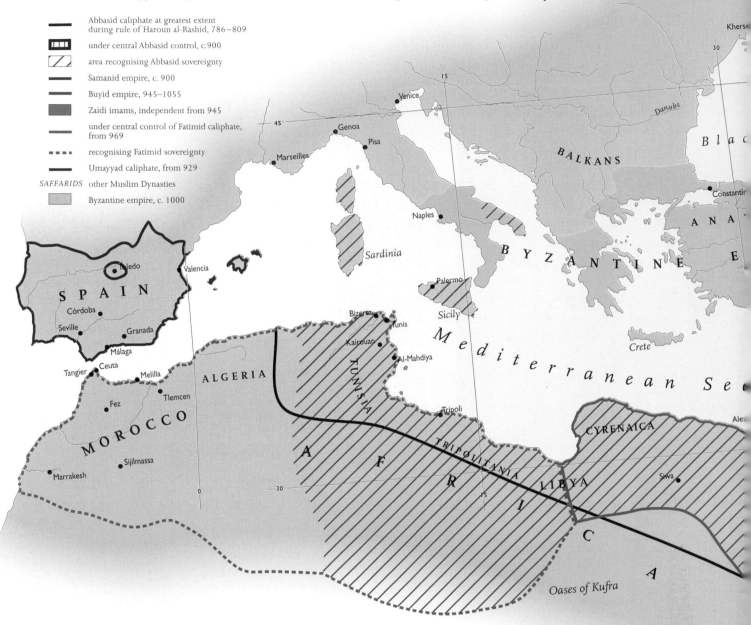

Legend:
- Abbasid caliphate at greatest extent during rule of Haroun al-Rashid, 786–809
- under central Abbasid control, c.900
- area recognising Abbasid sovereignty
- Samanid empire, c. 900
- Buyid empire, 945–1055
- Zaidi imams, independent from 945
- under central control of Fatimid caliphate, from 969
- recognising Fatimid sovereignty
- Umayyad caliphate, from 929
- *SAFFARIDS* other Muslim Dynasties
- Byzantine empire, c. 1000

The lifestyle and the conditions of the Arabs diversified and extended. They reached the limit in this and entered into the stage of sedentariness and luxury in the ways in which they lived, the exquisiteness of their food and drink, clothing, buildings, weapons, carpets, artefacts and all other household utensils and furnishings. Similar, too, was their lifestyle in the matter of banquets, celebrations and wedding feasts. Indeed, in this they went beyond the limit.

IBN KHALDUN (D. 1406), *THE INTRODUCTION TO HISTORY*

KHAZAR EMPIRE

Aral Sea

Caspian Sea

Itil

Caucasus Mts.

Derbent

Urgench

KHWARIZM

QARAKHANIDS
(960–1089)

Kashgar

Jaxartes (Syr Darya)

Tiflis

Trebizond

Baku

Bukhara

Samarkand

Ardabil

Amida

Tabriz

AZERBAIJAN

Mery

Balkh

TRANSOXANIA

HAMDANIDS

JEZIRA

Nisibis

Mosul

Rai

Tus

Nishapur

Oxus (Amu Darya)

Hindu Kush Mts

Kabul

KASHMIR

Antioch

Aleppo

SYRIA

Hamadan

Herat

KHURASAN

Ghazni

GHAZNAVIDS

Latakia

Tripoli

Homs

Kermanshah

IRAQ

AFGHANISTAN

Cyprus

Beirut

Damascus

Baghdad

Isfahan

SAFFARIDS

SEISTAN

Kandahar

Lahore

PUNJAB

Acre

Kufa

Yazd

Zarani

Multan

PALESTINE

Euphrates

Tigris

PERSIA

Jerusalem

Basra

Shiraz

INDIA

EGYPT

HEJAZ

BAHRAIN

Siraf

Ormuz

SIND

Daybul

Persian Gulf

Tiz

Medina

Red Sea

Muscat

OMAN

Aydhab

Jedda

Mecca

ARABIA

YEMEN

Sana

Hodeida

Zabid

Taizz

Aden

81

Islam And
Islamic Culture

Islam (Submission to Allah) was revealed to the Prophet
Muhammad in the desert town of Mecca, a centre of pilgrimage
before the Revelation. It was revealed, via the Angel Gabriel, over
some forty years: these disparate instances of the Revelation
together make up the Qur'an, the Book of Allah.

By the year of his death (632), Muhammad had united the
tribes of the Arabian Peninsula under the banner of Islam
and attention had already been directed at the
representatives of the Byzantine Empire in the *limes* of
Syria and the Levant. Muhammad died without
nominating a successor to guide the newly fledged
Islamic community. His uncle Abu Bakr was proclaimed
caliph, a title that means successor or vice-gerent, and
this initiated the period of the Rashidun, the Rightly
Guided Caliphs. The issue of the leadership of the
Community proved the most significant feature of at
least three centuries of Islamic history, for the leadership
was not simply political but religious – the right to
represent the Prophet and Allah on earth.

Islamic Culture was a multifarious and vibrant series
of interpretations of various traditions in the Near and
Middle East: the austere nobility of the Arab desert, the
Graeco-Arabic and Indian philosophical and scientific
traditions (the Asian legacy of the Empire of Alexander the
Great), ancient Iranian and Sassanid imperial courtly

ISLAM AND
ISLAMIC CULTURE

By the end of the 15th Century, the routes of the Pilgrimage to
Mecca, the spread of the Sufi brotherhoods and the practice of
visiting local shrines provided Muslims with a series of arteries and
travel itineraries well enough established to allow the 14th Century
North African traveller Ibn Battuta (d. c. 1377) to claim that he
had journeyed for some 25 years across the Abode of Islam.

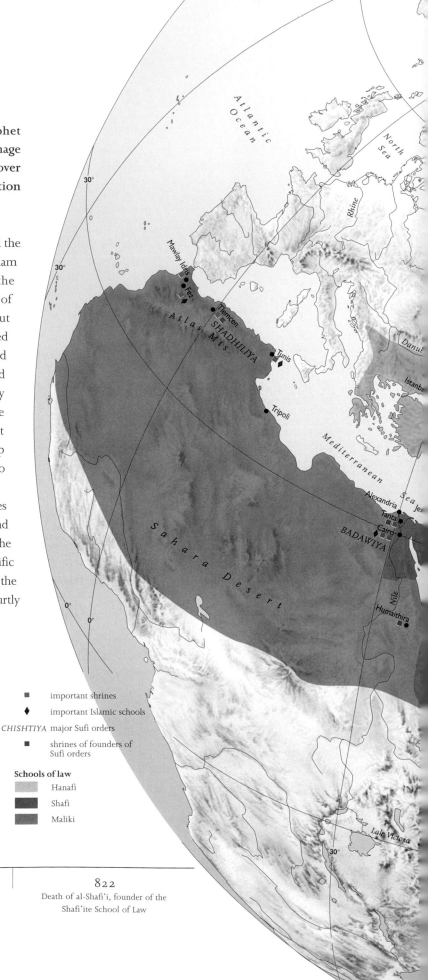

■ important shrines

♦ important Islamic schools

CHISHTIYA major Sufi orders

■ shrines of founders of
Sufi orders

Schools of law

Hanafi

Shafi

Maliki

632	691	822
Death of Muhammad in Medina	Construction of the Dome of the Rock in Jerusalem	Death of al-Shafi'i, founder of the Shafi'ite School of Law

82

LAWIYA

QADIRIYA

Damascus
Euphrates
Tigris
Kazimayn
Baghdad
Samarra
Karbala
Najaf
Umm Abida

SUHRAWARDIYA

Medinah

Mecca

Qom

Mashhad

Persian Gulf

Arabian Sea

Khiva

KUBRAWIYA

Bukhara

NAQSHBANDIYA
Oxus

Aral Sea

Caspian Sea

Volga

Caucasus Mts

k Sea

Ural Mountains

Ob

Irtysh

Jaxartes

Lake Balkhash

Turkestan

Issyk Kul

Tien Shan

Pamir Mts

Kunlun Range

Taklamakan Desert

Nan Shan

Gobi Desert

Yenisey

Lake Baikal

Amur

Sea of Japan

Yellow

Red

Mekong

South China Sea

Himalaya Mts

Brahmaputra

Indus

Ajmere

Ganges

CHISHTIYA

Bay of Bengal

Irrawaddy

Indian Ocean

60°

90°

120

83

The Umayyad Dome of the Rock was constructed in 691 by the Caliph 'Abd al-Malik, an event which coincided with the use of Arabic to replace Greek as the language of imperial administration and the minting of coinage with Arabic inscriptions. It is a clear and conspicuous statement of the temporal power of the one, true religion, Islam.

(Right) Taken from a manuscript copied and illustrated by al-Wasiti in Baghdad (1237), this scene depicts the arrival at a village of the picaresque hero Abu Zayd and the narrator al-Harith, who ask for directions from the figure on the left. The village has its own mosque, animals abound, the individual on the right is carding wool and a domestic quarrel is apparently taking place behind the principal characters.

culture, and the nomadic energy of the Turkic tribes. These interpretations were articulated within a Near-Eastern monotheistic tradition, which prized devotion to Allah and His Messenger Muhammad above all.

The eighth and ninth Centuries were the formative periods of Islam and Islamic culture. Numerous regional schools of law developed, out of which the four dominant schools emerged: the Maliki in Medina, and the Hanafi, Shafi'i and Hanbali in Iraq. By the tenth century, the development of these centres as "schools of thought", together with a hagiography of their founding fathers and foundational texts, was well under way. Malikism had spread to North Africa, where it was to persist, initially in tandem with Kharijism, a sect of extreme secessionists.

c. 764–1055	950	1037	1111
The Graeco-Arabic Translation Movement in Iraq	Death of al-Farabi, the Second Master (after Aristotle)	Death of Ibn Sina (Avicenna)	Death of al-Ghazali

Mawlana Jalal al-Din al-Rumi (d. 1273) was the founder of the Mawlawi Sufi Order, whose poetry continues to enjoy considerable popularity to this day and whose tomb in Anatolia is much visited. In this illustration (below) from a 16th Century Turkish manuscript, Mawlana ("our master") is recognized as unique when a cow miraculously bows down before him.

Hanafism, more inclusive in its definition of what constituted a Muslim (and thus conducive to conversion), was dominant in Khurasan and Transoxania. It is in this period also, that the Shi'a, the Party of the House of 'Ali, with their celebration of a charismatic and divinely inspired leader in whom all exegetical authority was located, fixed their identity and tradition against the emergent paradigm of Sunni Islam. Created by the Ulema who dominated religious thought and arrogated to themselves sole interpretative authority, Sunni Islam is the Islam of the Path of the Prophet Muhammad. The Shi'a themselves were to fragment into four groups: the Twelver Shi'a, who held that the Twelfth Imam had gone into occultation later to reappear and guide the Community; the Zaydis, who established communities in Iran, and, most successfully, the Yemen, and the Sevener Shi'a (also known as the Isma'iliyya), who held that the Imamate terminated with the figure of Isma'il, the son of the Sixth Imam, Ja'far the True. Central to the multiple and varied expressions of Islam is the notion of the right to speak authoritatively on behalf the Community, to act, in other words, as successor to Muhammad.

The Seljuk Sultanate, rigorous in its adherence to Sunni Islam and in opposition to the Fatimid Imam-Caliphs, inaugurated the codification of Sunnism as the dominant Islamic exegetical tradition of authority in the lands of the Caliphate. Central to this process is the figure of al-Ghazali (d. 1111), who defined for Islam, in addition to the textual processes of understanding the divine law and the Path of the Prophet, its component parts of Sufism (to be considered a personalized, unmediated approach to religious experience rather than as Islamic mysticism), speculative theology and the legacy of the Graeco-Arabic philosophy. In subsequent centuries, Sufism in its various guises was to unite credally the Islamic domains, facilitating trade and travel through the institution of its convents. The poetry of Jalal al-Din al-Rumi remains for many the pinnacle of Sufi thought and devotion, retaining its popularity even today in the West.

The Temple Kingdoms in India

The thousands of inscriptions that have come down to us from the temple kingdoms of medieval India reveal an intricate mosaic of kings, lords and priests resting upon a vast agrarian base. This period witnessed unparalleled agrarian expansion, the proliferation of different kinds of state forms and the triumph of theistic Hinduism over its rivals. From 950, political power gradually shifted south, as north India fragmented, making it vulnerable to Turkic incursions from the northwest.

The period 750–1200 saw the consolidation and expansion of the socio-political order established in the centuries following the demise of the Gupta empire (fifth century). While political power remained divided between regional dynasties, underlying social processes such as new patterns of urbanization and continued agrarian expansion gave the social order a certain unified character throughout the subcontinent.

Politically, the period may be split into two broad divisions. The first, spanning approximately 750–950, saw the emergence of three major imperial courts which struggled for supremacy: the Gurjara-Pratiharas, an aristocratic clan with pastoral origins who established a major empire from the north Indian city of Kanyakubja or Kanauj; the Rastrakutas, vassals who in 757 displaced their overlords, the Calukyas of Badami (they had built a major empire in the Deccan and South India); and finally, the Palas of Eastern India, famous for their patronage of Buddhism, who rose to prominence in modern Bihar and Bengal. The second period, commencing from about 950, saw the rise of the Cholas in south India (they even made military expeditions to the kingdom of Srivijaya in Southeast Asia). Meanwhile, in the Deccan, a Rastrakuta vassal from the Calukya family founded a powerful new empire at Kalyani. In

Medieval temples, like this Brahmeshwar Siva temple at Bhubaneshwar built in the 11th century reflect the power structure of medieval society. Divine icons sat inside these temples like kings, entertained and bathed daily by a host of ministrants. In addition they enjoyed revenue in service, money and kind from huge tracts of land in the surrounding countryside.

757	860	972	998–1030	1010	1191–92
Rastrakuta king Dantidurga defeats Calukya king and claims overlordship of the Deccan	King Balaputra of Sumatra establishes a monastery at the Buddhist University at Nalanda	King Siyaka II of Paramara sacks Manyakheta, the Rastrakuta capital	Mahmud of Ghazni conducts some 17 raids into India, looting and desecrating several important north Indian temples	The Chola king Rajaraja completes construction of the famous Rajarajesvara temple in Tanjavur, South India	First and second battles of Tarain

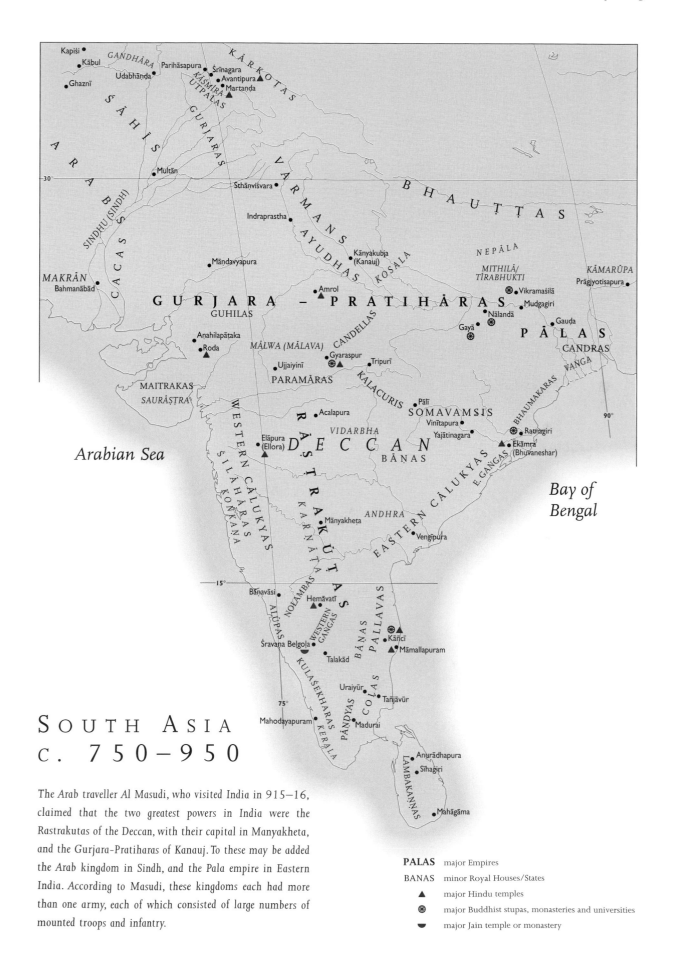

Kapiśi
Kābul
GANDHĀRA
Ghaznī
Udabhānda
Parihāsapura
KĀRKOTAS
Śrīnagara
KĀSMIRA
Avantipura ▲
UTPALAS
Martanda ▲

ŚĀHIS
GURJARAS
Multān

ARABS (SINDH)
SINDHU (SINDH)
CACAS
Sthānviśvara
BHAUTTAS
Indraprastha
VARMANS
AYUDHAS
Kānyakubja (Kanauj)
KOSALA
NEPĀLA

MAKRĀN
Bahmanābād
Māndavyapura
MITHILĀ/ TĪRABHUKTI
Prāgjyotiṣapura
KĀMARŪPA

GURJARA – PRATIHĀRAS
Amrol ▲
⊛ Vikramaśīlā
Mudgagiri
PĀLAS
GUHILAS
CANDELLAS
Gayā ⊛
Nālandā ⊛
Gauḍa
Anahilapāṭaka
Roda ▲
MĀLWA (MĀLAVA)
Gyaraspur ⊛ ▲
Tripurī
CANDRAS
Ujjaiyinī
KALACURIS
VANGA
PARAMĀRAS
Pālī
BHAUMAKARAS
MAITRAKAS
SAURĀṢṬRA
Acalapura
SOMAVAMSIS
Vinītapura
Yajātinagara
⊛ Ratnagiri
VIDARBHA
RĀṢṬRAKŪṬAS
Elāpura (Ellora) ▲
DECCAN
BĀNAS
Ekāmra ▲ (Bhuvaneshar)

Arabian Sea

WESTERN CĀLUKYAS
SILĀHĀRAS
KONKANA
Māṇyakheṭa
ANDHRA
EASTERN CĀLUKYAS
E. GANGAS

RĀṢṬRAKŪṬAS
KARṆĀṬA
Vengīpura

Bay of Bengal

Bāṇavāsi
NOLAMBAS
Hemāvatī ▲
ALŪPAS
WESTERN GANGAS
BĀNAS
PALLAVAS
Kāñcī ⊛ ▲
Śravana Belgoḷa
Talakād
KULASEKHARAS
Māmallapuram ▲

Uraiyūr
COĻAS
Tañjāvūr
Mahodayapuram
KERALA
PĀNDYAS
Madurai

Anurādhapura
Sīhagiri
LAMBAKANNAS
Mahāgāma

SOUTH ASIA
c. 750–950

The *Arab traveller Al Masudi, who visited India in 915–16,
claimed that the two greatest powers in India were the
Rastrakutas of the Deccan, with their capital in Manyakheta,
and the Gurjara-Pratiharas of Kanauj. To these may be added
the Arab kingdom in Sindh, and the Pala empire in Eastern
India. According to Masudi, these kingdoms each had more
than one army, each of which consisted of large numbers of
mounted troops and infantry.*

PALAS   major Empires
BANAS   minor Royal Houses/States
▲   major Hindu temples
⊛   major Buddhist stupas, monasteries and universities
⏝   major Jain temple or monastery

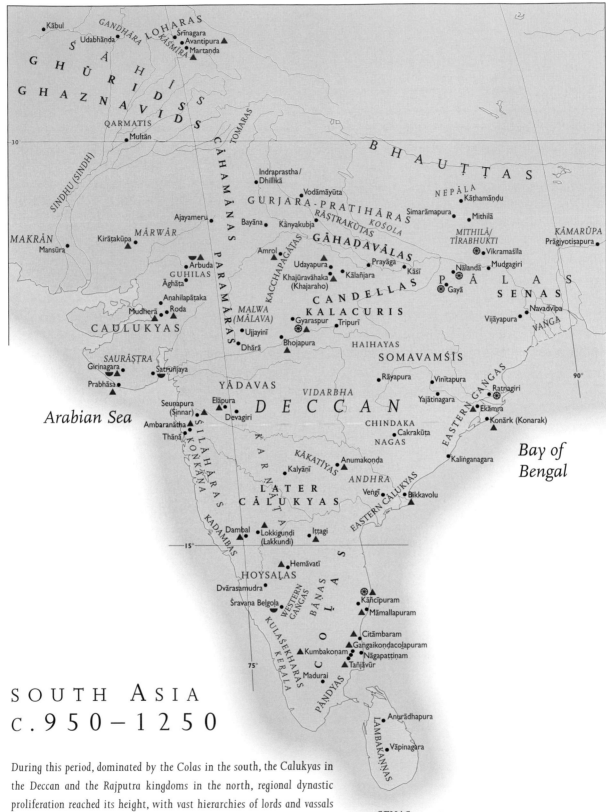

Kābul
GANDHĀRA
LOHARAS
Śrīnagara
Udabhānda
KĀŚMĪRA
Avantipura ▲
Martaṇḍa ▲

GHŪRIDS
GHAZNAVIDS

QARMATIS
Multān

SINDHU (SINDH)

MAKRĀN
Mansūra

MĀRWĀR
Ajayameru
Kirātakūpa ▲

Arbuda ▼▼
GUHILAS
Āghāta
Anahilapāṭaka
Mudherā ▲ Roda
CAULUKYAS

SAURĀṢṬRA
Girinagara ▲
Prabhāsa ▲
Satruñjaya ▲

Arabian Sea

Seunapura
(Sinnar)
Ambaranātha
Thāṇā
KOṄKAṆA
ŚILĀHĀRAS

KADAMBAS

CĀHAMĀNAS
TOMARAS
Indraprastha/
Dhillikā
Vodāmāyūta
GURJARA-PRATIHĀRAS
Bayāna
Kānyakubja
RĀṢṬRAKŪṬAS
KOŚOLA

GĀHADAVĀLAS

Amrol
KACCHAPAGHĀTAS
Udayapura
Khajurāvāhaka
(Khajaraho) ▲
CANDELLAS
KALACURIS
MALWA
(MĀLAVA)
Gyaraspur ⊛ ▲ Tripurī
Ujjayinī
Dhārā
Bhojapura ▲
HAIHAYAS
SOMAVAMŚĪS

PARAMĀRAS

YĀDAVAS
Elāpura ▲
Devagiri
VIDARBHA
DECCAN

KARṆĀṬA

CHINDAKA
NAGAS
Cakrakūṭa

KĀKATĪYAS
Anumakoṇḍa
Kalyāṇī
ANDHRA
LATER
CĀLUKYAS
Veṅgī ⊛ Bikkavolu
EASTERN CĀLUKYAS

Prayāga
Kālañjara
Kāśī
Nālandā ⊛
Gayā ⊛
Mudgagiri

PĀLAS
SENAS

Navadvīpa
Vijayapura
VAṄGA

NEPĀLA
Kāṭhamāṇḍu
Simarāmapura
Mithilā
MITHILĀ/
TĪRABHUKTI
Vikramaśīla ⊛

KĀMARŪPA
Prāgjyotiṣapura

BHAUṬṬAS

Rāyapura
Vinītapura
Yajātinagara
EASTERN GAṄGAS
Ratnagiri ⊛
Ekāmra ⊛
Konārk (Konarak) ▲

Kaliṅganagara

Bay of Bengal

Dambal
Lokkigundi
(Lakkundi)
Iṭṭagi ▲

Hemāvatī ▲

HOYSALAS
Dvārasamudra
Śravana Belgola

WESTERN GAṄGAS
BĀṆAS
KULAŚEKHARAS
KERALA
Madurai
PĀṆDYAS

CŌḶAS

Kāñcīpuram ⊛ ▲
Māmallapuram ▲
Citāmbaram ▲
Kumbakoṇam ▲
Gaṅgaikoṇḍacolapuram ▲
Nāgapaṭṭiṇam
Tañjāvūr ▲

Anurādhapura

Vāpinagara
LAMBAKAṆṆAS

30
90°
15
75°

SOUTH ASIA
c. 950–1250

During this period, dominated by the Colas in the south, the Calukyas in
the Deccan and the Rajputra kingdoms in the north, regional dynastic
proliferation reached its height, with vast hierarchies of lords and vassals
stretching throughout the countryside. The Hindu theory of diplomatic
relations envisioned this hierarchy as a vast set of concentric circles
composed of successive tiers of allies and enemies. As Hindu kings defeated
contiguous kingdoms, they often shifted their allegiances against their
former allies.

SENAS Major Empires
BANAS Minor Royal Houses/States
▲   Major Hindu temples
⊛   Major Buddhist stupas, monasteries and universities
▼   Major Jain temple or monastery

north India, the Pratihara empire disintegrated into smaller kingdoms some of whom claimed the same lineage and also to be "rajputras" (the sons of kings). The most powerful of these were the Chahamanas of Ajayameru, the Paramaras of Dhara, the Gahadvalas of Kasi, the Candellas of Kalanjar and the Kalacuris of Tripuri. These kingdoms bore the brunt of the raids by the powerful Muslim empires of the Ghaznavids and Ghurids from the 11th century. Between the years 998 and 1030, Mahmud of Ghazni made some 17 raids into northern and western India to obtain wealth from temples.

The dynasties of eastern India – particularly the Palas and the Cholas – established trade links and cultural exchanges with the kingdoms of Southeast Asia. Several Buddhist kings of Southeast Asia patronized Buddhist institutions in eastern India and maintained trading enclaves in coastal cities. Despite these trading links, medieval Indian empires remained primarily agrarian in nature, though temple towns, in trading with cities in other regions, integrated the countryside more closely than ever before. The royal families, courtly intellectuals and ritual specialists who composed the ruling classes of these kingdoms enjoyed the revenue from vast tracts of land cultivated by the lower orders, which in turn were divided into hierarchies of cultivators, tenants and labourers. The expansion of the agrarian order during this period led to two related social processes: the transformation of tribal pastoralists, hunter-gatherers and raiders into settled "revenue producing" peasant communities, and the ability of élites from these groups and already established landowning classes readily to convert their power into aristocratic or lordly status.

The major Hindu theistic orders, Vaisnavism and Saivism, gained near complete hegemony during this period (except at the fringes of the subcontinent), as Hindu temples and Brahmin religious communities enjoyed extensive royal and lordly support. The famous temples of the Rastrakutas at Elapura (Ellora) and Cholas at Tanjavur are spectacular examples of this process. The vast wealth that accumulated in temples through "devdana" (gifts of land and gold) explains some of their attraction for the raiding Ghaznavids.

Vaidyanatha temple, Baijnath, Himachal Pradesh. Located in the idyllic Kangra valley, this temple was founded by two merchants in the early 13th century. The gently curving spire, typical of north Indian temples, rests above a linga (aniconic image) of Siva known as Vaidyanatha, or "Lord of the Physicians".

Religion and Empire in Southeast Asia, c. 700–1000

Southeast Asia was a fulcrum of the global networks of trade, migration and belief of the medieval world. Commercial and cultural connections were central to the development of states. Early Southeast Asia was a fluid world of local chiefs and kings who left little material residue. But in the last three centuries of the first millennium, larger polities emerged, with more rooted centres of power.

Patterns of authority differed across a diverse region. The centralized domains of the mainland and Java were based on fertile river plains and wet-rice production. Political power in the maritime world rested upon control of the river systems and their trade in forest products. Here, where the hinterland was less accessible and populations more dispersed, it was more difficult for rulers to concentrate wealth and power than on the mainland.

Yet there were shared experiences. Interactions with the outside world became increasingly important to the success of states. Hindu and Buddhist cosmologies were adapted by Southeast Asian rulers, to enhance their authority. Their ritual sought to recreate a sense of the heavenly order on earth. Indic influence brought religion, economy and kingship closer together, and this made possible the construction of great temple complexes.

This was not a one-way process of "Indianization": borrowings of Sanskrit vocabulary, and Hindu and Buddhist concepts of state and kingship occurred through indigenous initiative, and show the creative ways in which Southeast Asians localized new ideas into their cultural

worlds. This was a common feature of the states that, by the end of the first millennium, were widening in imperial vision.

The outstanding example of this is the Khmer state. It emerged as a dominant force on the mainland with the establishment, by Jayavarman II (c. 770–854), of a new capital at Angkor. He and his successors incorporated local principalities into an empire which made unprecedented ritual claims, and, by the time of its consolidation under Rajendravarman (944–c. 968), claimed suzerainty as far as Burma and China.

In the northeast, a cluster of states previously under the dominance of Tang China coalesced into the Dai Viet kingdom, and carved out a more independent path. Although the state continued to be shaped by Chinese influence, the creation after 1000 of a more stable frontier and a new centre of political power on the area around Thang-Long (Hanoi), has been seen as "the birth of Vietnam", and is central to the historical memory of the modern nation-state.

Within the urbanized culture of the Irrawaddy basin there were competing centres of power, of which the cities of the Tibeto-Burman Pyu peoples, Sri Ksetra and later Hanlan, were the most important. By the ninth and tenth centuries the Burman state of Pagan arose to eclipse its principal rival, the Mon kingdom of Thaton. In this competitive world, states felt strongly the need to affirm the ethical basis of their authority in Buddhist terms.

From the last half of the seventh century the paramount power in the maritime world was Srvijaya. It was a conglomerate of Malay coastal communities created out of a shared interest in trade. Srivijaya's core region in south-eastern Sumatra was a "favoured coast" in long distance commerce, particularly for the Arab trade in aromatics and drugs, and its ships displaced other merchants in the carriage of exotic goods to China.

Srivijaya possessed no agrarian base and has left few monumental remains. It extended its power through suzerainty, tribute and control of piracy. Although it was an important centre of Buddhist scholarship – and celebrated as such by the Chinese pilgrim, I Ching – its experience shows that great cities and temples were not the only measure of a state's achievement, and Srivijaya was to become a model for later states in the Malay world.

SOUTHEAST ASIA 700–1000

In Java, a civilization based on hydraulic systems of wet rice farming had, by the eighth century, embarked on a large-scale temple construction. The most monumental site was the multi-terraced Buddhist stupa of Borobodur, built by the Mahayana Sailendra dynasty. The pedagogical stone reliefs that line its walls are rich in Javanese influences: the panel shown here (opposite left) illustrates early Southeast Asian shipping. By the later ninth or early tenth century, a rival, Saivite dynasty had responded in kind by constructing a temple complex at Prambanan. Little is known of these Javanese kingdoms; however, their rich cultural legacy is an outstanding example of the Southeast Asian ability to appropriate and enrich religious traditions from South Asia and elsewhere.

The Tang Dynasty

By consolidating and standardizing administrative practices that had evolved since the downfall of the Han dynasty in 219, the Tang dynasty (618–906) established, for only the second time in Chinese history, a long-lasting empire for both north and south China. Its administrative structure, court culture, official organization, law and ritual codes, and Buddhist learning and organization would be emulated, largely in vain, by other East Asian states and later Chinese dynasties.

In its early decades Tang government was simple and cheap. Court positions were retained largely by aristocratic families from previous dynasties of north China. The newly introduced examination system eventually attracted some aristocrats anxious to outperform competitors for the top appointments, but overall it produced less than ten per cent of the dynasty's officials. The dynasty's income came mainly from peasant land taxes, labour service, and sometimes military service, paid in return for roughly equal land grants. After securing rule within its own territory, successive seventh-century emperors like Taizong (599–649) oversaw the farthest expansion westward of any Chinese dynasty before the 18th century. They decisively defeated the Turks in the 640s, advanced west of the Tarim Basin, and attracted to their capitals of Changan and Loyang embassies from Persia and even the Byzantine Empire. By the close of the long rule of Empress Wu (625–705), Turk forces had revived and Tibetan soldiers were threatening Tang hegemony. But, the enthronement of Xuanzong in 712 saw a restoration of Tang dynastic power at home and abroad, a cultural efflorescence at the court, and a revival of aristocratic politics in 736 under the chief minister Li Linfu.

At this peak of Tang splendour, the emperor Xuanzong was distracted from government

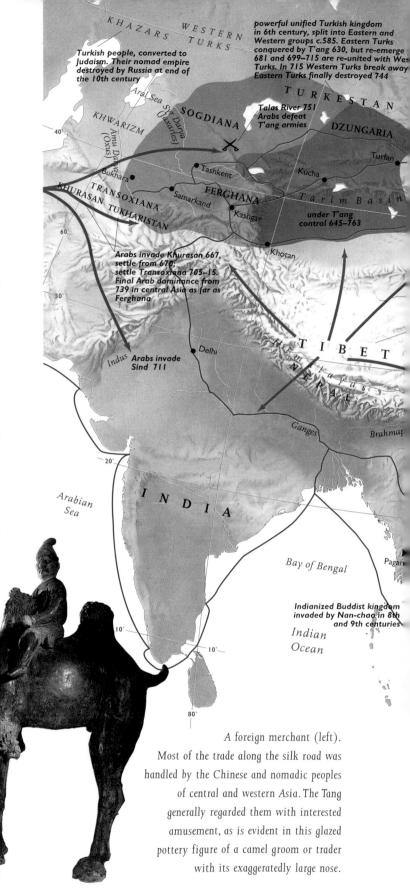

A foreign merchant (left). Most of the trade along the silk road was handled by the Chinese and nomadic peoples of central and western Asia. The Tang generally regarded them with interested amusement, as is evident in this glazed pottery figure of a camel groom or trader with its exaggeratedly large nose.

Turkish people, converted to Judaism. Their nomad empire destroyed by Russia at end of the 10th century

powerful unified Turkish kingdom in 6th century, split into Eastern and Western groups c.585. Eastern Turks conquered by T'ang 630, but re-emerge 681 and 699–715 are re-united with Wes Turks. In 715 Western Turks break away Eastern Turks finally destroyed 744

Talas River 751 Arabs defeat T'ang armies

under T'ang control 645–763

Arabs invade Khurasan 667, settle from 670; settle Transoxiana 705–15. Final Arab dominance from 739 in central Asia as far as Ferghana

Arabs invade Sind 711

Indianized Buddist kingdom invaded by Nan-chao in 8th and 9th centuries

631	684	751	780	c. 810	842–45
Gospel brought to Chang'an by Nestorian Christians	Empress Wu seizes power	Chinese armies under Korean general Gao Xianzhi defeated by Arabs near Alma Ata, along the River Talas	Basic land tax reform by Yang Yan	First bankers' bills	Ban on Buddhism and other foreign religions

KIRGHIZ

Shih-Wei

AMUR

MALGAL

KHITAN (LIAO)
proto-Mongol people, raid Tang border from 695, sometimes vassals of Turks. Set up own empire (Liao) in Manchuria in early 10th century

TURKS
to 744

UIGHURS
Uighurs replace Turks in the steppe 745–840; more stable, less anti-Chinese than Turks. Destroyed by Kirghiz

powerful kingdom on the Tang model set up by remnants of Korean ruling clan of Koguryo. Independent from 710. Destroyed by Khitan 934

before 660 there were three states in Korea: Koguryo, Paekche and Silla. The T'ang destroyed Paekche in 660, Koguryo in 668 and occupied N. Korea. Strong resistance led to Chinese withdrawal in 676, leaving all Korea under Silla, a powerful, centralized state on T'ang lines

Gobi Desert

PO HAI (PARHAE)

still occupied by Emishi aboriginal peoples

NINGSIA

Yellow River

Tun-huang

to Tibet 763–843

KANSU

Tang occupation 668–676

SILLA

Sea of Japan

independent politically; increasing Chinese cultural influence from 6th century. In 7th century a strong centralized kingdom developed, based on T'ang institutions

...ified kingdom c.600. ...pansion after 650; ...der Chinese cultural ...luence until c.750 then ...lian influence. ...ntral control collapsed ...40

T A N G

Loyang

Changan

E M P I R E

Ch'eng-tu

Yangtze

O F

C H I N A

Yang-chou

Ning-po

Po Hai

J A P A N

Kyoto • Nara

NAN-CHAO
kingdom formed by federation of tribal groups organized on Tang model

850–70

Canton

Chiao-chou

South China Sea

800

khothai

KHMER

Hue

CHAMPA

ANNAM

Mekong

kingdom centred on Hue. Strong Indian influence

...ngdom under strong ...dian/Hindu influence

affairs by his concubine, Yang Guifei. Her brother's succession to Li Linfu's post in 752 so disgruntled An Lushan, a Tang general of Sogdian and Turkish ancestry, that three years later he initiated one of the most famous and disruptive rebellions in all of Chinese history. He led 150,000 border troops into the north central plain, plundered the capitals and drove the emperor and his court into exile in Sichuan province. Within eight years the dynasty had suffered a dramatic reversal of its fortunes. Uighur troops had helped the remaining Tang forces regain control of central China, but its northeastern provinces would henceforth be semi-autonomous, and its other provinces held unprecedented powers in law, finance, and military.

Its land grants were replaced by private and unequal plots acquired by purchase or inheritance, and its tax base was dependent first on state salt-monopoly revenues and then, from 780, on a land tax that effectively recognized private property. In response to these reforms, provincial leaders rebelled between 781 and 786 and almost brought the dynasty (under emperor Dezong) to its knees. A limited revival followed, thanks to clever eunuch generals and the throne's increased control over provincial revenues. Nonetheless, constant court intrigue, peasant rebellions, and weak emperors undermined these efforts and left the dynasty vulnerable to military mutinies in the early 10th century.

This dynastic tale of rise and fall conceals significant long-term social and economic changes that culminated in the wealthier more commercialized world of south China in the 11th century. Also, Tang political and cultural norms long retained much attraction in Japan, particularly in the organization and operation of the imperial courts in Nara and then Kyoto. Chinese schools of Buddhism, propagated by Japanese monks after study in China, had considerable influence on Japanese art and literature. Yet, with the increasing construction of temples throughout Japan, its monks developed indigenous approaches to Buddhist learning.

THE CHINESE WORLD 7TH–8TH CENTURIES

During the 660's and 670's Chinese military power reached a peak and briefly extended the power of the Tang from Sogdiana to north Korea. The Tarim Basin and parts of northwest China fell to the Tibetans in 763–83 after Tang garrisons were withdrawn. Chinese institutions and literary culture extended over parts of the Far East which although never ruled by China still came under Chinese hegemony.

- under permanent T'ang civil administration
- area of temporary occupation during 7th century
- under T'ang military control
- zone of Chinese cultural dominance
- trade routes
- canals
- Tibetan expansion
- advance of Islam

Religion And Missionaries: The Expansion Of Christianity

The expansion of Christianity through missionary work went hand in hand with the political expansion of both the western Frankish and eastern Byzantine empires. Although both the pope and the patriarch of Constantinople respectively played a key role in the support of missionaries, there was rivalry between Greek and Latin secular and religious leaders in the exertion of influence in the newly converted regions.

The missionary activity of Christians in the early Middle Ages extended the expansion of Christianity in the Roman world, notably after 310. Early conversions were often independent Christianizations of whole communities, such as the Copts, Syrians, Armenians and Goths. In the case of the latter, their native missionary Bishop Ulfilas provided them with a written language, Gothic, based on Greek into which he then translated the Bible and some liturgical texts. Other early missionaries, such as Augustine of Canterbury in Kent, had papal backing. Travelling monks and preachers, such as Columbanus in Merovingian Gaul or Boniface in Hesse and Thuringia have been labelled as

Liudger reliquary now in Essen. Oak boards covered in carved bone showing Christ between two angels. It was made in Francia c. 700 and is associated with the English missionary Liudger, first bishop of Münster.

597	685	690	716	741/42	754	782
Augustine of Canterbury converts King Aethelbert of Kent	Wilfrid converts the Isle of Wight	Willibrord arrives in Frisia and five years later establishes his see at Utrecht.	Duke Theodo asks the pope for help in the reorganization of the church in Bavaria.	Bishoprics established at Erfurt, Büraburg and Würzburg	Murder of Boniface at Dokkum in northern Frisia	Widukind the Saxon rebel baptized

Gold and enamel nail reliquary made in Lotharingia in the second half of the tenth century and now in Trier. When the True Cross was found in the fourth century, so were the nails used at the Crucifixion, and they became highly-prized holy relics. This reliquary contained what was supposedly one of the nails used for the crucifixion of Christ.

missionaries, though they did not so much convert pagans as instil ascetic rigour or ecclesiastical discipline into the existing Christianity of the regions they visited.

Political support was essential for the enterprise of missionaries and reformers alike. Many enterprises were part of political expansion especially on the Continent. From the seventh to tenth centuries, Franks – especially the Carolingian rulers – protected the Anglo-Saxons in Frisia, Hesse and Thuringia; Franks were active in Bavaria; Bavarians were preaching in the Slav regions; the Franks attempted to convert the Danes, and then brutally forced the Saxons to convert. Furthermore, there were religious dealings between Franks and Moravians, and German expansion and religious consolidation into the eastern Slav lands. Many new bishoprics were established in the course of the ninth and tenth centuries in Saxony, Poland, Bohemia and Hungary. Conversion became a form of very effective cultural imperialism, whether as a diplomatic tool or as part of a process of conquest.

The careers of Irish, English, Frankish, and subsequent missionary bishops to the Danes, Bulgars, Magyars, Slavs

(Right) Baptism as portrayed in an illustrated version of the story of the finding of the True Cross made in Augsburg, c. 814.

At intervals you should compare their superstitions with our Christian doctrines ... so that the pagans, thrown into confusion rather than angered, may be ashamed of their absurd ideas and may understand that their infamous ceremonies and fables are well known to us.

BISHOP DANIEL OF WINCHESTER, LETTER TO BISHOP BONIFACE OF MAINZ, 723–24

799–806	797	818/825	826	830–31	832	861
Bishoprics established at Münster & Werden, Worms, Bremen, Paderborn and Osnabrück	*Capitulare Saxonicum* and forced conversion of the Saxons	Mojmir of Moravia converted	King Harald Klak the Dane baptized at Ingelheim with the Emperor Louis the Pious as his godfather	Anskar's mission to Scandinavia	Hamburg made an archbishopric with jurisdiction granted by the pope, Gregory IV, over Swedes, Danes and Slavs	conversion of the Khazars to Judaism

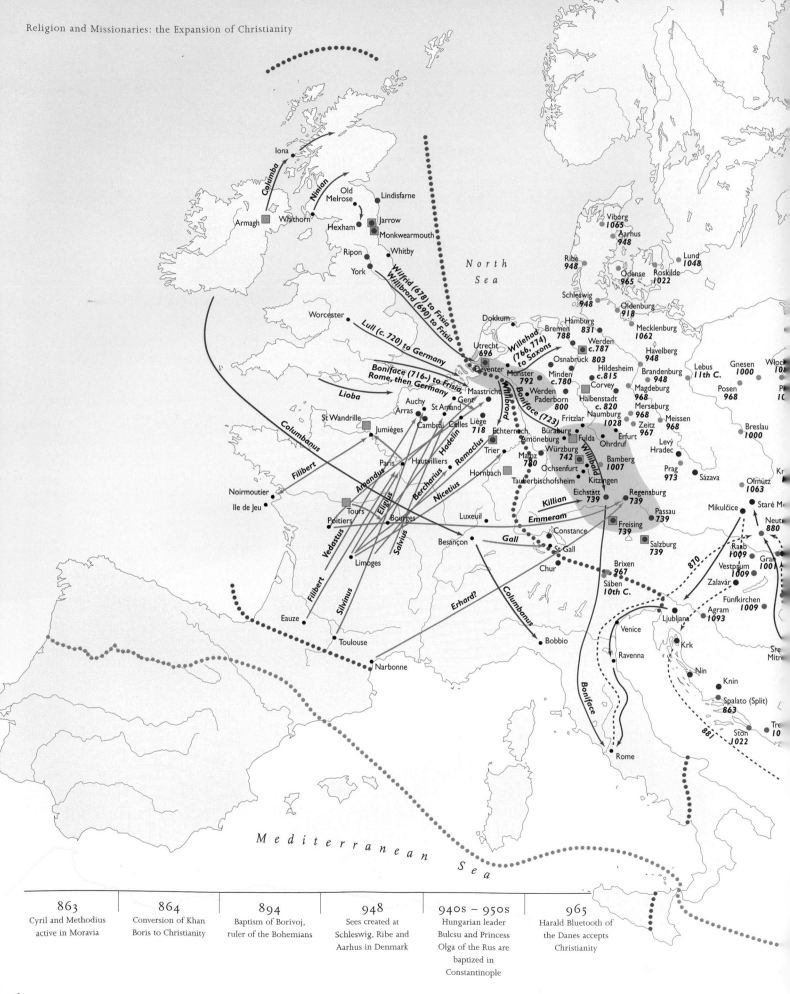

Iona
Columba
Ninian
Armagh
Whithorn
Old Melrose
Lindisfarne
Hexham
Jarrow
Monkwearmouth
Ripon
Whitby
York
Worcester
Wilfrid (678) to Frisia
Willibrord (690) to Frisia
Lull (c. 720) to Germany
North Sea
Dokkum
Utrecht 696
Deventer
Willehad (766, 774) to Saxons
Münster 792
Willibrord
Boniface (716–) to Frisia Rome, then Germany
Lioba
Maastricht
Gent
St Amand
Auchy
Arras
Cambrai
Celles
Liège 718
St Wandrille
Jumièges
Filibert
Columbanus
Paris
Hautvilliers
Hadelin
Remaclus
Nicetius
Bercharius
Salvius
Eligius
Amandus
Vedastus
Bourges
Tours
Poitiers
Limoges
Noirmoutier
Ile de Jeu
Filibert
Silvinus
Eauze
Toulouse
Narbonne
Echternach
Amöneburg
Büraburg
Trier
Hornbach
Tauberbischofsheim
Mainz 780
Würzburg 742
Ochsenfurt
Kitzingen
Eichstätt 739
Killian
Emmeram
Fulda
Willibald
Bamberg 1007
Ohrdruf
Erfurt
Regensburg 739
Freising 739
Salzburg 739
Passau 739
Gall
St Gall
Constance
Besançon
Luxeuil
Chur
Erhard?
Columbanus
Bobbio
Brixen 967
Säben 10th C.
Bremen
Hamburg 831
Werden c.787
Osnabrück 803
Minden c.780
Hildesheim c.815
Corvey
Werden
Paderborn 800
Halberstadt c.820
Fritzlar
Naumburg 1028
Zeitz 967
Levý Hradec
Prag 973
Sázava
Boniface (723)
Boniface
Ribe 948
Schleswig 948
Viborg 1065
Aarhus 948
Odense 965
Roskilde 1022
Lund 1048
Oldenburg 918
Mecklenburg 1062
Havelberg 948
Brandenburg 948
Magdeburg 968
Merseburg 968
Meissen 968
Lebus 11th C.
Gnesen 1000
Posen 968
Breslau 1000
Olmütz 1063
Mikulčice
Neutra 880
Raab 1009
Vestprim 1009
Zalavár
Gran 1001
Fünfkirchen 1009
Agram 1093
Ljubljana
Venice
Ravenna
Krk
Nin
Knin
Spalato (Split) 863
Ston 1022
Staré M
870
881
Rome
Mediterranean Sea

863	864	894	948	940s – 950s	965
Cyril and Methodius active in Moravia	Conversion of Khan Boris to Christianity	Baptism of Borivoj, ruler of the Bohemians	Sees created at Schleswig, Ribe and Aarhus in Denmark	Hungarian leader Bulcsu and Princess Olga of the Rus are baptized in Constantinople	Harald Bluetooth of the Danes accepts Christianity

THE EXPANSION OF CHRISTIANITY FROM THE 7TH CENTURY

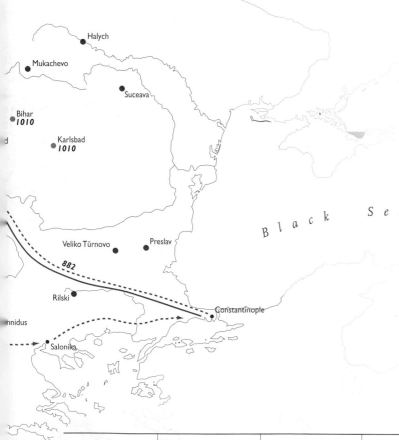

Bishoprics and centres founded 7th–11th centuries, with date of establishment

● ● ● ● approximate extent of Catholic Christianity, c. 700

● Christian expansion in the 7th century

● English, Irish and Bavarian missionary sees of the 7th–8th centuries

● Saxon bishoprics of the late 8th and early 9th centuries

● German expansion of the 10th and 11th centuries

● Byzantine expansion of the 10th and 11th centuries

▪ centres commissioning or producing missionary hagiography

Missionary journeys

●→ routes of English missionaries from England to Francia and Germany

→ Aquitanian and Frankish missionaries to Northern Gaul and Bavaria

→ Irish missionaries

▭ areas of strongest insular English and Irish influence

→ route of Cyril and Methodius to Greater Moravia (863–4) and Rome (867)

- - → later travels of Methodius

● centres of Old Slavonic culture

● ● ● ● northern frontier of expansion of Islam, 1050

Kiev

Halych

Mukachevo

Suceava

Bihar
1010

Karlsbad
1010

Veliko Tŭrnovo

Preslav

882

Rilski

Constantinople

nnidus

Salonika

Black Sea

Missionaries from Ireland, England and Francia in the west and from Byzantium were active east of the Rhine and north of the Danube from the seventh century onwards. The spread of Christianity can be charted through the foundation of many new monasteries and bishoprics (map left).

and Rus are presented in a distinctive genre of missionary hagiography. This has its own conventions and dynamic, so that it is often difficult to be certain of their details or emphases. Boniface of Mainz, for example, is one of many celebrated in such a life, though Boniface has also left us many of his letters recounting his efforts to reform the Frankish church.

Missions to the Danes were initially prompted by diplomatic imperatives: a process of softening up was perhaps envisaged before conquest, or else it was felt that it might be easier to deal with fellow Christians. In the event the Frankish missions of Archbishop Ebbo to the Danes and Anskar to the Swedes had very temporary success. It was not until the later tenth and the early 11th century that Christianity was successfully established in Scandinavia, by rival missionaries from England as well as Hamburg-Bremen. Iceland accepted Christianity c. 1000.

Ecclesiastical rivalries were not only between different polities. In Moravia and the Slav, Bulgar and Rus regions to the south and east, western efforts overlapped and even clashed with Byzantine missions from the east, most notably that of Cyril and Methodius in Moravia who devised the Glagolitic script for Slav versions of liturgical texts. The greatest Byzantine successes were in Bulgaria, where Simeon of Bulgaria turned to the Orthodox Church for inspiration and support, despite papal cajoling, and in the lands of the Rus. There, as in Germany and Moravia in the ninth century, the missionaries provided the new converts with a written language for the first time. With Christianity came Christian culture and learning (including the classical heritage), church building and organization, monasticism, new moral standards (especially in sexual relations) and new social rhythms reflected in the Christian rites of passage of baptism, marriage and death.

966	967/972-999	968	988	997	1000-1001	1000
Miesko I, king of Poland, is baptized	Prague is made a bishopric	Foundation of the bishopric of Magdeburg and at Poznán	Prince Vladimir of Kiev accepts Christianity	Adalbert, bishop of Prague, martyred by the Prussians	Waik, king of Hungary marries Gisela sister of the emperor Henry II, and takes the name of Stephen on baptism	The Althing in Iceland formally accepts Christianity; earliest churches constructed on Greenland

Towns And Trade in the Early Middle Ages

Throughout the early Middle Ages the relationship between urban centre and agricultural hinterland remained crucial, whatever the commercial activity of the town. Administrative functions and the existence of a mint were important elements in the development of cities, as were patterns of local, regional and international trade. The early Middle Ages saw the development of Irish, North and Baltic Sea trading networks to complement the major area of activity in the Mediterranean. The church, with the bishop usually based at the centre of his see in the town, played a pivotal role in forming the identity and even ensuring the survival of many towns in the west.

The late antique network of cities where artisans and a governing elite resided had been supported by taxes on the agricultural population. In the course of the sixth century many urban concentrations in the west broke up into smaller settlements, though institutions and social structures did not change as much in the east. Nonetheless, the different regions of the west experienced change in a variety of ways: ruralization was far greater in Frankish Gaul and the notion of a capital or political centre less important than in Italy and in Spain. In the successor states of the Roman empire many old Roman cities continued to act as a focus for their region.

In the course of the seventh century, new emporia or *wics* were established on either side of the North Sea.

Trading networks, amply attested by the archaeological and numismatic evidence, developed apace, with Frisian merchants in particular playing a key role as middlemen. As Viking trading activity extended ever further into the Atlantic, Baltic and Irish seas, new trading centres were established in Ireland, Scandinavia and the Baltic Sea regions and down the Volga and Dnieper rivers into Russia. Many of these new emporia were carefully planned with street grids and diversified buildings, warehouses and wharves, which housed, among other things, industrial and craft working districts. These new settlements enjoyed a close relationship with the hinterland and depended on a supply of agricultural products as well as imported goods from elsewhere. Wine from the Rhineland and Moselle, for example, was imported into England through Ipswich. Further inland, annual fairs and markets also attested to the key role of commerce, and many cities, especially in Italy, benefitted from both coastal trade and goods carried overland and on inland waterways.

Urban elites in places such as Milan, Pisa, Lucca and Rome

The reformed coinage of Charlemagne. In 794 the new "heavy penny" was accepted coin all over the empire and effectively a single European currency for much of the ninth century, though Anglo-Saxon England had its own strongly controlled coinage. This coin of the Class IV type (812–814) shows the symbol and inscription for the port and mint of Quentovic and a portrait bust of the Emperor Charlemagne on the obverse.

c. 750	794	833–37	c. 880	c. 900	c. 907
Trading post established at Staraia Ladoga	Council of Frankfurt reforms the coinage and regulates weights and measures throughout the Frankish empire	Vikings attack the wic of Dorestad	Othere the Norwegian reaches the White Sea	Rus start trading with Byzantium from middle Dnieper	first written trading privilege granted by Byzantium to Rus

Lake Ladoga

*North
Sea*

Bergen
Kaupang
Stigtuna · Staraia Ladoga
Stockholm
Birka · Helgö
Skara
Edinburgh
Turku
Reval
Gorodishche
Novgorod
Nizhniy
Novgorod
Volga
Carlisle
Lödöse
Kungahälla
Pskov
Paviken · Gotland
Köpingsvik
Moscow
Århus
Riga
Western Dvina
York
Ribe
Löddeköpinge
Baltic
Sea
Polotsk
Oxford
Chester
Lincoln
Hedeby
Reric · Ralswiek
Gnëzdovo
Wroxeter
Worcester
Leicester
Derby
Stamford
Emden
Hamburg
Menzlin · Wollin
Danzig
Truso
Desna
Liubech
Chernigov
Hereford
Northampton
Thetford
Norwich
Medemblik
Bremen
Deventer
Kolobzreg
Don
Gloucester
Cirencester
St Albans
Ipswich
Utrecht
Dorestad
Vistula
Shestovitsy
Winchester
Southampton
London
Canterbury
Westenschouwen
Pripet
Vyshgorod
Kiev
Sandwich
Domburg
Wilta
Kiataevo
Quentovic
Ghent
Antwerp
Cologne
Dnieper
Arras
Nivelles
Tournai
Liège
Leipzig
Quillebeuf
Huy
St James de
Beuvron
Caen
Sèes
Evreux
Rhine
Tana
Paris
Chalon sur Marne
Nuremberg
Pontlevoy
Burgus Briensi
Sens
Cracow
prie de
rossay
Burgus S.
Ambrosii
Burgus by Marcènay
Augsburg
Beaulieu
Bourges
Bourg
Vienna
Levroux
Dijon
Besançon
d'Angely
Poitiers
Chalons-sur-Saone
Salins
Saintes
Cluny
Poligny
Cognac
Lyons
Burgus Grosonensis
rdeaux
Flers
Genas
A L P S
Le Puy
Vienne
Romans
Castelseprio
Grado
Caffa
Zaragossa
Vizille
Milan
Bergamo
Torcello
Trieste
Albi
Donzere
Brescia
Venice
Cittanova
Cherson
Forcalquier
Cremona
Mantua
Chioggia
Pola
Genoa
Ferrara
Comacchio
Black Sea
Arles
Savona
Parma
Bologna
Barcelona
Narbonne
Marseilles
Florence
Danube
Trebizond
Pisa
Corsica
alencia
Sardinia
Tiber
Ragusa
Constantinople
Herakliea
Palma
Rome
Durazzo
Nikomedeia
Naples
Salerno
Bougie
Taranto
Lesbos
Phocea
Lajazza
Carthage
Palermo
Messina
Cephallonia
Athens
Smyrna
Antioch
Mediterranean
Sea
Cyprus
Rhodes
Damascus
Candia
Tyre
Acre
Tripoli
Alexandria
Cairo

TOWNS AND TRADE IN MEDIEVAL EUROPE

Europe's economic development reflects great diversity, with strong lines of
continuity as well as many new developments from the seventh century onwards.
The strategic location of new towns on land, river and sea routes is clear.

- Roman civitates that retained their importance
- new emporia, wics, trading settlements
- newly important towns emerging from
  previously unimportant towns

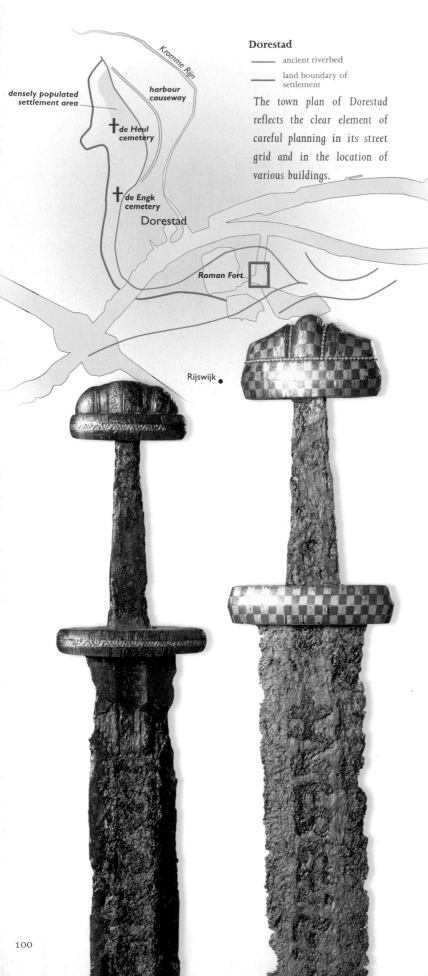

Dorestad

— ancient riverbed

— land boundary of settlement

The town plan of Dorestad reflects the clear element of careful planning in its street grid and in the location of various buildings.

Kromme Rijn

densely populated settlement area

harbour causeway

† *de Heul cemetery*

† *de Engk cemetery*

Dorestad

Roman Fort

Rijswijk

Byzantine silk in Aachen, c. 800. It may have reached the Frankish kingdom as part of a diplomatic gift or as a result of trade in luxury goods.

You have written to us also about merchants, and by our mandate we allow that they shall have protection and support in our kingdom, lawfully, according to the ancient custom of trading.

LETTER OF CHARLEMAGNE, KING OF THE FRANKS TO OFFA, KING OF MERCIA. 796

maintained their dominance and prosperity and the doges of Venice consolidated their political position as well as their wealth at the head of the Adriatic. In the Mediterranean, Jewish and Arab merchants played an increasingly active role. New trading centres in northern Africa, Sicily, southern Italy and Egypt emerged, and the wealth of their populations was manifested in many fine new buildings and merchants' town houses. Seeking fiscal benefits, rulers and local lords were enthusiastic participators in economic activity. Merchants channelled goods, such as spices, gold and other luxuries, from the east into Italy and northern Europe in exchange for wood, iron, furs, weapons and, above all, slaves. Byzantine towns in the east, by contrast, were dominated by landowning elites, and many towns, such as Constantinople and Theassalonika, were primarily centres of consumption rather than craft and trade.

More traditional views of the birth of the medieval city failed to take sufficiently into account consumption, social complexity, or fortifications and the great variety of functions of a town other than commerce. Merchants, nevertheless, particularly in the tenth and eleventh centuries, certainly exercised a strong influence over the development of urban topography, institutions and social networks. New episcopal cities, established as Christianity expanded, provided further new concentrations of population and diversified activity as administrative centres, military bases and mercantile settlements. Certainly this period was one of steady economic expansion.

Frankish swords (left) were highly desirable as a commodity all over Europe. Made of plaited steel, they were very strong and tensile.

Buildings And Power

Medieval society was characterized by a plurality of locations of power. Thus not only cities, but also palaces, fortifications, monasteries and churches became public expressions of the power of kings as well as of secular and ecclesiastical elites.

The topography of power, in terms of sites, buildings and the organization of space was linked in the Middle Ages, as much as in other eras, with both the perception and exertion of physical, mental and spiritual power. Places of power in their turn enhanced the authority of those who created them. In the religious context, particular places, such as Rome, Jerusalem and Mecca constituted crucial concentrations of sacred power and holiness. Many monasteries and churches, moreover, were places where the power of the holy saints was both focussed and venerated.

Yet in medieval Europe in particular, it is striking how many rulers linked their own worldly power to God's authority and how often this is reflected in the juxtaposition of royal palaces and cathedrals (as at Frankfurt or Paderborn in the ninth century or Magdeburg in the tenth century), or the close association between a royal court and a new monastic foundation (as at Anglo-Saxon Winchester). Alternatively, a sumptuous chapel could be incorporated into the palace complex. Aachen, Ingelheim and Compiègne, for example, were completed in the reigns of Charlemagne, his son Louis the Pious and grandson Charles the Bald respectively.

Rulers all over the world also exploited buildings and topography to insist upon or assert their status, display their power and wealth, dominate the landscape, and provide planned sites, often of extraordinary magnificence and complexity. From these places they exercised government, the administration of justice, control of the economy and reception of plaintiffs, visitors and envoys both from within and without their territories. Fortifications, such as castles, walls and huge earthworks could also have an effective defensive function, as in the range of castles built by the Norman kings to enable them to subdue Wales or those of the Crusaders in the Holy Land.

Cities and buildings alike provided a venue for the display of power in the medieval world,

The emperor then sped peacefully along the road to Ingelheim with his wife and children. That place is sited near to the swift course of the Rhine in the midst of cultivated lands producing many kinds of foods. A spacious palace stands there, firmly supported by a hundred columns, with different kinds of passages leading to it and many sorts of buildings, a thousand entrances and exits and a thousand inner chambers built by the handiwork of master craftsmen. … To the imperial conquests of the excellent city of Rome are linked the Franks and their marvellous achievements… then there is a painting of the first Charles, masterly victor in the Frisian war, and with him the great exploits he performed; then a splendid picture of Pippin, restoring the rule of law to the Aquitainians, and annexing them to his realms through success in battle. Wise Charlemagne's frank expression is clear to see, his head is crowned, as his lineage and achievements demand… With these and other deeds that place shines brightly; those who gaze on it with pleasure take strength from the sight.

THE PALACE ITSELF AND THE FRESCOES OF PAST HEROES AND EMPERORS IN THE *AULA REGIA* AT INGELHEIM, DESCRIBED IN THE POEM IN HONOUR OF LOUIS THE PIOUS BY ERMOLD THE BLACK, *c.* 827.

The Temple of Angkor Wat, Cambodia. The extraordinary range of buildings at Angkor, especially from the reign of Jayavarman II (802–56) was greatly extended with the Baphuaon, built under King Udayadityavarman II (1050–66) and Angkor Wat itself, the City Temple, built under Suryavarman II (1130–50).

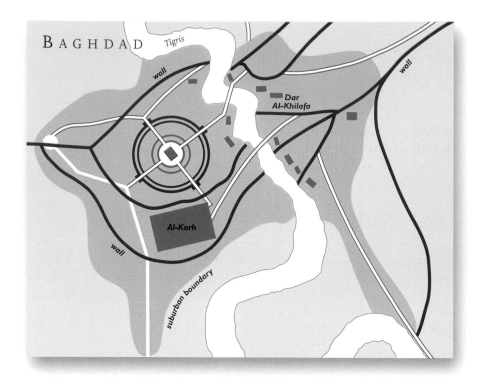

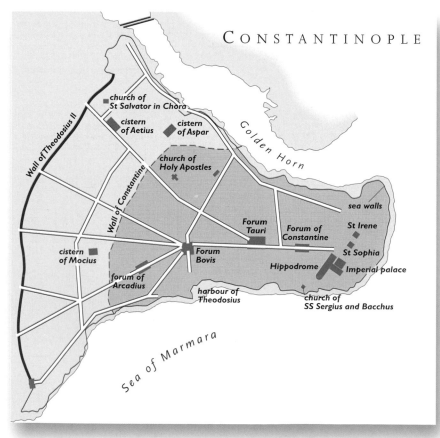

(Left) The round city of Baghdad, capital of the *Abbasids*, founded in 762 by the caliph al-Mansur. The circular city, with a diameter of 2.64km, was surrounded by a rampart with 360 towers. By the early ninth century, it was one of the world's largest city.

(Opposite above) Changan. Planned as a massive rectangle, 9.4km from east to west and 8.4km from north to south, with 11 great north-south avenue, the main avenue led from the imperial palace to the south gate. It was no less than 153m wide, intersecting 14 east-west thoroughfares and dividing the city into 106 separate wards. Changan probably had a million inhabitants within the walls and another million in the suburbs outside. Already by 722 it contained 91 Buddhist and 16 Taoist places of worship, four Zoroastrian temples and two Nestorian Christian churches.

(Left) Constantinople never grew beyond the walls of Theodosius II (c.447) and within the walls there was much vacant space. Historians have tended to exaggerate its population, which at the beginning of the ninth century was probably less than a quarter of a million. Nevertheless, it was with the possible exception of Córdoba, far excelling any city in the Christian west, including Rome.

c.600	754	780s	c.800	836
City of Tihuanaco in Peru begun	Madinat al-Salan, the round city of Baghdad built by al-Mansur	Aachen palace complex constructed	Building of the temple at Borobodur by the Sailendra dynasty in Java	Samarra created by al-Mu'tasim to house his army

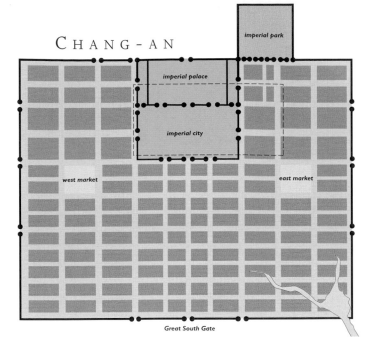

CHANG-AN

imperial park

imperial palace

imperial city

west market

east market

Great South Gate

The palace complex at *Aachen* was constructed around a massive courtyard over 200 metres long and built on a grid plan to emphasize its symmetry and harmony. It included a large reception hall, possibly modelled on the late Roman *aula palatina* at Trier. At one end was the magnificent chapel, which is now all that remains. It forms, with its later medieval additions, the present-day Aachen cathedral. Its ceiling, arching above the gallery where the marble throne of the emperor may have been placed, was decorated with a rich mosaic portraying the worship of the lamb by the twenty-four Elders from the Book of Revelations. The marble pillars included late antique *spolia* brought over the Alps from the Mediterranean made of bronze and green porphyry. The huge candelabrum was added by the Emperor Frederick II.

providing routes for processions and parades, grand halls for feasts, assemblies, entertainment and audiences, often with strict hierarchies imposed by the buildings themselves (as at Madinat al Zahra outside Cordoba, the Great Palace at Constantinople and Angkor Wat). Even in essentially mobile societies, such as those of inner Asia, a tent city such as that of the Mongol Khan Güyük or the mobile camps of Sartaq and Batu, not only imposed control on space and the movement of individuals, but derived their importance from the ruler's presence.

Although the notion of a capital city was not fostered among the Franks, who preferred a network of royal residences and hunting lodges throughout their realm, others of the barbarian successor states maintained an urban concentration of political power, in places such as Toledo, Ravenna, Pavia and Carthage, which owed much to their Roman past. These combined the royal court and household with an administrative centre and a specific religious role in one place. Similarly, Byzantine and Arab political centres such as Constantinople, Baghdad, Cordoba and, indeed, Rome, hub of the Republic of St Peter (*see* pp. 130–31), were urban in character. Such places, which had developed over time as locations of secular power, where historical resonances augmented the symbolic position of the contemporary ruler as well as offering eloquent physical reminders of it, also contributed greatly to the sense of identity of the peoples of these regions as a whole.

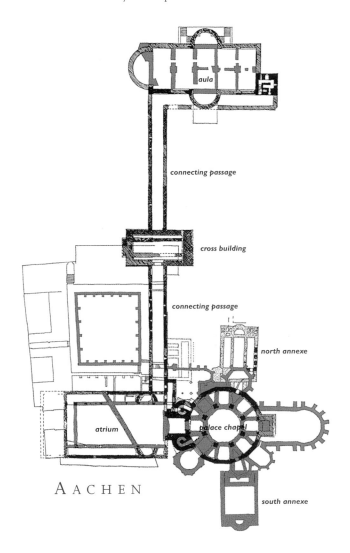

aula

connecting passage

cross building

connecting passage

north annexe

atrium

palace chapel

AACHEN

south annexe

837–80	c. 850	960	c.1000	c. 1010
Xian Changan the vast capital of the Tang dynasty, is reduced to ruins	Sacred enclosure of Chichén Itzá in the Yucatán established	Foundation of the Toltec capital of Tula in central America	Construction of Monks' Mound of Cahokia in the Mississippi Plain	Completion of Rajaràjestvara temple

PART II

This copy of the commentary of Beatus of Liebana on the
Apocalypse is one of twenty-six extant illustrated copies of
this eighth-century text. The 'Facundus Beatus' was painted in
1047 by the artist Facundus in the royal scriptorium of Léon for
King Fernando I and Queen Sancha of Léon-Castile. The style is
the extraordinary 'Mozarabic' style of Spain, so strikingly
different from styles of painting north of the Pyrenees

PART II

cotidie ab agno superatur. quiabeius
pacientia confunditur.

INCIPIT DE AGNO ET BESTIA SUPERATA.
Hii decem reges cu agno pugnabunt.
&agnus uincet eos. qin dns dnorum
est et rex regu etqui cu eo uocati et sut
electi et fideles. Et dicit michi. haec
udes ubi mulier sedet. ppts & turbe
sunt. et gens. et lingue. et dece cor
nua que uidisti hii odio habent &de
serta ea facient et nuda et carnes eius
commedent & ipsam comburet igni.
ds em dedit in corde eorum facere senten
ciam et et dare regnu suu bestie. usq;
dum finiatur dicta di. Et mulier
qua uidisti est ciuitas magna que hab;
regnu sup reges terrae.

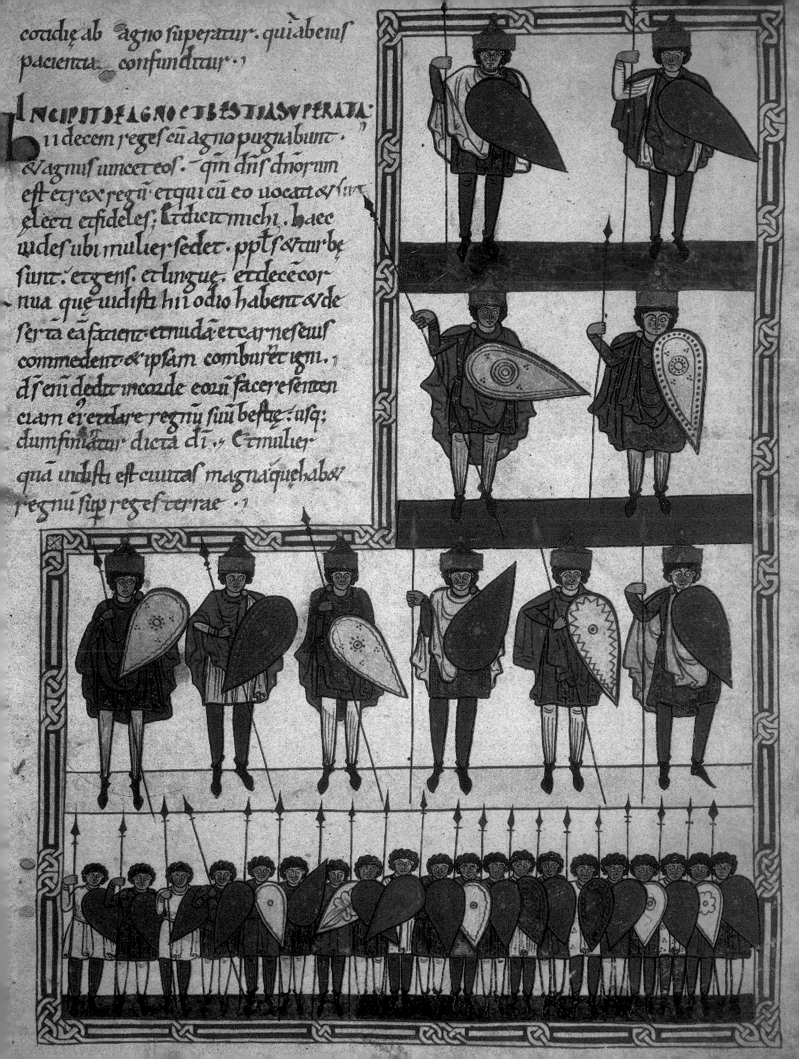

The World In 1000

Modern historians and archaeologists have been able to identify and document many states in the process of formation around the year 1000. The German empire, for example, appears to have been consolidating its power and expanding the territories over which it had control. So were the rulers of the kingdoms of Benin, Ife, Igbo Ikwu and the holy city of Yoruba in the savannahs and rainforests of Nigeria; the kingdom of Wessex in Anglo-Saxon England; and the Chola in southern India and Ceylon. There is evidence, too, of cities organized and ruled on a communal basis such as Jenne-Jeno in sub-Saharan Africa and the Italian city-states. Furthermore we see the continuance of great empires such as Byzantium, China and Ethiopia (based on Aksum). Still other polities, notably the Frankish empire, Spain and the empire of Srivijaya in Indonesia were undergoing a process of restructuring and transformation. Around the year 1000, moreover, New Zealand – the Land of the Long White Cloud – was colonized from southern Polynesia and the Easter Islanders began to carve their spectacular statues. On the other side of the world the Viking Leif Ericsson reached the northeast coast of North America and the farmers of Iceland converted to Christianity.

Thus no general formula adequately characterizes the world in 1000. Even in the European context, the year 1000 was just another year. The processes of economic expansion, of the consolidation of the powers of local aristocracies, and the move towards the centralization of government in the course of the 12th century were very extended and gradual. They varied much, moreover, in emphasis and pace from region to region. Similarly, the year 1000 is of no significance in charting the transformation of religious belief and practice, despite the claims of the 11th-century reformers. In the perception of the past, and in the minds of 12th-century intellectuals, cultural roots stretched back through the crucial work of the writers and scholars of the early Middle Ages to antiquity. But it could be said that there was indeed far greater and far more dynamic interaction between the ever-expanding horizons of Latin Christendom, of orthodox Christianity and of the Islamic world and beyond. It was a world, as ever, of great richness and diversity.

St Sever Beatus Map of the world, 13th century. Paris, Bibliothèque Nationale

The map of the world (right) in the illustrated copies of Beatus of Liebana's commentary on the Apocalypse (written c. 776) introduces the commentary to Revelations chapter 2 discussing the mission of the apostles and the fields of their work: Rome, Achaia, India, Spain, Asia Minor, Macedonia, Egypt, Jerusalem and "the entire world of the gentiles". Thus the map represents the spread of Christianity as well as geographical knowledge. Here the existence of a southern continent is charted. At the top of the map is the Garden of Eden and the outer ocean is full of ships and fish. Other physical details such as mountains and rivers are also included and the Red Sea is coloured red. Dimensions (taken from Pliny) are provided for some of the islands, such as Britain, and little buildings symbolize the cities, such as Rome and Constantinople. The church of St Sever itself has a bigger symbol than the rest. The map is crowded with place names. Notes about wonders in the regions outside Europe are provided from the encyclopaedic Etymologiae by Isidore of Seville.

THE WORLD IN c.1000

GREENLAND

L'Anse aux Meadows

TOLTEC EMPIRE

MAYA EMPIRE

Law and the Judicial Process

Medieval society relied on a received body of law, which was continually augmented and adapted to social conditions and institutional developments. Medieval rulers guaranteed the working of justice and the law, the observance of which was a mark of political allegiance and social alignment throughout the Middle Ages. Extant legal transactions and enactments provide a remarkable reflection of social and political interaction in this period. Moreover, the study of law was a vital intellectual discipline in the medieval schools and universities.

In the earlier Middle Ages, most of the barbarian successor states produced their own law codes. The purely "germanic" content of the Salic Frankish, Ripuarian Frankish, Anglo-Saxon, Lombard, Burgundian, Bavarian, Alemannian, Saxon, Frisian and Visigothic codes is disputed, for there are indications that late Roman legal ideas existed side by side with such non-Roman concepts as *mund* (legal protection) and *wergild* (life price). The laws, moreover, were essentially Roman in format and were written in Latin, with the exception of the vernacular codes of the Irish, the Anglo-Saxons and the Icelandic *Gragas*. Laws were generally issued by rulers with the advice and consent of their leading men, and made specific provision for the Christian church. Whether these laws continued to be applied in the various kingdoms and smaller principalities into the tenth and eleventh centuries depended on the extent to

The most noble Rothari, king of the Lombards, together with his principal judges, issues this lawbook in the name of the Lord. "We have perceived it necessary to improve and to reaffirm the present law, amending all earlier laws by adding that which is lacking and eliminating that which is superfluous. We desire that these laws be brought together in one volume so that everyone may lead a secure life in accordance with law and justice."

FROM THE *EDICT OF ROTHARI*,
KING OF THE LOMBARDS, 643

(Left) *A Muslim qadi (judge) resolves a dispute between two litigants. From the Abbasid period, oral testimony was preferred over written. A judge could also refer to a fatwa (legal opinion) in making a judgement.*

438	533–4	802	1139	1158	1187–89	1218
Theodosian Code	Digest and Code of Justinian	Charlemagne encourages writing down of the laws of all the peoples within the Carolingian Empire	1st recension of *Gratian's Decretum*	2nd recension of *Gratian's Decretum*	Ralph Glanville, *Tractatus de legibus et consuetudinibus regni Angliae*	Henry de Bracton, *De legibus et consuetudinibus regni Angliae*

which they were subsumed into the changing social and legal customs of the new polities and augmented or replaced by new legislation. In this process, contemporary thinking about status and power was embodied in legal compilations and applied to issues of government and order in society.

Nevertheless, Roman law remained widely in use throughout early medieval Europe and Byzantium, both as a source of jurisprudential ideas and as law in practice (though it underwent a process of abbreviation, excerpting and adaptation). Thus the so-called "rediscovery" of Roman law in the 11th century has been rather exaggerated. Roman law was known primarily in the form of the Theodosian Code in the west, though knowledge of Justinian's (later) *Corpus iuris civilis*, widely used in the Byzantine empire, is attested in western Europe in ninth- and tenth-century fragments and codices.

The implementation of law implies legal knowledge and specialist personnel who gradually became institutionalized with the training of legal notaries and professional lawyers. This was linked with the emergence of schools and universities specializing in the law, such as Bologna, Oxford and Paris. In these institutions the study of civil (Roman) law flourished side by side with that of canon law.

Canon law comprised the ecclesiastical provisions agreed at the major councils of the early Christian church, papal decisions and Roman law on matters of

A copy of Gratian's Decretum, England c. 1310–30, now in Cambridge, Sidney Sussex College Library, illustrating the tree of consanguinity which set out the degrees of kinship within which marriage was prohibited.

13th century	1234	1220–40	1303	1317	before 1357	before c. 1400
Libri feudorum (non-Roman law)	Pope Gregory IX's *Extravagantes*	Accursius's exposition of Justinian's *Corpus iuris civilis*	*Glossa ordinaria*	*Constitutiones Clementinae*	Bartolus of Sassoferrato commentaries on the law	Ubaldis de Ubaldis commentaries on the law

toto legitimo opere perfectos· posse etiam nram rem

puplicam inpartibus eius uobis credendam gubernare·

DATA xkt DEC DN IVSTINIANO PP TERTIO COS·

DOM IVSTINIANI GRATISSIMIAUGUSTI INSTITUTORUM·

SIUE ELEMENTORUM· INCIPIT LIBER·I· DEITITIAETIURE·R·

VSTITIAEST CONSTAN

ET PERPETUA VOLUNTAS· IVSSUUM CUIQUETRI

buens·/ Iuris prudentia est· diuinaru atq̄ hu

manaru reru notitia· iusti atq̄ iniusti scientia·/

His generaliter cognitis· & incipientibus nobis

exponere iura popli romani· ita maxime ui

dentur posse tradi commodissime· si primo leui

ac simplici postdeinde diligentissima atq̄ exac

tissima interpretatione singula tradantur·/

Alioquin· si statim ab initio rudem adhuc & in

firmum animum studiosi· multitudine ac ua

rietate rerum onerauerimus· duorum alteru

aut desertorem studiorum efficiemus· Autcu̅

magno labore eius· sepe etiam cum diffidentia·

que plerumq̄ iuuenes euertit· serius ad id per

ducemus· ad quod leuiore uia ductus sine mag

no labore· & sine ulla diffidentia maturius pduci

potuisset·/ Iuris precepta sunt hec· honeste uiuere

ecclesiastical discipline and organization. A number of informal collections with different emphases and arrangements had been formed in the early Middle Ages, but in the course of the tenth and eleventh centuries individual efforts were made to reorganize canon law. This culminated in the formal systematization known as *Gratian's Decretum* put together as a textbook for teaching law at Bologna in the middle of the 12th century. This corpus was subsequently augmented under papal auspices to form a solid body of law that was central to legal study and ecclesiastical practice.

Both civil and canon law were international systems working simultaneously with royal, "feudal", manorial, municipal, mercantile and maritime law in the various medieval polities. Legal transactions and court proceedings were recorded in charters in a manner derived originally from Roman practice. These survive in their thousands from all over Europe and from Christian, Jewish and Muslim societies, together with law books, legislation and statutes of many different associations, attesting to the constant practical application of law and justice, served by hierarchies of officials.

(Left) *A page from Justinian's* Institutes. *A fine copy of Roman law written in Rome, c. 960–970. The book was probably given by the Emperor Henry II to Bamberg cathedral at the beginning of the 11th century.*

Notes in Judaeo-Arabic (early 12th century) of the rabbinic court concerning the love affair of al-Wuhsha (known as 'the broker', daughter of a banker), a successful Jewish businesswoman at the end of the 11th century. Witnesses testify to the court that she committed adultery with a married man by whom she had a son (though she married the man before a Muslim notary, a form of civil marriage at the time). The purpose of the testimony is to demonstrate that although her son was born out of wedlock through an irregular relationship, it was not an illegal relationship (for instance, incestuous) that would disqualify the son from marrying a Jewish wife. The testimony is thus a vindication of the son's legitimacy probably at a time when he himself wished to marry.

... we have granted to all men living in Val Scalve the opportunity and dispensation of trading and of selling their iron or whatever they wish through the vastness of our empire to Kreuzberg and La Cisa without contradiction or molestation of any mortal man or a duty of any royal exaction beyond 1,000 pounds of iron which they have supplied up to now and must give henceforth every year to our royal estate called Darfo on the conditions and following the custom and habit of their ancestors or predecessors.

THE GERMAN EMPEROR HENRY III PERMITS THE INHABITANTS OF VAL SCALVE TO TRADE IN IRON

Languages In The Medieval World

Most of the languages spoken throughout the world in the Middle Ages have developed modern forms. Some, such as Cornish or Tasmanian, have become extinct as a result of communities being integrated into groups speaking a different language or dying out. The languages known and recorded are generally classified into twenty-nine large but not entirely autonomous linguistic families. While the written form of many ancient languages, such as Greek, Latin and Hebrew survives from antiquity, that of many of the others is documented for the first time in the Middle Ages.

The earliest records of Japanese and Korean, both written in Chinese characters, date from the eighth and 12th centuries, respectively. Records of Albanian date from the 15th century. In the Altaic group, written forms of Turkic survive from the eighth century and Mongolian from the 13th century. Among the Dravidic languages of southern India, there are records of Kanada, Telugu and Malayalam as early as the fifth, seventh and ninth centuries respectively. In the Austro-Asiatic group of Southeast Asia, Khmer inscriptions have been found from as early as the late sixth century. Among the Sino-Tibetan languages there are records on Buddhist religious subjects in Tibetan from the eighth century and in Burmese from the 11th century. Nubian texts in modified Coptic script are extant from the eighth century, and Malay is found in seventh century written inscriptions from Sumatra. Among the Q-Celtic (Goidelic) languages, Old Irish is found in texts as early as the seventh century. The P-Celtic forms (Welsh, Breton and Cornish) are attested in medieval manuscripts.

In Europe and even farther afield the written form of many languages is associated with the conversion of a people to a "religion of the book", such as Christianity, Islam or Judaism. The coming of the Anglo-Saxon missionaries to Germany was the stimulus for the writing down of Old High German and missionaries from England and Germany introduced Latin and encouraged written forms of Old Norse in Scandinavia. Not until the 14th century and the conversion of the Lithuanians to Christianity do we find texts in Lithuanian. Maltese, on the other hand, developed from Arabic.

The provision of a written language sometimes entailed the provision of a grammar and even a special alphabet.

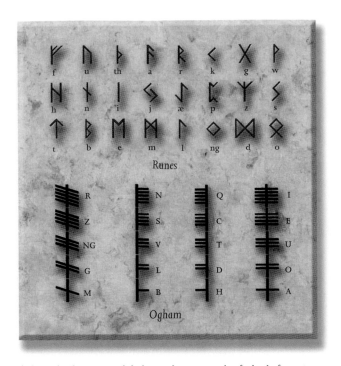

(Above) *The Runic alphabet — known as the futhark from its initial letters — and Ogham were well suited for carving on wood and stone.*

Thus when Ulfilas converted the Goths in *c.* 350 he created a Gothic alphabet and used it to write his translations of the liturgy and the Bible (allegedly omitting only the Book of Kings on the grounds that it might exacerbate the warlike tendencies of the Goths). Similarly the missionaries St Mesrop invented a 38-letter alphabet for the Armenians in the fifth century and Cyril and Methodius devised the Cyrillic alphabet for the Slavs in the ninth century. The process of writing in itself accelerated the process of standardization of languages. Yet alphabets originally for one language could be used to record another, such as the use of Arabic letterforms by many Jews in Cairo when writing Hebrew. Other apparently independent alphabets such as ogham or runes are in fact clearly based on the Roman/Latin writing system. Alphabets, with their sign-for-sound correlation as distinct from picturegram or syllabic character systems, appear to have been more readily adaptable across languages, with new signs devised to represent different sounds. Throughout Christendom, moreover, the dominance of the liturgical and biblical languages in written texts of all categories gradually gave way before the emergent local vernaculars, especially in the Romance regions. Nevertheless, Latin and Greek in west and east continued in use as the languages of religion, learning and in many cases law as well. Latin in particular served as a *lingua franca* until well into the modern period.

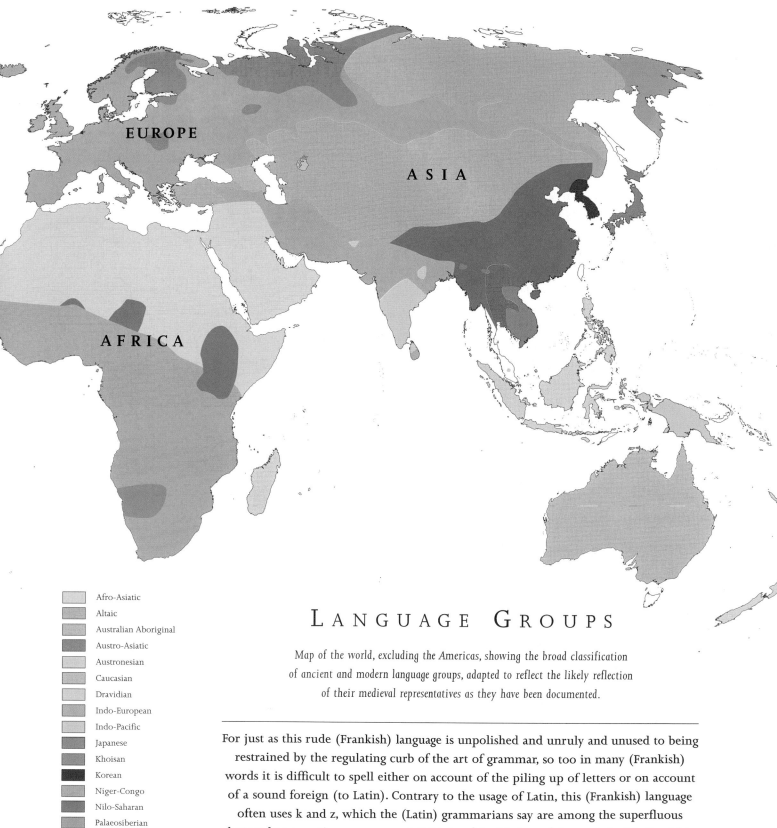

LANGUAGE GROUPS

*Map of the world, excluding the Americas, showing the broad classification
of ancient and modern language groups, adapted to reflect the likely reflection
of their medieval representatives as they have been documented.*

Legend:
- Afro-Asiatic
- Altaic
- Australian Aboriginal
- Austro-Asiatic
- Austronesian
- Caucasian
- Dravidian
- Indo-European
- Indo-Pacific
- Japanese
- Khoisan
- Korean
- Niger-Congo
- Nilo-Saharan
- Palaeosiberian
- Sino-Tibetan
- Tai
- Uralic
- Isolate/unclassified languages and uninhabited areas

For just as this rude (Frankish) language is unpolished and unruly and unused to being restrained by the regulating curb of the art of grammar, so too in many (Frankish) words it is difficult to spell either on account of the piling up of letters or on account of a sound foreign (to Latin). Contrary to the usage of Latin, this (Frankish) language often uses k and z, which the (Latin) grammarians say are among the superfluous letters; but sometimes on account, I think, of the hissing of the teeth in this Frankish language z is used and k on account of the back-sound quality (in certain words).

OTFRID OF WEISSENBURG, DEDICATORY PREFACE OF HIS *LIBER EVANGELIORUM*,
A VERSION OF THE FOUR GOSPELS WRITTEN IN OLD HIGH GERMAN IN *c.* 840

ΕΛΑΙΟC ΚΑΙ ΕΠΙ ΤΟΝ IHΛ ΤΟΥ ΚΥ
    laboris   mihi   nemo
ΤΟΥ ΛΟΙΠΟΙ ΚΟΠΟC ΜΟΙ ΜΗΔΕΙC
  exhibeat
ΠΑΡΕΧΕΤΩ ΕΓΩ ΓΑΡ ΤΑ CΤΙΓΜΑ
ΤΑ ΤΟΥ ΚΥ ΗΜΩΝ ΙΥ ΧΥ ΕΝ ΤΩ
CΩΜΑΤΙ ΜΟΥ ΒΑCΤΑ ΖΩ Η ΧΑΡΙC
ΤΟΥ ΧΥ ΗΜΩΝ ΙΥ ΧΥ ΜΕΤΑ ΤΟΥ
ΠΝC ΥΜΩΝ ΑΔΕΛΦΟΙ ΑΜΗΝ

ΕΤΕΛΕCΘΗ ΕΠΙCΤΟΛΗ
ΠΡΟC   ΓΑΛΑΤΑC

ΑΡΧΕΙΔΙ   ΠΡΟC
ΕΦΕCΙΟΥC

Π ΑΥΛΟC ΑΠΟCΤΟΛΟC
    IHΥ   ΧΡΥ
ΔΙΑ ΘΕΛΗΜΑΤΟC ΘΥ ΤΟΙC ΑΓΙΟΙC
ΤΟΙC ΟΥCΙΝ ΕΝ ΕΦΕΩ ΚΑΙ ΠΙC
ΤΟΙC ΕΝ ΧΡΩ ΙΥ ΧΑΡΙC ΥΜΙΝ
ΚΑΙ ΙΡΗΝΗ ΑΠΟ ΘΥ ΠΑΤΡΟC ΗΜΩΝ
ΚΑΙ ΚΥ ΙΥ ΧΥ ΕΥΛΟΓΗΤΟC
Ο ΘC ΚΑΙ ΠΑΤΗΡ ΤΟΥ ΚΥ ΗΜΩΝ
ΙΥ ΧΡΥ Ο ΕΥΛΟΓΗCΑC ΗΜΑC
ΕΝ ΠΑCΙ ΕΥΛΟΓΙΑ ΠΝΕΥΜΑΤΙΚΗ
ΕΝ ΤΟΙC ΕΠΟΥΡΑΝΙΟΙC ΕΝ
ΧΩ ΚΑΘΩC ΕΞΕΛΕΞΑΤΟ ΗΜΑC
ΕΑΥΤΩ ΠΡΟC ΚΑΤΑΒΟΛΗC ΚΟC
ΜΟΥ ΕΙΝΑΙ ΗΜΑC ΑΓΙΟΥC ΚΑΙ

---

misericordia et super israhel di
De cetero nemo mihi mo
lestus sit. Ego enim stigmata
ihu in
corpore meo posito. Gratia
dni nri ihu xpi cum
spirtu uro fratres. Amen

EXPLICIT EPISTOLA
AD GALATAS.

INCIPIT AD
EFESIOS.

P aulus aposts
    ihu xpi
per uoluntatem di scis
omnib; quis ephesi & fideli
bus in xpo ihu Gratia uobis
& pax a do patre nostro
& dno ihu xpo Benedictus
ds et pater dni nri
ihu xpi Qui benedixit nos
in omni benedictione spitali
in caelestib. in
xpo sicut elegit nos in
ipso ante mundi constitutio
nem ut essemus sci &

The Greek-Latin Epistles, Trinity College, Cambridge, produced at Reichenau at the end of the ninth century. This copy of the Pauline Epistles in Greek and Latin is an important witness to the knowledge of Greek (confined to a minority of scholars) in the early Middle Ages, as well as a scholarly interest in the text of the New Testament. It is one of a number of such two-language Biblical texts extant from this period.

OLD NORSE

Germanic
Celtic
Slavic
Latin/Romance
Uralic
Greek
Arabic
Isolates
Linguistic frontier between
Romance and Germanic in 8th century

OLD NORSE

OLD NORSE

BALTIC
LANGUAGES

IRISH/
GAELIC

(and Pictish
to 9th century)

WELSH   ENGLISH
              (OLD & MIDDLE)
              AND FRENCH

CORNISH   FRISIAN

RUSSIAN

LOW GERMAN

POLISH

WALLOON

CZECH

BRETON

LANGUE D'OÏL

HIGH GERMAN

HUNGARIAN

FRANCO-
PROVENÇAL

SLOVENE

LEONESE

BASQUE

LANGUE D'OC

RHAETO-
ROMANCE

CROATIAN

ROMANIAN

GALICIAN &
PORTUGUESE

CASTILIAN

ARAGONESE

CATALAN

SERBIAN

CORSICAN

LATIN/
ITALIAN

BULGARIAN

MACEDONIAN

(and Hebrew)

SARDINIAN

ALBANIAN

(and Turkish
from 12th century)

LANGUAGE GROUPS IN MEDIEVAL EUROPE

The languages of medieval Europe, showing the broad distribution of the four main language families — Latin, Slavic, Celtic, and Germanic — and
their subdivisions, together with the early medieval linguistic frontier between spoken Latin/Romance and German and areas in Europe where other
representatives of the world's language families were spoken. Latin begins slowly to diversify into the various Romance forms in the course of the eighth
and ninth centuries and takes far longer in some regions than in others. Fragments survive from the ninth century but it is not until the tenth and 11th
centuries that substantial written texts with new orthography to take account of the sound changes in Romance vernaculars are created. In many areas,
moreover, language might differ according to social status, and bilingualism was common.

One of the Rusiyyah stood beside me and I heard him speaking to my interpreter. I quizzed him about what
he had said, and he replied. He said, "You Arabs are a foolish lot!" So I said: "Why is that?" And he replied
"Because you purposely take those who are dearest to you and whom you hold in highest esteem and throw
them under the earth, whereas we burn them in the fire there and then so that they enter paradise immediately."

IBN FADLAN ON THE RUS, A TENTH-CENTURY ACCOUNT OF AN ARAB MERCHANT TRAVELLING IN
THE REGION OF KIEV OR NOVGOROD AND ENCOUNTERING A GROUP OF RUS (PROBABLY SWEDES)

Networks Of Communication

Travellers in the Middle Ages exploited both new land routes connecting newly established centres of population and those parts of the Roman road system that had been maintained. They also travelled by boat on river, canal and sea routes. Many different goals took men and women from their homes: short trips to a local market; journeys to a local, regional or royal court to seek justice; long sea voyages or overland expeditions on commercial ventures; military campaigns; diplomatic embassies; religious missions and pilgrimages; travel round a kingdom on government business; or gathering together in civic and ecclesiastical assemblies.

The Roman road network, army routes, the postal service and the exploitation of river systems provided the basic framework for travel within Europe at the beginning of the Middle Ages. Over 4000 milestones are known to mark the distances en route on the old Roman road network. These original routes were further extended, with some routes gaining prominence at the expense of others, as a result of changes in economic, governmental and social organization.

Sea routes across the English Channel and the North Sea, as well as the Atlantic and Baltic regions became ever more frequented. The Mediterranean was navigable for many more months of the year than the more northern seas; it also lacked the tides and dangerous storms of the Atlantic. Nevertheless, the sets of currents and prevailing winds, land and sea breezes and the complex contours of the coast, made extraordinarily complex by the proximity of land masses, had as profound an influence on ship design as conditions in the northern seas had on choice of route and seasonal sailings. Sailing technology for voyages further east drew on local expertise as well adapting existing practice to new conditions.

In addition to the weather conditions and the terrain, a major factor for all medieval travellers was the duration of the journey. But the latter was not to alter much until the invention of steamships, railways, metalled roads and, in due course, the catastrophically destructive internal combustion engine. Wealth could pay for faster ships and frequent changes of horses, or simply horse or mule and

The Bayeux Tapestry. Horses being led from Norman ships before the Battle of Hastings.

680s	723–33	726	793
Adamnán of Iona writes up Arculf's account of the Holy Land in his *De locis sanctis*	Willibald's pilgrimage to Jerusalem	Kanhave canal built in Denmark	Charlemagne attempts to join the Rhine/Main and Danube rivers by constructing a canal between the rivers Rednitz and Altmühl, but is defeated by the swampy terrain and wet weather.

When strangers who plan to go to Rome come to our borders, the judge should inquire diligently whence they come. The judge shall issue a passport (*clusarius syngraphus*), placing it on a wax tablet and setting his seal upon it, so that afterwards the travellers may show this notice to our appointed agents. After this notice has been sent to us, our agents shall give the travellers a letter to enable them to go to Rome; when they return from Rome they shall receive the mark of the king'sseal ring.

FROM THE *LAWS OF KING RATCHIS OF THE LOMBARDS* (746).

RATES OF EXCHANGE AGAINST THE FLORENTINE FLORIN, 1252–1500

Florence 20s
(weight, 3.54 grams of gold)

Lucca 20s (veteri)

Pisa 20s

Siena 20s

Sicily 10 pirreali (1298)

Naples 12 gigliati

Rome 20s

Bologna 24s

Venice 48s

Verona/Tirol 33 grossi or
kreuzer (1303)

Milan 10s (in imperiali)

Genoa 8s (in gold genovini)

Savoy 12s 6d (in 1275)

Barcelona 11s (1276)

Aragon 9s (1280)

Castile
5 marvedis 8 dineros =
1 Fl. Florin (1291)

Paris 8s (1265)

London 2s 6d (1277)

Flanders
13 groten
3 miten (1317)

Cologne 2s 6d (1277)

Lübeck 8s (1288)

Nuremburg 10s

Prague 12 groschen
(c. 1300)

Vienna 6od
(1262: (1 pfund =8 schillings;
1 schilling=30 pfennige)

(All systems are used according to the ratio L.s.d: 12 denarii or pennies = 1 solidus or shilling 20 solidi or shillings = 1 libra or pound.)

880s	922	949 and 968	c. 1000	1230s
Othere the Norwegian reaches the White Sea via the North Cape	Ibn Fadlan visits the upper Volga	Liutprand of Cremona's embassies to Constantinople	First landings of Scandinavians on the Atlantic seaboard	Bridge constructed at Schöllenen increases transalpine traffic via the Gotthard pass.

cart transport of some kind, but for most of the peoples of Europe the normal mode of travel would have been on foot. A relatively trouble-free journey from Canterbury to Rome, for example, could take six weeks; Willibald of England (700–787) was on the road or at sea for ten years. His pilgrimage included wintering in Rome, Jerusalem and Cyprus and a two-year journey which took him from Hamwic in England to the Holy Land via France, Italy, Sicily, Palestine (under Muslim rule) and Asia Minor before settling in his new diocese of Eichstätt in Germany. The news of the murder of Charles the Good in Bruges on 2nd March 1127, on the other hand, was reported in London the next morning.

Along these networks of communication inns, hospices, monastic guest houses, holy shrines and support for the traveller provided a means of livelihood for many, not least the local populations in the foothills of the Pyrenees and Alps (who made their living as porters and couriers, guides and protectors of travellers), and the seamen who operated the cross-Channel ferries. They served many categories of traveller, not least pilgrims to holy places such as Compostella, Rome and Jerusalem, whose religious interest was assimilated to a long-standing tradition of "learned tourism", that is, travel for intellectual or scholarly purposes. Students travelling to different schools and universities, government agents, merchants and long-term travellers also numbered among their customers. These people would have made arrangements for transferring money to support themselves on their journeys. Others relied on local customs of charity and hospitality, or, in the case of itinerant artisans, craftsmen and musicians, on receiving their pay on the spot. Group travel for safety reasons was common and systems of passes were devised by local rulers.

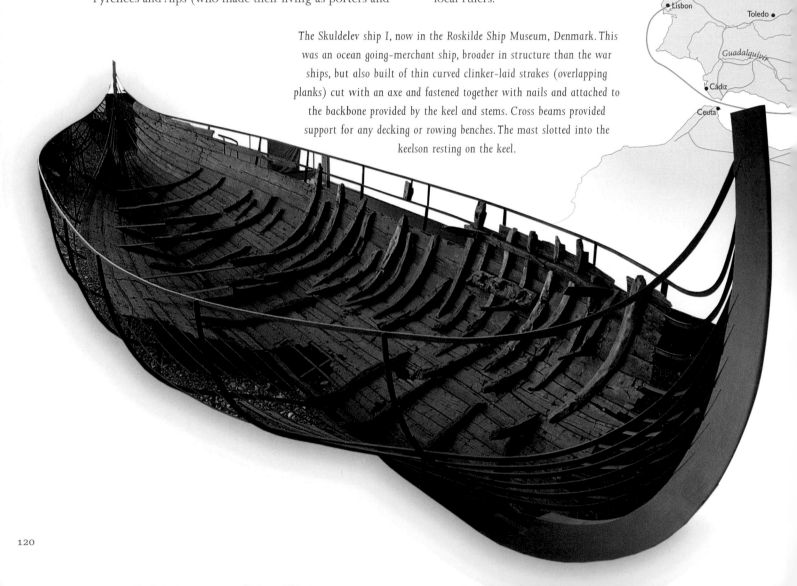

The Skuldelev ship I, now in the Roskilde Ship Museum, Denmark. This was an ocean going-merchant ship, broader in structure than the war ships, but also built of thin curved clinker-laid strakes (overlapping planks) cut with an axe and fastened together with nails and attached to the backbone provided by the keel and stems. Cross beams provided support for any decking or rowing benches. The mast slotted into the keelson resting on the keel.

Bergen

Lake Ladoga

North
Sea

Turku

Stockholm

Reval

Novgorod

Edinburgh

Gotland

Volga

Århus

Riga

York

Ribe

Baltic
Sea

main sea routes (Viking, Frisian, Anglo-Saxon)

main sea routes (Mediterranean merchants)

Roman roads

major Alpine passes

Elbe

Oder

Vistula

royal routes in German empire, c. 1000

Don

Hanwic

London

outward journey of Willibald

return journey of Willibald

Antwerp

Cologne

Leipzig

Rouen

Seine

Dnieper

Paris

Cracow

Nuremberg

Eichstätt

**site of Charlemagne's failed canal
connecting the Rednitz (from Main)
and Albmül**

Angers

Rhine

Augsburg

Langres

Vienna

deaux

Gt. St
Bernard

St Gotthard

Brenner

Lyons

Lit. St
Bernard

Simplon

Vienne

San Bernardino

Rhône

Mt Cenis

Milan

Caffa

Mt Genevre

Turin

Pavia

Venice

Pyrenees

Genoa

Black   Sea

Col di Tendo

Narbonne

Lucca

Ravenna

Trebizond

Florence

Barcelona

Corsica

Danube

Tarragona

Tiber

Rome

Pliska

Adrianople

Constantinople

encia

Sardinia

Naples

Nicaea

Thessalonica

Lesbos

Smyrna

Cephallonia

Ephesus

Antioch

Catania

Athens

Miletus

Emesa

Corinth

Tunis

Syracuse

Cyprus

Salamis

Damascus

Monemvasia

Rhodes

Beirut

Mediterranean
Sea

Sidon

Tyre

Candia

Tiberius
Nazareth

Caesarea

Jerusalem

Tripolis

Alexandria

Cairo

NETWORKS OF COMMUNICATION
IN MEDIEVAL EUROPE

The physical terrain as well as the weather presented considerable difficulties for all travellers, but each local government had
the care of roads and bridges under its control, with varying degrees of maintenance.

The British Isles And France To The Twelfth Century

Between the tenth and mid-twelfth centuries the power of many of the French magnates overshadowed the Capetian kings of France. At a more local level, the widespread construction of castles secured the power of lesser nobles. In 1066 one of the greatest French magnates, William of Normandy, conquered England with warriors from all over northern France; their successors also advanced into Wales and Ireland. The fusion of Anglo-Saxon and Norman traditions made England a rich and effectively governed kingdom, but by 1223 the revitalized French monarchy was without equal in western Europe.

In 900 the Carolingian kings of the West Frankish kingdom could claim to rule the whole of the territory from the River Scheldt to the Pyrenees. They faced great competition from their nobles, however, and in 987 the most powerful of them, Hugh Capet, was elected king, establishing a lineage that would rule France until 1328. Yet the first two centuries of Capetian kingship were very troubled. In most regions regalian rights had fallen into the hands of magnates such as the dukes of Aquitaine, Normandy and Burgundy and the counts of Anjou, Blois and Toulouse. By 1060 effective royal power was restricted to the north-eastern quarter of the kingdom, and the royal domains had shrivelled to a cluster of territories around Orléans and Paris. Nevertheless, the king of France enjoyed enormous prestige as the successor of Charlemagne, whose popularity in legend spread through songs such as the *Chanson de Roland*.

Both kings and magnates faced challenges to their authority from their own barons and knights. In the 11th and 12th centuries castles (military strongholds and aristocratic residences that embodied noble power) came to dominate the French landscape. For many monastic chroniclers the castle was a potent symbol of baronial disorder, but Capetian France was far from anarchic. Castles were the mainstay of royal as well as seigneurial power, and castellans often provided order in districts where kings or magnates were too ineffective to do so. The reorganization of society around castles had a creative impact upon the local economy, concentrating resources and manpower under the leadership of the castellan. Undoubtedly acquisitive and brutal, the castellans nevertheless represented the most dynamic force in French society in this period. Since power was concentrated around fortified points, much of France was not divided into solid blocs of territory that can be easily represented upon a map. The frontiers of the kingdom were also rarely of great political significance in this period. Along most of the tortuous border with the Empire, for instance, neither king nor emperor exerted much direct control (and in any case, until 1032 a third kingdom, Burgundy, survived in the valley of the Rhône).

The spread of castles across the landscape of western Europe: from simple towers on artificial mounds, to the impressive Château-Gaillard in Normandy, raised by Richard I of England between 1196 and 1198 at a cost of over £12000 sterling (left). Philip Augustus of France captured château-Gaillard in March 1204.

987	1016–42	1066	1154	1169	1204
Capetian dynasty replaces the Carolingians as kings of West Francia (France)	Danish rule in England	Norman Conquest of England	Henry of Anjou, duke of Normandy and Aquitaine, becomes king of England	English invasion of Ireland begins	Philip II Augustus, king of France, annexes Normandy, Maine, Anjou and Poitou to his domain

THE BRITISH ISLES AND FRANCE, c.1080

areas firmly held by Normans, c.1100

areas under Norman hegemony, c.1100

France

French royal domain, 987

added by 1032

added by c.1130

Church lands

Kingdom of Burgundy, c.1130

Fiefs held from the County of Flanders

other French fiefs

possessions of the House of Blois

✝ royal bishoprics

England

—— English shires, 1086

✝ English bishoprics, 1086

● fortresses built after Norman conquest of England, to 1086

—— northern limit of Domesday Book

Scotland

—— maximum area held by David I, c.1140–45

—— Norwegian territory from 1098

—— autonomous regions within Scotland, to c.1164

Wales

Welsh control, 1094

Ireland

Irish kingdoms in the 8th century, nominally subject to High Kingship of Brian Boru, 1005

In the wake of the unification of England, the late Anglo-Saxon kings developed a highly advanced administration that functioned through a system of local divisions (shires) and royal officers (sheriffs). Almost uniquely in 11th century western Europe, they made their will known throughout their kingdom by means of writs and levied direct taxes (geld); they also minted the finest coinage in the West. The unity of the English kingdom survived conquest by the Danish kings Swegn and Cnut (1013-16) and by the duke of Normandy, William the Conqueror, in 1066. The Norman Conquest transformed the English landscape, language and culture, but William I (1066-1087) built his régime upon Anglo-Saxon foundations: the most famous record of William's reign, the Domesday Book (1086), is pervaded by Anglo-Saxon influences. In the 12th century English

123

royal finance and justice continued to be the most sophisticated in western Europe. The emergence of a central auditing body, the exchequer, made royal officials far more accountable, and a single system of justice based around royal courts encouraged the growth of a "common law of the realm". The kings, however, remained loath to abide by the law, which they enforced upon their subjects, until a baronial reaction in 1215 forced King John (1199-1216) to concede the great charter of liberties known as Magna Carta.

In Scotland, a monarchy that already ruled Gaelic, Anglo-Saxon, Scandinavian and Welsh-speaking peoples welcomed many French settlers after 1066, and borrowed policies and institutions from its English neighbour in order to consolidate royal power. In contrast, the inhabitants of Wales and Ireland remained fundamentally divided, despite attempts by successive rulers of Deheubarth and Gwynedd to bring the whole of Wales under their sway, and similar efforts by the kings of Leinster and Connacht to dominate Ireland. Both countries found themselves prey to Anglo-Norman aggression; by 1200 large tracts of Welsh and Irish territory lay under English rule.

The Norman Conquest reinforced political and cultural links between the British Isles and France; until 1204 England and Normandy had a single aristocracy and usually the same ruler. In 1154 Count Henry of Anjou, duke of Normandy and, by marriage to Eleanor of Aquitaine, ruler of much of southwestern France, succeeded to the English throne as Henry II (1154-89). Henry's Angevin or Plantagenet dynasty effectively dominated half the kingdom of France; not surprisingly, the Capetian kings strove to reduce the power of these mighty subjects wherever possible. Under Philip Augustus (1180-1223) the French monarchy dramatically expanded its power. Through marriage Philip acquired Vermandois and Artois, and through war he won Normandy, Maine, Anjou and most of Poitou from John of England. Philip's territorial acquisitions were matched by advances in governance that enabled the Capetians to tap the burgeoning wealth of their kingdom as never before. From then on the kings of France had no rival within their kingdom; the greatness of France within Europe had begun.

No free man shall be seized or imprisoned, or stripped of his rights or possessions, or outlawed or exiled, or deprived of his standing in any other way, nor will we proceed with force against him, or send others to do so, except by the lawful judgment of his equals or by the law of the land.

KING JOHN'S CHARTER OF LIBERTIES FOR THE
ENGLISH ("*MAGNA CARTA*"), 1215, CLAUSE 39

The king in his counting house: the English exchequer in the mid-12th century. Before 1200 similar accounting systems developed in Normandy, Flanders, Capetian France, and the kingdom of Sicily.

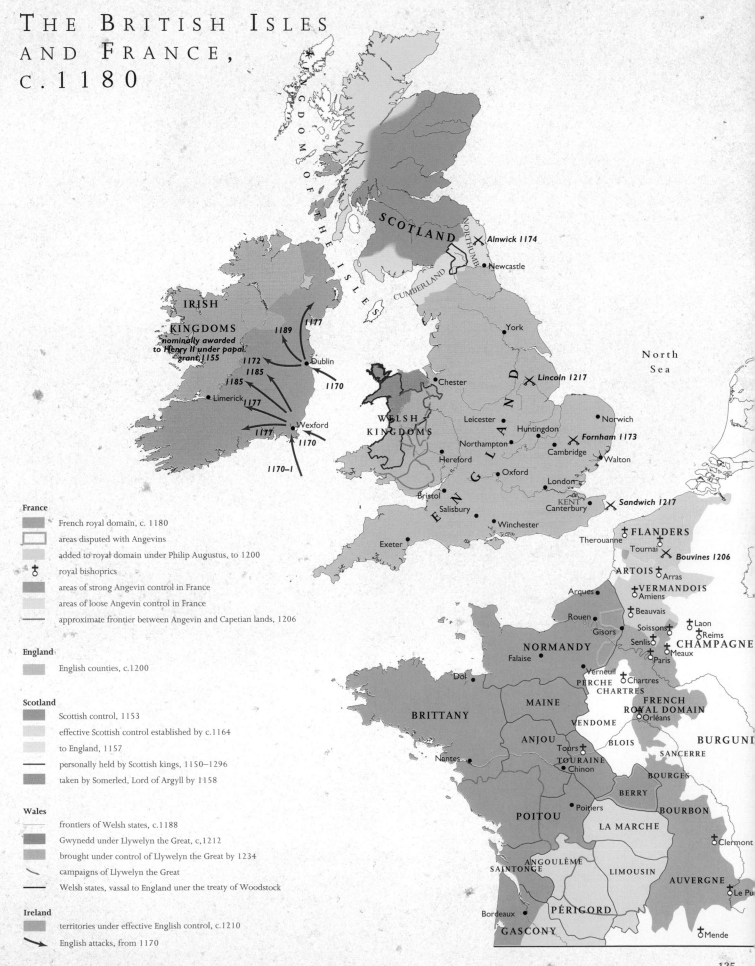

The British Isles
and France,
c.1180

SCOTLAND

KINGDOM OF THE ISLES

NORTHUMB.

✕ **Alnwick 1174**

Newcastle

CUMBERLAND

IRISH

KINGDOMS
nominally awarded to Henry II under papal grant, 1155

1177

1189

Dublin

1172
1185

1185

1170

Limerick

1177

Wexford

1177

1170

1170–1

York

✕ **Lincoln 1217**

North
Sea

Chester

WELSH
KINGDOMS

Leicester

Northampton

Hereford

Oxford

Bristol

Salisbury

E N G L A N D

Huntingdon

Cambridge

Norwich

✕ **Fornham 1173**

Walton

London

KENT

Canterbury

✕ **Sandwich 1217**

Exeter

Winchester

Therouanne

✝ **FLANDERS**

Tournai

✕ **Bouvines 1206**

ARTOIS

Arras

✝ **VERMANDOIS**

Arques

Amiens

✝

Rouen

Beauvais

✝

Laon ✝

Soissons ⚲

✝ Reims

⚲

✝ **CHAMPAGNE**

Gisors

Senlis

Meaux

NORMANDY

Falaise

Verneuil

Paris ⚲

PERCHE

✝ Chartres

CHARTRES

Dol

MAINE

VENDOME

FRENCH
ROYAL DOMAIN

Orléans ○

BRITTANY

ANJOU

BLOIS

BURGUND

Nantes

Tours ✝

TOURAINE

Chinon

SANCERRE

BOURGES

BERRY

POITOU

Poitiers

BOURBON

LA MARCHE

Clermont ✝

ANGOULÊME

SAINTONGE

LIMOUSIN

AUVERGNE

Bordeaux

PÉRIGORD

Le Pu ✝

GASCONY

✝ Mende

France

- French royal domain, c. 1180
- areas disputed with Angevins
- added to royal domain under Philip Augustus, to 1200
- ✝⚲ royal bishoprics
- areas of strong Angevin control in France
- areas of loose Angevin control in France
- —— approximate frontier between Angevin and Capetian lands, 1206

England

- English counties, c.1200

Scotland

- Scottish control, 1153
- effective Scottish control established by c.1164
- to England, 1157
- —— personally held by Scottish kings, 1150–1296
- taken by Somerled, Lord of Argyll by 1158

Wales

- frontiers of Welsh states, c.1188
- Gwynedd under Llywelyn the Great, c,1212
- brought under control of Llywelyn the Great by 1234
- campaigns of Llywelyn the Great
- —— Welsh states, vassal to England uner the treaty of Woodstock

Ireland

- territories under effective English control, c.1210
- ➘ English attacks, from 1170

The German Empire

The German empire consisted of kingdoms, themselves divided into provinces. These became the basis of growing regional power from the 12th century on. Lay and ecclesiastical princes established their territorial lordship, under their own jurisdiction and with quasi-independent powers. What on the surface could be seen as an alternation of periods of crisis with the rule of strong emperors was due to the structure of the empire, where the balance of power sometimes favoured, and at other times disadvantaged the emperor.

The Ottonians resurrected the imperial title and expanded the boundaries of the empire. The monarchy was elective, but in practice the son of a ruler was usually elected and thus inheritance had an important role in establishing ruling dynasties. Bishops played a significant part in imperial government; this was still true under the "priestly kingship" of Henry III (1039–56). When the papacy began to contest the right of the emperor to invest bishops, this led to a clash between Pope Gregory VII and Emperor Henry IV.

From the late 11th century, the territorial aristocracy acquired military and judicial powers; their role in peace unions also enhanced their authority. While the emperor focused on external affairs such as Italian expeditions, princes became the effective "lords of the land". The principal means of government remained personal presence. One cannot speak of "German" unity on any level; social, legal, economic and linguistic diversity characterized the period. Yet the imperial ideal was strong. Frederick Barbarossa (second of the Hohenstaufen dynasty and Emperor from 1152–90) promoted the cult of Charlemagne, having him canonized at a court assembly in 1165. Frederick also put down major ducal revolts, but powerful territorial families continued to dominate their own regions, and territorial lordship remained the basis of power. Changes in society led to the enlargement of the nobility in the 13th century. Ministeriales, originally of unfree legal status, rose through

Henry IV asking Abbot Hugh of Cluny and Countess Matilda of Tuscany to intercede for him with Pope Gregory VII. Gregory VII had excommunicated Henry and annulled all oaths to him. Henry gained absolution and thus reestablished his power by submitting to the pope as a penitent. Secretly crossing the Alps in January, he asked Gregory for forgiveness at Canossa. Matilda, countess of Canossa, and Henry's godfather, Abbot Hugh, were among those who interceded with the pope on Henry's behalf.

919–1024	1077	1024–1125	1138–1254	1250–73
Saxon (Ottonian) dynasty	Henry IV at Canossa	Salian dynasty	Staufen dynasty	interregnum

THE GERMAN EMPIRE

The German Empire consisted of different parts, including the kingdom of Germany, the kingdoms of Burgundy and Italy and later Bohemia, as well as duchies and other lands. Family lands as well as ecclesiastical domains were frequently not contiguous. The marches along the empire's eastern frontier, which originally served a defensive function, developed into duchies. Ecclesiastical centres provided missionaries and clerics to spread Christianity. German emperors strove to extend their power over newly created kingdoms, which led to territorial acquisitions in the northeast. German settlement was also important in lands that were not incorporated into the empire.

Legend:

— borders of the Ottonian empire, 962

— imperial frontier, 1152

— imperial frontier in the 13th century

/// Staufen demesne lands mid-12th century

||| Welf demesne lands mid-12th century

Kingdom of Italy, 1152

Kingdom of Burgundy, 1152

Kingdom of Bohemia, 1152

ecclesiastical lands, 1152

✝ important monastery

■ archdioceses

○ Lombard league members

Henry the Lion (d. 1195), Welf duke of Saxony and Bavaria, was the most powerful prince of the empire. After he refused to send troops to help Frederick Barbarossa, the emperor took advantage of the bishop of Halberstadt's complaint and had Henry tried according to feudal law. The princes deprived Henry of his two duchies, which were split up and granted by the emperor to rivals of Henry.

military service and administration, and became territorial lords. Frederick II (elected king of the Romans in 1211 and crowned emperor in 1220) used the kingdom of Sicily, which he had inherited, as the base of his power. An ambitious monarch, he continued the traditions of a strong centralized monarchy in the kingdom of Sicily, but favoured the territorial princes by granting them extensive powers in Germany. He even intervened on the side of the princes against his own son Henry, who had been elected king of the Romans prior to Frederick's own imperial coronation. The papal curia was suspicious of the increasing power of the Staufen family, although the crowns of Germany and Sicily were technically separate. Open conflict erupted when Pope Gregory IX excommunicated Frederick in 1227, under the pretext that the emperor had broken his vow to go on crusade. Warfare alternating with uneasy peace continued for the rest of Frederick's reign. Hostile propaganda presented Frederick as dissolute and irreligious. He was even deposed by Pope Innocent IV in 1245, but until his death in 1250 papal attempts to diminish his power did not, in fact, succeed. This, however, did not mean a unification of the empire; Germany became a juxtaposition of autonomous territories.

Territorial fragmentation increased after Frederick's death during the "interregnum". In this period, rather than having no ruler, Germany was often divided between two elected kings, but none had effective power. Rudolf of Habsburg (at the time one of the less important territorial lords) was elected king in 1273 and started to build Habsburg power. Despite a policy of reform and of recuperating imperial properties, he was more successful in increasing familial, rather than imperial, power. At the end of the 13th century, the seven electors, who had emerged as the body responsible for royal election, demonstrated their power by electing, then deposing, Adolf of Nassau.

"[Frederick Barbarossa], having brought all matters in Saxony into good order and inclined to his own will all the princes of that province, entered Bavaria ... There indeed did the prince, having displayed a strong will in arranging all to his satisfaction within the confines of his empire, think to display abroad a stout arm. He wished to declare war on the Hungarians and to bring them under the might of the monarchy. But being ... unable to secure the assent of the princes ...[he was] thus powerless to put his plans into effect.'

(From Otto of Freising, *The Deeds of Frederick Barbarossa*)

Augustalis coin of Emperor Frederick II, issued in 1231 for his Sicilian kingdom. Frederick's policies, legislation, and even money-minting differed between his kingdoms. Issued only in the kingdom of Sicily, the gold coin was of unprecedented purity. Moreover, the name of the coin, the "portrait" on it modelled on classical Roman emperors and the presence of the imperial eagle impressed on the viewer that Frederick was Roman emperor.

Italy And The Papacy

The pope was secular ruler over territories in central Italy, but his real power – at its height in the 13th century – stemmed from his position as head of Christendom. The Norman kingdom of Sicily, in the south of Italy, was one of the most powerful monarchies of the time; it became the power-base of the German Emperor Frederick II. Power-struggles between these two rival powers, the German emperors and popes, contributed to the emergence of city-states in northern Italy.

The kingdom of Italy was part of the German Empire. As imperial authority in northern Italy grew weaker from the late 11th century, cities gained de facto independence. The northern Italian cities resisted Frederick Barbarossa's attempt to reassert imperial rights. They formed the Lombard League (1167) and in 1176 at Legnano defeated Frederick's army, forcing him to recognize urban self-government, although the cities did remain under imperial overlordship. In southern Italy and Sicily the Normans displaced Byzantine and Muslim rule. After initially providing military service in local power-struggles, they conquered Calabria and Apulia. In 1059, Pope Nicholas II recognized the Norman leaders Richard of Aversa and Robert Guiscard. The latter's brother, Roger, took Sicily (1061–72) from the Muslims. Roger II (1130–54) assumed royal title in Sicily and brought the Norman territories of southern Italy under his rule. He imposed strong royal administration and taxation, but local institutions and religious observance continued to exist.

The Staufen inherited the Norman kingdom in 1194. Thus the territories under their rule encircled the papacy

Debates about the relationship between the spiritual and temporal power were central for both papal and imperial claims. In this canon law manuscript (below), Christ, the source of all power, gives the key, symbol of spiritual authority, to St Peter, and the sword, symbol of temporal rule, to the emperor. Thus the two powers are separate, yet St Peter's halo indicates the superiority of papal office – the popes were seen as the successors of St Peter.

The Roman pontiff can exercise his pontifical judgment … over any Christian of any condition whatsoever… and particularly by reason of sin. Thus he may decree that any sinner whose contumacy has brought him to the depths of depravity is to be held … outside the body of the faithful, so that, by implication at least, he is deprived of the power of any temporal rulership that he had … For our Lord Jesus Christ … was a true king and true priest… and he established not only a pontifical but a royal monarchy in the apostolic see, committing to Peter and his successors control over both an earthly and a heavenly empire…

(POPE INNOCENT IV JUSTIFYING THE DEPOSITION OF FREDERICK II)

1060	1183	1215	1234	1240s	1243–54
Norman conquest of Calabria completed	Treaty of Constance between Lombard League and Frederick Barbarossa	Fourth Lateran Council	Gregory IX's *Decretals*, official canon law collection of papal letters	Last Muslim rebellion in Sicily	Pope Innocent IV

Southern Italy and the Normans

- - - - northern limit of Byzantine rule, c.1025

conquered by Normans by 1059

additional conquests by 1085

additional conquests by 1130

additional conquests by 1154

1060 date of acquisition by Normans

The Growth of the Papal State

original Duchy of Rome ('Patrimonium Petri'), to 756

claimed 756 under donation of Pippin, King of the Franks

acquired 757–74

acquired 781–89

acquired 1053

area "recuperated" under Innocent III 1198–1216 or acquired 1217–78

- - - - northern Frontier of Papal States 1201–13

• members of Lombard League of 1177

● members of Lombard League of 1226

maternal inheritance of Frederick II

- - - - Kingdom of Italy, c.1152

Corsica

Sardinia

Feltre
Belluno
Como
Monza
Bergamo
Brescia
Treviso
Novara
Cortenuovo
Vicenza
Vercelli
Milan
Verona
Padua
Lodi
Mantua
Venice
Pavia
Cremona
Po
Asti
Piacenza
Alessandria
Tortona
Parma
Modena
Ferrara
Reggio
Bologna
Ravenna
Faenza
Lucca
Pistoia
Urbino
Pisa
Florence
Arno
Siena
Arezzo
Gubbio
Cortona
Assisi
Spoleto
Nursia
Orvieto
Terano
Viterbo
Tiber
Tagliacozzo
Rome
Tivoli
Ermoli
Monte Cassino
Lucera *1042*
Siponto
Gaeta *1073*
Capua *1058*
Benevento
Trani
Bari *1071*
Naples *1130*
Conza
Ravello
Salerno *1077*
Acerenza
Brindisi *1071*
Amalfi *1127*
Agropoli
Taranto *1060*
Otranto
Rossano
Cosenza

Tyrrhenian Sea

Squillace *1060*

Monreale
Palermo *1072*
Messina *1061*
Reggio *1060*
Paormina
Sicily
Catania *1071*
Girgenti *1086*
Syracuse *1088*
Tagusa

ITALY
756–c.1300

The northern and southern parts of Italy were under different rule for much of the period. Cities, many developing into city-states, played an important political role in the north; the Lombard League fought against emperors in the 12th and 13th centuries. The Patrimony of St Peter was the area the popes claimed as their own on the basis of the forged Donation of Constantine. In addition, emperors and Countess Matilda of Tuscany (1102) donated territories to the popes. In the 11th–13th centuries the creation of an independent papal state, rather than overlordship over scattered territories, became important for the papacy, but the borders were continuously changing and popes often lacked effective control. Innocent III did more for the consolidation of the papal state than any of his predecessors had done.

ROMAN CHURCHES

Rome, the seat of the papacy, had strong symbolic significance for medieval Christians. Believed to be the place where the apostle Peter was imprisoned, crucified, and buried, the relics of the "prince of the apostles" became the centre of a cult. From the 11th to the end of the 13th century, urban expansion led to the creation of new quarters, the restoration of the walls and some bridges. Innocent III restored and enlarged the papal palace next to St Peter's Basilica and had new administrative buildings built to the north. Innocent IV and his successors added a papal palace there, which became the Vatican. Yet political conflicts with local noble families and the commune of Rome eventually contributed to the move of the papacy from Rome.

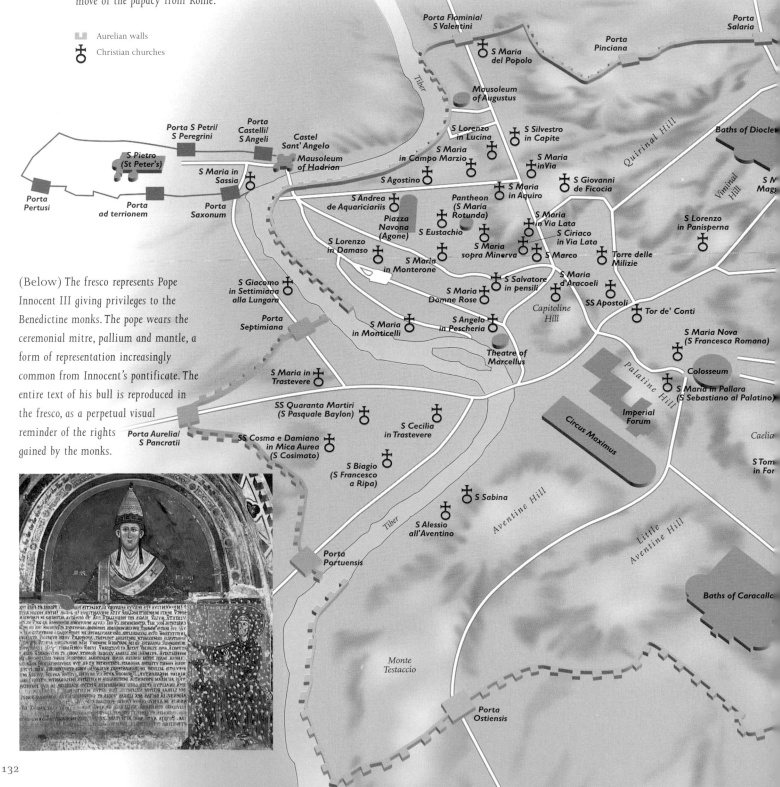

Aurelian walls

Christian churches

(Below) The fresco represents Pope Innocent III giving privileges to the Benedictine monks. The pope wears the ceremonial mitre, pallium and mantle, a form of representation increasingly common from Innocent's pontificate. The entire text of his bull is reproduced in the fresco, as a perpetual visual reminder of the rights gained by the monks.

Porta Flaminial
S Valentini

Porta Salaria

Porta Pinciana

S Maria
del Popolo

Mausoleum
of Augustus

Tiber

S Lorenzo
in Lucina

S Silvestro
in Capite

Baths of Dioclet

Quirinal Hill

Viminal Hill

S M
Mag

Porta S Petril
S Peregrini

Porta Castellil
S Angeli

S Pietro
(St Peter's)

Castel
Sant' Angelo

Mausoleum
of Hadrian

S Maria in
Sassia

S Maria
in Campo Marzio

S Maria
in Via

S Giovanni
de Ficocia

Porta
Pertusi

Porta
ad terrionem

Porta
Saxonum

S Agostino

S Andrea
de Aquariciariis

Piazza
Navona
(Agone)

Pantheon
(S Maria
Rotunda)

S Maria
in Aquiro

S Maria
in Via Lata

S Lorenzo
in Panisperna

S Eustachio

S Ciriaco
in Via Lata

S Lorenzo
in Damaso

S Maria
sopra Minerva

S Marco

Torre delle
Milizie

S Maria
in Monterone

S Giacomo
in Settimiana
alla Lungara

S Salvatore
in pensili

S Maria
d'Aracoeli

SS Apostoli

Porta
Septimiana

S Maria
Domne Rose

Capitoline
Hill

Tor de' Conti

S Maria Nova
(S Francesca Romana)

S Maria
in Monticelli

S Angelo
in Pescheria

Theatre of
Marcellus

Palatine Hill

Colosseum

S Maria in
Trastevere

Imperial
Forum

S Maria in Pallara
(S Sebastiano al Palatino)

SS Quaranta Martiri
(S Pasquale Baylon)

S Cecilia
in Trastevere

Circus Maximus

Caelia

S Tom
in For

Porta Aurelial
S Pancratii

SS Cosma e Damiano
in Mica Aurea
(S Cosimato)

S Biagio
(S Francesco
a Ripa)

S Sabina

Aventine Hill

Little
Aventine Hill

Tiber

S Alessio
all'Aventino

Porta
Portuensis

Baths of Caracalla

S Tom
in For

Monte
Testaccio

Porta
Ostiensis

and this exacerbated the tensions between popes and German emperors. The highpoint of these conflicts was the reign of Frederick II. War with the Lombard cities continued until his death in 1250. Thereafter, the city-states exploited the vacuum of political power, but local rivalries also grew. Guelphs and Ghibellines fought against each other; factionalism finally facilitated the emergence of dynastic rule over some city-states.

By 1268, after the defeat and death of the heirs of Frederick II, Charles of Anjou gained rule over the *regno* (the Staufen kingdom in the South). He also tried to extend his power to Northern Italy. In 1282, however, the Sicilian Vespers led to the break-up of the *regno*. While the Angevins remained lords in Naples, the Aragonese took power in Sicily. In central Italy, the papal states acquired political autonomy in the 13th century.

Around 1000, the papacy was under the control of emperors and local factions. Popes were often appointed and sometimes deposed by the German emperor, and they were caught up in the rivalries of aristocratic factions in Rome. From the mid-11th century, ecclesiastical reform, initially fostered by the entourage of the emperor, began to change the nature of papal power. Lay control over ecclesiastical matters was rejected, and papal election by cardinals established (1059). The reform movement redefined the relationship between spiritual and temporal power, claiming the superiority of the former. This led to the investiture controversy in the 11th century (*see* pp 126–7), but by the late 12th and 13th centuries the pope became an effective leader of Christendom. "Papal monarchy" meant that the pope, head of the institutional Church, gained progressively more power not only over the clergy, but also over the lives of the laity. The pope was at the centre of an increasingly sophisticated jurisdictional and administrative system, taxation, and bureaucracy. Through councils, legates, and papal letters, papal power radiated to every corner of Christendom. The growth in the average number of papal letters per annum, from 35 in the 1130s to over 3,000 by the early 14th century, indicates this. Papal decisions extended to diverse spheres, including canonization, marriage cases, and politics.

Porta Nomentana
S Prassede
Esquiline Hill
Porta Tiburtina/ S Laurentii
ppian Hill
Porta Maior
S Croce in Gerusalemme
S Clemente
Porta Asinaria/ S Iohannis
SS Quattro Coronati
S Giovanni in Laterano (St John Lateran)
S Stefano Rotondo
Porta Metronia
Porta Latina
Porta Appia

(Left) The fresco (c. 1275) represents the investiture of Charles I of Anjou in 1266 with the kingdom of Naples and Sicily. Pope Clement IV holds the keys of St Peter, symbol of his apostolic authority. He gives a bull (a letter with a pendant seal) to Charles, making him a vassal of the Holy See. Charles, younger brother of King Louis IX of France, was invited by the pope to intervene in the regno. After securing his domination over the South, Charles wished to extend his influence over the rest of Italy.

The Kingdoms of Central Europe: Bohemia, Hungary and Poland

Around 1000, after local rulers converted to Christianity, new polities emerged in Central Europe. Christianization and state building were inextricably linked. Borrowing from western Europe was complemented by adaptation and local specificities. The balance of power was determined by the consolidation of one dynasty, or one branch of a particular dynasty, at the expense of others, and relations to the German and Byzantine empires. By 1300, central Europe was an integral part of Latin Christendom.

Ecclesiastical structures and rulership emerged and were consolidated simultaneously, through the defeat of "pagan revolts", which were linked to political rivalry, the creation of dioceses and counties, and the installation of ecclesiastical personnel and royal officials. Government was based on the ruler's household, with more specialized institutions developing gradually. German emperors tried to extend their influence over the emerging states, often backing one party in internal political rivalries and sometimes intervening by military force.

Bohemia was the earliest to be Christianized. The Premysl dynasty succeeded in establishing itself by the end of the tenth century and the bishopric of Prague was founded in 973 as a suffragan of the archbishop of Mainz. Ties to the German Empire were not simply ecclesiastical. Apart from brief interludes of political independence, Bohemia remained part of the Empire, although it had a special status. Its rulers were crowned kings from 1158 on, and Otakar I (1198–1230) transformed Bohemia into a leading power. Otakar II attempted to become emperor but failed.

Hungary became an independent kingdom with its own archbishopric, Esztergom (and soon also Kalocsa). Stephen I, the first Christian king of Hungary (crowned c. 1000, d. 1038) defeated his rivals, divided the kingdom into counties and imposed conversion to Catholicism on his subjects. Nonetheless, Byzantine influence was still strong in 12th-century Hungary. Its

St Stanislaw, bishop of Cracow. Implicated in a plot to overthrow King Boleslaw II, he was executed on the order of the king in 1079. Seen as a reformer, who criticized an evil king and was thus martyred, he was canonized in 1253. His cult was very important in Poland from the 13th century on. According to his Legend, *the dismembered body of the bishop was miraculously reassembled; he was to help reunify fragmented Poland.*

1020	1083	1222	1226	1241–42
Moravia attached to Bohemia	Canonization of Stephen I, king of Hungary	Golden Bull of Hungary	Conrad of Mazovia invited Teutonic Knights into Prussia	Mongol invasion of Hungary and Poland

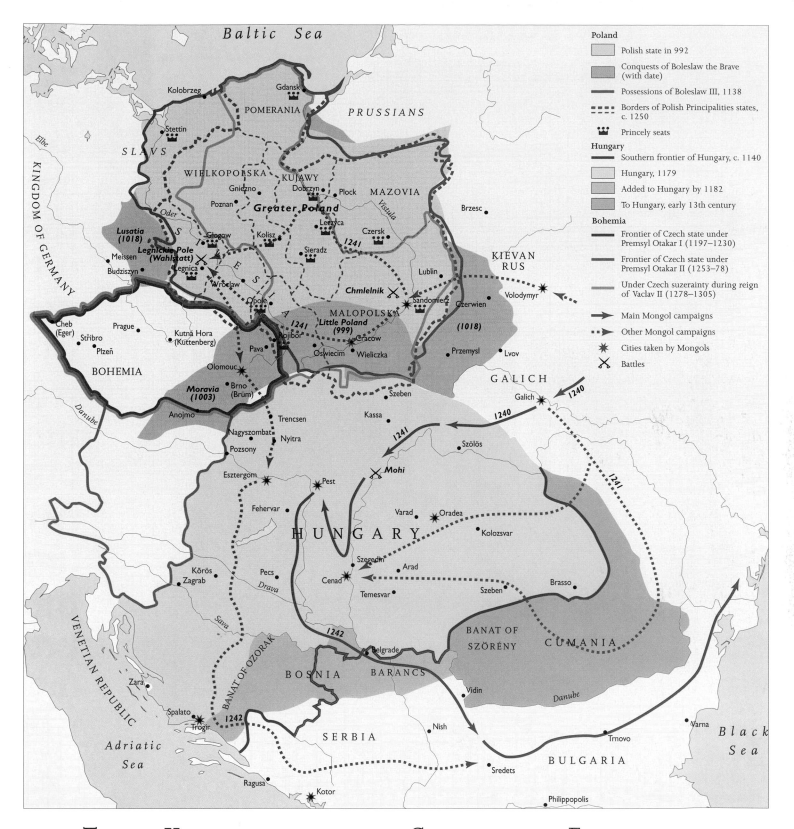

Poland
- Polish state in 992
- Conquests of Boleslaw the Brave (with date)
- Possessions of Boleslaw III, 1138
- Borders of Polish Principalities states, c. 1250
- Princely seats

Hungary
- Southern frontier of Hungary, c. 1140
- Hungary, 1179
- Added to Hungary by 1182
- To Hungary, early 13th century

Bohemia
- Frontier of Czech state under Premsyl Otakar I (1197–1230)
- Frontier of Czech state under Premsyl Otakar II (1253–78)
- Under Czech suzerainty during reign of Vaclav II (1278–1305)
- Main Mongol campaigns
- Other Mongol campaigns
- Cities taken by Mongols
- Battles

THE KINGDOMS OF CENTRAL EUROPE: BOHEMIA, HUNGARY AND POLAND

Bohemia's rulers extended their power over large territories at the end of the period, but could not consolidate their rule over them. Hungary's kings added some new areas to the kingdom, which was divided into counties. Immigrant Turkic Cumans were settled on the plain in the middle of the kingdom. The territorial extent of the kingdom of Poland changed many times; both the borders and the internal divisions shifted. Greater Poland, Little Poland, Mazovia, Kolisz and the other constituent parts of the kingdom increasingly came under the rule of separate princes. The ecclesiastical network of bishoprics and parishes evolved in all three polities, with an influx of clerics and monks from the west.

...tor De ui... tis ad ...u regi
cum gaudio. De construcde e
waradiensis ecce ꝛ d'mote reg'
ladi.

sua t
amo
mon
char
mma
inan
ꝛ di
non
omi
respt
moꝛi
dute
rum
tima
ditet
pet t
suo t
ꝛ su

(Left) *This illumination from the 14th-century Hungarian Illuminated Chronicle depicts the building of a church during the reign of Ladislas I (d. 1095, canonized 1192). Royal control over the church continued over the whole period. Ecclesiastics filled high positions in government, the chancery and diplomacy, with more and more ecclesiastics studying at western European universities.*

(Right) *A 13th-century Cistercian monastery in Osek. Architectural styles resembled western European models. Monastic orders established their houses in central Europe, drawing these areas into international networks. Ecclesiastics were one among the many groups who arrived in the new states: knights and peasants also settled there.*

rulers gradually incorporated Slovakia, Croatia-Slavonia, and Bosnia into its territories and tried to expand into the Adriatic and Rus. With the growth of noble power in the 13th century, conflicts between kings and the nobility were recurrent, leading to the fragmentation of political power under the territorial barons ("kinglets") at the end of the period.

After the conversion of Mieszko (d. 992), Boleslaw I created administrative, military and ecclesiastical structures (including the archbishopric of Gniezno in 1000), and was crowned the first king of Poland. Poland had about 3000 parishes and 300 monasteries by 1300. New areas were Christianized and conquered in the Baltic in the 12th century. Yet Poland, although nominally one kingdom, came to be subdivided into a growing number of provinces and duchies (ruled by members of the Piast dynasty), with no overall ruler. Political disintegration continued for almost two centuries after 1138. By the late

13th century, over 50 provinces existed; this, however, did not prevent economic growth.

Throughout central Europe, areas under cultivation grew – in Bohemia and Hungary from the 12th century, in Poland from the 13th. Silver mining became important in Bohemia and Hungary. Urbanization took off, through the establishment of royal cities and the use of German urban law. Immigrants from German lands settled in all three countries, often organized by local "locators". The privileges and freedoms of "German law" were also granted to local settlers. Immigrants arrived from east and west; by the 13th century the population of Hungary included Saxons, Flemings, French, Jews and Cumans. Kings of Hungary and Poland also fought nomads, who invaded from the east. The most important of these were the Mongols, one of their raids reaching as far as Moravia. They left destruction and a fear of their return in their wake.

… everyone, both great and small, men and women, with the exception of those who guard the fire, [must] gather on Sundays in the church. If someone remains at home … let them be beaten and shorn … If some people, upon coming to church to hear the divine service mutter among themselves and disturb others by relating idle tales during the celebration of mass … if they are … common folk, they shall be bound in the narthex of the church in front of everyone and punished by whipping and by the shearing off of their hair.

FROM THE LAWS OF KING STEPHEN I OF HUNGARY

Byzantium From Manzikert To The Fourth Crusade

Byzantium's dominance of the eastern Mediterranean was severely weakened at the end of the 11th century by a series of external adversaries. Although the empire's strategic, administrative and monetary position was to recover under the Comnenian dynasty, crisis within the imperial family and renewed external attacks at the end of the 12th century led to further fragmentation, a process that culminated in 1204 with the fall of Constantinople to the Fourth Crusaders.

Between the 1060s and 1090s Byzantium, until recently the dominant power of the eastern Mediterranean, came under military pressure from Normans, Pecheneg nomads and Seljuq Turks. Traditional Byzantine military and diplomatic methods proved inadequate in the face of a simultaneous triple attack. In 1071 Bari, the empire's last outpost in southern Italy, fell to the Normans. In the same year the Byzantines were defeated by the Seljuqs at Manzikert. These defeats proved the catalyst for a disastrous civil war.

Internal stability was only restored with the accession of Alexius I Comnenus, who slimmed down administration, reformed the coinage and put the governance of the empire on an explicitly dynastic footing, reserving the most important titles and offices, both in Constantinople and the provinces (themes), for the imperial family. Securing external security took somewhat longer, although the death of the Norman Robert Guiscard in 1085, and the defeat of the Pechenegs in 1091, eventually enabled the emperor to tackle the Turks. Requests were sent to western states for troops to fight the Seljuqs in Asia Minor, demands that contributed to the calling of the First Crusade. Yet, harmony between Byzantines and the Crusaders proved elusive. After a successful joint action against Nicaea in 1097, deep strains appeared. When the Crusaders retook Antioch they refused to return the city to Byzantine control.

Despite Byzantine setbacks at Antioch, the empire's territorial recovery continued after Alexius' death. Consolidation was achieved by military and diplomatic

Byzantine frontiers		external attacks in late 11th century	
1060		Seljuk and Turk	Byzantine protectorates
1118		Pecheneg	fortifications
1170		Norman	STRYMON 12th century provinces (themes)
	heartland of Empire, c.1143		

1071	1091	1097	1176	1185	1204
Imperial defeat by Seljuq Turks at Manzikert and loss of Bari to Normans	Imperial armies defeat Pechenegs at Levunium	Recapture of Nicaea from the Turks by Byzantine armies and First Crusaders	Defeat of imperial armies by Turks at Myriocephalon	Sack of Thessalonica by the Normans of Sicily	Sack of Constantinople by Fourth Crusaders

BYZANTIUM, 1071–1204

Large areas of Byzantium's eastern borderlands were dominated in the 11th century by Armenian communities. By 1080 these regions had fallen to the Seljuq Turks. Some Armenian monasteries survived conquest and continued to produce illuminated manuscripts. While many Armenians remained in the east, others moved south, settling in upland Cilicia where they periodically acknowledged the overlordship of Byzantium. By the end of the 12th century these groups had coalesced into an independent kingdom ruled by the Rupenids.

"It was my misfortune to find the Empire surrounded on all sides by barbarians, with no defence worthy of consideration against the enemies who threatened it." Alexius Comnenus' reflections on the strategic crisis that characterized the beginning of his reign are reported in The Alexiad. Written by the emperor's daughter Anna, the Alexiad is a skilfully crafted and wide ranging history of Alexius' reign, which includes extensive comments on the passage of the First Crusaders through Byzantium.

(Above) *Canon Table from an Armenian Gospel book from the monastery of Awag Vank' near Erzindjan, located in modern-day eastern Turkey (c. 1200).*

(Left) *Coronation portrait of John II Comnenus and his son Alexius. This image reflects Byzantine belief in the divine origin of imperial power. The enthroned Christ is flanked by personifications of Charity and Justice. Alexius died before his father in a hunting accident. This image forms part of a Gospel book that may have been used for devotional purposes by a member of the imperial family, possibly Alexius himself.*

channels. The army was refinanced through the use of *pronoia* grants (the non-hereditary allocation of fiscal revenues to soldiers). Fortresses, such as the one at Neacastra, were constructed. Emperors led armies to the frontiers to demonstrate imperial might and rulers of neighbouring powers, including some of the Crusader States, periodically became imperial clients. Nonetheless, relations between Byzantines and westerners continued to be mixed. While Byzantium and the Crusader States sometimes engaged in marriage deals and joint campaigns against local Muslim powers, the passage of the Second and Third Crusade armies through the empire provoked distrust. The empire's dealings with the increasingly powerful Italian maritime city-states, principally Venice, were also ambiguous. Trading concessions were frequently granted, but also frequently rescinded.

Increased commercial contact between Byzantium, Italian traders and the Crusader States encouraged economic expansion across the empire. The construction of new rural churches indicates that prosperity was generated in even the most remote regions. Yet, paradoxically, this growing economic vitality contributed to the collapse of Byzantium, particularly once dynastic conflict within the imperial family erupted after the death of Manuel Comnenus in 1180. The power vacuum at the centre encouraged provinces to distance themselves from Constantinople. Outsiders also began to view the empire as easy prey. In 1147 the Normans of Sicily raided Thebes in central Greece, taking the city's silk workers back to Palermo as economic prisoners of war. In 1185 they briefly occupied Thessalonica. The denouement of the interplay between dynastic weakness, economic prosperity and increasingly aggressive neighbours was reached in 1204 when the armies of the Fourth Crusade, ostensibly acting in the interests of the imperial claimant Alexius IV, sacked and occupied Constantinople.

Fatimid And Mamluk Egypt And North Africa

The Fatimids established an Imam-Caliphate in 919 in al-Mahdiyya in Tunisia, in opposition to the Sunni Caliphate of the Abbasids in Baghdad. They conquered Cairo in 969 and ruled Egypt until 1169, when the Ayyubids captured Cairo. Trade flourished under their rule and they contended with the Byzantines and the Umayyads of Muslim Spain for hegemony of the Mediterranean. The Mamluk Sultans of Egypt were slave-soldiers by origin who came to power in 1250 and enjoyed three centuries of independent rule until Egypt was conquered by the Ottomans in 1517.

The Fatimids were members of the Isma'ili branch of the Shi'a, the party of 'Ali, which disputed the legitimacy of the Umayyad and Abbasid Caliphates, preferring a conception of the Imamate which held that mankind needed a leader (imam) who was both beyond sin and under divine inspiration to provide guidance and instruction to the community of believers. They traced their descent to Fatima, daughter of the Prophet Muhammad and wife of 'Ali, but accorded equal prominence to charismatic illumination.

At the beginning of the tenth century, after a period of missionary activity from their base in Syria, and aided by the sedentary Berbers of Lesser Kabylia, they extended their power westwards defeating the Aghlabids in Ifriqiya (Tunisia and eastern Algeria), the Rustamids in Algeria and the Idrisids in Morocco. In 909, an Isma'ili kingdom was established. In 910 'Ubayd Allah declared himself the Mahdi, the Rightly Guided One, and established the Fatimid Imam-Caliphate, the first Shi'i Caliphate and a serious rival to the Abbasid Caliphate of Baghdad. They

FATIMID CALIPH-IMAMS
(WITH DATES OF ACCESSION)

1. Al-Mahdi, 909.	9. Al-Musta'li, 1094.
2. Al-Qa'im, 934.	10. Al-Amir, 1101.
3. Al-Mansur, 946.	11. Al-Hafiz, 1132
4. Al-Mu'izz, 953.	(regency from
5. Al-'Aziz, 975.	1130–1132).
6. Al-Hakim, 996.	12. Al-Zafir, 1149.
7. Al-Zahir, 1021.	13. Al-Fa'iz, 1154.
8. Al-Mustansir, 1036.	14. Al-'Adid, 1160.

919	969	1169	1250	1260–1277	1390–1399	1517
Foundation of al-Mahdiyya in Ifriqiya	Conquest of Cairo	End of Fatimid rule, when Ayyubids seize control of Cairo	Bahri Mamluks (Kipchak Turks) seize power in Egypt	Reign of Sultan Baybars	Reign of Sultan Barquq heralds the Sultanate of the Burji Mamluks (Circassian Turks)	Conquest of Syria and Egypt by the Ottoman Sultan, Selim I

MAMLUK SULTANS (WITH DATES OF ACCESSION)

BAHRI MAMLUKS

1. Shajar al-Durr, 1250
2. Al-Mu'izz Aybak, 1250
3. Al-Mansur 'Ali, 1257
4. Al-Muzaffar Qutuz, 1259
5. Al-Zahir Baybars, 1260
6. Al-Sa'id Baraka Khan, 1277
7. Al-'Adil Salamish, 1279
8. Al-Mansur Qalawun, 1279
9. Al-Ashraf Khalil, 1290
10. Al-Nasir Muhammad, 1293, 1299, 1310.
11. Al-'Adil Kitbugha, 1294
12. Al-Mansur Lachin, 1296
13. Al-Muzaffar Baybars, 1309
14. Al-Mansur Abu Bakr, 1341
15. Al-Ashraf Kujuk, 1341
16. Al-Nasir Ahmad, 1342
17. Al-Salih Isma'il, 1342
18. Al-Kamil Sha'ban, 1345
19. Al-Muzaffar Hajji, 1346
20. Al-Nasir Hasan, 1347, 1354
21. Al-Salih Salih, 1351
22. Al-Mansur Muhammad, 1361
23. Al-Ashraf Sha'ban, 1363
24. Al-Mansur 'Ali, 1377
25. Al-Salih/Al-MAnsur Hajji, 1381, 1389

BURJI MAMLUKS

1. Al-Zahir Barquq, 1382, 1390
2. Al-Nasir Faraj, 1399, 1405.
3. Al-Mansur 'Abd al-'Aziz, 1405
4. (Al-Musta'in, Abbasid Calpih and Sultan in Cairo, 1405)
5. Al-Mu'ayyad Shaykh, 1412
6. Al-Muzaffar Ahmad, 1421
7. Al-Zahir Tatar, 1421
8. Al-Salih Muhammad, 1421
9. Al-Ashraf Barsbay, 1422
10. Al-'Aziz Yusuf, 1438
11. Al-Zahir Jakmaq, 1438
12. Al-Mansur 'Uthman, 1453
13. Al-Ashraf Inal, 1453
14. Al-Mu'ayyad Ahmad, 1460
15. Al-Zahir Khushqadam, 1461
16. Al-Zahir Yalbay, 1467
17. Al-Zahir Timurbugha, 1468
18. Al-Ashraf Qa'it Bay, 1468
19. Al-Nasir Muhammad, 1495
20. Al-Zahir Qansawh, 1498
21. Al-Ashraf Janbalat, 1499
22. Al-'Adil Tumanbay, 1501
23. Al-Ahraf Qansawh al-Ghawri, 1501
24. Al-Ashraf Tumanbay, 1516

This 14th-century Qu'ran Box bears the names of the two master craftsmen who supervised its manufacture: Hajj Yusuf and Muhammad b. Sunqur al-Baghdadi. The Tenth Mamluk Sultan al-Nasir Muhammad commissioned their services on many occasions. The panels are of bronze, decorated with verses from the Qur'an and arabesque patterns.

FATIMID AND MAMLUK EGYPT AND NORTH AFRICA

founded al-Mahdiyya as their capital in Ifriqiyya in 919. The ambition of the Imam-Caliphs was to remove the Abbasids from the Caliphate in Baghdad and defeat the Byzantines and the Umayyads of Spain, and thus control both the Mediterranean and the Middle East. In 969 they founded Cairo (literally "the Victorious") three miles north of Fustat and in 970 the Holy Cities of Mecca and Medina placed themselves under the protection of the Fatimids. Despite their subsequent conquest of Syria, it proved impossible for them to control the Berbers of North Africa. After assuming the status of a protectorate of Frankish Jerusalem from 1163–68, they were toppled from power in 1171 by Saladin, founder of the Ayyubid dynasty.

The Fatimid Imam-Caliphate presided over the manufacture of an astonishing plethora of artefacts and a burgeoning of architectural activity in their domains. Major mosques, such as the al-Azhar Mosque in Cairo, were built. The Fatimids also exerted considerable cultural influence over Norman Sicily and Southern Italy, in particular the court of Roger II.

During the reign of the Mamluk (slave) Sultans, Egypt enjoyed three centuries of independence. Their history can be divided into two periods, based on the ethnicity of the ruling Sultans: the Bahri Mamluks, who were Kipchak Turks, enjoyed the ascendancy from 1250–1390; and the Burji Mamluks, who were Circassian Turks, ruled from 1390 to 1517. The Bahri Mamluks were originally slave-soldiers from Southern Russia brought to Egypt by the last Ayyubid, Najm al-Din. Baybars, who was Sultan from 1260–77, immortalized in folk epics, overcame Crusaders and Mongols alike, defeating Louis IX of France at al-Mansura (1250). His military policies in Syria and Palestine led to the collapse of the Kingdom of Jerusalem in 1291 at the hands of Sultan al-Ashraf Khalil, a son of Sultan Qalawun. The Sultanate of the Burji Mamluks was established by Barquq. After his death in 1399, Mamluk control of the Levant was terminated by the Mongol Conqueror Timur Lenk (Tamerlane), who took control of Syria in 1401. Timur's meeting with the great historian Ibn Khaldun, at that time a judge in the employ of the Mamluk Sultan, is one of the defining moments of the period. There was a brief period of rejuvenation under Sultan Qa'it Bay (1468–69), but the Mamluk star was in the descendant and in 1517 Egypt became a province of the Ottoman Empire.

By the second half of the 11th Century, the Fatimid Imam-Caliphs controlled Ifriqiya, Sicily (which they lost in 1072), Egypt, the Levant and the Red Sea Coast of Arabia, including guardianship of Mecca and Medina. The Mamluk Sultanate extended from autonomy in Egypt in the early 14th Century to include Frankish Outremer and the Red Sea Coast, including Mecca and Medina, in the 16th century.

- Fatmid territory in 1st half of 11th century
- Fatmid territory in 12th century
- Mamluk territory in 1st half of 14th century
- Mamluk territory in early 16th century
- Christian states

ICELAND

SCOTLAND

IRELAND

WALES ENGLAND

London

NORWAY

SWEDEN

NOVGOROD

60

MUSCOVY

Bruges

Elbe

Rhine

FRANCE

HOLY ROMAN
EMPIRE

POLAND-
LITHUANIA

Aigues-
Mortes

AUSTRIA

Genoa

Venice

HUNGARY

Dniester

Dnieper

Don

Volga

PORTUGAL

CASTILE

Barcelona

Pisa

Florence

ARAGON

Corsica

OTTOMAN SUZERAINTY

SPAIN

Majorca

Ragusa

Danube

Isbon

Seville

Valencia

Naples

Granada

Sardinia

B
A
L
K
A
N
S

Black Sea

45

Malaga

Almeria

Palermo

Constantinople

Caspian
Sea

euta

Melilla

Oran

Algiers

Bougie

Sicily

O
T
T
O
M
A
N

E
M
P
I
R
E

Tlemcen

b

Bejaia

Tunis

Trebizond

r

Ashir

Qala of the
Banu Hammad

Sousse

Malta

ZAYYANIDS

Kairouan

Mahdia

Crete

Rhodes

Sfax

Mediterranean Sea

Gabes

HAFSIDS

Tripoli

Aleppo

Mosul

Cyprus

SYRIA

uat

Beirut

Acre

Damascus

Tigris

Alexandria

Damietta

Jerusalem

Euphrates

Baghdad

Cairo

Ghat

Murzuk

PERSIA

MAMLUKS

EGYPT

Basra

a

Nile

S
a
h
a
r
a

Ormuz

Aydhab

Red

Medina

P
e
r
s
i
a
n

G
u
l
f

Sea

A R A B I A

Muscat

Mecca

NUBIA

ETHIOPIA

RASULIDS

15

Aden

30

45

15

The Crusades

The Crusades, military expeditions that offered participants the spiritual benefits of a pilgrimage with the glory of fighting as God's warriors, grew from the Christian concept of holy war. Crusaders set out to recover former Christian territory or to defend Catholic Christendom. The concept of crusading developed to include wars against heretics, such as the Albigensian Crusades, and wars against pagans on the north-eastern frontier of Catholic Europe, such as the Baltic Crusades.

The first crusade (1095–99) was in response to Seljuq conquests, which threatened pilgrimage routes and Christian holy places in the Middle East. Prompted by an appeal from the Byzantine emperor Alexios Comnenus (1081–1118), at the Council of Clermont in November 1095, Pope Urban II (1088–99) urged Catholic Christian warriors to recover the Holy Land, Christ's inheritance. The crusaders captured Nicaea and Antioch (lost to the Turks in 1080 and 1084 respectively), and took over Christian Edessa, finally capturing Fatimid-held Jerusalem in July 1099.

The castle of Crac des Chevaliers: given to the military religious order of the Hospital of St John of Jerusalem by Count Raymond II of Tripoli in 1142–4, this became one of the Hospitallers' most significant castles, famous as an early example of concentric castle design. It was finally captured by the Mamluk sultan Baibars in 1271.

The European conquerors or "Franks" who settled in the newly conquered territories established the "crusader states", centred on Antioch, Edessa, Tripoli and Jerusalem. Pilgrims and crusaders came from Europe to help to defend these states. In addition, military religious orders developed to care for pilgrims and to protect Christian territory – The Order of the Temple, the Hospital of St John of Jerusalem, and the Teutonic Order. Relations with native Christians were good: in 1198 Prince Leon of Cilician Armenia was given a crown by the western Emperor Henry VI.

Between 1099 and 1193 Muslim leaders such as Zangi of Mosul (d. 1146), his son Nur al-Din (d. 1174) and Saladin (d. 1193) won lasting territorial gains from the Franks. Zangi's capture of Edessa in 1144 prompted the second crusade (1147–49). This crusade recovered no territory in the East, but crusaders *en route* to the East by sea assisted in the capture of Muslim strongholds in the Iberian peninsula (in the Reconquista). The capture of Jerusalem by Saladin in 1187 provoked the third crusade (1189–92), which recovered sufficient coastal territory for the kingdom of Jerusalem to survive, its capital now at Acre.

After Saladin's death in 1193, his empire was divided between his brother and sons, the Ayyubids, who formed alliances with the Franks in their wars against each other. The Mamluks, who came to power in Egypt in 1250, had less need of Frankish support, and after defeating the Mongols at 'Ain Jalut in Galilee in 1260 they moved against the crusader states. Christian strongholds were captured by a series of Mamluk generals, culminating in the capture of Acre by al-Ashraf Khalil in May 1291. The kingdom of Cyprus (established following the capture of the island from the Byzantines in 1191 by Richard I of England) survived until the 16th century. Campaigns in the eastern Mediterranean continued, with the long-term aim of recovering Jerusalem.

1095	1099	1187	1229	1244	1291
Pope Urban II calls the first crusade	First crusade captures Jerusalem. Crusader states are established in the Holy Land	Saladin, sultan of Egypt, captures Jerusalem	The emperor Frederick II recovers Jerusalem by treaty	Jerusalem lost to al-Salih, sultan of Egypt	Acre captured by al-Ashraf Khalil, sultan of Egypt. Only Cyprus survives of the crusader states

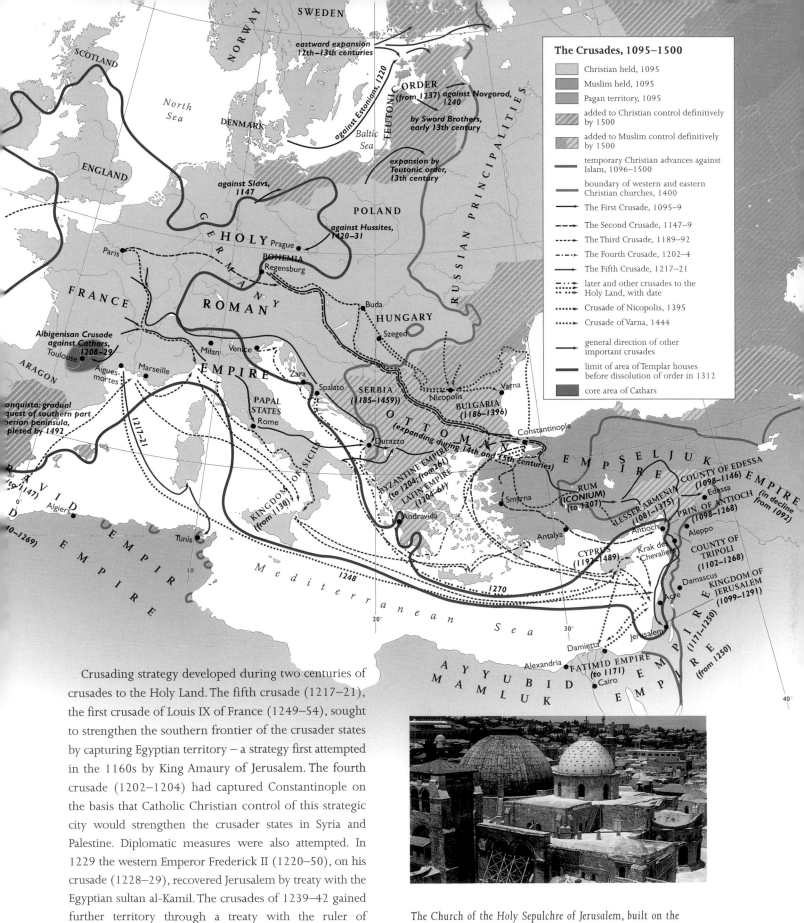

The Crusades, 1095–1500

- Christian held, 1095
- Muslim held, 1095
- Pagan territory, 1095
- added to Christian control definitively by 1500
- added to Muslim control definitively by 1500
- temporary Christian advances against Islam, 1096–1500
- boundary of western and eastern Christian churches, 1400
- The First Crusade, 1095–9
- The Second Crusade, 1147–9
- The Third Crusade, 1189–92
- The Fourth Crusade, 1202–4
- The Fifth Crusade, 1217–21
- later and other crusades to the Holy Land, with date
- Crusade of Nicopolis, 1395
- Crusade of Varna, 1444
- general direction of other important crusades
- limit of area of Templar houses before dissolution of order in 1312
- core area of Cathars

Map labels:

SCOTLAND · SWEDEN · NORWAY · DENMARK · North Sea · Baltic Sea · ENGLAND · eastward expansion 12th–13th centuries · TEUTONIC ORDER (from 1237) · against Estonians, 1220 · against Novgorod, 1240 · by Sword Brothers, early 13th century · expansion by Teutonic order, 13th century · against Slavs, 1147 · POLAND · RUSSIAN PRINCIPALITIES · GERMANY · HOLY · Prague · BOHEMIA · against Hussites, 1420–31 · Regensburg · FRANCE · Paris · ROMAN · Buda · HUNGARY · Szeged · Milan · Venice · EMPIRE · Zara · Spalato · Varna · Nicopolis · SERBIA (1185–1459)) · BULGARIA (1186–1396) · OTTOMAN (expanding during 14th and 15th centuries) · Albigenisan Crusade against Cathars, 1208–29 · Toulouse · ARAGON · Aigues-mortes · Marseille · PAPAL STATES · Rome · Durazzo · BYZANTINE EMPIRE (to 1204; from 1261) · LATIN EMPIRE (1204–61) · Constantinople · EMP SELJUK EMPIRE · Conquista: gradual conquest of southern part of Iberian peninsula, completed by 1492 · 1217–21 · KINGDOM OF SICILY (from 1130) · Andravida · Smyrna · RUM (ICONIUM) (to 1307) · LESSER ARMENIA (1081–1375) · COUNTY OF EDESSA (1098–1146) · EMPIRE (in decline from 1092) · PRIN. OF ANTIOCH (1098–1268) · ALMORAVID EMPIRE · Algiers · Tunis · CYPRUS (1191–1489) · Antalya · Antioch · Aleppo · Krak des Chevaliers · COUNTY OF TRIPOLI (1102–1268) · Mediterranean Sea · 1248 · 1270 · Damascus · Acre · KINGDOM OF JERUSALEM (1099–1291) · Damietta · Jerusalem · EMPIRE (1171–1250) (from 1250) · Alexandria · FATIMID EMPIRE (to 1171) · AYYUBID MAMLUK EMPIRE · Cairo

---

Crusading strategy developed during two centuries of crusades to the Holy Land. The fifth crusade (1217–21), the first crusade of Louis IX of France (1249–54), sought to strengthen the southern frontier of the crusader states by capturing Egyptian territory – a strategy first attempted in the 1160s by King Amaury of Jerusalem. The fourth crusade (1202–1204) had captured Constantinople on the basis that Catholic Christian control of this strategic city would strengthen the crusader states in Syria and Palestine. Diplomatic measures were also attempted. In 1229 the western Emperor Frederick II (1220–50), on his crusade (1228–29), recovered Jerusalem by treaty with the Egyptian sultan al-Kamil. The crusades of 1239–42 gained further territory through a treaty with the ruler of Damascus. Yet the religious divisions that underlay the territorial conflict ultimately made peaceful resolution politically unacceptable to both Christians and Muslims.

The Church of the Holy Sepulchre of Jerusalem, built on the traditional site of Christ's empty tomb, and a centre of Christian pilgrim from the late Roman era. It played a central role in crusader religious devotion and was the ultimate destination for all crusades to the Holy Land.

The New Monasticism And Religious Alternatives, Heresies And Dissent

Reform, advocating religious renewal based on the Benedictine Rule, started in monastic circles, but soon affected the whole of society. The increased participation of lay people, men and women, in religious life took the form of mass movements, some of which were condemned by the institutional church as heretical, whereas others were incorporated and granted official status. In the 13th century, the emerging mendicant orders responded to both lay aspirations and papal fears.

Cluny became the head of hundreds of monasteries, but from the 12th century monastic orders proliferated and offered increasingly diverse forms of religious life. The Cistercian order pioneered a new international monastic organization. This consisted of a network of monasteries, each under an abbot, brought together in annual General Chapter meetings. Visitations and customaries also ensured unity. Cistercian advocacy of a return to the purity of monastic ideals was expressed in their plain architectural

style, undyed habits and a rhetoric of the decadence of Cluniac monasticism. Reform also led to organized forms of life for hermits (Camaldoli, Fonte Avellana), and a combination of the eremitic and cenobitic life was born with the Carthusians (1084). The ideal of following a rule in a community affected the canons as well; the most popular order of regular canons was the Premonstratensians (founded in 1120), using the Rule of St Augustine. Some founders (Order of Sempringham, 1130s and house of Fontevrault, c.1101) expressed new attention to women. The crusades had an impact on monasticism as well, with the formation of military orders.

The laity were also influenced by the ecclesiastical striving for religious renewal. In the 12th and 13th centuries, mass movements suddenly emerged, seeking to re-establish the purity of early Christianity, but not all were accepted by the clergy. Some were anti-clerical; they saw the church and the clerics as corrupt and sinful.

Francis of Assisi was quickly transformed by his followers into a "second Christ". Receiving the stigmata, the five wounds of the crucified Christ, was the ultimate proof in this identification. Francis, who insisted on complete poverty, wears a simple tunic with a cord, and is barefoot. Although a layman, Francis came to be represented with a clerical tonsure, reflecting the clericalization of the order.

1098	1134	1153	1227–31	1253
Cîteaux founded	Death of Norbert of Xanten, founder of Premonstratensian order.	Death of St Bernard of Clairvaux, leading abbot of the Cistercian order	Establishment of papal inquisition	Death of Clare of Assisi, founder of the female branch of the Franciscan order

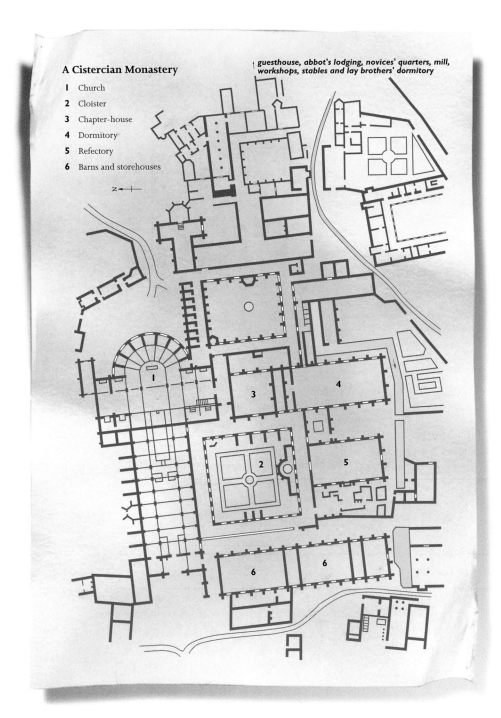

A Cistercian Monastery

1 Church
2 Cloister
3 Chapter-house
4 Dormitory
5 Refectory
6 Barns and storehouses

guesthouse, abbot's lodging, novices' quarters, mill, workshops, stables and lay brothers' dormitory

A Cistercian Monastery
Cistercians often settled in uninhabited areas, creating vast domains. They supported themselves by agricultural work involving lay brothers, and came to play an important role in bringing new lands under cultivation. Cistercian monastic complexes included not only buildings used by the monks to live and pray: a church and cloister, refectory, dormitory, kitchen, but also barns, stables, a mill and workshops. The Cistercians enjoyed great economic success and quickly became involved in the developing market economy, selling raw materials and produce. The order grew rapidly from five houses in 1119, to 650 by the mid-13th century.

The friars should be delighted to follow the lowliness and poverty of our Lord Jesus Christ, remembering that of the whole world we must own nothing; 'but having food and sufficient clothing, with these let us be content', as St Paul says. They should be glad to live among … the poor and helpless, the sick and lepers … they should not be ashamed to beg alms, remembering that our Lord Jesus Christ, the Son of the living, all-powerful God … was poor and he had no home of his own and he lived on alms, he and the Blessed Virgin and his disciples.

FROM THE FIRST RULE (1221) OF FRANCIS OF ASSISI

THE NEW MONASTICISM AND HERESY

During this period, international orders were born that spread rapidly. Within 50 years of the foundation of Cîteaux, Cistercians already appeared in England, Iberia, Hungary and Poland. The success of the mendicant orders was even more spectacular; the Franciscans and Dominicans created a dense network of friaries, based in towns, all over Christendom. Unlike monks, friars did not belong to a particular house, and could move from place to place. Other religious movements, such as that of the Beguines, were more localized. Condemnation, crusade and then inquisition stemmed the diffusion of Catharism from Languedoc. After the Albigensian crusade, inquisitors continued the eradication of Cathars for over a century.

Monastic houses

- •   10th/11th century centres of monastic reform (with foundation date)
- •   Franciscan houses to c.1300
- ○   Dominican houses to c.1300
- △   Cistercian houses, with date of foundation
- ▽   Premonstratensian houses, with date of foundation
- ■   Major Beghard centre
- ▣   Minor Beghard centre (more than one house)
- ▢   Beguine houses
- ○   Other houses, with date of foundation

Heresy

     Areas with large concentrations of heretics, c.1200

     Area affected by Albigensian crusade, c.1200–c.1240

(Left) This drawing depicts Cathars being led out to be burnt at the stake. After the Albigensian crusade, mainly Dominican inquisitors replaced local bishops in investigating and rooting out heresy. Stubborn heretics were handed over to the secular authorities and were generally burnt. Overall, these represented a small minority; most heretics were imprisoned or given various types of penance.

Doctrinal and/or organizational differences as well as disobedience to the papacy could lead to condemnation. Many movements had as their aim the return to apostolic poverty. Beguines, pious lay women living in celibacy from manual labour, but without taking irrevocable vows, and the Humiliati, living in family groups, had to accept strict clerical supervision or face censure. The most important heretical movements were the Waldensians (followers of Valdès), who were condemned for preaching despite episcopal prohibition, and the Cathars, who had their own liturgy, hierarchical structure and belief-system (strictly separating the spiritual and material world).

Heretics sometimes differed from each other more than they did from the Catholic Church. The Waldensians even preached against the Cathars. Pope Gregory IX initiated a new mechanism to search out and eradicate heresy: investigation by inquisitors, who were mainly members of a new mendicant order, the Dominicans.

Mendicant orders followed the ideal of an apostolic life, interpreted as preaching and voluntary poverty, partly as a reaction to the social and economic tensions in Italian towns. Francis of Assisi (c.1181–1226), son of a wealthy merchant, enjoyed both great popularity and the backing of the papacy. Although he simply wished to live a devout

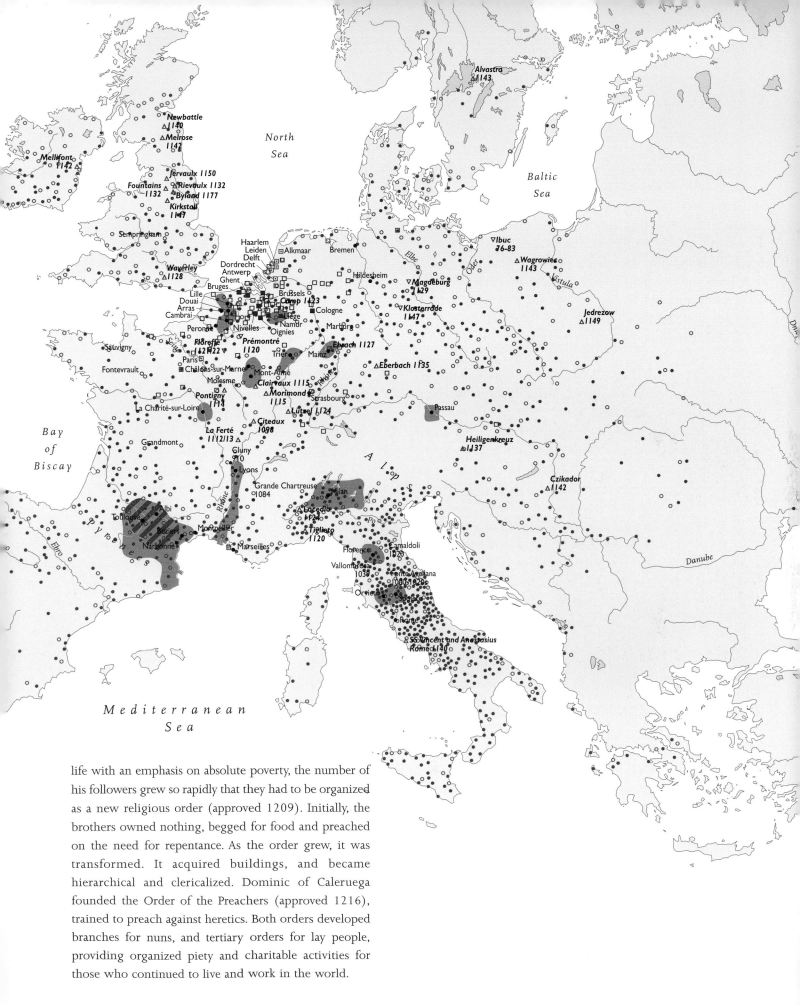

North Sea

Baltic Sea

Alvastra △1143

Newbattle △1140
△Melrose 1142

Mellifont △1142

Jervaulx 1150
Fountains △1132 △Rievaulx 1132
1132 △Byland 1177
Kirkstall 1147

Sempringham

Waverley △1128

Haarlem
Leiden
Delft
Dordrecht
Antwerp
Ghent
Bruges
Lille
Douai
Arras
Cambrai
Péronne
Nivelles
Floreffe 1121/22
Prémontré 1120
Trier

Alkmaar
Brussels
Camp 1123
Liège
Namur
Oignies
Cologne
Marburg

Bremen
Hildesheim

▽Ibuc 76-83
△Wagrowiec 1143

▽Magdeburg 1129

▽Klosterrode 1147

△Jedrezow 1149

Ebrach 1127
Mainz
△Eberbach 1135

Sauvigny
Paris
Châlons-sur-Marne
Fontevrault
Molesme
Mont-Aimé
△Clairvaux 1115
△Morimond 1115
Strasbourg
△Lützel 1124
△Cîteaux 1098
△Pontigny 1114
La Charité-sur-Loire
La Ferté 1112/13
Grandmont
Cluny 910
Lyons

Passau

Heiligenkreuz △1137

Czikador △1142

Grande Chartreuse 1084

A l p s

Milan
△Lucedio 1124
Tiglieto 1120
Florence
Camaldoli 1020
Vallombrosa 1039
Fonte Avellana 1000-1200
Orvieto
Sublaco
Rome
SS. Vincent and Anastasius Rome 1140

Bay of Biscay

Pyrenees

Toulouse
Albi
Béziers
Narbonne
Montpellier
Marseilles

Ebro

Mediterranean Sea

Elbe
Oder
Vistula
Dniester
Danube

Seine
Rhône

life with an emphasis on absolute poverty, the number of his followers grew so rapidly that they had to be organized as a new religious order (approved 1209). Initially, the brothers owned nothing, begged for food and preached on the need for repentance. As the order grew, it was transformed. It acquired buildings, and became hierarchical and clericalized. Dominic of Caleruega founded the Order of the Preachers (approved 1216), trained to preach against heretics. Both orders developed branches for nuns, and tertiary orders for lay people, providing organized piety and charitable activities for those who continued to live and work in the world.

Schools And Universities In Europe

The university, a direct development from the cathedral and monastic schools of the early Middle Ages, is arguably the most important and certainly the most distinctive and universally influential of Europe's contributions to world civilization. Universities proved extraordinarily adaptable to each major current of change. They were a part of, as well as an expression of, their social environment but were also based on a composite ideal of the love of learning for its own sake and a recognition of the social utility of knowledge and the fruits of academic study.

The institutional framework of the early medieval schools had been the cathedrals and monasteries. Those who studied there went on to careers in the church or in the outside world. Even in the eighth, ninth and tenth centuries it was not uncommon for students and scholars to travel from one school to another to study a particular subject under a renowned master. One such student was Richer, who went to Reims in order to study dialectic, arithmetic, astronomy and music under the great master Gerbert, later Pope Sylvester II (999–1003). In the course of the 11th and 12th centuries, independent masters, such as Fulbert and Bernard of Chartres, gathered circles of students and scholars around them and in due course these groups, usually on their own initiative, became institutionalized in ways which reflected contemporary legal and organizational forms. These associations of teachers with students laid the basis for the *studium generale* or university. In the later 12th century at Bologna, for example, the *doctores* (also active as lawyers and judges) joined with their pupils to form a corporation divided into nations. In Paris in 1208 teachers and students of various disciplines formed a single corporate body. Popes and monarchs conferred legal recognition on the corporate bodies of the universities and other rulers and municipalities founded universities by grants of privilege. By 1500 there were 63 universities in Europe.

The interchange between secular authorities and the corporation of masters and students involved the according of certain rights to those within the *studium generale*, such as administrative autonomy, the realization of the course of study, research and the award of publicly recognized degrees. An institutional setting was provided for the quest for and transmission of knowledge. At the heart of the university was the so-called "ivory-tower", that is, intellectual training for its own sake, but the universities' latent function from its earliest foundations was also to prepare professional experts for practical affairs.

When as a lad I first went to Gaul for the cause of study I addressed myself to the Peripatetic of Palaos (Abelard) who then presided upon Mount Saint Genovefa, an illustrious teacher and admired of all men. There at his feet I acquired the first rudiments of the dialectical arts and snatched according to the scant measure of my wits whatever passed his lips with entire greediness of mind. Then when he had departed, all too hastily as it seemed to me, I joined myself to master Alberic who stood forth among the rest as a greatly esteemed dialectician and verily was the bitterest opponent of the nominal sect.

JOHN OF SALISBURY, *METALOGICON*

1155	1208	1209–14	1214	1215/31	1252
Bologna comes under the protection of the Emperor Frederick II	Paris masters form a guild	Following the arrest and execution of a student, a "swarm" of masters and students leave Oxford and found the University of Cambridge	First papal statues for Oxford	Statutes granted to the University of Paris	Statutes of Bologna define it as a students' university

SCHOOLS AND UNIVERSITIES IN EUROPE

The rapid expansion of universities before 1500 all over western Europe established institutions of learning in most major cities, though some specialized in particular subjects.

■ university foundations before 1300, with date

■ university foundations before 1300–78, with date

■ university foundations before 1300–1500, with date

□ □ □ ephemeral, lasted for a few years only or status as university uncertain

■ ■ ■ universities which disappeared and were refounded later

□ □ ephemeral universities which disappeared and were refounded later

Uppsala *1477*

Aberdeen *1495*

SCOTLAND

Glasgow *1451*

St Andrews *1411*

North Sea

Copenhagen *1475*

Baltic Sea

D E N M A R K

NORWAY

S W E D E N

TEUTONIC ORDER

LITHUANIA

IRELAND

Dublin *1312*

WALES

ENGLAND

Cambridge *1209–25*

Oxford *beginning of s.XIII*

Rostock *1419*

Griefswald *1456*

Frankfurt an Oder *1498*

BRANDENBURG

S M A L L

S T A T E S

POLAND

NETHERLANDS

Leuven *1425*

Cologne *1388*

Leipzig *1409*

Erfurt *1379*

Mainz *1476*

Würzburg *1402–13*

LANDS OF THE

BOHEMIAN CROWN

Prague *1347*

Cracow *1364–c. 1370; refounded 1397*

Caen *1432*

Trier *1454*

Paris *beginning of s.XIII*

Heidelberg *1385*

Tübingen *1459*

Ingoldstadt *1459*

Angers *1250*

Orléans *1235*

Frieburg *1457*

Nantes *1460*

FRANCE

Poitiers *1431*

Bourges *1464*

Dôle *1422*

Basle *1459*

SWISS CONFED. *1361–98; transfered to Piacenza; refounded 1412*

Vienna *1365*

AUSTRIA

Pozsony *1459–end s.XV*

HUNGARY

Buda *1389–1400; refounded 1410–60*

Bordeaux *1441*

Cahors *1332*

Grenoble *1339–s.XIV med*

Vàlance *1452*

SAVOY

Vercelli *1228*

Pavia

Turin *1404*

Vicenza *1204–9*

Mantua *1433*

Treviso *1318 to c.1407*

Venice *1470 college of physicians*

Padua *1222*

Ferrara *1391–4; refounded 1430*

Toulouse *1229*

BÉARN

NAVARRE

Orange *1365*

Montpellier *beginning s.XIII*

Avignon *1303*

Piacenza *1248*

Reggio *1188*

Bologna *end of 12th C.*

V E N E T I A N   R E P U B L I C

Valladolid *end of 13th C.*

Huesca *1354–s.XVII; refounded 1464*

Perpignan *1350*

Aix *1409*

1349; transfered to Pisa; closed 1472

Florence *1343–60; refounded 2nd s.XV in*

Pisa

Arezzo *1215–60; refounded 1355–73*

OTTOMAN

Coimbra *–38; 1354–77*

Salamanca *before 1218–19*

Sigüenzal *1489*

Saragossa *1474*

Lérida *1300*

ARAGON

Barcelona *1450*

Siena

Perugia *1308*

PAPAL STATE

Rome

EMPIRE

PORTUGAL

Lisbon *1290; transfered to Coimbra 1308–38 and 1354–77*

Alcalá *1499*

SPAIN

CASTILE

Valencia *1500*

Balearics

Palma *1483*

SARDINIA

1246–52; refounded 1357

1303–end; s.XIII studium urbis refounded 1431

Naples *1224*

Salerno *status unclear*

NAPLES

Mediterranean Sea

SICILY

Catania *1444*

Seville *1254*

(Above) *A cutting from a manuscript produced in Bologna in the 14th century, depicting Henry of Germany lecturing to his students in Bologna.*

There were differences among the medieval universities as far as organization was concerned. Some, such as Paris, Oxford and Cambridge were masters' universities. Only they were full members of the corporation (hence the significance of the now misunderstood Oxford and Cambridge MA granted some years after the conferral of the BA). Other universities were "students'" universities. In Bologna or Padua, for example, the masters were hired through annual contracts agreed with the university or the commune. In many universities, moreover, students, foreigners by definition for whom the journey to a new place to study was considered an essential part of the experience, were divided into nations. Universities were also subdivided into faculties of arts, theology, law (both civil and canon) and medicine. A few, such as Bologna, Padua and Montpellier, devoted themselves to a single discipline (whether law or medicine). Paris, Cambridge and Oxford became particularly important for theology. A student began with the *artes* and proceeded towards wisdom by means of the higher subjects – theology, law or medicine. These pedagogic divisions followed current hierarchical classifications of knowledge bequeathed to the universities from late antiquity and the early medieval schools.

The 16th-century chained library of Trinity Hall, Cambridge.

xxxv. pc

A pecia copy of Thomas Aquinas' Commentary on the Metaphysics of Aristotle. This is an example of the peciae system by which multiple copies of the texts students needed in the universities were produced. University stationers (controlled by the university authorities) owned exemplars of university texts books kept unbound. Each of the gatherings making up a book was numbered and known as a piece or pecia. The peciae were hired out one at a time by the stationer to scribes and students so that they could make their own copies. This example with the pecia note "xxxv.pc" in the left-hand margin indicates where the scribe noted he had started pecia xxxv.

Art and Architecture: Cathedrals, Sculpture, Metalwork and Book Painting

The three centuries between 1000 and 1300 witnessed major transformations in the art and architecture of Western Europe, under the auspices of increasingly powerful, confident and wealthy patrons. Collectively, the Church was the most important of these, and the period is often called the Cathedral Age, although many of the most important works were monastic. Stylistically, architecture, sculpture, metalwork and book painting between 1000 and 1300 are classified under the headings Romanesque and, from the second half of the 12th century, Gothic.

Around 1030, the Cluniac monk Raul Glaber wrote of the world "cladding itself everywhere in a white mantle of churches", an allusion to the many building projects initiated around the turn of the first millennium. This fashion for renewal, which continued beyond 1300,

encouraged stylistic and technological advances such as the rib vault and flying buttress, which made possible increasingly large and better-illuminated churches.

Romanesque architecture developed out of Cluniac (French) and Ottonian (German) church design, although it had many precedents and embraced many variants. It is characterized by round arches, thick walls and relatively small windows. Among the defining monuments of the style are the cathedrals of Durham, Ely, Norwich (England), Arles, Autun (France), Mainz, Speyer (Germany), Monreale, Pisa (Italy) and Santiago de Compostela (Spain). Gothic architecture proper appeared around 1140 at the abbey church of St Denis, north of Paris. By the 1160s the new style had reached England, but did not flourish elsewhere until after 1200. Gothic's defining characteristics include pointed arches, rib vaults, and windows incorporating stone tracery, all combining in a microcosm of the Heavenly Jerusalem. Renowned examples include the cathedrals of Notre Dame at Paris, Amiens and Rheims, and outside France the cathedrals of Prague (Czech Republic), Canterbury, Lincoln, York (England), Cologne (Germany), Florence, Siena (Italy), Trondheim (Norway) and Burgos (Spain). Byzantine church architecture developed in different directions between 1000 and 1300, elaborating upon the cross-in-square design in which the expression of unity was more important than size or the admission of light.

Autun cathedral, Romanesque sculpture above the west doorway. Carved by Gislebertus c. 1130, and signed "Gislebertus hoc fecit" (Gislebertus made this). The scene here is the Last Judgement, a popular subject for the west portals of cathedrals during the Romanesque and Gothic periods. Physiognomically, the main figure of Christ and the smaller figures surrounding him demonstrate the limited repertoire of pose and gesture employed by Romanesque sculptors.

(Right) Durham cathedral, the Romanesque nave (south side), c. 1115–30. Like Norwich, Ely, and a number of other English cathedrals, Durham is a mixture of Romanesque and Gothic architecture. The round arches, weighty stone piers, deep gallery at the central level and small windows are all characteristic of the Romanesque style. However, Durham's rib vaults are a harbinger of the Gothic style although as yet only the main transverse arches are properly pointed.

981	1093	1140	c. 1185–1200	1211	1260
Second church of Cluny abbey consecrated: a seminal Romanesque building	Romanesque cathedral of Durham begun	Inception of the Gothic style proper at St Denis and Sens	Shrine of Three Kings, Cologne cathedral, built	Rheims cathedral begun	Nicola Pisano carves pulpit of Pisa cathedral baptistery

(Left) The prophet Habakkuk, from the Shrine of the Three Kings in Cologne cathedral (c. 1185–1200). The Old Testament prophets of the shrine's lower register are by Nicholas of Verdun, the leading artist of the Mosan school of metalworkers. Aspects of the work, among them the pose, draperies, hairstyle and profile of the face, hark back to ancient sculptural conventions. However, his naturalism also anticipates Gothic developments.

Sculpture, metalwork and book painting were influenced by these architectural developments. The 11th century witnessed the revival of monumental stone sculpture after a virtual lacuna of six centuries. The medium evolved with astonishing speed, primarily as an embellishment to ecclesiastical architecture. In the carvings of Gislebertus at Autun (c. 1130) Romanesque sculpture attained a degree of refinement paralleled in Germany, Italy and Spain but never surpassed. Gothic sculpture, which steadily superseded Romanesque between 1150 and 1200, reached its apogee in the 13th-century portal sculpture of cathedrals such as Chartres and Rheims, and the works of the Italians Nicola Pisano (d. c. 1284) and Arnolfo di Cambio (d. c. 1302). Sculptors, metalworkers and book painters of the Gothic period placed an increasing emphasis upon naturalism in their representations of people, animals and plants. This is exemplified by book painting after c. 1200. The finest Romanesque book painting, occurring in 12th-century liturgical books such as the Bibles of Bury and Winchester (England), offered a more expressive but less convincing picture of man and his environment than that developed by Gothic artists during the 13th century, a century which culminated in the emergence of Giotto (1267–1337). In metalwork, figure style developed from the stiff, spare figures of the bronze reliefs at Hildesheim (c. 1010–20), to the coherent, cogently articulated figures that adorn French Gothic reliquaries like the shrine of St Taurin at Evreux cathedral (1247–55). Metalwork also embraced the classicizing naturalism of Nicolas of Verdun, at once retrospective and precocious. His work on the Shrine of the Three Kings at Cologne cathedral (begun c. 1185) captures the spirit of a creative and restless age as well as any that has come down to us.

A page from a breviary (liturgical book containing psalms, hymns, lessons etc.) made in 1296 for the French king Philip the Fair (1285–1314) by the Gothic book painter Master Honoré. The illustration shows the anointing of David by Samuel and, below, David's battle with and decapitation of Goliath. Gothic painters often employed continuous narrative, showing two or more episodes from a story within the same pictorial space.

The Economy: Agriculture And Trade

Europe's population was overwhelmingly rural (perhaps 85 per cent by 1300), but the hardy belief that its economy was entirely one of subsistence agriculture is a caricature. Latin Christian Europe had long enjoyed an economy focused on different social and political structures and reflected a very different landscape to those of the Muslim and Byzantine worlds. Between about 950 and 1350, however, western Europe's economic organization became much more similar to that of the east as a consequence of rapid commercial expansion. Agrarian output greatly increased, serfdom declined in much of western Europe and the development of trade and handicrafts transformed the lives of the rural majority as well as the urban minority.

Population and agricultural output both increased markedly from the tenth century onwards. What triggered these increases is unclear, but the cessation of external attacks (from Muslims, Vikings, Hungarians and Slavs), the revival of powerful central authorities and the lubrication of the economy by silver mining (essential for currency), all played a part. This agrarian expansion was accompanied, in many regions, by a reorganization of the countryside. Scattered settlements were agglomerated into nucleated villages as centres for more efficient arable cultivation, often in large open fields.

The economic revolution began in Italy, where agrarian output was boosted by the reclamation of forests, marshes and hillsides. Similar "internal colonization" followed in other lands, including France, the Low Countries, England and the Rhineland. As colonists filled up the empty spaces, settlers, in turn, migrated to thinly populated regions in a form of "external colonization". They went to the Iberian plateau and to large parts of eastern and northern Europe: German migration into Slav territories was especially extensive and specialized middlemen called *locatores* helped to put entrepreneurial lords in touch with land-hungry settlers. The expansion of cultivated area was accompanied by more efficient techniques in cropping systems, by the development of new technology (notably the introduction of windmills) and by the specialization of land-use. Large-scale sheep farming brought about the beginnings of a major textile industry.

961–68	c. 1086	c. 1160–80	c. 1175–1250	1252
Start of silver mining in Saxony	Domesday survey of England	First recorded windmills in western Europe (1170 England)	Great age of the Champagne fairs	Resumption of gold coinage in western Europe (Genoa, Florence)

PRINCIPAL TRADE ROUTES IN THE 13TH CENTURY

Europe's commercial revolution led to a proliferation of both land and water routes by 1300. The Mediterranean sea routes were dominated by the Venetians and Genoese, those of the Baltic and North Seas by the Hanse.

— land trade routes

— sea trade routes

□ Champagne trade fairs

V Venetian possessions

G Genoese possessions

■ towns of the Hanseatic League

Map labels: Turku, Stockholm, Reval, Novgorod, Bulgar, Visby, Gotland, Nizhniy Novgorod, Riga, Moscow, Ural, Baltic Sea, Memel, Königsberg, Danzig, Elbing, Thorn, Oder, Vistula, Breslau, Kiev, Don, Volga, Cracow, Dnieper, Astrakhan, Vienna, Tana, Caspian Sea, Caffa, Danube, Black Sea, Ragusa, Trebizond, Tabriz, to Samarkand, Durazzo, Constantinople, Lesbos, Mosul, Cephallonia, Lajazza, Antioch, Baghdad, Rhodes, Cyprus, Candia, Damascus, Messina, Mediterranean Sea, Tyre, Acre, Basra, to Ormuz, Alexandria, to Bokhara

A selection of luxury items. The French city of Limoges specialized in making enamelled caskets for holy relics, which were traded widely across western Europe. This example (opposite) from around the 1160s is of enamelled and gilded copper, and depicts the martyrdom of St. Stephen. An apothecary's jar (above) made in Umbria in the 16th century, and depicting St Martin dividing his cloak with a beggar. Such fine earthenware, called majolica, was a typical luxury item of Renaissance Italy. A sumptuous carving of the Virgin and Child (left), made about 1250–60 for Louis IX's new Sainte-Chapelle in Paris, and now in the Louvre. Ivory was always a luxury material, and much in demand for delicately carved church furnishings.

Because the land was uninhabited, [the count] sent messengers into all the regions, namely Flanders, Holland, Utrecht, Westphalia and Frisia, saying that whoever was oppressed by shortage of land to farm should come with their families and occupy this good and spacious land …

ADOLF II OF HOLSTEIN IN THE 1140s, AS REPORTED BY HELMOLD OF BOSAU, *CHRONICLE OF THE SLAVS*

Increased output provided surpluses, which could be traded for necessities, such as salt, for the many, and luxuries for the wealthy. Local trade triggered the creation of thousands of small towns where foodstuffs and raw materials could be sold, and manufactures bought, in weekly markets and seasonal fairs, while larger or more valuable purchases could be made in the larger towns or in specialized international fairs. The two most advanced commercial zones (northern Italy and the Low Countries) were linked by roads through the Alpine passes. The counts of Champagne profited from the passing traffic by sponsoring a cycle of fairs, the Champagne fairs, which were for a time the most important in Europe. Such overland trade was possible because roads were better than is popularly believed: much effort went into maintaining major routes and building bridges.

Nevertheless, waterborne trade was more important. Most commercialized areas before 1300 were located either around the Mediterranean, the Baltic and North Seas or in the valleys of navigable rivers. Muslim and Jewish merchants traded widely around the Mediterranean, and Constantinople remained the largest European city because of its nodal position in seaborne trade as well as its capital status. It is significant that the earliest Italian commercial centres were ports under nominal Byzantine sovereignty (including Venice), or at least trading with the eastern Empire (especially Pisa and Genoa). Moreover, in northern Europe it was shipping that linked together London, Novgorod and the Flemish textile towns with those groups of towns in north Germany and the Baltic lands which developed into the Hanse. All this trade encouraged not only improvements in navigation and shipping, but also more efficient instruments of commerce, all of them first developed in Italy: banking and credit, business partnerships and marine insurance as well as the restoration of gold currency for high-value transactions.

Towns And Urban Life

The agricultural and commercial growth of this period was accompanied by a dramatic and sustained urbanization. The greatest expansion of existing towns lay within the four centuries between 950 and 1350. During the same period many villages were expanded into towns, and yet other towns and cities (in the largest numbers to date) were founded on virgin sites. By the eve of the Black Death (1347–50), at least a dozen cities had populations of over 50,000, though none yet rivalled Constantinople in size.

> Developments from the turn of the millennium – growth of population, agriculture and commerce – entailed urbanization. Lords and peasants needed market towns; long-distance merchants needed secure bases

[You are] to elect men from among your wisest and ablest who know best how to devise, order and array a new town to the greatest profit of ourselves and of merchants.

EDWARD I'S SUMMONS TO 24 ENGLISH TOWNS, 1296

with commercial facilities. Industries, though they did not have to be based in towns, tended to concentrate there for the benefits of a ready market and also for security (most towns of any size were walled). Moreover, rulers of provinces and kingdoms were beginning to need capital cities as fixed bases for their households, bureaucrats and treasuries. By 1300 Paris and London, Palermo and Barcelona were true state capitals.

Between 1000 and 1300 existing towns in favourable locations were thriving, while many "new towns" were also established. The most important urban zone in this period was northern and central Italy, where its four giants – Venice, Florence, Genoa and Milan (the first two with perhaps 100,000 people each by 1300) – were only the largest of many. Nowhere else was so highly urbanized, though Sicily and Flanders came close. Outside these areas London and Paris dominated their respective national urban networks. Indeed Paris, with perhaps 200,000 people, was the largest western city by 1300, and many lesser towns, while insignificant in size

1075–1122	1120	1143	1155	1277–95
Achievement of full self-government by many Italian towns	First town foundation of dukes of Zähringen (Freiburg-im-Breisgau)	Lübeck founded by Count Adolf II of Holstein	Customs of Lorris (a widely influential model for French royal towns)	Ten planned Welsh towns founded by Edward I

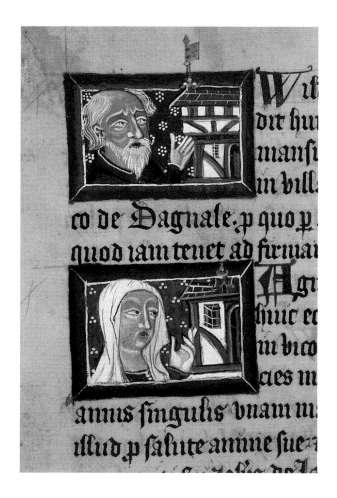

Two miniatures from the register of benefactors of St Albans Abbey, England, showing William Langleye and Agnes Langeford with the houses they donated to the monastery.

Lorenzetti's frescos in the Palazzo Pubblico at Siena include this scene of the city's daily life, including shops, a school, building work in progress and countryfolk coming in with livestock and produce.

by 21st–century standards, were vital to their regional economies. Even under-urbanized England had some 650 towns, collectively housing as much as 15 per cent of the national population.

All of the towns so far named were established before 1000, but such was the urban revolution of the high Middle Ages that many other towns were established *de novo*, either on virgin sites or adjacent to existing settlements. Some were created initially to service an adjoining castle, palace or monastery, but others were wholly commercial speculations, intended to tap burgeoning trade and industry for the profit of both lords and burgesses. Hundreds of these new towns (or to use the French term, *bastides*) were founded and many are still distinguishable today by the repetitive names that advertise their newness (Neustadt, Villeneuve) or free status (Freiburg, Villefranche). Some rulers became specialist town founders, including the dukes of Zähringen in the south German and Alpine lands, Henry the Lion in Bavaria and Saxony, and King Edward I in England, Wales and Gascony. Most of these new towns were planned, though usually piecemeal in successive phases; the grid-plan town of a single phase was quite common in the smaller bastides, but large towns of the type (like Salisbury in England) were always exceptional.

Most towns, even small ones, developed a society and culture that differentiated them from their rural hinterland (though economically town and country were closely intertwined). Their social distinctiveness, caused partly by their size and density of population and partly by their wide range of occupations, was reinforced by customs and by-laws, usually asserting a greater degree of freedom for their inhabitants. Many towns in France, Flanders, England and the Holy Roman Empire obtained the privilege that any serf living there for a year without being reclaimed by his master was to be free (though not, confusingly, in the full sense of the privileged "freemen" or burgesses). Large and wealthy towns also aimed at corporate freedom from external authority; the most successful were Imperial towns in Italy and Germany as the authority of the emperor weakened. By 1200 some 300 Italian towns were effectively independent city–states.

Kievan Rus, c. 964–1242

The history of the Kievan Rus' is part of the history of European Russian as a whole, including the Byzantine Crimea, the Khazar Khaganate and the Volga Bulgar emirate. The ruling elites dominated the diverse peoples of the steppe, the forests and the river plains. The Rus' established their capital at Kiev which became the archbishopric when the Rus' were converted to Christianity. They expanded their territory greatly but internal rivalries weakened their kingdom and left them vulnerable to the Golden Horde.

The leaders of the Rus' who established themselves at Kiev and other bases on the middle Dnieper river were probably Scandinavian merchants rather than Slavs. It is most likely that the Rus' as a whole formed a multi-ethnic group of merchants, mercenaries and peasants, including many Slavs, Balts and Finns. Their settlements were on the trade routes, and from their small beginnings at Staraya Ladoga throughout their history there is a strong emphasis on exploiting the resources of their lands.

This created a certain tension between the different requirements of the steppe nomads and the pastoralists and agriculturalists. The rivers played a crucial role within the polity. The principal waterway apparently ran from the Gulf of Finland up the river Neva, through Lake Ladoga to the river Volkhov. From thence the Rus' transported their boats over land to the Dnieper river and so on to the Black Sea and Byzantium. Most of our information about the early Rus' comes from archaeological excavations, especially at Staraya Ladoga and at Kiev, and from the written sources which began to be produced after the conversion of the Rus at the end of the tenth century. The most important of these are the Russian Primary Chronicle, written in the middle of the 11th century but giving an account of events from 850, and the Pravda Russkaia or law code.

Descriptions of the people have also been provided by the Arab merchants Ibn Fadlan, and Ibn Rustah. The ambiguities of much of this material has led to a considerable amount of inconclusive speculation about the origin and early history of the Rus'.

Their trading actiirty also extended across the Caspian Sea into central Asia. Baltic amber, furs and slaves were particularly prized commodities. The Rus' were aggressive neighbours as well as enterprising merchants. They gradually expanded their territory into the lands once dominated by the Khazars (a people who had converted to Judaism in the ninth century) and by the Bulgars. They had initially threatened Constantinople but in due course trading agreements were reached with the Greeks and it was from Byzantium that the Kievan Rus' under their ruler Vladimir Syatoslavich (980–1015) received Christianity. Conversion opened up the Kievan Rus' to Byzantine influence; the church introduced literacy and an alphabet, Greek artisans and monasticism. It was in the aftermath of the acceptance of Christianity that the first history and the first law code of the Rus' were produced. Kiev became increasingly prosperous and famous for the high level of its culture, its crafts and its lovely buildings. Of these the church of St Sophia is the most celebrated. The conversion of Vladimir may have been seen as a way to unify a very heterogeneous realm. Certainly the princes of Kiev exploited the ideological potential of Christian rulership.

Politically, however the Kievan state was unstable and prone to civil wars, largely as a result of the uncertainties of the succession. Potentially any one of the king's sons were eligible to be his heir for their was no system of either primogeniture or of particle inheritance. Iaroslav the Wise in the early 11th century tried to change the succession laws by dividing his kingdom before he died, He also built up a strong network of family alliances by astute marriage arrangements for his sons and daughters with Hungary,. Norway, France, Byzantium, Poland and Germany. But the civil wars persisted. These internal weaknesses left the Kievan state less able to withstand attacks from outside the realm, especially those of the Pechenegs. But is was ultimately the invasion of the Mongol armies of Batu, grandson of Chinggis Khan, which fatally undermined Kiev's supremacy.

750s	839	911	922	941	944	945–985
Settlement at Staraya Ladoga	Rus' embassy to the Franks at Ingelheim near Mainz	Trade agreement with Byzantium	Ibn Fadlan's visit to the Middle Volga	Rus' attack on Constantinople	Trade agreement with Byzantium	Rus' campaign against the Volga Bulgars

The Golden Gates of Kiev (above) were part of the extended system of fortifications Iaroslav the Wise had constructed around Kiev in the 11th century. They incorporated the dramtic Golden Gates which included the fortified and moated church of the Blessed Virgin ornamented with frescoes, ceramics and woodcarvings.

KIEVAN RUSSIA, 964–1242

In 1054 there was still a unified Rus' state, but by the early 13th century it had disintegrated. Southern centres, such as Kiev, were weakened by nomadic attacks, leaving northern towns, such as Novgorod, Vladimir and Moscow to expand.

—— Kievan Russia, 1054	- - - waterway trade routes
Yatvagi tribes of the East Slavs	defensive works built against nomads
MARI other peoples	Russian principalities, c.1200
→ movements of steppe nomads in the 11th century	Prince Igor Svyatoslav's campaign against Polovtsy, 1185
→ campaigns of Svyatoslav, 964–71	

c. 988	1037–47	1041	1054	1097	1169
Conversion of the Rus' to orthodox Christianity and the marriage of Vladimir to the Byzantine princess Anna	building of St Sophia's church in Kiev	Disastrous expedition of Ingvar the Widefarer	Iaroslav the Wise tries to divide the kingdom between his sons	Conference at Liubech	Sack of Kiev by native princes

The Balkans, c. 1000–1300

This period witnessed first the recovery and subsequently the loss of Byzantine political authority throughout the Balkan peninsula, and the establishment of independent kingdoms by the Serbs and Bulgarians. Balkan potentates began to look west, not east, for their political symbols and ideas. This was not, however, the result of national or ethnic sentiment, but rather Realpolitik in the face of the decline of the eastern empire.

In the year 1000 the northern Balkans was dominated by a realm centred on Ohrid and Prespa in modern Macedonia, which its ruler Samuel regarded as a continuation of the earlier Bulgarian empire. Warfare and diplomacy by Emperor Basil II (976–1025) led to the defeat and annexation of this realm, and the restoration of Byzantine political authority across the peninsula. However, this authority was subject to regular threats

from without and within. In the mid-11th century the Pechenegs, nomads who dwelt beyond the Danube, posed the principal threat, which was largely neutralized by the payment of tribute. Diplomatic strategies were also implemented to secure the loyalty of the various Slav potentates who dominated the mountainous interior of the Balkans and the northern Adriatic littoral. Imperial ranks and titles were granted by the emperor, and the accompanying silks and stipends served as recognized symbols of authority. Such measures prevented independent Slav incursions into the Byzantine districts of Thrace, Macedonia and Thessaly. Moreover, by the end of the 11th century the loyalty of the Balkan potentates was required to prevent encroachments by external powers: Hungary, Norman Sicily, Venice and, later, Germany. The Comnenian emperors were largely successful in limiting losses and controlling rebellions in the Balkans. Indeed, in the 1160s the empire's frontiers were advanced beyond the Danube, and imperial agents and troops were active in northern Italy for the first time in centuries, despatched by Manuel I Comnenus (1143–80), who feared the imperial pretensions of the German emperor, Frederick I Barbarossa (1152–90).

Byzantine fortunes declined rapidly after 1180. However, it was not ethnic awareness that led various Balkan peoples to reject Byzantine suzerainty, but rather the emergence of alternative, powerful patrons in the west. From the mid-12th century the Balkan peoples, courted and threatened from both sides, were offered unprecedented choices. While the Dalmatians continued to enjoy Byzantine patronage, which became ever more lavish, the Serbs began to make overtures to the German

Portrait from the Psalter of Emperor Basil II showing him in military costume before prostrate enemies and subjects. Biblioteca Nazionale, c. 1000

1018	1025	1180	1204	1217	1282
Death of Tsar Samuel of Bulgaria	Death of Emperor Basil II	Death of Emperor Manuel I	Coronation of Kalojan, King of the Vlachs and Bulgarians	Coronation of Stefan "the First-Crowned", King of Serbia	Accession of Stefan Urosh II Milutin, King of Serbia

The Northern Balkans and Beyond, 1140–1240

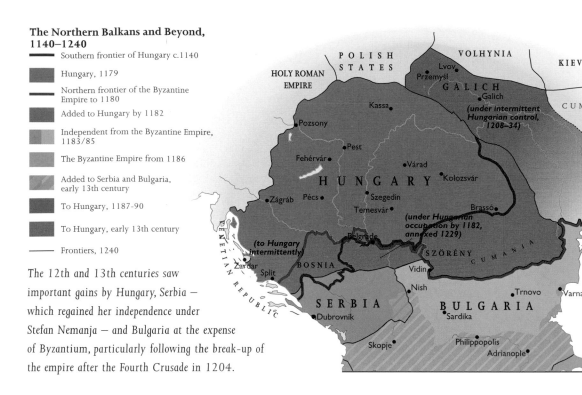

Southern frontier of Hungary c.1140

Hungary, 1179

Northern frontier of the Byzantine Empire to 1180

Added to Hungary by 1182

Independent from the Byzantine Empire, 1183/85

The Byzantine Empire from 1186

Added to Serbia and Bulgaria, early 13th century

To Hungary, 1187-90

To Hungary, early 13th century

Frontiers, 1240

The 12th and 13th centuries saw important gains by Hungary, Serbia — which regained her independence under Stefan Nemanja — and Bulgaria at the expense of Byzantium, particularly following the break-up of the empire after the Fourth Crusade in 1204.

emperor, as well as, on various occasions, to the Hungarian and Sicilian Norman kings, showing an informed preference for a more distant suzerain. It was for this reason that Manuel Comnenus stage-managed trials in the Serbian highlands with envoys of numerous foreign rulers in attendance, demonstrating the extent and nature of his rule in the Balkans. After Manuel's death in 1180, the independent ambitions of the emperor's kin led to a succession of coups, and the empire endured a series of ephemeral reigns which were punctuated by rebellions. Increasingly, Balkan potentates saw no reason to tie their own interests to those of a series of eastern emperors who were unable even to control their own kin. A rapid escalation in the value of prizes offered from Constantinople did not change this trend. The daughter of a reigning Byzantine emperor was rejected by the son of Serbian ruler, the *veliki zhupan* Stefan Nemanja, and the ruler of the Bulgarians and Vlachs rejected a patriarch and imperial diadem from Constantinople, preferring to receive symbols of his regnal status from Rome.

After 1204, when the forces of the Fourth crusade sacked Constantinople, the rulers of Bulgarians and Vlachs were able to annex former Byzantine territory in Thrace and Macedonia and, after 1230, Epiros as far as Dyrrachium. A Bulgarian patriarchate was established in 1235. However, internal and external threats, particularly the Mongol onslaught, saw a change in Bulgarian

fortunes. Serbia, similarly, benefited initially from Byzantine misfortune. Nemanja's elder son, Stefan, became the "first-crowned" king of Serbia in 1217. In 1219, a second son, Sava, was recognised as autocephalous archbishop. Serbian rulers maintained relations with other powers established in the Balkans, including the Byzantine despots of Epiros and Mystra, and the restored emperors in Constantinople. However, Stefan Urosh I (1243–76) joined an anti-Byzantine alliance, and his son Stefan Urosh II Milutin (1282–1381) annexed much of Macedonia and the Vardar valley. Conversely, in this period Serbian institutions and architecture became more markedly influenced by Byzantine models.

A rare wooden icon of St Clement of Ohrid carved in the later 13th century. It is now housed in the Church of the Virgin Peribleptos, Ohrid, in the Republic of Macedonia. Clement is the subject of two lives, both composed by Archbishops of Ohrid: Theophylact Hephaistos and Demetrios Chomatenos.

The Seljuqs
And Ayyubids

In 1055, the Seljuqs ousted the Buyids from power and took control of Baghdad. They ruled as Sultans, in the name of the Abbasid Caliphate, over a vast empire, maintaining, via agnate groups, their presence in Iraq and Iran in the 11th and 12th Centuries, and dominating Anatolia, where their agnates were known as the Seljuqs of Rum, until the 13th Century. The Ayyubids, the dynasty founded by Salah al-Din (Saladin) in 1171, ruled Egypt and the Levant until the advent of the Mamluk Sultanate in 1250.

The Seljuqs were a clan of the Oghuz Turks, originally from the Siberian steppes, who had converted to Islam. In the tenth century they occupied the steppes between the Aral and Caspian Seas. At the battle of Dandanqan, in 1040, they destroyed the Ghaznavids, and in 1055 their leader Tughril Beg entered Baghdad and put an end to Buyid domination of the Abbasid Caliphate. The Seljuqs were Sunni Muslims, in contrast to the Buyids who, for all their preservation of the Abbasid Caliphate, were Shi'i Muslims. Tughril Beg saw himself as the rightful protector of the Abbasid Caliph, and directed his energies as much against the Fatimid Imam-Caliphs of Egypt as against the Buyids. He perpetuated the Turkic nomadic pattern of rule, with primacy going to the family, and the tribal organization represented in various quasi-autonomous local rulers. Thus, the Seljuqs of Rum (Anatolia) were as good as independent of the Great Seljuqs of Iraq and Iran, as were the Atabegs (literally, "tutors of princes") of Syria and Mesopotamia. The Seljuq Sultans followed the common military pattern of mustering standing armies of Turkish slave soldiers (mamluks).

Salah al-Din (Saladin), son of Ayyub was a Kurdish soldier in the service of the Zengid, Nur al-Din Mahmud Son of Zengi of Aleppo. A relatively minor figure in the history of the Islamic Middle East, Saladin was quickly established in the western imagination as a paragon of noble, chivalric values.

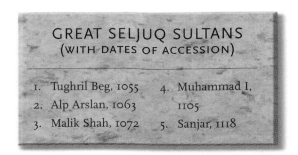

GREAT SELJUQ SULTANS
(WITH DATES OF ACCESSION)

1. Tughril Beg, 1055
2. Alp Arslan, 1063
3. Malik Shah, 1072
4. Muhammad I, 1105
5. Sanjar, 1118

While I was standing thus Saladin turned to me and said: "I think that when God grants me victory over the rest of Palestine I shall divide my territories, make a will stating my wishes, then set sail on this sea for their far-off lands and pursue the Franks there, so as to free the earth of anyone who does not believe in God, or die in the attempt.

IBN SHADDAD (D. 1234) –
SALADIN ON THE HOLY WAR

Alp Arslan, a nephew of Tughril Beg, replaced him as Sultan in 1063. He was responsible for appointing Nizam al-Mulk as his chief minister in 1065. Nizam al-Mulk remained chief minister until his death in 1092. He was the chief architect of the organization of the Seljuq empire, favouring a move away from the fragmented Turkic nomadic polity to a centralized government, and played a seminal role in the codification and development of Sunni Islam, with the foundation of madrasas, schools for religious education. Under his tutelage, the Third Great Seljuq Sultan, Malik Shah further developed the policies of Alp-Arslan. Both men died in 1092 at the hands of assassins working on behalf the Isma'ili leader Hassan-i Sabagh, known to the Crusaders as the Old Man of the Mountains, from his mountain fastness in Alamut. In the power-struggle following the death of Sultan Malik Shah and his vizier Nizam al-Mulk, the Khwarazm-Shahs wrested the province of Khwarazm from the Seljuqs and established their own dynasty. With the death of Sultan Sanjar in 1157, the Great Seljuq Empire was at an end.

In the 12th century, the Seljuqs had appointed the

1040	1055	1071	1157	1169–71	1228–29	1250
Subjugation of the Ghaznavids by the Seljuks	Tughril Beg seizes Baghdad	Alp Arslan defeats the Byzantines and captures the Emperor Romanus IV Diogenes at Manzikert	Collapse of Great Seljuq Sultanate	Saladin overthrows the Fatimid Imam-Caliphs and creates the Ayyubid state	Al-Kamil returns Jerusalem to Frederick II	End of Ayyubid rule, when Mamluks seize control of Cairo

170

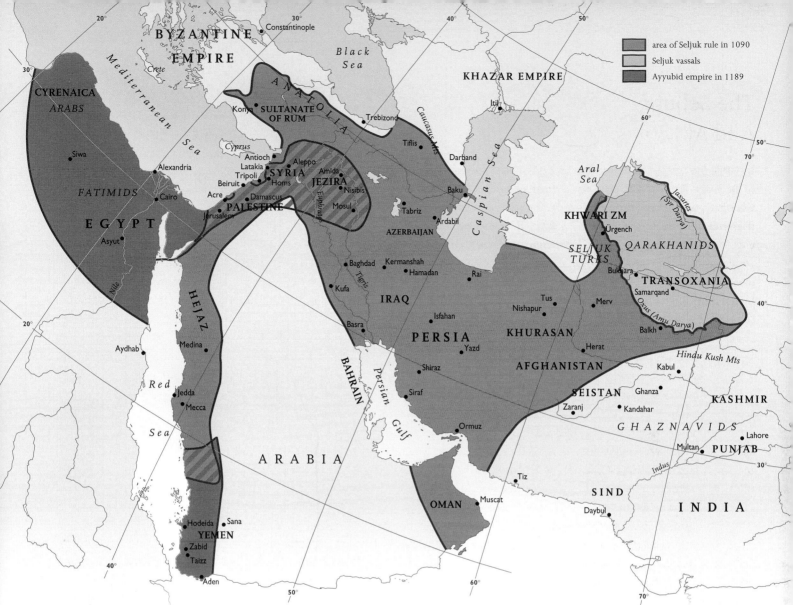

Zangids of Damascus and Mosul as Atabegs of the Seljuqs. The Zangids became independent soon thereafter. In their service was a Kurdish general named Ayyub. His offspring became the dynasty known as the Ayyubids. Ayyub's son Saladin (in Arabic: Salah al-Din) was also in the service of the Zangids. Saladin, together with his patron Nur al-Din Mahmud, son of Zangi, led the Muslim military response to the first Crusades. As Sunni Muslims, however, their vision of the Jihad (Holy Struggle) was directed as much against the Fatimid Caliph-Imams as against the Franks of Outremer. In 1171, Saladin and his uncle Shirkuh, son of Shadi, having in 1169 driven the Franks out of Egypt at the request of the Fatimids, put an end to the Isma'ili Imam-Caliphate of the Fatimids in Cairo, and Saladin founded the Ayyubid dynasty. In 1174 he conquered Damascus and in 1187, after the Battle of Hattin, retook Jerusalem from the Franks. At the end of the Third Crusade in 1192, Saladin and the Franks agreed a peace treaty, granting the Franks right of entry to Jerusalem. Al-'Adil succeeded Saladin in 1200, and he, in

THE SELJUQ EMPIRE

The migration westwards of the Seljuq Turks from the steppe-lands of the Caspian and Aral Seas had long-lasting consequences for the configuration of power in the Middle East and Inner Asia. In the wake of their defeat of the Ghaznavids in 1040, they established themselves as Sultan Protectors of the Abbasid Caliphate in 1050 and ruled from Transoxania and Khurasan to Anatolia. Defeat of the Byzantines at the Battle of Manzikert in 1071 led to the establishment of the Seljuq Sultanate of Anatolia, which they controlled until 1307. The Ayyubids, under the impetus of their founder Saladin, removed the Fatimids from power in Cairo and set about the reconquest of the Levant from the Crusaders. Their dynasty also enjoyed control over the Yemen until they were ousted from power by the Mamluk Sultans in 1250.

turn, was succeeded by Al-Malik al-Kamil in 1218, who returned Jerusalem to the Crusaders in a treaty with Frederick II in 1229. The Mamluk slave-soldiers, introduced to the region by the Seljuqs Tughril Beg and Alp-Arslan, put an end to Ayyubid rule in 1250.

The Mongols

The Mongol empire represented the high point of encroachment by nomads on the territories of sedentary peoples. Although their initial conquests were often accompanied by considerable devastation, certain towns being completely destroyed, and their approach to government was, at first, highly rapacious, in its more mature phase (from c. 1250 onwards) the empire also had beneficial effects. Closer economic and cultural links were fostered between the Iranian world and China, and for the first time since Classical Antiquity western Europe was brought into contact with the Far East.

Like earlier rulers of the eastern steppes, Chinggis Khan warred against China – then divided into three states: the Chin in the north, the Sung in the south and the Hsi-Hsia (Tangut) in the west. The conquest of Sung China was completed only under his grandson, the *qaghan* (Great Khan) Qubilai (1260–94). In the far west, a campaign by Chinggis Khan himself overthrew the Muslim empire of Khwarazm (1218–24), and another led by his grandson Batu subdued the remaining steppe tribes, reduced the Rus' principalities (1237–40), and briefly ravaged Poland and Hungary. Qubilai's brother Hülegü conquered Iran and Iraq, obliterating the Assassin strongholds in Persia (1256) and the Abbasid Caliphate (1258).

Beyond these limits, expansion halted. Successive invasions of Syria achieved only short-lived success, so that the Ilkhans were obliged to seek the co-operation of western European states against the Mamluks; and attempts by Qubilai at seaborne invasions of Japan and Java ended in disaster. The principal reason was that the resources of the empire were now being deployed in internal conflict. In 1261–2 the empire had dissolved into a number of rival khanates, each a major power in its own right: the Golden Horde; the khanate of Chaghadai (Chinggis Khan's second son) in Central Asia; the Ilkhanate (founded by Hülegü); and the dominions of the qaghan, whose dynasty was officially known in China as the Yüan (from 1271). For a time the situation was

Temüjin, who in 1206 was proclaimed Chinggis Khan at an assembly of tribes in what is now Mongolia, was born in c. 1162. Before his rise to power, the Mongols were simply one of a number of steppe and forest peoples beyond the northern borders of China. His victories over tribes who resisted were usually followed by the annihilation of the chiefs and the division of the tribes among new, artificially created units which transcended tribal allegiances and which owed loyalty to him alone.

complicated by the rise of Qubilai's cousin Qaidu, who, defying the qaghan until his death (1303), welded the Chaghadayids and other Central Asian Mongol princes into a rival power-bloc. The Golden Horde's easternmost territories were virtually separated off to form the White Horde, and the Negüderis (or Qaraunas), an independent Mongol grouping which had emerged in Afghanistan, were brought under Chaghadayid control only c. 1300.

The end of the empire is usually reckoned to date from the Mongols' expulsion from China by the Ming dynasty in 1368. The Ilkhanate had disintegrated between 1335 and 1353. But the other two main polities survived for much longer, the Golden Horde until 1502 (of its successor-states, the Crimean khanate lasted until 1783) and the Chaghadai khanate until 1678.

1206	1227	1241–2	1260	1279	1295
Temüjin proclaimed Chinggis Khan at a tribal assembly in Mongolia	Death of Chinggis Khan	Mongol invasion of eastern Europe: Poles defeated near Liegnitz, and Hungarians at Móhi	Mongols defeated by the Mamluks at Ain Jalut in Palestine	Conquest of China completed	The Ilkhan Ghazan adopts Islam

The archer, armed with the famous composite recurved bow, shoots at a pursuing enemy. It is unlikely that the Mongols' renowned skills in mounted archery and their extraordinary discipline are enough to explain the success of their campaigns. The calibre of the high command, logistical capabilities, the use of psychological warfare, and the disunity of their enemies must all be taken into account as well.

The Mongols readily utilized the administrative talents of their subjects. Members of the indigenous bureaucratic class retained access to high office (though in China the highest posts went to foreigners), and in certain regions sovereignty was mediated through local tributary rulers. Some of these, like the Rus princes, represented continuity; others, like the Kartids of Herat, were new dynasties promoted by the conquerors.

The Mongol states were characterized by religious pluralism, which made it possible for Catholic missionaries from western Europe to penetrate much further into Asia than previously. During the years 1307–18 the popes created an episcopal network that embraced the whole of the Mongol world. Nevertheless, by 1400 the European mission had collapsed, and Nestorian Christianity was in full retreat. The ultimate beneficiaries were Christianity's rivals. Under Mongol rule Buddhism gained ground in China and its borderlands. The Ilkhans, the khans of the Golden Horde, and the Chaghadayid khans adopted Islam, which intensified its hold in Central Asia and the Russian steppes and even spread as far as Yün-nan, in southwestern China.

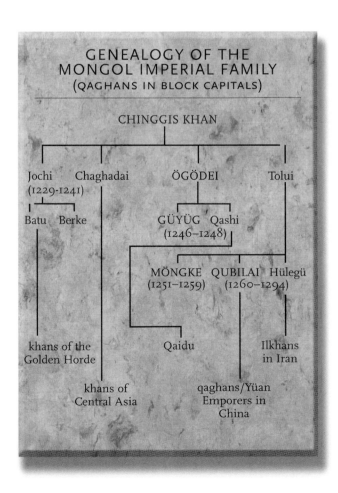

GENEALOGY OF THE
MONGOL IMPERIAL FAMILY
(QAGHANS IN BLOCK CAPITALS)

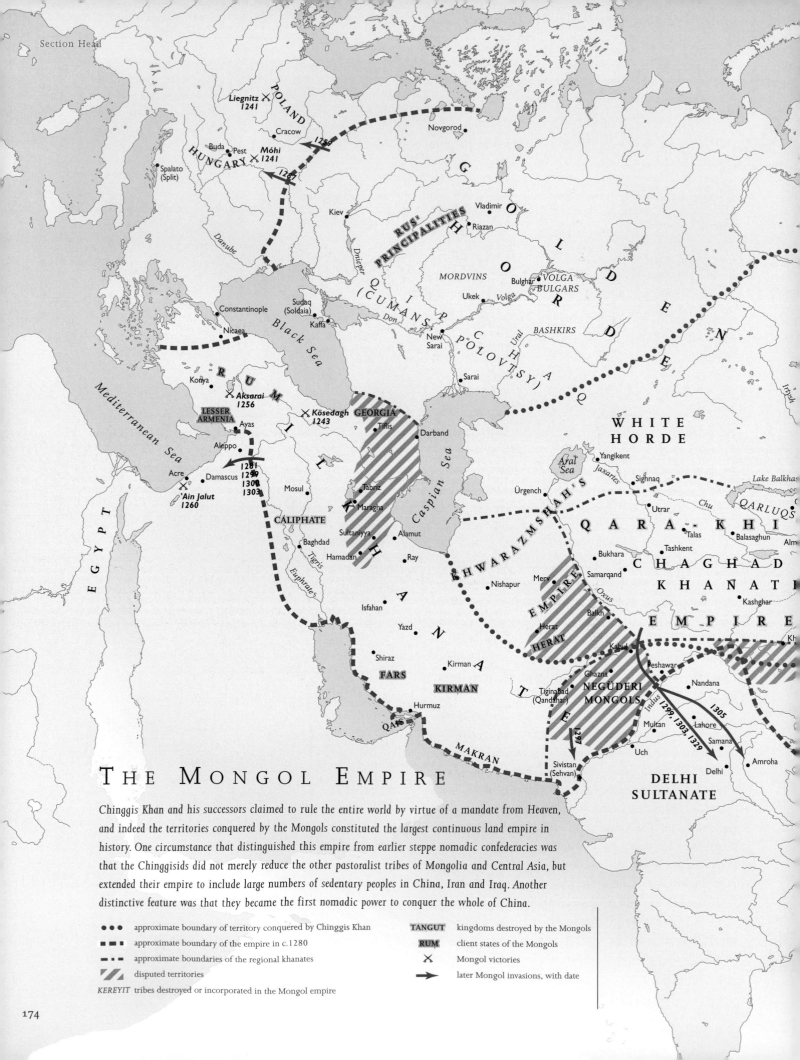

THE MONGOL EMPIRE

Chinggis Khan and his successors claimed to rule the entire world by virtue of a mandate from Heaven, and indeed the territories conquered by the Mongols constituted the largest continuous land empire in history. One circumstance that distinguished this empire from earlier steppe nomadic confederacies was that the Chinggisids did not merely reduce the other pastoralist tribes of Mongolia and Central Asia, but extended their empire to include large numbers of sedentary peoples in China, Iran and Iraq. Another distinctive feature was that they became the first nomadic power to conquer the whole of China.

•••• approximate boundary of territory conquered by Chinggis Khan	**TANGUT** kingdoms destroyed by the Mongols
▬▬▬ approximate boundary of the empire in c.1280	**RUM** client states of the Mongols
▬·▬·▬ approximate boundaries of the regional khanates	✕ Mongol victories
▨ disputed territories	➜ later Mongol invasions, with date
KEREYIT tribes destroyed or incorporated in the Mongol empire	

Map labels: Liegnitz 1241, POLAND, Cracow, 1259, Novgorod, Buda, Pest, Móhi 1241, HUNGARY, 1287, Spalato (Split), Danube, Kiev, RUS' PRINCIPALITIES, Vladimir, Riazan, GOLDEN, MORDVINS, Bulghar, VOLGA BULGARS, Ukek, Volga, BASHKIRS, Constantinople, Sudaq (Soldaia), Kaffa, Black Sea, QIPCHAQ (CUMANS POLOVTSY), Don, New Sarai, Sarai, Ural, HORDE, Irtysh, Nicaea, RUM, Konya, Aksarai 1256, Kösedagh 1243, GEORGIA, Tiflis, Darband, WHITE HORDE, Yangikent, Lesser Armenia, Ayas, Aleppo, Mediterranean Sea, Acre, Damascus 1281 1299 1300 1303, 'Ain Jalut 1260, Mosul, Tabriz, Maragha, CALIPHATE, Sultaniyya, Alamut, Baghdad, Hamadan, Ray, Caspian Sea, Aral Sea, Ürgench, Jaxartes, Sighnaq, Utrar, Chu, Lake Balkhash, QARLUQS, KHWARAZMSHAH'S, Talas, Tashkent, QARA-KHI, Balasaghun, Alm, Bukhara, Samarqand, CHAGHAD, KHANATI, EMPIRE, Kashghar, EGYPT, K H A N A T E, Isfahan, Nishapur, Merv, Oxus, Herat, HERAT, Balkh, Kabul, Peshawar, Kh, Yazd, Shiraz, Kirman, FARS, KIRMAN, Tiginabad (Qandahar), Ghazna, NEGÜDERI MONGOLS, Nandana, Indus 1299, 1303, 1329, 1305, Multan, Lahore, Hurmuz, QAIS, MAKRAN, 1291, Sivistan (Sehvan), Uch, Samana, Delhi, Amroha, DELHI SULTANATE, Dnieper, Tigris, Euphrates

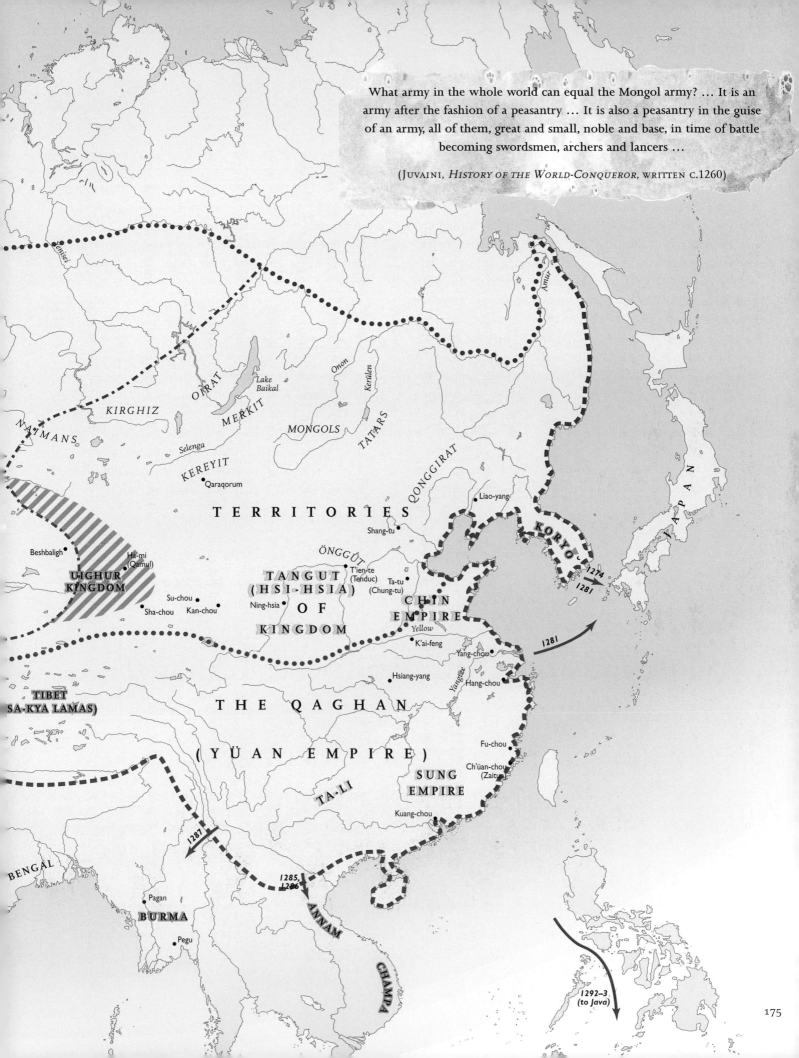

What army in the whole world can equal the Mongol army? ... It is an army after the fashion of a peasantry ... It is also a peasantry in the guise of an army, all of them, great and small, noble and base, in time of battle becoming swordsmen, archers and lancers ...

(JUVAINI, *HISTORY OF THE WORLD-CONQUEROR*, WRITTEN C.1260)

Yenisei

Amur

Onon

Kerülen

OIRAT

KIRGHIZ

Lake Baikal

MERKIT

Selenga

MONGOLS

TATARS

NAIMANS

KEREYIT

Qaraqorum

QONGGIRAT

• Liao-yang

T E R R I T O R I E S

Beshbaligh •

Ha-mi (Qamul) •

• Shang-tu

ÖNGGÜT

KORYO

1274

UIGHUR KINGDOM

TANGUT (HSI-HSIA)

T'ien-te (Tenduc) •

Ta-tu (Chung-tu) •

1281

Su-chou •

OF

Ning-hsia •

CHIN EMPIRE

Sha-chou •

Kan-chou •

KINGDOM

Yellow

1281

• K'ai-feng

TIBET SA-KYA LAMAS)

T H E   Q A G H A N

• Hsiang-yang

Yang-chou •

Yangtze

Hang-chou •

(Y Ü A N   E M P I R E)

TA-LI

Fu-chou •

SUNG EMPIRE

Ch'üan-chou (Zaitun) •

1287

Kuang-chou •

BENGAL

1285, 1286

Pagan •

ANNAM

BURMA

Pegu •

CHAMPA

1292–3 (to Java)

J A P A N

175

Iran And Central Asia, c. 1000–1220

This period witnessed the widespread immigration of steppe peoples into Iran and Transoxiana. Since at least the ninth century pagan Turks had been entering the Islamic world as elite slaves, receiving both instruction in Islam and training for high military and administrative office. Turkish slave officers often founded dynasties of their own, the Ghaznavids for example. The late tenth century saw the beginning of the first mass influx of recently-converted free Turks in tribal groups, notably the Seljuqs. Subsequent upheavals in the Far East brought Islamic Central Asia under the rule of the pagan Qara-Khitan, and in the early 13th century most of the eastern Islamic world was conquered by the advancing Mongols, whose armies included a high proportion of nomadic Turks.

During the tenth century Islam had been carried from Transoxiana into the steppes beyond, and had been adopted by large numbers of Turkish nomads. In 999 these Turks, under a dynasty known to historians as the Qarakhanids, pushed into the moribund Samanid amirate, partitioning its territories with the Ghaznavids (962–1186), a dynasty founded by a Turkish slave lieutenant of the Samanids. Under its greatest ruler, Mahmud (997–1030), the Ghaznavid amirate was powerful enough to war both against the Buyids in the west and against Hindu rulers beyond the Indus, laying the foundations of Islam in Afghanistan and the Punjab. But soon both the Ghaznavids and the Qarakhanids were obliged to give ground to the Seljuqs, a clan from the Oghuz Turkish confederacy north of the Aral Sea. The Qarakhanids acknowledged Seljuq overlordship. The Ghaznavids, defeated at Dandanaqan in 1040, were confined to their easternmost territories. From c. 1140 they were under mounting pressure from the Ghurids (the rulers of Ghur, the mountainous region east of Herat), who in 1186 suppressed the Ghaznavids and for a time dominated eastern Iran and the Punjab.

> **"The Turk is like a pearl that lies in the oyster in the sea. For as long as it is in its habitat, it is devoid of power and worth; but when it emerges from the oyster and from the sea, it acquires value and becomes precious, decorating the crown of kings and adorning the neck and ears of brides"**
>
> Fakhr-i Mudabbir, writing c. 1206

999	1040	1055	1141	1194	1218–24
Qarakhanid Turks suppress the Samanid amirate	Ghaznavids defeated by the Seljuqs at Dandanaqan	Seljuq leader Toghril Beg enters Baghdad	Sultan Sanjar defeated by the Qara-Khitan in the Qatwan steppe	End of the Seljuq Sultanate in Iran	First Mongol invasion of the eastern Islamic world

THE SELJUQ EMPIRE

The Seljuqs created the most extensive and impressive Islamic state since the break-up of the Caliphate in the ninth century. But in accordance with the nomadic idea that the empire's territories belonged to the ruling dynasty as a whole, the Sultans granted out provinces as appanages to members of their family; both Kirman and Anatolia (Rum), for instance, were ruled throughout by separate branches of the Seljuq dynasty. In addition, a number of existing dynasties, like the Shaddadids in Ganja and the Kakuyids in Yazd, were allowed to retain their territories as the Sultan's subordinates.

—————— Approximate boundary of Seljuk empire, c.1200

SHIRVAN Dynasties and states subordinate to the Seljuk sultan

KIRMAN Territories ruled by separate branches of the Seljuk dynsaty

Qipchaq Tribal names

In 1055 the Seljuq leader suppressed the Buyids and assumed protection of the Caliph, who granted him the new and exalted title of Sultan. The Seljuqs reduced the whole of Iran, though they were never able to crush the heterodox Assassins in their strongholds in the Caspian region after the 1090s. The system of authority in the Seljuq empire was less diffuse than that of the Qarakhanids,

and the sultans encouraged unruly nomadic Turkish ("Türkmen") tribal groups to move out towards Syria and Anatolia on the empire's periphery. In the east, however, the nomads proved a more intractable problem, and in 1153 Sultan Sanjar (d. 1157) was defeated and captured by insurgent Oghuz tribes in Khurasan. By this time, he had already abandoned Central Asia to the Qara-Khitan ("Black

Map labels (selection as shown):

Lake Baikal · Merkit · Kirghiz · Kereyit · Qipchaq (Qangli) · GEORGIA · Tiflis · RUM · SHIRVAN · AZARBAIJAN · Tabriz · Naimans · Yenisei · Irtysh · Lake Zaysan · Lake Balkhash · Imil · Ili · Qarluqs · Almaligh · Bishbaligh · Qaraqocho · Hami (Qomul) · Aral Sea · KHWARAZM · Jand · Siqhnaq · Jaxartes · Utrar · Tashkent · Talas (Taraz) · Balasaghun · Issik Kul · UIGHUR KINGDOM · Lop Nor · TANGUT (HSI-HSIA) KINGDOM · 'ABBASID CALIPHATE · Baghdad · Qazvin · Hamadan · Ray · GILAN · MAZANDARAN · GURGAN · Caspian Sea · TRANSOXIANA · Urgench · Bukhara · Qatwan · Samarqand · Khojend · Uzkend · FARGHANA · Kashghar · Tarim · Yarkand · Khotan · Euphrates · Tigris · Basra · KHUZISTAN · Isfahan · Yazd · Nasa · Abivard · Tus · Nishapur · Sarakhs · Merv · KHURASAN · Oxus · Tirmud · Balkh · SHUGHNAN · BADAKH-SHAN · VAKHAN · Shiraz · FARS · Bardasir · KIRMAN · Jiruft · SISTAN · Herat · Jam · GHUR · JUZJAN · Andkhud · Shuburghan · Bamiyan · Ghazna · Bust · Tiginabad (Qandahar) · Kabul · Kabul · BINBAN · Peshawar · KURRAM · BOLOR · KASHMIR · TIBET · NEPAL · Ray · MAKRAN · Sivistan (Senvan) · Indus · Multan · Uch · Khokhars · Lahore · Hansi · Meerut · Delhi · CHAUHAN KINGDOM · Ajmer · Anhilvara (Patan) · GUJARAT · Yamuna · Ganges · BENGAL · INDIA

Legend:
— approximate boundary of Qara-Khitan and Ghurid empires, c.1200
— approximate boundary of the Khwarazmshah's empire, c.1216
/// territory disputed between the Khwarazmshahs and the Ghurids
Qipchaq tribal names

THE GHURID, QARA-KHITAN AND KHWARAZMIAN EMPIRES

The Ghurids, a dynasty of Iranian stock in an era otherwise dominated by Turks, engaged in a duel for Khurasan with the Khwarazm-Shahs and their Qara-Khitan overlords. The Qara-Khitan sovereigns were Buddhists, although they appear to have tolerated other faiths and their victories over Muslim princes like Sanjar turned them into candidates for the role of the mythical Christian ruler, "Prester John". Their conquests represented the first serious encroachment on Islamic territory by non-Muslims, thereby prefiguring the more cataclysmic advance of the Mongols a hundred years later.

Khitan"), refugees from the Khitan (Liao) empire in northern China, who had established themselves in Central Asia and reduced the Seljuqs' Qarakhanid clients to tributary status.

The outlying provinces of the declining Seljuq empire fell under the control of its Turkish slave officers, often nominally acting on behalf of a junior Seljuq prince and hence styled *atabeg* ("guardian"). The Zangids in Mosul, the Ildegüzids in Azerbaijan and the Khwarazm-Shahs (1097–1221) in the fertile oasis region around the lower Oxus, all originated in this fashion. The Khwarazm-Shah overthrew the last Seljuq Sultan of western Iran (1194), repudiated Qara-Khitan overlordship, and eliminated the Ghurids (1206, 1215) and the surviving Qarakhanids (1217), only to provoke an attack by a formidable new eastern neighbour. In 1218–24 the Mongols of Chinggis Khan destroyed the Khwarazmian empire and began the conquest of much of the eastern Islamic world.

The minaret at Jam (left) was constructed under the Ghurid Sultan Ghiyath al-Din Muhammad (1163-1202), probably not far from the town of Firuzkuh, which the Ghurids had built in c. 1145 and which had become the dynasty's principal centre. Ghiyath al-Din Muhammad, conqueror of Herat and later of Ghazna, was one of the two rulers who effectively founded Ghurid power; the other was his younger brother Mu'izz al-Din Muhammad (d. 1206), who was responsible for the conquest or reconquest for Islam of a significant area of northern India.

Iran And Central Asia, c. 1330–1500

The decline of the Mongol states did not destroy the prestige of Chinggis Khan's legacy and dynasty. The Central Asian conqueror Timur (more properly, Temür; d. 1405), who was not a descendant of Chinggis Khan but a member of a Turkicized Mongol tribe within the Chaghadai khanate in Transoxiana, acted throughout in the name of a puppet Chinggisid khan, taking no title higher than amir. He sought to reconstitute the Mongol empire of the 13th century. Controversy over the respective authority of the Shari'a and of Mongol law, and the validity of Mongol as against Islamic taxes, still raged in Iran and Central Asia in the mid-15th century.

Reconstruction of Timur's head from his skull in the Gur-i Mir, Samarqand (far right). Timur shared Chinggis Khan's military genius, but not his capacity to create lasting institutions, and after his death his empire swiftly fell apart. His campaigns were often marked by cruelty even more appalling than that of the Mongols; and although they were mounted in the name of Islam, the victims were all Muslim powers, with the minor exception of the Christians of Georgia, the Knights of St John in Smyrna, and a few Hindu chieftains.

Since the 1330s the Chaghadai khanate in Central Asia had been divided. In Transoxiana the khans were merely a façade for the rule of the various tribal amirs, and the Turco Mongol nomads were increasingly Islamicized and sedentarized; whereas in Moghulistan ("Mongol territory") the khans enjoyed real power and pagan, nomadic Mongol tradition still held sway. By 1370 Timur was the master of Transoxiana, and he then set about restoring Chinggis Khan's empire, acting until his death in the name of a puppet Chinggisid sovereign. The only other consistent element in his policy was the transplantation of painters and skilled craftsmen from captured cities to his capital at Samarqand. His campaigns against the khans of Moghulistan and of the Golden Horde, like his victories over the Ottomans and the Mamluks, achieved little more than the temporary humiliation of these powers. In Iran, however, the effect of his operations was more enduring.

Four powers competed in the vacuum left by the collapse of the Ilkhanate. A dynasty of Mongol (though not Chinggisid) origin, the Jalayirids (c. 1340–1432), ruled over Iraq and Azarbaijan from Baghdad, blocking the efforts of the Muzaffarids (c. 1340–93), a family of Arab extraction who held Kirman, Isfahan and Fars, to extend their power to the north-west. In eastern Khurasan, the Karts (c.1245–1389) maintained themselves in face of the threat from the Sarbadars (1337–81), a movement headed by an unstable combination of local notables and dervishes of largely Shi'ite proclivities. In a series of invasions, Timur destroyed all these powers with the exception of the Jalayirids, who were confined to Iraq.

Timur's numerous progeny, who divided up his empire, inherited neither his vigour nor his military skill, although his youngest son, Shah Rukh (d. 1447), and subsequently another descendant, Husain Baiqara (d. 1506), ruled over an impressive territory from Herat. But soon after 1500 the Timurid rulers of Herat and Transoxiana were ousted by the Uzbeks, a nomadic confederacy based north of the Jaxartes and led by a cadet branch of the dynasty of the khans of the Golden Horde. The Timurid prince Babur, who had vainly tried to maintain himself in Samarqand, withdrew to India and in time founded the Moghul empire.

Much earlier, the Timurids' territories in western Iran had passed into the hands of two dynasties founded by Türkmen tribal chiefs: the Qara Qoyunlu (c. 1365–1467), who had absorbed the Jalayirid principality, and the Aq Qoyunlu (c. 1352–1507). The Aq Qoyunlu prince Uzun Hasan (d. 1478), who eliminated the Qara-Qoyunlu prior to inflicting a crushing defeat on the Timurids in 1469, even figured as a possible ally for Catholic Europe against the Ottomans until the latter routed him at Bashkent in 1473. The Aq Qoyunlu were finally destroyed by the mass Türkmen rising which had brought to power the Safavid dynasty in Tabriz in 1501.

1335–53	1370	1402	1473	1507	1511
Collapse of the Ilkhanate	Timur becomes *de facto* master of the Chaghadai khanate	Timur defeats the Ottoman Sultan Bayazid at Ankara	Ottoman victory over the Aq Qoyunlu at Bashkent	Uzbeks capture Herat	Final capture of Samarqand by the Uzbeks

THE EMPIRE OF TIMUR, 1360–1445

Timur's campaigns took him as far afield as the steppes of southern Russia (1395), Delhi (1398), Smyrna (1402) and Damascus (1404), and a plan to invade China was interrupted only by his death. But his empire embraced little more than Iran and Transoxiana. He was generally satisfied with the submission of local rulers and was often content, following a victory over a recalcitrant enemy, merely to put the clock back. In the wake of his triumph at Ankara (1402), he simply reinstated as his clients in Anatolia the various Turkish princelings that had earlier been dispossessed by the Ottomans.

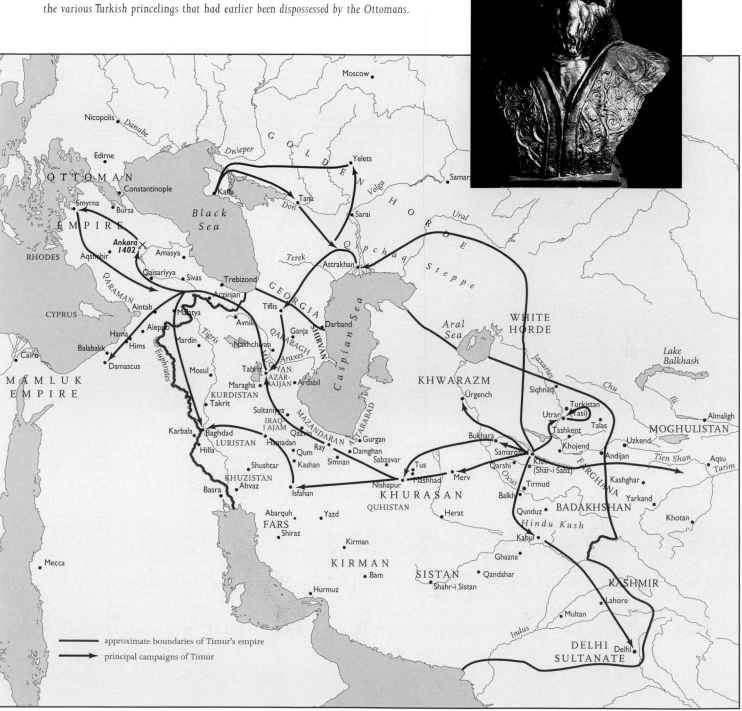

approximate boundaries of Timur's empire

principal campaigns of Timur

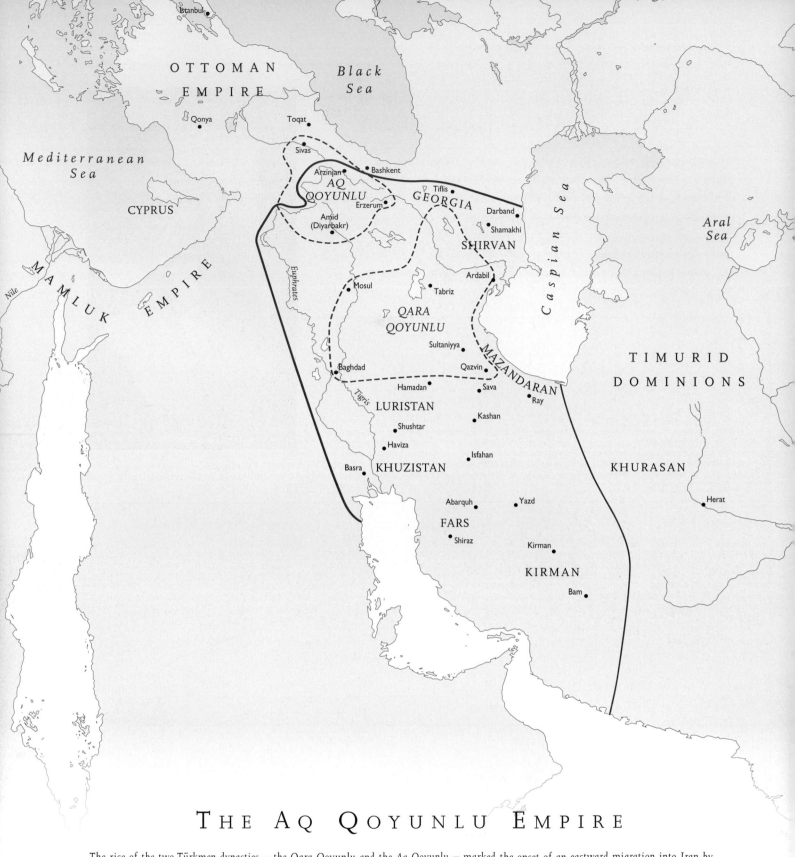

THE AQ QOYUNLU EMPIRE

The rise of the two Türkmen dynasties — the Qara Qoyunlu and the Aq Qoyunlu — marked the onset of an eastward migration into Iran by tribes that had moved into Anatolia two centuries earlier, during the Seljuq era. They had profited, like other tribal groups there, from the collapse of the Ilkhanate. The final phase of this "Türkmen interlude" was the migration of Türkmen tribes that accompanied the takeover of power in Iran by the Safavids from c. 1500 onwards and which was responsible for the ethnic map of Iran in modern times.

- - - - - - approximate boundaries of Qara Qoyunlu and Aq Qoyunlu principalities, c.1435
———— approximate boundary of Aq Qoyunlu empire under Uzun Hasan, to 1478

Gauhar Shad mosque, Mashhad (right). This building was erected in
1418–19 on the orders of Shah Rukh's wife Gauhar Shad, and marks the
transportation to eastern Iran of architectural styles from
Transoxiana, then undergoing a cultural renaissance.
The Timurid rulers were keen builders, as well as
notable patrons of painting, calligraphy and the
sciences. Shah Rukh's son Ulugh Beg (d. 1449)
is most celebrated for the magnificent
astronomical observatory he caused to be built
at Samarqand.

The Delhi Sultanate And Vijayanagara
India, c. 1200–1500

In the early 13th century Turkish Muslim rule was established at Delhi. The Delhi Sultanate, which controlled most of north India for nearly 300 years, saw a gradual transformation of Indian society through processes of conflict, accommodation and assimilation. In the south a smaller sultanate struggled with the last old-style Hindu empire at Vijayanagara, which witnessed a renaissance of orthodox learning and disseminated a new military elite throughout the southern peninsula.

While the Ghaznavids had seen "al-Hind" (India), as a rich source of plunder, their successors, the Ghurids, increasingly viewed India as a zone of imperial expansion. The Ghurid slave general Qutb-ud-din Aybak won important victories against Hindu monarchs across north India at the end of the 12th century. In 1206, Aybak received "Hindustan" with a scarlet canopy of state. Though recognizing the sovereignty of the Ghurids, his residence in the city of Delhi made Aybak's

dominions in India less a Ghurid frontier and more a fully-fledged state. This marks the beginning of the Delhi Sultanate, which was actually composed of several dynastic periods. Aybak's immediate successors were know as the "slave rulers" because of their original status as prestigious military slaves of Turkish origin. Among these, Iltutmish (b. 1211) received sanction for independent rule from the Caliph in 1229. The Sultanate was henceforth formally autonomous from outside political powers, though Delhi continued to receive a flow of immigrants from central Asia.

The slave sultans were replaced by the Afghan Khaljis in 1290, who were in turn overthrown by the Turkish Tughluqs in 1320. Under these dynasties the Sultanate consolidated power. Alauddin Khalji (1296–1316) sent and expedition as far south as Madurai, defeating Yadava, Kakatiya, Housel and Pandya kings. Later, to protect the Sultanate from the Mongol scourge ravishing the Muslim

Quwwat al-Islam mosque with Qutb Minar in the background. The picture shows the arched screen of the Quwwat al-Islam (Might of Islam) mosque, built by Qutb-ud-din Aybak inside a captured Hindu citadel, close to Delhi, on the platform of a demolished Hindu temple. He also built the Qutb Minar as a tower of victory to symbolize the supremacy of Islam in India.

1206	1288, 1293	1336	1526	1538	1539
Qutb-ud-din Aybak founds Delhi Sultanate.	Marco Polo visits south India.	Harihara and Bukka found the kingdom of Vijayanagar.	Babur defeats Ibrahim Lodi, the last ruler of the Delhi sultanate, at the battle of Panipat.	Bahmani kingdom gives way to five new Deccani Sultanates: Bijapur, Golconda, Ahmednagar, Bidar and Berar.	Fall of the Vijayanagar kingdom to the armies of the combined sultanates of the Deccan.

SOUTH ASIA,
c. 1200–1400

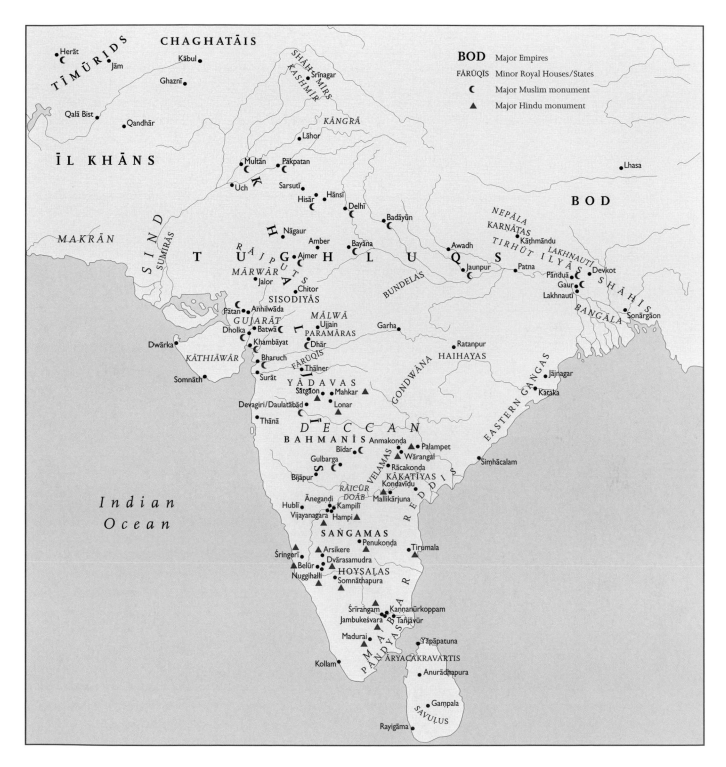

BOD Major Empires
FĀRŪQĪS Minor Royal Houses/States
☾ Major Muslim monument
▲ Major Hindu monument

CHAGHATĀIS

TĪMŪRIDS
Herāt
Jām
Kābul
Ghaznī
Qalā Bist
Qandhār

ĪL KHĀNS

MAKRĀN

SIND
SUMIRĀS

SHĀH MIRS
KASHMĪR
Srīnagar

KĀNGRĀ
Lāhor

Lhasa

Multān
Uch
Pākpatan
Sarsutī
Hisār
Hānsī
Delhī
Badāyūn

NEPĀLA
KARNĀTAS
Kāthmāndu
Awadh
Jaunpur
Patna

TIRHŪT ILYĀS
LAKHNAUTĪ
Devkot
Pānduā
Gaur
Lakhnautī

SHĀHĪS
BANGĀLA
Sonārgāon

BOD

Nāgaur
Amber
Ajmer
Bayāna

RĀJPUT
TUGHLUQS
GUTS
HS

MĀRWĀR
Jalor
Chitor
SISODIYĀS

Pātan
Anhilwāda
GUJARĀT
Dholka
Batwā
Khambāyat
Bharuch
Thālner
Surāt

MĀLWĀ
Ujjain
PARAMĀRAS
Dhār

Garha

Ratanpur

BUNDELAS

Dwārka
KĀTHIĀWĀR
Somnāth
FĀRŪQĪS

GONDWĀNA
HAIHAYAS

Jājnagar
Kataka

EASTERN GANGAS

YĀDAVAS
Sātgāon
Mahkar ▲
Devagiri/Daulatābād ▲
Lonar ▲
Thāna

DECCAN

BAHMANĪS
Bīdar
Gulbarga
Bijāpur

Anmakonda
Palampet ▲
Wārangal ▲
Rācakonda ▲
KĀKATĪYAS
Kondavīḍu
Mallikārjuna ▲

VELAMAS
REDDIS
Simhācalam

**Indian
Ocean**

RĀICŪR
DOĀB
Hublī
Ānegandi
Kampilī
Vijayanagara
Hampi ▲

SANGAMAS
Penukonda
Arsikere
Śringerī ▲
Belūr ▲
Nuggihalli ▲
Dvārasamudra ▲
HOYSALAS
Somnāthapura ▲

Tirumala ▲

Śrīrangam ▲
Jambukeśvara ▲
Kannanūrkoppam ▲
Tañjāvūr ▲
Madurai
PĀNDYAS
ĀRYACAKRAVARTIS
Kollam

Yāpāpatuna
Anurādhapura

Gampala
SAVULUS
Rayigāma

The political centre of India returned to the north with the establishment of the Delhi Sultanate under various dynasties of Turkish slave-nobles in the 13th and 14th centuries, a dominance partly challenged by the rise of the independent Bahmani Sultanate and the Vijayanagara empire in the south in the middle of the 14th century. Many royal houses (particularly Hindu dynasties of the south and north) during this period operated from impressive upland fortresses.

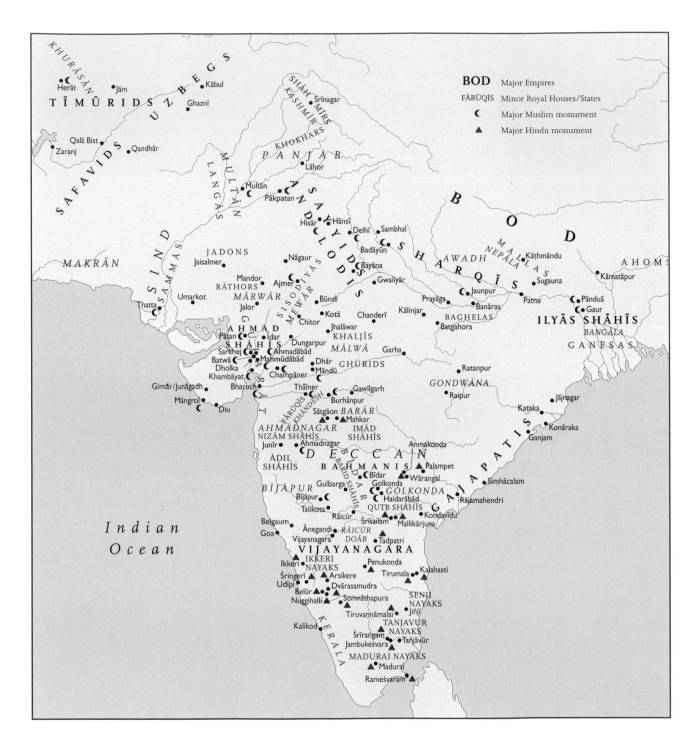

BOD — Major Empires
FĀRŪQĪS — Minor Royal Houses/States
☪ — Major Muslim monument
▲ — Major Hindu monument

KHURĀSĀN
Herāt • Jām • Kābul
TĪMŪRIDS UZBEGS Ghaznī •
SHĀH MIRS • Srīnagar
KASHMĪR
Qalā Bist • KHOKHARS
Zaranj • Qandhār • PANJĀB
SAFAVIDS Multān LANGAS Lāhor
Pākpatan • Hānsī
MAKRĀN SIND Hisār • Delhī • Sambhal
JADONS SAYYIDS Badāyūn
Jaisalmer • Nāgaur • Bayāna LODIS AWADH NEPĀLA Kāthmāndu
MANDOR RĀTHORS Ajmer Gwaliyār Prayāga Jaunpur SHARQĪS Sugauna • AHOM
Kāmatāpur
Umarkot • MĀRWĀR Būndī Kālinjar Banāras Patna • Pāndua
Thatta SAMMĀS Jalor MEWĀR Kotā Chanderī Batgahora BAGHELAS Gaur
SISODIYAS Chitor KHALJĪS Garha ILYĀS SHĀHĪS
AHMAD Jhalāwar MĀLWĀ BANGĀLA
SHĀHĪS Pātan Idar Dungarpur Garha GANESAS
Sarkhej Ahmadābād Dhār Ratanpur
Batwā Mahmūdābād Mānḍū GHŪRIDS GONDWĀNA
Dholka Champāner Raipur Jājnagar
Khambāyat Thālner Gawīlgarh Kataka
Girnār/Junāgadh Bharuch FĀRŪQĪS Burhānpur Konāraka
Māngrol KHĀNDESH Sātgāon BARĀR Mahkar Ganjam
Diu AHMADNAGAR IMĀD GAJAPATIS
NIZĀM SHĀHĪS SHĀHĪS Anmakonda
Junīr Ahmadnagar DECCAN Palampet
ĀDIL BAHMANIS Bīdar Wārangal Simhācalam
SHĀHĪS Gulganga Golkonda GOLKONDA
BĪJĀPUR Bīdar Haidarābād Rājamahendri
Bījāpur QUTB SHĀHĪS
Talikota Rāicūr Srīsailam Kondavīdu
Belgaum Ānegandi RĀICŪR Mallikārjuna
Goa DOĀB Tadpatri
Vijayanagara VIJAYANAGARA
Penukonda
IKKERI Tirumala Kalahasti
NĀYAKS
Śringerī Arsikere
Udīpi Belūr Dvārasamudra
Nuggihalli Somnāthapura SENJI
NĀYAKS
Tiruvannāmalai Jiñji
Kalikod TANJAVUR
NĀYAKS
Śrīrangam
Jambukeśvara Tanjāvūr
MADURAI NĀYAKS
Madurai
Rāmeśvaram

Indian Ocean

SOUTH ASIA, C. 1400–1550

Independent Hindu and Muslim dynasties flourished across northern and central India, with the succeeding rulers of the Sultanate occupying temporary and limited power at best, until the final collapse of the Delhi throne in 1526 at the hands of the first Mughal emperor, Babur. In the south, successors of the Bahmanis together overthrew the kingdom of Vijayanagara in 1565 at the battle of Talikota, leaving their southern vassals, called nayaks, to rule independently.

world, and to control unruly southern districts, Muhammad bin Tughluq (1300–1351) moved his capital from Delhi to Daulatabad (Devagiri). Though the Mongols were repulsed, the dream of an India-wide empire soon faded. The Daulatabad experiment was abandoned and the court returned to Delhi. Shortly thereafter, rebel governors established an independent Muslim Sultanate in the northern Deccan known as the Bahmanis. Further south, two erstwhile governors of the Tughluqs, brothers of the Sangama clan, founded the last great Hindu empire, named after its capital "Vijayanagara" (City of Victory), in 1336. From 1400 independent sultanates were established in Bengal (Ilyas Shahis), Gujarat (Mahmud Shahis), and later in Khandesh (Faruqis) and Jaunpur (Sharqis). The Sayyids (1414–1451) and Lodis (1451–1526) ruled a weakened Sultanate before its final collapse at the hands of the Mughals in 1526.

Political stability was no less elusive in south India, where the Bahmani sultanate, based in Gulbarga and Bidar, and the Vijayanagar kingdom, now spreading far southward, battled for the fertile Raichur Doab. In 1538 the Bahmani kingdom fragmented into five successor sultanates at Bijapur, Golconda, Bidar, Berar and Ahmadnagar while Vijayanagar kings sought to control military governors (Nayaks) in Madurai, Jinji, and Tanjavur. In 1565, the combined Deccani sultanates defeated Vijayanagar forces at Talikota and sacked its capital.

The introduction of Muslim rule in India led to important religious changes. The most remarkable fact in this process is that large-scale conversion did not happen. As in other Islamic empires, Muslim rulers in India governed huge non-Muslim populations. Forced conversion was never a serious option (widespread conversion occurred only in Punjab and Bengal). Instead Hindus were treated as "zimmis" (non-Muslim believers) to be tolerated if they paid a special protection tax. Throughout society Hindus and Muslims lived together, sometimes in harmony, sometimes in conflict, as mutual interests often triumphed over religious differences. Hindu rajputs, for example, took their place among Muslim governors as integral but intractable elements of the larger political context. Undoubtedly, the political power enjoyed by Hindu elite classes was seriously compromised under the Sultanate. Nonetheless, Islam became a new religious option for tribal groups, peasants and nobility alike with Islamic mysticism (Sufism) playing and important role in conversion. Within Hinduism, high-caste society gained a new unity and conservatism, while new religious movements from below stressed devotion (bhakti) and challenged cast hierarchy.

Vitthala temple, Hampi, Karnataka. View of stairs leading into a ornately columned pavilion at the Vitthala temple in the city of Vijayanagara, built in the middle of the 15th century. Though never dedicated, the Vitthala temple remains one of the city's most ornate and celebrated monuments.

Southeast Asia, the Golden Age of Pagan and Angkor

In the two centuries after 1000, the mainland Southeast Asian empires of Pagan and Angkor reached the meridian of their power, and their court cultures left ehin dsome of the greatest monumental works of the medieval world. By the 13th century, as the mainland empires declines, new states staked their claim to power by orienating themselves more closely towards long-distance trade.

The expansion of Pagan illustrates well the ability of Southern Asian states to incorporate diverse cultural elements. Although principally a Burman kingdom, achieving hegemony over the Mon state of Thaton by military expansion, Pagan built on the legacies of earlier Pyu kingdoms and recruited Mon artisanal and scribal expertise. However, by the 12th century, there was a reaction against such syncretism, and the emergence of a more sharply defined Burman Theravada Buddhist tradition is reflected in the temple construction of the era (see picture).

By the later 12th and the first half of the 13th century, Pagan had brought political unity to the Irrawaddy basin and parts of

Tenasserim and Arakan. The Buddhist clergy, the *sangha*, reached the height of its wealth and influence, to such a level that the last great king of Pagan, Narapatisithu (c. 1173–1211) cut back on its lands and purified its institutions. His successors, however, were less successful in their defence of royal power.

In Angkor, the personal ascendancy of its Khmer rulers was perhaps more pivotal to the success of the empire than the administrative institutions they created. Strong kings cast their shadow in great works of construction, and the ebbs and flows of Angkor's power in the 11th to 14th centuries can be traced through these (see map).

The Dai Viet kingdom achieved greater institutional stability. Under the Ly rulers (1009–1224) it established its own dynastic tradition. In an attempt to assert its power over the South China Sea, it was in intermittent conflict with the more maritime-orientated Cham kingdoms to the south, particularly over the border zone of Quang Nam. The Chams were also a principal military adversary of Angkor in this period. After 1225, a new Tran dynasty

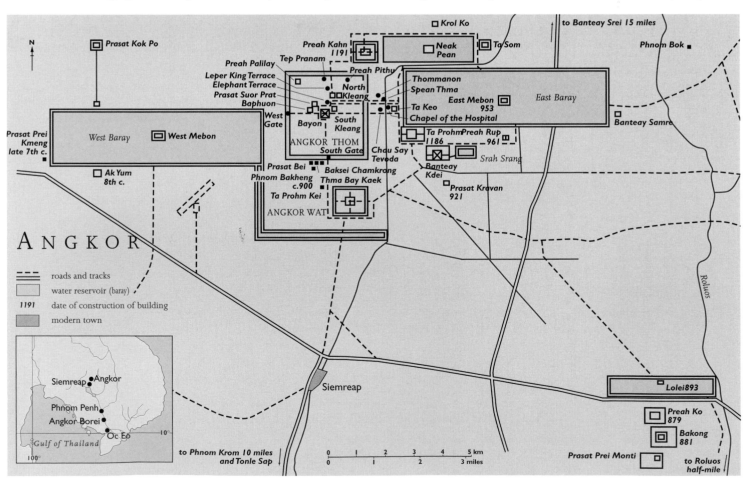

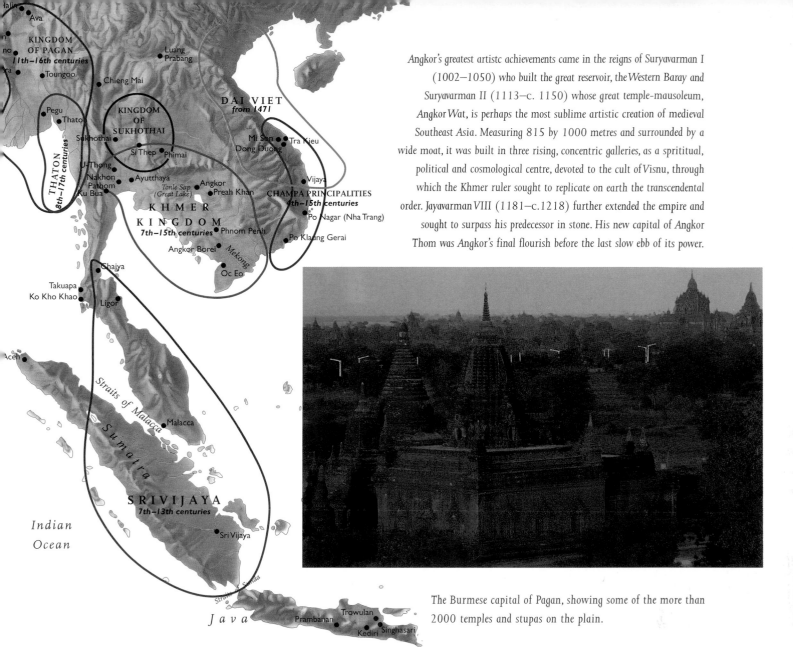

Angkor's greatest artistc achievements came in the reigns of Suryavarman I (1002–1050) who built the great reservoir, the Western Baray and Suryavarman II (1113–c. 1150) whose great temple-mausoleum, Angkor Wat, is perhaps the most sublime artistic creation of medieval Southeast Asia. Measuring 815 by 1000 metres and surrounded by a wide moat, it was built in three rising, concentric galleries, as a sprititual, political and cosmological centre, devoted to the cult of Visnu, through which the Khmer ruler sought to replicate on earth the transcendental order. Jayavarman VIII (1181–c.1218) further extended the empire and sought to surpass his predecessor in stone. His new capital of Angkor Thom was Angkor's final flourish before the last slow ebb of its power.

The Burmese capital of Pagan, showing some of the more than 2000 temples and stupas on the plain.

was established in the Dai Viet: it introduced a Confucian examination system on the Chinese model, and its more centralized regime was able to repulse Mongol-Chinese invasions in 1284 and 1287–8.

These incursions show how connections with the wider world could precipitate political change. From the 1280s, the Mongols also tore into Burma, fatally weakening Pagan, and struck as far south as Java. The dislocation of war also helped precipitate a southward move of the Tai peoples. Ramkamhaeng (1279–98) founded a more centralized domain at Sukhothai. The new capital attracted Chinese traders, and Sukothai's economy profited from its proximity to Angkor.

In the maritime world, trade was pivotal to shifts in power. Srivijaya reached the peak of its influence in the ninth and tenth centuries. Its wealth attracted predators from far afield: the Colas of Tamil Nadu plundered it in 1025, and Javanese and Chinese shipping undermined its maritime hegemony.

Merchants dealt in new commodities, such as cottons

and porcelain from China, in addition to the staple exotic goods. Trade routes dispersed: the communities of north and east Sumatra and began to deal directly with foreign traders; new centres of exchange, such as Kedah in the north of the Malay peninsula, grew in importance, and played an important role in the commerce of Pagan and Angkor.

As Srivijaya declined, commercial and political initiative in the archipelago shifted eastwards to Java. Chinese records rank the island's commercial importance as second only to the Arab lands. The historical record of political change is fragmentary from the time of Airlingga (c.1020s–49), whose extensive Javanese realm was divided after his death, until Kertanagara (1268–92) emerged in eastern Java as a new contender for regional power. Java's cultural life reached perhaps its highest expression after 1293, when Kertanagara's son, Kertarajasa, established the empire of Majapahit, from which the rulers of Java claimed paramountsy over most of island Southeast Asia.

Sung China, 960–1279

The Sung dynasty (960–1279) is celebrated in Chinese history for its civil service examination system, neo-Confucian thought, commercial growth, and refined accomplishments in printing, porcelain, and landscape painting. However, these social, economic, and cultural accomplishments were repeatedly undermined by weak border defence and increasingly divisive conflicts among officials.

In 977 the Sung government set up an open and competitive examination system that by the mid-11th century became virtually the sole route to official appointment. With the end of the Tang aristocratic class and its privileged entry to official status, aspiring officials had to spend decades mastering the Confucian canon and classical composition. Promoted also by state printing projects, this Confucian learning eventually replaced Buddhism as the central intellectual concern of educated Chinese, and from the mid-11th century developed varied schools of thought. By 1237 the School of True Way, advocated by the scholar-official Zhu Xi, had overcome political oppression to become the throne's orthodox learning for these examinations. Zhu's complex espousal of textual learning, cosmology, self-cultivation, and moral behaviour, adroitly mixed Buddhist terms and concepts with Confucian answers and so gained widespread acceptance amongst scholars, officials, and even the countless examination failures.

These intellectual accomplishments were matched by remarkable economic advances. An expansion of rice paddy cultivation, double cropping of grain, and specialized commercial agriculture led to a doubling of China's population, to 110,000,000, between the censuses of c. 755 and c. 1080. As the home of 60 per

Spring Festival on the River, as depicted in this handscroll, Spring Festival on the River, life in the capital Kaifeng.

1041	1068–	1090	1142	1163	1233
First printing by moveable type	Wang Anshi's New Reforms	First reported use of compass in Chinese ships	Sung peace treaty with Jurchen	Synagogue in Kaifeng	Mongols capture Kaifeng

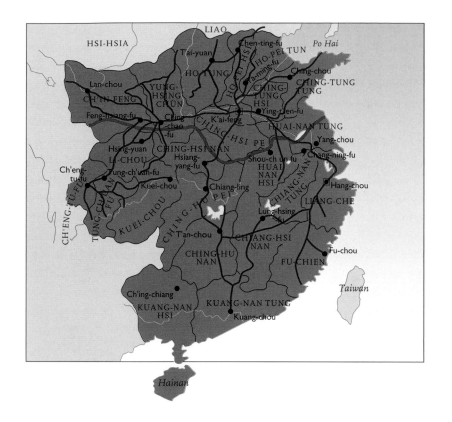

SUNG CHINA 960–1279

The Sung never recovered all of the territory of Tang China: Annam had broken away; the Khitan state of Liao still occupied the border areas to the northeast; and the Tangut state of Hsi-hsia the northwest. The centre of the Sung empire was the great commercial city of Kaifeng, hub of the canal system and road network, and seat of industries.

- ● provincial capitals
- —— canals
- —— principal roads
- ▬ boundary between Southern Sung and Chin after 1127

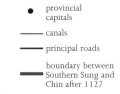

cent of this vast populace, south China replaced the north as the empire's economic centre. Trade and traders largely escaped earlier dynasties' controls on their movements, prices, and consumption. They expanded domestic markets for commercial agriculture and specialized products, such as silk, porcelain, tea. They also broadened the markets for the products of the printing, coal mining, iron manufacture, and copper mining industries and developed more complex means of exchange like paper money and promissory notes. Overseas, they traded in Korea, Japan, and in southeast Asia (where some settled permanently). Government income increasingly depended on taxes from private commerce and state salt and tea monopolies. By 1065 its annual cash tax revenue was 20 times greater than at any time during the Tang dynasty.

The arts likewise saw persistent growth. Generations of artists created monumental and intimate landscapes, refined and impressionistic bird-and-flower paintings, and remarkably detailed descriptions of daily life. Potters developed regional styles of decoration, glazes, and shape for porcelain ware. Silk textiles were woven with patterns of unrivalled complexity. And, educated men increasingly aspired to the lifestyle of the literati as their culture's highest ideal.

The Sung, however, encountered repeated political and military setbacks. The Sung court in Kaifeng ceded increasing portions of its territory: to the Liao in 1004, then to the Xixia in 1044, and, most disastrously, to the Jurchen in the early 12th century. Its advanced weaponry, wealth, and some able generals like Yue Fei failed to rescue it from the shame of paying annual tribute to these foreigners. From the 1040s, three generations of reformist officials, particularly Wang Anshi, advocated greater state involvement in economic transactions, education, and local militia. After the Sung unexpectedly lost north China to the Jurchen in 1126, court politics fell under the control of political bosses reluctant to support the neo-Confucian mission to recover north China. The 150 years of southern Sung rule, centred in Hangzhou, saw a slowing of economic growth and the loss of military initiative first to the Jurchen state in north China and then its successor, the Mongol Yuan dynasty.

Africa, 1000–1300

During the period 1000–1300 Africa was home to various kingdoms, sultanates and empires: Ghana in West Africa; the Christian kingdoms of Sudanese Nubia; Great Zimbabwe in southern Africa; the successors to Aksum in Ethiopia; and the trade centres of the eastern African coast. These indigenously founded political entities claim a distinguished ancestry stretching back to the period during which both urbanism and complex society were developed in Africa – the late first millennium BC to the early first millennium AD.

Charting the process of state development in Ethiopia, where the kingdom of Aksum (first to seventh centuries) was itself preceded by the enigmatically named D'MT kingdom (fourth to fifth centuries BC), reveals the origins of the polities that were to follow. Aksum was also the first Christian state in Africa, following the conversion of King Ezana by the Syrian Coptic monk Frumentius in 330. Trading through its port of Adulis in oils, ivory, spices and slaves, Aksum was also a major international commercial power. Yet it was not immune to decline and by the late seventh century it had disappeared, perhaps due to a loss of trade. Islam was thereafter a significant power, and from the 10th century it spread inland from the coast as indicated by the development of the sultanate of Shoa, which was in turn absorbed by Ifat in the 1280s.

Although Christianity continued to thrive as a political force in the Ethiopian highlands until the deposition of the last emperor Haile Selassie in the early 1970s, elsewhere Christianity disappeared, as in Sudanese Nubia. Here Muslims gained territory through a variety of processes, both peaceful and warlike. Initially, Christian Nubia was divided into three kingdoms, Alwa, Makuria and Nobadia, though by the mid-seventh century Nobadia had fused with Makuria. With the assumption of power in Egypt by the Mamluks in the mid-13th century the fate of Alwa and Makuria was sealed, and the army of Makuria was defeated at Dongola by the Mamluks in 1276.

In other areas of Africa this was also a time of important historical events. On the eastern African coast numerous Muslim trade centres were flourishing, having developed over the course of the first millennium AD, and their inhabitants having converted to Islam from c. 800. In west Africa the kingdom of Ghana reached its peak in the late 11th century, having similarly developed via indigenous

Great Zimbabwe is made up of many different elements, which served different purposes. The site is dominated by a large stone-built hill complex with the Acropolis or Hill Ruin at the top. The lower slopes of the hill are covered with several hut terraces, with the base of the hill partly surrounded by the inner perimeter wall. A further outer perimeter wall also exists enclosing the hill and several structures in the lower valley. The sacred leader, the divine king, was secluded within this complex, whilst the bulk of the population lived below and beyond the hill.

330	896	c. 1060	1276	1250–1450
King Ezana converted to Christianity	Foundation of the Muslim sultanate of Shoa.	Al-Bakri describes Ghana	Defeat of Christian armies of Makuria at Dongola by Muslim forces.	Heyday of Great Zimbabwe

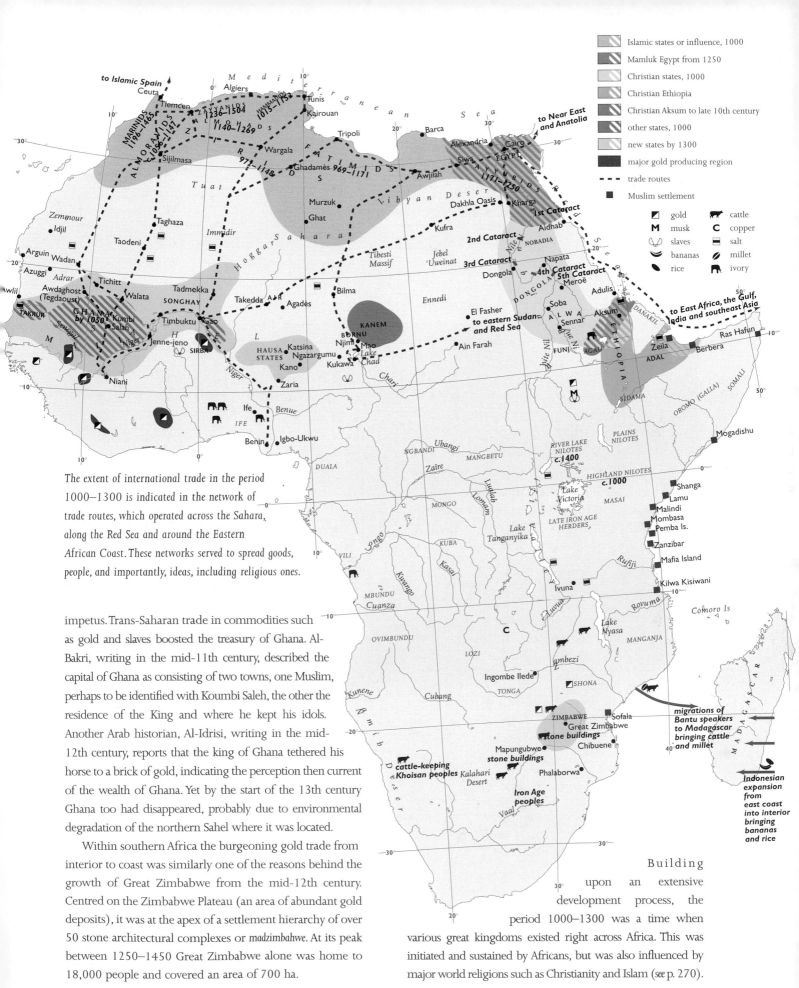

The extent of international trade in the period 1000–1300 is indicated in the network of trade routes, which operated across the Sahara, along the Red Sea and around the Eastern African Coast. These networks served to spread goods, people, and importantly, ideas, including religious ones.

impetus. Trans-Saharan trade in commodities such as gold and slaves boosted the treasury of Ghana. Al-Bakri, writing in the mid-11th century, described the capital of Ghana as consisting of two towns, one Muslim, perhaps to be identified with Koumbi Saleh, the other the residence of the King and where he kept his idols. Another Arab historian, Al-Idrisi, writing in the mid-12th century, reports that the king of Ghana tethered his horse to a brick of gold, indicating the perception then current of the wealth of Ghana. Yet by the start of the 13th century Ghana too had disappeared, probably due to environmental degradation of the northern Sahel where it was located.

Within southern Africa the burgeoning gold trade from interior to coast was similarly one of the reasons behind the growth of Great Zimbabwe from the mid-12th century. Centred on the Zimbabwe Plateau (an area of abundant gold deposits), it was at the apex of a settlement hierarchy of over 50 stone architectural complexes or madzimbahwe. At its peak between 1250–1450 Great Zimbabwe alone was home to 18,000 people and covered an area of 700 ha.

Building upon an extensive development process, the period 1000–1300 was a time when various great kingdoms existed right across Africa. This was initiated and sustained by Africans, but was also influenced by major world religions such as Christianity and Islam (see p. 270).

PART III

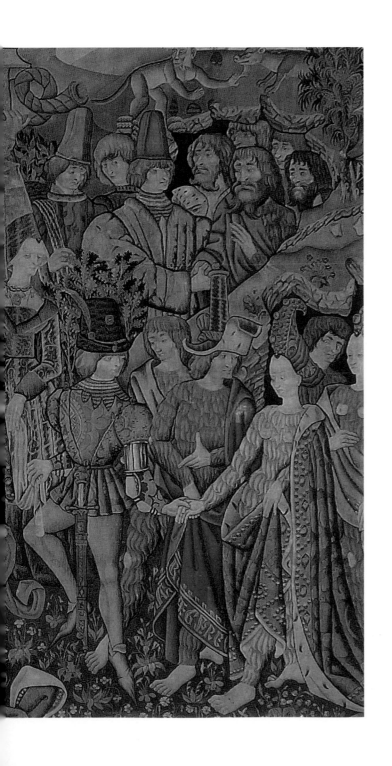

"The savages ball". Tapestry, Nantilly Church, Saumur. The original is 16' 5" x 9' 10". This scene from the late 15th century may either relate to an unknown story or to the famous masked ball in 1393 at the Hôtel Saint-Pol in Paris. King Charles VI of France and other young nobles attended in costumes covered in fleecy wool stuck on with resin. The Duke of Orléans tried to identify one of the revellers by holding a flaming torch close to him and the resin caught fire. The king himself was saved by the Duchess of Berry who quenched the flames with her cloak. But the fact that there are also clearly women covered in fur as well may point to some strange legend.

Scandinavia
And The Baltic

Towards the end of the Viking period the three Scandinavian kingdoms emerged, more or less intact, and were consolidated in the following centuries, although this development was surprisingly slow. Sweden, ostensibly united from Svealand and Götaland by the middle of the 11th century, did not come under the leadership of one king until nearly a century later. After the defeat in battle of Olaf II (1014–30), the Norwegians submitted to the Danes. Denmark was the hub of a huge empire comprising England, Norway and parts of Finland. In 1262 both Iceland and Greenland gave up their independence and submitted to the king of Norway; their most valuable export to the European market, walrus ivory, was being outstripped by elephant ivory, making them more dependant on links with Norway.

Ecclesiastically the Scandinavian countries originally belonged to the archdiocese of Hamburg-Bremen. Dioceses were created in the second half of the 11th century, and in 1104 an archbishopric for Scandinavia was created in Lund. This church province was, however, split up in 1152, when Norway got its own archbishop in Nidaros; an ecclesiastical province for Sweden was created in 1164 and its location in Uppsala, well out of the Danish sphere of influence, helped consolidate the kingdom of Sweden. The papacy promoted these developments to reduce the scope for imperial influence in Scandinavia via Denmark. The province of Nidaros also comprised the bishoprics of Orkney and Man, of Skálholt and Hólar in Iceland and Garðar in Greenland. Kings or members of the royal family normally funded bishoprics and the building of cathedrals, and also sponsored monasteries, but the lay aristocracy of Scandinavia seems to have been involved as well. The chapter in Odense was a Benedictine community brought in from Evesham in England, and later all the major orders established themselves in Scandinavia. The Dominicans had 17 houses in Denmark, the Franciscans, arriving first in 1232, had 29.

In the 12th century the Scandinavian countries participated in the conversion of pagan peoples in the Baltic. Danes evangelized and colonized west Slav peoples such as the Abodrites and the Liutitzians, making the island of Rugen part of the diocese of Roskilde. Daughter houses of Danish monasteries were established in Pomerania. Whether these campaigns were predominantly crusades or sheer imperialism is debatable, but the later campaigns of Valdemar the Victorious (1202–41), who extended his power over many of his north German neighbours, were definitely imperialist; in 1219 parts of Estonia were conquered by the Danes. Finland came under heavy Swedish influence and was a Swedish province till 1809.

In the 13th century a new power emerged in the Baltic: the merchant towns of the Hanse. They gradually monopolized the trade in the Baltic between Russia and western Europe and by virtue of their economic and military power became an important factor in Scandinavian politics. Lübeck based its strength on salt (used to preserve herring at the Skåne market) from Lüneburg, and Norwegian cod, both in demand as Lenten fare.

In 1387, upon the death of her husband, Haakon VI of Denmark, Margaret (daughter of Valdemar IV of Norway) was made lady and principal of Denmark and Norway. She proceeded to defeat the king of Sweden, and with the Union of Kalmar (1397), Denmark, Norway and Sweden accepted Margaret's great-nephew Erik of Pomerania as king of all three countries. In fact, Margaret, herself, ruled on her nephew's behalf until her death in 1412. The Swedish magnates were soon dissatisfied with this situation and rebelled several times. The Nordic union was dealt a final blow with the Massacre of Stockholm in 1520, when Christian II crowned the celebration of his coronation as king of Sweden with the execution of more than 80 Swedish magnates. The election of Gustavus I (1523–60) as king of Sweden brought an end to the Kalmar Union. Norway remained part of the Danish monarchy until 1814 when it was joined in a personal union with Sweden, leaving Iceland and Greenland as well as the Faeroes within the Danish monarchy.

c. 1060	1104	1152	1161	1223	1226
Diocesan organization of Denmark	Lund replaces Hamburg-Bremen as metropolis of all Scandinavia	Nidaros becomes independent archbishopric for Norway and the Atlantic isles	Karl Sverkersson the first king to rule all Sweden	First Dominican house in Scandinavia in Lund	Lübeck receives imperial charter

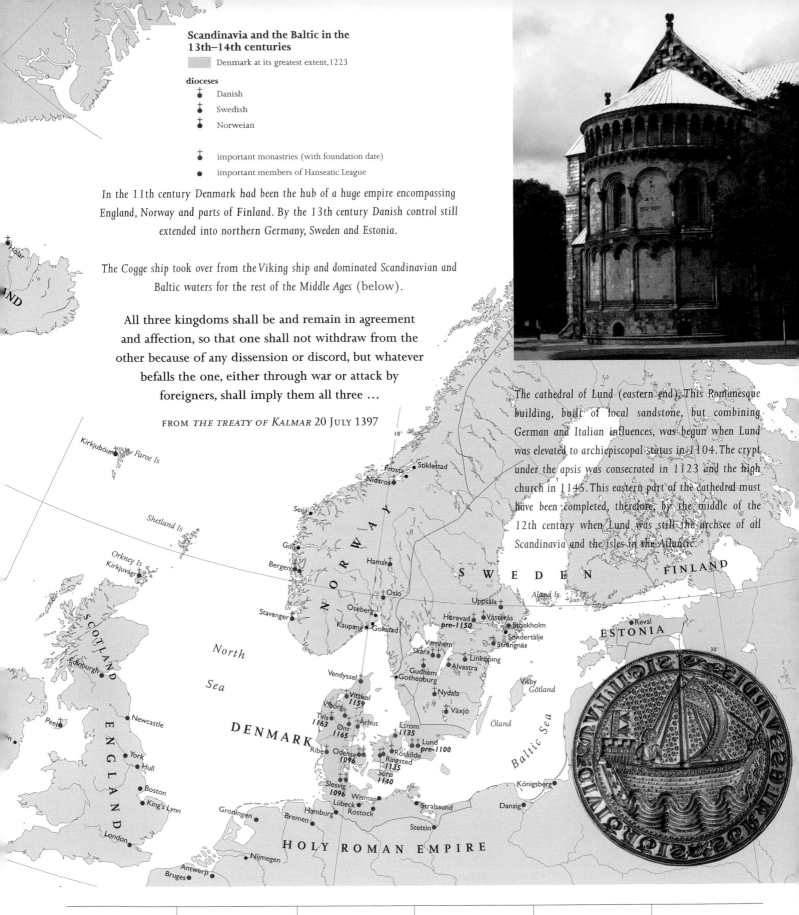

Scandinavia and the Baltic in the 13th–14th centuries

Denmark at its greatest extent, 1223

dioceses
✝ Danish
✝ Swedish
✝ Norweian

✝ important monasteries (with foundation date)
● important members of Hanseatic League

In the 11th century Denmark had been the hub of a huge empire encompassing England, Norway and parts of Finland. By the 13th century Danish control still extended into northern Germany, Sweden and Estonia.

The Cogge ship took over from the Viking ship and dominated Scandinavian and Baltic waters for the rest of the Middle Ages (below).

All three kingdoms shall be and remain in agreement and affection, so that one shall not withdraw from the other because of any dissension or discord, but whatever befalls the one, either through war or attack by foreigners, shall imply them all three …

FROM *THE TREATY OF KALMAR* 20 JULY 1397

The cathedral of Lund (eastern end). This Romanesque building, built of local sandstone, but combining German and Italian influences, was begun when Lund was elevated to archiepiscopal status in 1104. The crypt under the apsis was consecrated in 1123 and the high church in 1145. This eastern part of the cathedral must have been completed, therefore, by the middle of the 12th century when Lund was still the archsee of all Scandinavia and the isles in the Atlantic.

1232	1262–64	1332–40	1350	1397	c. 1450
First Franciscan house in Ribe, and one in Visby the year after	Iceland and Greenland give up their independence and submit to Norway	Interregnum in Denmark	Foundation of the Brigittine Order by St. Birgitta of Vadstena	Denmark, Norway and Sweden form the Kalmar Union and elect Erik of Pomerania king of all three countries	Norse settlements in Greenland become depopulated

The German Empire And Central Europe

The German empire, unlike most other European kingdoms, did not develop as an increasingly centralized monarchy. Instead, it consisted of many political units, the number of which grew over the late medieval period. The driving force behind German development was localism; the emperors themselves mainly furthered the landed power of their own family. Bohemia played an important role, first as the power-base of the Luxemburg dynasty, then as a centre of reform.

The German empire consisted of a multitude of territories, under lay or ecclesiastical lords who, to a large degree, had political autonomy. Seven electors among the German princes elected the "king of the Romans", crowned

Efft der Zug Kaifer Sigismund und feiner

emperor by the pope. The *de facto* power of the electors increased in the 14th century; they imposed conditions and deposed kings. The Golden Bull (1356), approved by the electors at diets in Nuremberg and Mainz, formalized the system of a College of Electors. Electoral principalities were to be indivisible. The subjects of an elector could not appeal to any court outside his territory, and conspiracy against an elector became lèse-majesté. Electors also held rights to mines, and to the minting of coins. The German princes acquired rights over people, strengthening local government.

Imperial institutions included the chancery, the treasury and the Diet (the governing council). Yet the chancery negotiated not only with foreign rulers but also with German princes. Imperial revenues as such hardly existed; even ordinances that were approved often did not go into effect. The Empire had no fixed capital, no archives, and no standing army. Each territorial principality had its own, more effective institutions. The local power of German princes was not due to usurpation; it received royal approval. Emperors did not possess the political capacity to create a centralized empire; the imperial title, however, remained a prestigious one.

Sigismund (1368–1437), son of Charles IV, married the queen of Hungary and was elected king of Hungary in 1387. Plagued by baronial resistance in Hungary, he also failed to stop Ottoman expansion and was defeat at Nicopolis in 1396. As king of the Romans, he convoked the Council of Constance (1414–1418) to solve the papal Schism. He inherited the Bohemian throne on his brother's death in 1419, but could not take power until he granted concessions to the Hussites in 1436. Uniting the crowns of Hungary, Bohemia and the Empire, he attempted to reform the Empire, but failed to create an effective power-base.

1346–1437	1410–37	1415	from 1438	1434	1458–71
Luxemburg dynasty	Sigismund, king of Hungary and Bohemia and German emperor	Jan Hus executed	Habsburg dynasty	Defeat of radical Hussites at Lipany	George of Podebrady king of Bohemia

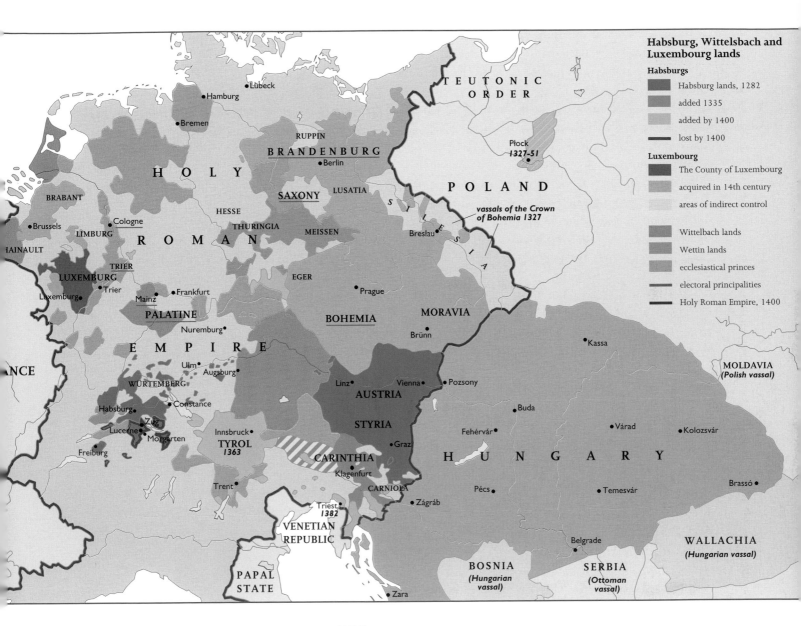

Habsburg, Wittelsbach and Luxembourg lands

Habsburgs
- Habsburg lands, 1282
- added 1335
- added by 1400
- lost by 1400

Luxembourg
- The County of Luxembourg
- acquired in 14th century
- areas of indirect control

- Wittelbach lands
- Wettin lands
- ecclesiastical princes
- electoral principalities
- Holy Roman Empire, 1400

HABSBURG, WITTELSBACH AND LUXEMBOURG LANDS

The map of the later medieval German Empire shows the growth of Wittelsbach, Luxembourg and Habsburg family lands. Yet even these families did not hold unified areas. The electoral principalities were not necessarily more powerful bases than other duchies. Urbanization led to the growth of different types of towns. Imperial towns, at first towns belonging to the king, were by the 15th century autonomous, independent from outside control. The political importance of towns was manifest in the Rhenish and Swabian town leagues. Towns played a major role in the kingdom of Bohemia as well, in the Hussite movement. Rulers of Bohemia extended their power over Hungary, Austria, Silesia, Poland and Brandenburg for shorter or longer periods.

The Habsburg, Wittelsbach, and Luxemburg families vied for the imperial title, and used it to build their dynastic power, extending their lands by marriages and imperial grants to family members. Conflicts with the papacy continued. After Pope John XXII (1316–1334) refused to recognize Ludwig of Bavaria (1314–47), election, rather than papal coronation, was proclaimed to be at the basis of the exercise of full imperial authority. New political forces also appeared on the scene. With the aim of keeping the peace and ensuring safe transit, leagues of towns, emerged from the 13th century, and continued to be important into the 14th (in 1349 under the leadership of Ulm and Augsburg; in 1376 the Swabian league, which incorporated the reformed Rhenish league in 1381; and the urban Swiss cantons in 1385). The princes mainly saw these as political and military rivals and waged war against them. From the second half of the 14th century, the Estates (local legislative assemblies) developed. By the end of the 15th century an imperial supreme court was established on a permanent basis, and projects for imperial reform emerged.

Bohemia, the centrepiece of Charles IV's (1346–78) imperial policies, became a centre of revolt in the 15th century. Jan Hus, a preacher of clerical reform, criticized ecclesiastical wealth and involvement in worldly affairs. At the request of Sigismund, king of the Romans (1411–37), Hus travelled to the Council of Constance. Here he was burnt at the stake, despite having received a safe-conduct from Sigismund. Thereafter, his followers united in the Hussite league. Moderates and radicals created diets. They refused to recognize Sigismund, who led crusades against them in Bohemia, as king. Religious reform and the cause of the Czech-language community were combined. Sigismund was only accepted after he granted moderate demands. Hussitism continued in Bohemia despite papal condemnation, culminating in the reign of George of Podebrady, a Hussite leader.

A priest carrying a monstrance in front of Jan Zizka. Zizka (c. 1370–1424) was a Taborite, and the most important Hussite military leader. He organized the Hussite army and defeated the crusaders who attacked Bohemia from 1420. The infantry, using wagon-fortresses and artillery, revolutionized central European warfare. The chalice on the flag is a symbol of utraquism (communion in both kinds).

After … the electors or their envoys shall have entered the city of Frankfort, they shall … cause a mass to be sung to the Holy Spirit … After such mass has been performed, [they] shall … together … take the oath … And from now on they shall not disperse from the said city of Frankfurt until the majority of them shall have elected a temporal head for the world and for the Christian people; a king of the Romans and prospective emperor. But if they shall fail to do this within thirty days… they shall live on bread and water… unless through them, or the majority of them, a ruler … shall have been elected.

FROM THE GOLDEN BULL OF 1356

Leta panie M cccc ❀ j❀ w kralow stwi czeskem powstali su lide proti wssem
duchowm pro neslechetnost gich Neb si se były przelssti w zdony se myłte Y
hrzeczky nesmierne wydali s panny pame marzelk wzdowy symistwe nestudme
porussima A hrzeczy rustian skem Upigenni kostkurstwim latonstwim la
nim se zanteprzumsti A lide zwuole boze zem to del teprie nemohu ze bili
paslili topili wiezeli z zeme wyhaneli Bich kostely klastery kaply domy
paslili bozili russili Ibrazy kalichy knihy palili sekali a wzmetali tomu
thtegir az aby kniez byli dobrzy rztio stin a nabozm nasledugur prwmeh
swatych Eztenie wssem lidem kazali hrzechy na sobie y na lidu kazyli
lk terzyto to gasu lide swoystem ❀ wozy z bram pozem gezdili a o mate
neodiene❀ lidu mnozstwie w odiengwow porazeli Magir haytmana
bratan zizki slepeho❀ S l przednim knie ne sa monstranky

zizku na so bra
tr wiernu ; :4

Neprzatele se nelekay te na mnozstwie nehledte pa❀ swe❀
wssudy mnegte proti a smym bowuicte a przedneprzately
neutiekay te nesslo Ny sudem pamantugme buoh nass
pan brztkmeine a nakorzistech se nezasstawugme
Her zdeoslemmisa ade Czechtis

The Grand Duchy Of Lithuania

The Grand Duchy of Lithuania grew and prospered through control of the Nemunas, Dvina and Dnieper trade routes as her Baltic rulers expanded through Slavonic western Rus. King Mindaugas's policy of rapprochement with the Catholic merchant world (1251–63) was continued, despite civil war, by his successors, most notably Grand Dukes Vytenis (1295–1315) and Gediminas (1316–41/2), who exploited divisions in Catholic Livonian society as they fought against the Teutonic Order.

In 1323 Gediminas made peace with Livonia (later ratified by the Pope) and invited north German merchants, soldiers and craftsmen to settle in his lands. He rejected baptism in 1324. Lithuania balanced between Orthodoxy (gaining a metropolitan see on occasion) and Catholicism (playing with baptism pledges) but remained pagan. In a daring solution to internal dynastic power disputes Grand Duke Jogaila (1377–1434) married Queen Jadwiga of Poland and ascended the throne of Poland (1386–1434), promising in return the baptism of pagan Lithuanians in the Roman rite, a process begun in 1387. Christian practices were adopted quickly over the 15th century, especially when they blended with old local practices, such as memorial cults of the dead. During the reign of Vytautas (1392–1430), the Grand Duchy with its polyethnic, multireligious community of largely Catholic Lithuanians, Orthodox west Rus'ians, Jews, Karaites, and muslim Tatars, spread from Palanga on the Baltic to the Black Sea coast.

The new religion, in concert with political power developing with nobles outside the ruling family, saw many changes in Lithuanian society. The war with Livonia and Prussia (1283–1422) continued until after the victory at Grunwald (1410) and the Treaty of Torun (1422). Subsequently, the old military frontier became a thriving economic zone containing the cities Kaunas, Polotsk, Smolensk and Vilnius on the one side, and Riga, Königsberg and Gdansk on the other, linking into the Polish routes in Kraków, Poznan and Lublin. Merchants traded largely in grain, linen and forest products (furs, wax, honey, and timber), and imported mainly salt, iron and iron products.

Catholic boyars increased their influence in administration and politics under Jogaila and Vytautas. By the mid-15th century the Council of Lords, whose unofficial origins stretched back to the reign of Gediminas, was ready to administer policy in the ruler's absence. In 1492 a grand-ducal charter promised the ruler would take no major political decision without the

"a region whose population is strong and brave, warlike and fierce. The land is fruitful but boggy in many places and extremely wooded, replete with rivers and waterways, full of beasts and marshes, having few defences other than rivers, forests and wetlands. The realm can barely be conquered in summer; it is best to attack in winter when the waters and rivers are frozen".

BARTHOLOMEW, ENGLISH FRANCISCAN BISHOP OF MAGDEBURG DESCRIBING 'LECTONIA' IN THE 13TH CENTURY

1386	1387	1410	1422	1501
Grand Duke Jogaila of Lithuania ascends throne of Poland	Cathedral in Vilnius founded	Battle of Grünwald	Treaty of Torun	Treaty of Melnik declares Poland and Lithuania indivisible

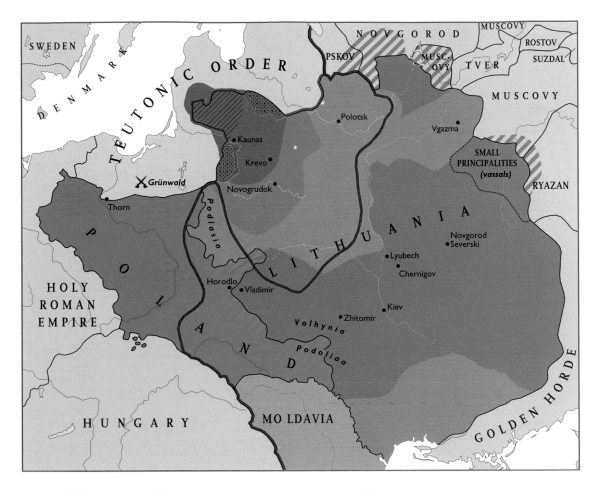

THE GROWTH OF LITHUANIA FROM 1430

Founded in the 13th century by Mindaugas (d. 1263), Lithuania's expansion towards the Baltic was blocked initially by the activity of the Teutonic knights. Instead it grew eastward, particularly in the earlier 14th century which saw the seizure of Polotsk as well as Podlasia. During the joint reign of Algirdas (1345–77) and Kestutis (1345–82) the southern lands of Kievan Rus were overrun: Novgorod-Severski fell in 1363 and Kiev in 1362–3. Further advances in to Russia meant that by 1392 the Lithuanians had reached the Black Sea to the west of the Dnieper. In 1385 a succession crisis in Poland led to a treaty by which the Lithuanian Grand Duke, Jogaila, became King of Poland. In 1410 the united Polish-Lithuanian forces advanced into Prussia and crushed the Teutonic Knights at Grünwald, thereby largely neutralizing the Order's threat to Poland-Lithuania.

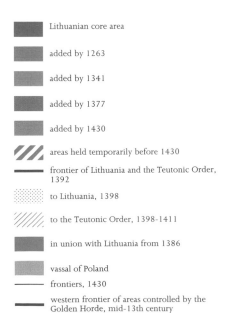

- Lithuanian core area
- added by 1263
- added by 1341
- added by 1377
- added by 1430
- areas held temporarily before 1430
- frontier of Lithuania and the Teutonic Order, 1392
- to Lithuania, 1398
- to the Teutonic Order, 1398-1411
- in union with Lithuania from 1386
- vassal of Poland
- frontiers, 1430
- western frontier of areas controlled by the Golden Horde, mid-13th century

advice of his council. Proto-parliaments, or *seims*, for noblemen to consider important issues are known from the mid-15th century and developed into joint assemblies with the Polish nobility.

Christianity brought schools attached to parish churches and the cathedral in Vilnius (1387), Trakai (1409) and Varnai (1469). Between 1402 and 1440 there were approximately thirty-eight Lithuanian students in Jogaila's refounded University of Krakow. Such studies were important for the growth of a native governing apparatus of church and state in the Grand Duchy.

When Casimir IV of Poland (a descendant of Grand Duke Jogaila) died in June 1492 he was succeeded by his sons John Albert (as king of Poland) and Alexander (as grand duke of Lithuania). Their brother Wladyslaw was king of Bohemia and Hungary. In October 1501 Alexander inherited the kingdom of Poland and sealed the never-ratified treaty of Melnik whereby Poland and Lithuania were acknowledged to be one indivisible body, one race, one nation under the rule of one elected head. Nevertheless, separate state machinery including separate legal systems was to be maintained in both places.

"In the town of Trakai and the surrounding villages there are very many Tatars living in family groups, true sarracens who know nothing of the faith of Jesus Christ and speaking their own language, called Tatar. In the town dwell Germans, Lithuanians, Russians and very many Jews. Each of these peoples has its own language."

The castle at Trakai, south-west of Vilnius. Constructed by Grand Duke Gediminas in the 14th century, Trakai became an important political and administrative centre. It was also famous for its very cosmopolitan community: there were groups of Karaites, Tartars, Lithuanians, Russians, Jews and Poles all living in the town.

Russia, c. 1221–1510

The principalities of Russia in the later middle ages were part of the Mongol Empire, but the princes of Muscovy and Tver and the city republics of Novgorod and Pskov in particular were able to build distinctive political states nevertheless. It was Ivan III of Muscovy who triumphed over them all at the end of the 15th century and he even refused to pay tribute to the Mongols. The Russian Orthodox church continued to flourish in this period providing some measure of cohesion; the seat of the Metropolitan (patriarch of the Muscovites) eventually moved from Kiev to Moscow and major artists were commissioned to adorn the many new churches that were built.

The Mongol invasion of the lands of the Rus' in the middle of the 13th century was far from being a catastrophic change. By 1262 all the lands of the Rus' had been brought under Mongol administrative and fiscal control. The Mongol Kipchak Khanate based at Sarai on the lower Volga tolerated the Christian church

and the local Rus' rulers acted as their agents. Even so, the Mongols had a severe economic impact and there was a major shift in patterns of trade at Kiev's expense. The Riurikid principalities of Kiev, whose political life had been marked by a changing pattern of alliances and family rivalries, had to adjust to the new regime. Certainly the fall of Kiev to the Mongols in 1240 marked a shift in the political focus of the region, though Aleksandr Nevskii, immortalized by Sergei Eisenstein's film, did his best to stem the tide. Kirill, (Metropolitan 1242/3–1281/2) also did much to create an overall sense of cohesion, not least in the promotion of a new compilation of secular and ecclesiastical law. The most decisive blow to Kiev's pre-eminence, however, was Archbishop Maksim of Kiev's move of the Metropolitan seat of the Russian orthodox church from Kiev to Vladimir in 1299/1300 and the archbishop's own move of his residence to Moscow.

In the aftermath of the Mongol invasions a collection of principalities in the Ukraine, Belarus' and Greater Russia, including Tver and the urban republics of Novgorod and Pskov formed, among which Moscow became increasingly pre-eminent. Moscow's rulers were aggressive towards their political rivals and ambitious in the expansion of the territory under their control. They developed a strong administration with a marked military emphasis, and a tight network of bonds of dependency, which became in due course a centralized autocracy with a dominant boyar elite. In 1331 Moscow's ruler was awarded the title of grand prince, and their attacks on other princes, such as those of Tver, had the support of the

Andrei Rublev (1360/70-1430 was a Muscovite pupil of the great artist Theophanes the Greek. His work adorns many buildings, including the frescoes of the Assumption church in Vladimir. The Old Testament trinity depicted here is possibly his most famous icon. in it he depicts the spiritual harmony of the three persons of the trinity, with a distinctively bright and complex use of colour.

1221	1240	1240	1252	1260	1299/1300	1325
Novgorod founded by Iurii Vsevolodovich	Fall of Kiev to the Mongols	Aleksandr Nevskii defeats the Swedes at the Battle of the Neva	Khan Möngke instigates a general census throughout the Mongol empire	Novgorod submits to Mongol rule	Archbishop Maksim of Kiev moves the metropolitan seat to Vladimir	The Metropolitan takes up residence in Moscow

THE GROWTH OF MUSCOVY 1466

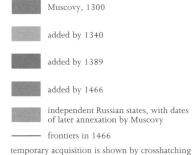

The expansion of Muscovy was a slow process that owed much to the determination of its ruling house. Ivan I (1328–41) gained the right to act as the tax collector for the Tatars and thus benefited from their power. Gradually the Muscovites brought the lands of other Rus rulers under their sway. By 1485 Tver had succumbed, Novgorod fell in 1478 and Pskov in 1510.

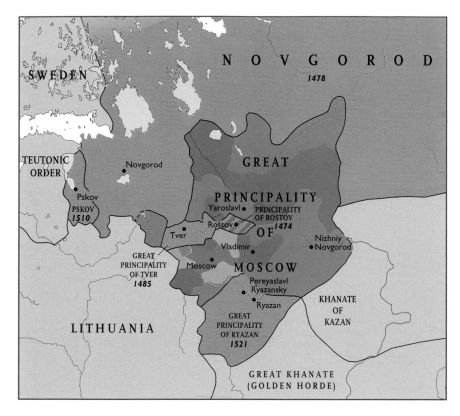

Muscovy, 1300

added by 1340

added by 1389

added by 1466

independent Russian states, with dates of later annexation by Muscovy

—————— frontiers in 1466

temporary acquisition is shown by crosshatching

Mongols. They successfully extended their commercial interests and control of trade routes. A major political player in Rus' and especially Muscovite affairs throughout the later middle ages, moreover was the Grand Duchy of Lithuania (*see* pp. 202–5).

Novgorod, by contrast, founded in 1221 by Iurii Vsevolodovich, had a political system based on an assembly of freemen and was at the height of its success and prosperity in the 14th century. It enjoyed the profits of the Baltic trade handled by the German Hansa merchants resident in the city. In the 15th century its independent position was challenged by the princes of Moscow. The challenge threw Novgorod back on the resources of its earlier glories and an astonishing array of major chronicles documenting the history of the city was produced. These, the cults of the Novgorod victors

of 1109 and the canonization of nine former Novgorod archbishops and several former princes promoted by Archbishop Evfimii (1429–1458), seemed to be an attempt to evoke the past to shore up defences in the present. All was in vain and Novgorod was defeated by the Muscovite prince Ivan III in 1471.

Much of the social and cultural patterns of life of the Rus' continued and developed throughout the period and in the sphere of art, law and history the period was particularly rich. Artists of the calibre of Andrei Rublev adorned many churches in Moscow such as the Kremlin and the monastery of St Sergii, as well as the Dormition cathedral in Vladimir and the church of the Trinity in Zvengorod. The Muscovite princes invoked Rome, Byzantium and Kiev as their historical antecedents and gradually increased their contacts with the rest of Europe.

1331	1339	1458	1471	1484–1504	1493	1502	1510
Moscow's ruler awarded the title of grand prince by the Kipchak khanate	Canonization of Metropolitan Peter (1308–1326)	Rus' church breaks away from Byzantium	Defeat of Novgorod by Muscovite prince Ivan III	Slav translation of the Bible	Ivan III takes title of Sovereign of all Russia	Moscow conquers Crimean khanate	Moscow conquers Pskov

Burgundy And The Swiss Confederation, 1300–1500

The neighbouring territories of Burgundy and the Swiss Confederation experienced a "golden age" in the late 14th and 15th centuries. A comparative examination reveals similarities, such as the small size of their constituent parts, but also two contrasting socio-political systems. As a model of noble culture and monarchical government, Burgundy differed sharply from the Swiss Confederation, a loose alliance of small urban and rural republics. By the early 16th century, however, both states had passed the peaks of their influence on European affairs.

The Swiss Confederation originated as an alliance between the rural areas of Uri, Schwyz and Unterwalden around Lake Lucerne. An early treaty of 1291 cites the upkeep of public peace, mutual assistance and a

Charles the Bold holds a Chapter of the Golden Fleece c. 1470. Founded by Philip III the Good in 1430, the order provided Burgundy's social elite with a platform for the display of noble virtues and an organization to defend their land and religion. Forming the central axis of the illustration, prince and clergyman represent the towering role of the monarchy and the Church in Burgundian society.

From the accession of Philip the Bold to the Duchy of Burgundy in 1363, the Burfundian princes gradually acquired a choherent set of territories between the kingdom of France and the Holy Roman Empire. The lands were divided into two main parts: the Duchy and the Franch-Comté in the South and the prosperous urban landscape of Flanders and Brabant in the North. In addition, Burgundy exercized strong influence over a number of neighbouring areas and bishoprics. Charles the Bold succeeded in linking his possessions in the north and south by conquering the Duchy of Lorraine in 1475, but his abrupt death at the Battle of Nancy brought Burgundy's expansion to an abrupt end.

resentment of foreign jurisdiction as reasons for the union. By 1513, the Confederation had grown to 13 members, including cities such as Bern (1353). In a series of military conflicts – most notably the Battle of Sempach (1386) – the House of Habsburg gradually lost its hold over the region and the Confederates managed to consolidate their lands. There was no single treaty linking all members, but a complex network of bi- and multilateral alliances with a few constitutional principles agreed by the *Tagsatzung*. Apart from full membership, there were two other ways of "belonging" to the Confederation. Several areas sought military or political protection as "associated territories"; others were "dependent lordships" subject to two or more of the Confederates.

The long-term survival of a medieval alliance of rural and urban republics is a truly extraordinary phenomenon in European history. So is the socio-political system. The old feudal hierarchy disintegrated, while peasants overcame the burdens of serfdom. Free burghers and peasants elected ruling councils composed of merchants, artisans and major landholders. The Confederation benefited from an early division of labour. Alpine areas evolved a lucrative cattle and transport trade (over the Gotthard Pass), while the lower lands offered grain, urban services and export products. Early traces of republican pride and a Swiss identity manifested themselves in numerous illustrated chronicles. Internal

1291	1363	1386	1430	1477	1513
First surviving treaty of the Swiss Confederation	Philip II ("the Bold"), from the French royal house of Valois, created Duke of Burgundy	Battle of Sempach effectively ends Austrian claims on Swiss territories	Foundation of the Order of the Golden Fleece	Charles the Bold's death in the Battle of Nancy initiates the disintegration of Burgundy	Swiss Confederation admits the last of its 13 urban and rural member republics

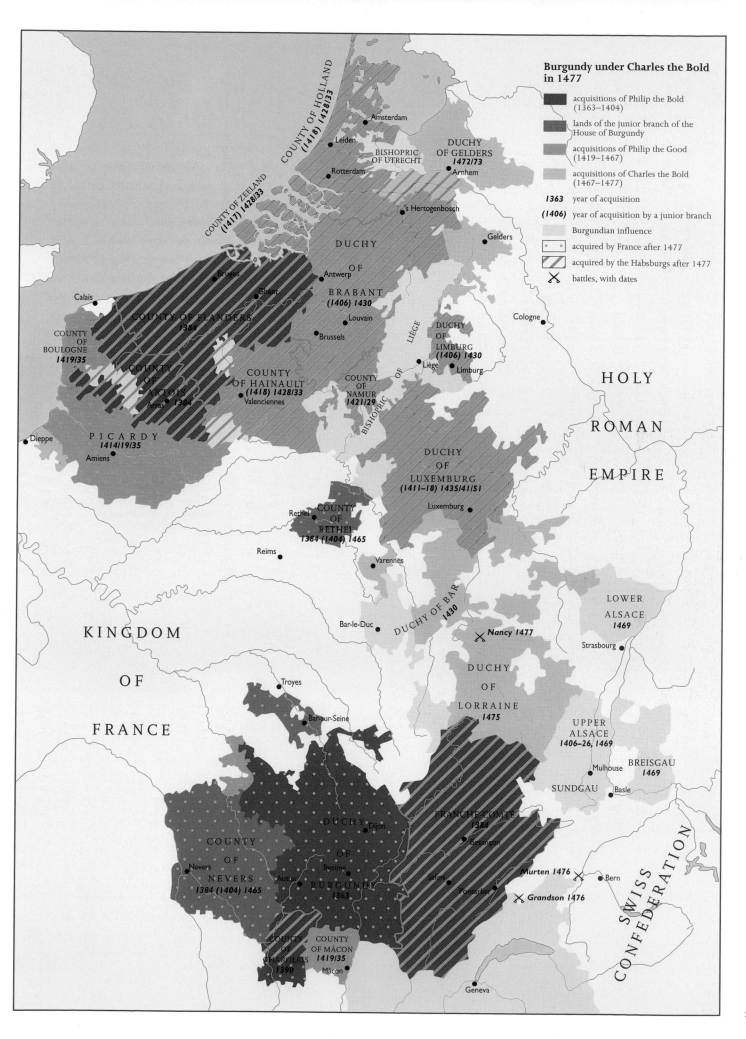

Burgundy under Charles the Bold in 1477

- acquisitions of Philip the Bold (1363–1404)
- lands of the junior branch of the House of Burgundy
- acquisitions of Philip the Good (1419–1467)
- acquisitions of Charles the Bold (1467–1477)
- *1363* year of acquisition
- *(1406)* year of acquisition by a junior branch
- Burgundian influence
- acquired by France after 1477
- acquired by the Habsburgs after 1477
- battles, with dates

COUNTY OF HOLLAND (1418) 1428/33

Amsterdam

Leiden

BISHOPRIC OF UTRECHT

Rotterdam

DUCHY OF GELDERS *1472/73*

Arnhem

COUNTY OF ZEELAND (1417) 1428/33

's Hertogenbosch

Gelders

Cologne

DUCHY OF BRABANT (1406) 1430

Bruges

Calais

Ghent

Antwerp

Louvain

LIÈGE

DUCHY OF LIMBURG (1406) 1430

COUNTY OF FLANDERS *1384*

Brussels

Liège

Limburg

COUNTY OF BOULOGNE *1419/35*

COUNTY OF ARTOIS *1384*

Arras

COUNTY OF HAINAULT (1418) 1428/33

Valenciennes

COUNTY OF NAMUR *1421/29*

BISHOPRIC OF

HOLY

ROMAN

EMPIRE

Dieppe

PICARDY *1414/19/35*

Amiens

DUCHY OF LUXEMBURG (1411–18) 1435/41/51

Luxemburg

Rethel

COUNTY OF RETHEL *1384 (1404) 1465*

Reims

Varennes

DUCHY OF BAR *1430*

LOWER ALSACE *1469*

Bar-le-Duc

Nancy 1477

Strasbourg

KINGDOM

OF

FRANCE

Troyes

Bar-sur-Seine

DUCHY OF LORRAINE *1475*

UPPER ALSACE *1406–26, 1469*

BREISGAU *1469*

Mulhouse

SUNDGAU

Basle

DUCHY OF BURGUNDY *1363*

Dijon

FRANCHE-COMTÉ *1384*

Besançon

COUNTY OF NEVERS *1384 (1404) 1465*

Nevers

Auxerre

Beaune

Salins

Pontarlier

Murten 1476

Bern

Grandson 1476

COUNTY OF CHAROLAIS *1390*

COUNTY OF MÂCON *1419/35*

Mâcon

SWISS

CONFEDERATION

Geneva

political divisions, however, halted further expansion, most notably in the Italian Wars.

Burgundy, in contrast, was much admired for its model court, noble values and innovative government. Compared to other European countries, state administration was remarkably efficient and based on extensive written records. The ruling elite aspired to high standards of chivalry and knightly valour, exemplified by the foundation of the Order of the Golden Fleece (1430).

When the French king John II the Good gave the duchy of Burgundy to his son Philip II the Bold in 1363, the princedom embarked on a remarkable period of expansion. A number of different strategies were employed. In 1384, for instance, Philip inherited Flanders, the Franche-Comté and other lands as a result of his marriage to Margaret of Flanders. Allying himself with England against France in the Hundred Years' War, Philip III the Good (1419–67) reaped great territorial rewards in the Treaty of Arras (1435). In the 1470s, Duke

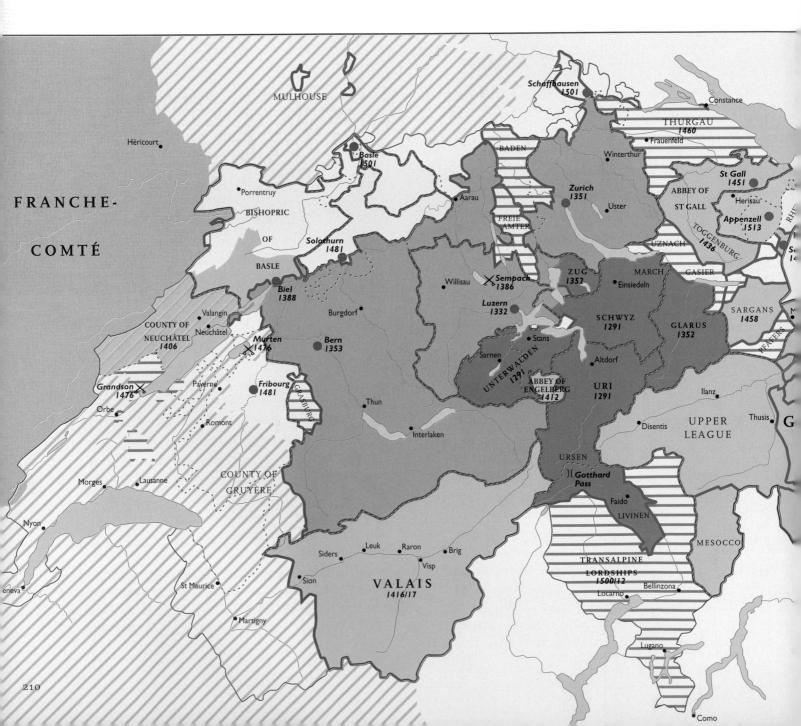

Burghers of the Swiss city of Lucerne swear their annual oath at the close of the Middle Ages. This key communal ceremony served the dual purpose of re-enacting the original civic union and reminding its members of their rights and duties. The men are armed and the religious imagery implies divine backing for the urban constitution.

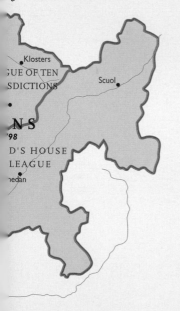

he Swiss Confederation on the eve
f the Burgndian wars, 1474
with major additions to 1513)

— boundaries of confederate territories c.1500

— boundaries of modern Switzerland

- - - current cantonal boundaries

363 year of association with the Confederation

full rural members of the Confederation

full urban members of the Confederation
(with dependent rural areas)

full rural member from 1513 (Appenzell)

full urban members joining 1481–1501
(with dependent rural areas)

dependent lordships (subject to two
or more Confederates)

associated territories

areas under Burgundian influence 1474

battles, with dates

Klosters

GUE OF TEN
SDICTIONS

Scuol

N S

98

D'S HOUSE
LEAGUE

nedan

UCHY OF

MILAN

From its core areas of Uri, Schwyz and Unterwalden, north of the Gotthard Pass and around Lake Lucerne, the Swiss Confederation expanded to eight members by 1352 and 13 by 1513. Together with dependent lordships and associated territories, a substantial part of the Alps obtained a Republican form of government. The formation of "Leagues" was quite common in the later Middle Ages, but the Swiss Confederation is unusual in the combination of rural and urban members and its long-term survival.

Charles the Bold (1467–77) strove to establish a powerful "intermediate" kingdom between France and the German empire, both of which claimed overlordship over parts of the Burgundian lands. The urban wealth of the Netherlands boosted the economic resources for the pursuit of such ambitious plans and he eventually closed the gap between his northern and southern possessions by conquering Lorraine. In the long run, however, he was outmanoeuvred by the French king Louis XI (1461–83) and defeated in successive battles by the Swiss Confederates, for whom the powerful neighbour posed a significant threat. After his death at the Battle of Nancy (1477), Burgundy disintegrated. The Duchy was annexed by France and the lion's share of the remaining lands passed to the Austrian archduke Maximilian of Habsburg, who married Charles' daughter Mary of Burgundy. The seeds of Austrian–French tensions over the Burgundian heritage, a source of decades of conflict, were sown.

The Black Death and its Aftermath: Health and Disease In Europe

The Black Death swept into western Europe in the Autumn of 1347 from the eastern Mediterranean on the ships of Italian merchants. Contemporary chroniclers recorded that these merchants had become infected with plague after being besieged in the port of Kaffa in the Crimea. Dead bodies of plague victims had been catapulted into the city by the army of the Khan of the Golden Horde. Whether or not this story is true is difficult to prove; what we do know is that foreigners and minority groups were often blamed as the cause and carriers of epidemics in late medieval and early modern Europe. From southern Italy the plague spread with remarkable rapidity throughout Europe, reaching London by November 1348. The extraordinary event left much of Europe devastated; up to 50 per cent of the people in some countries, cities, towns and villages died during these few years.

The causative agent of the Black Death is traditionally thought to have been the infected flea of the black rat (*Pulex irritans*). More recently, though, historians have begun to challenge the flea's supremacy. Some historians now suggest that some other epidemic disease may have been the cause of the devastating mortality, though so far no convincing candidate has been identified, while yet others think it was more likely to have been a deadly cocktail of diseases.

Despite the demographic devastation caused by the Black Death, it cannot be studied in isolation. It accentuated an existing population decline over the past half-century, which was caused by other outbreaks of epidemic disease and famines. However, we should remember this was not

The increasing popularity of the image of The Triumph of Death from the second half of the 14th century coincided with the recurrent waves of plague almost every decade. The aim of this horrifying image was to concentrate the viewer's mind on the horrors and inevitability of death, which spared neither popes nor peasants, and to induce the spectator to take proper cognisance of his way of life and repent his sins before it was too late!

MEDIEVAL HOSPITALS: A FEW EXAMPLES

651	c. 1150	1198	1288	1245
Hotel Dieu, Paris founded (300 beds in 14th century)	St. John's Hospital, Brugges founded (75 beds in 14th century)	Hospital of S. Spirito, Rome founded (300 beds)	Hospital of S. Maria Nuova, Florence founded (looking after 220 patients in 1347)	The Great Hospital in Norwich founded (30 beds in 14th century)

This picture shown the façade of Santa Maria Nuova, the largest hospital in late medieval Florence, which by the end of the 15th century came to treat up to 6,500 male and female patients each year. The importance of the hospital in the life of the city is shown by the presence, at this ceremony, of representatives of the leading secular and ecclesiastical authorities in Florence.

just a demographic crisis. It also accentuated pre-existing economic decline. In the preceding decades poverty had increased and severe crises had shaken Europe's financial centres and industrial sectors.

The effects of the Black Death should not be seen in totally negative terms. For many of those who survived standards of living improved and new job opportunities were created in the expanding textile and commercial sectors. Then the vast inheritances unlocked by high mortality led in some places to the commissioning of lavish buildings and works of art to adorn new religious and charitable foundations. From the mid-14th century new themes emerged in religious sensibility, in particular a new emphasis on death and the afterlife. One new image was the *Triumph of Death* in which the skeletal death is seen as the great leveller. Another was representations of plague saints, most important of whom was St Sebastian often shown like a pin-cushion riddled with arrows.

Just as the significance of cultural and socio-economic changes caused by the Black Death cannot be understood

in isolation, so we cannot understand properly society's reactions to plague without examining how it dealt with endemic disease. As cities expanded in western Europe from the early 13th century so they became aware of the necessity to cope with the ravages of recurrent epidemics and to improve the general health of the population. This was achieved in two ways. Town and city councils began to develop sanitary legislation, which required citizens to keep the streets clean of human and animal waste in order to prevent the spread of smell and "corrupt vapours", seen as the cause of disease. Then many towns and cities, in particular in southern Europe, appointed physicians and surgeons to provide free medicine to the poor.

Another contributory factor in improving the general health of the population was the foundation of hospitals, often as a result of private benefactions, to provide free treatment for the poor sick. Though institutions known as "hospitals" had sprung up all over the West during the early Middle Ages — mostly to provide shelter for

SPREAD OF BLACK DEATH

1345–56 Caffa (now Feodosiya), Black Sea port	Late September 1347 Messina, Sicily	May 1348 Siena, Central Italy	May 1348 Barcelona, Spain	August 1348 Paris	November 1348 London

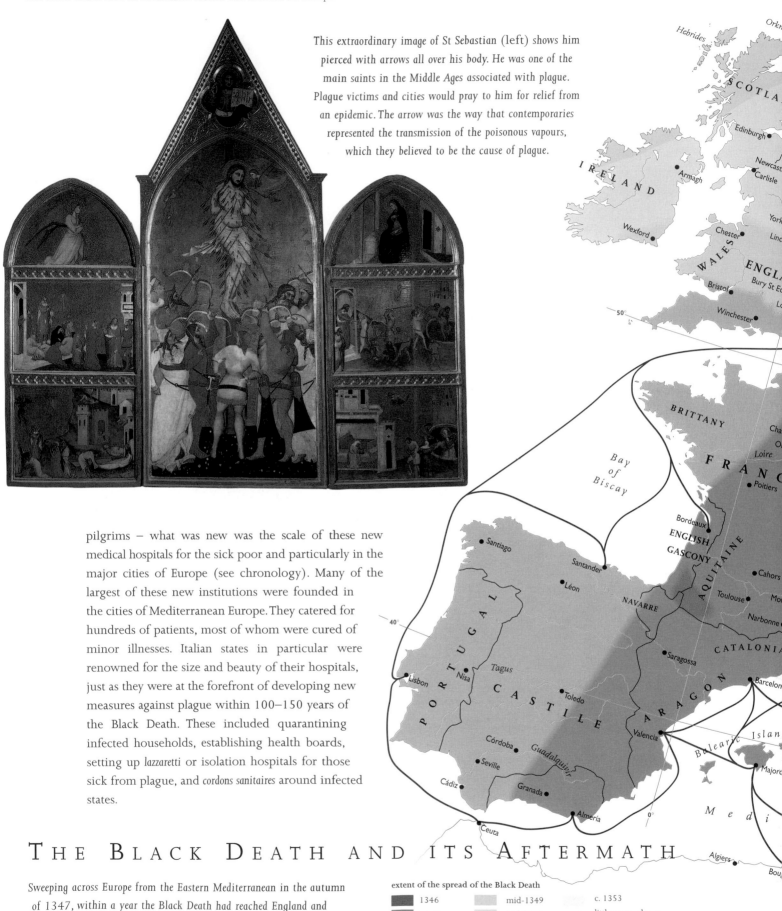

This extraordinary image of St Sebastian (left) shows him pierced with arrows all over his body. He was one of the main saints in the Middle Ages associated with plague. Plague victims and cities would pray to him for relief from an epidemic. The arrow was the way that contemporaries represented the transmission of the poisonous vapours, which they believed to be the cause of plague.

pilgrims – what was new was the scale of these new medical hospitals for the sick poor and particularly in the major cities of Europe (see chronology). Many of the largest of these new institutions were founded in the cities of Mediterranean Europe. They catered for hundreds of patients, most of whom were cured of minor illnesses. Italian states in particular were renowned for the size and beauty of their hospitals, just as they were at the forefront of developing new measures against plague within 100–150 years of the Black Death. These included quarantining infected households, establishing health boards, setting up *lazzaretti* or isolation hospitals for those sick from plague, and *cordons sanitaires* around infected states.

THE BLACK DEATH AND ITS AFTERMATH

Sweeping across Europe from the Eastern Mediterranean in the autumn of 1347, within a year the Black Death had reached England and Portugal, devastating the entire continent and leaving up to 50 per cent of the population dead in its wake.

extent of the spread of the Black Death

1346	mid-1349	c. 1353
1347	end 1349	little or no plague mortality
mid-1348	1350	main sea-trade routes
end 1348	c. 1351	

Shetlands

North
Sea

NORWAY

Bergen

60

Oslo

SWEDEN

Uppsala

Stockholm

DENMARK

Copenhagen

Baltic Sea

Visby

Riga

ORDER

Königsberg

TEUTONIC

Danzig

Lübeck

Hamburg

FRIESLAND

Bremen

HOLLAND

Amsterdam

Bruges

Ghent

Antwerp

Cologne

Ypres

Liège

Aachen

FLANDERS

Rhine

SAXONY

Brunswick

Magdeburg

POMERANIA

BRANDENBURG

SILESIA

Oder

Elbe

POLAND

Warsaw

Rheims

Troyes

BURGUNDY

Trier

Mainz

Frankfurt

FRANCONIA

ROMAN

Strasbourg

Regensburg

LORRAINE

SWABIA

Augsburg

Nuremberg

Basle

Constance

Munich

Passau

BOHEMIA

Prague

Tabor

MORAVIA

BAVARIA

Salzburg

AUSTRIA

Vienna

SWISS
CONFED.

EMPIRE

HOLY

Cracow

LITHUANIA

Kiev

UKRAINE

Dniester

Lausanne

SAVOY

Geneva

Alps

CARINTHIA

Buda

Pest

HUNGARY

Caffa

DAUPHINÉ

Milan

Turin

Trieste

Danube

PROVENCE

Genoa

Venice

Marseilles

Ravenna

REPUBLIC OF VENICE

BOSNIA

Belgrade

WALLACHIA

Bucharest

Black Sea

Pisa

Florence

Corsica

Siena

PAPAL

Ancona

Adriatic

SERBIAN

Danube

BULGARIA

Rome

STATES

PRINCES

Sea

Ragusa

Alghero

KINGDOM

OF

NAPLES

Bari

PRINCIPALITY OF ALBANIA

Adrianople

Constantinople

Sardinia

Naples

Amalfi

Salonica

Cagliari

OTTOMAN TURKS

Mediterranean

Sea

Messina

Palermo

KINGDOM
OF
SICILY

ACHAEA

DUCHY
OF
ATHENS

Athens

Tunis

Rhodes

Crete

Cyprus

10

20

30

France and England, 1300–1500

The age of the Hundred Years War saw the creation of a powerful French monarchy and the restriction of English royal power to little more than England and Wales. While Anglo-French conflict is the most prominent feature of these two centuries, it needs to be understood as part of a general process of territorial definition and political integration, in which kings and princes had frequently to defend their rule before increasingly well-organized and articulate subjects. Not only warfare, but success or failure in domestic politics helped to determine both the shape and the nature of the resulting kingdoms.

In this period, three monarchies with conflicting claims – those of England, France and Scotland – sought to impose their rule upon territories which were gradually gaining their own identities and means of organization. Complex conflicts took place not only between rival kings, but also between kings and communities, even within each kingdom. Where England's monarchy was limited by law and parliament, that of France was comparatively free, parliaments being difficult to organize in such a large country and the king wielding power absolutely wherever his officers and courts were able to prevail. In France, therefore, the traditional story is one of territorial consolidation, as the Capetian monarchy pushed outwards from its base in the Ile de France, reducing vassals whose obedience was purely nominal and increasing the royal *domaine* through a programme of judicial assertion and military intervention. This programme nearly came apart under the Valois amid the strains of the Hundred Years War (1337–1453), in which the interventions of English kings for a time provided the leading princes and outlying provinces of France with opportunities to re-assert their independence. Charles VII's (1422–61) success in expelling the English, and Louis XI's (1461–83) in defeating Burgundy and absorbing most of the remaining major fiefs, laid the foundations for the absolutist France first visible under Francis I (1515–47).

England, meanwhile, achieved early unity, made real by the spread of the common law in the 12th and 13th centuries and the emergence of parliament in the 13th and 14th. This unity too came under threat in the age of the Hundred Years War, and never more so than in the 15th century, with its history of usurpation and dynastic conflict. But the triumph of the English monarchy, when it came with Edward IV (1461–83), Henry VII (1485–1509) and Henry VIII (1509–47), was supposedly marked by the defeat of overmighty subjects and the restoration of authority, not the conquest of territory.

ENGLAND, FRANCE AND IRELAND, 1308–1429

The map shows the core areas of English, French and Scottish royal power, together with the uncertain peripheries and the vagaries of fortune over time. Lines show the progress of English royal power at three points in the period: 1305, when the warrior king Edward I was at the height of his powers, and a single realm uniting the British Isles with parts of France seemed a real possibility; 1360, when Edward III's victories in France had culminated in the great territorial settlement of the Treaty of Brétigny, but the English position in Britain had begun to slip; and 1429, when Henry V's son was temporarily master of northern France and English power in Ireland and Scotland had receded to almost nothing. Dates printed on the map record the final absorption of French lands into the orbit of the Valois crown, while the major battles and risings that marked the triumphs and failures of royal power in each space help to show the broad trends of recession and resurgence.

1328	1340	1360	1380–2	1420	1453
End of Capetian dynasty in France, succession of Philip of Valois; Treaty of Northampton acknowledges the independence of Scotland from England	Edward III of England announces his claim to the French throne and begins 20 years of active warfare in France	Treaty of Brétigny records Edward III's failure to secure the French crown, but concedes huge territories in France. By 1374, these are almost all back in French hands	Wave of popular revolts against high taxation and incompetent government sweeps through southern England and northern France	Treaty of Troyes reflects the Anglo-Burgundian victories secured following Agincourt in 1415 by making Henry V heir to the throne of France	Final expulsion of the English from all of France except Calais, achieved by Charles VII, "le Trèsvictorieux". Later English expeditions achieve little

France

- territory generally under direct royal control or controlled through loyal magnates
- fiefs generally under royal influence
- fiefs often free of royal influence, commonly allied to English
- fiefs of the English crown
- conquered or re-absorbed by French crown
- not part of France in 1300

1491/9 date of establishment of French royal control

- ✗ English victory
- ✗ French victory

THE PALE
1 LOUTH
2 MEATH
3 DUBLIN
4 KILDARE
5 CARLOW

PRINCIPALITY OF WALES
1 CAERNARVONSHIRE
2 MERIONETHSHIRE
3 CARDIGANSHIRE
4 CARMARTHENSHIRE
5 FLINTSHIRE

England, Wales and Scotland

- England
- Lowland Scotland (ceded to England 1334, largely or partly in English hands 1334–41, 1346–early 1350's, 1355–84)
- Scotland
- Marches of Wales
- Principality of Wales
- ✗ English victory
- ✗ Scottish victory

Ireland

- Fully under control of English government throughout the period (The Pale)
- counties, sherriffdoms and liberties still influenced by English crown in 15th century
- lordships slipping out of English influence in period
- under independent Gaelic control in 1297

Extent of English control in France, Scotland and Ireland
— 1305
— 1360
— 1429

English strongholds in France and Britain
- ● English-controlled for most of period
- ● English-controlled for more than 20 years
- ● Briefly English-controlled

- ⊗ siege
- rising

English Strongholds
1 Stirling (1304–14, 1334–42)
2 Edinburgh (1296–1314, 1334–41)
3 Berwick (1296–1318, 1333–55, 1356–1461, 1482 onwards)
4 Roxburgh (1296–1314, 1334–41, 1346–1460)
5 Jedburgh (1296–?1315, 1334–1409)

North Sea

SCOTLAND

Inverness
Aberdeen
Montrose
Arbroath
Perth • Dundee
Stirling Bridge 1297
Bannockburn 1314
Dunfermline
Halidon Hill 1333
Falkirk 1298
Glasgow • Linlithgow
LOTHIAN
Lanark
Homildon Hill 1402
Ayr
Otterburn 1388
Lochmaben
Dumfries
Newcastle
Wigtown
DUMFRIES
Coleraine
Carlisle
Neville's Cross 1346

Sligo
Armagh
ULSTER
Carrickfergus
Downpatrick
Dundalk
Kells
Drogheda
Yorkshire Rebellion 1489
THE PALE
Galway • Athenry
Dublin
York • Beverley
Towton 1461
Kingston upon Hull
Clonmacnoise
Kildare
Limerick
Kilkenny
LIMERICK
New Ross
Beaumaris
Denbigh
Chester
Lincoln
KERRY
TIPPERARY
Caernarvon
Ruthin
Nottingham
Cashel
Owain Glyn Dwr 1400–c.1409
Welshpool
Shrewsbury 1403
Boston
Cork
Waterford
Wexford
Aberystwyth
MARCHES OF WALES
Leicester
Lynn
Norwich
Youghal
PEMBROKE
Bosworth 1485
Coventry
Cambridge
Yarmouth
Carmarthen
Worcester
Northampton
Bury St Edmunds
Peasants' Revolt 1381
Haverfordwest
Abergavenny
Hereford
Tewkesbury 1471
Ipswich
Pembroke
Kidwelly
Monmouth
St Albans 1455
Colchester
Tenby
Caerleon
Gloucester
Barnet 1471
PRINCIPALITY OF WALES
Cardiff
Chepstow
Oxford
London
Bruges 1347
Sluys 1340
Bristol
Westminster
Canterbury
1379
Ghent 1338–45, 1380–5
Salisbury
Jack Cade's Revolt 1450
Dover
(1477)
Revolt of Flanders 1322–8
Winchester
Calais (1347–1558)
Lille
Tournai
Great Rumour 1377
Agincourt 1415
ARTOIS (1477–92)
Exeter
Southampton
Arras
1340
Western Rising 1497
Crécy 1346
Amiens
Plymouth
PONTHIEU (1337–47, 1369)
Cherbourg (1378–93)
Harfleur 1415
1435
Etienne Marcel 1358–60
HARCOURT
1419
Maillotins 1382
Rouen (1419–49)
Cabochiens 1413
Formigny 1450
1380
Jacquerie 1358
Rheims 1359–60
BAR (1481)
Brest (1372–97)
Caen
NORMANDY (1450)
EVREUX
Paris (1420–36)
CHAMPAGNE
Nancy 1477
Rennes
ALENÇON
Verneuil 1424
Montlhéry 1465
Troyes
BAR (1481)
BRITTANY (1491/9)
MAINE (1481)
Le Mans
Patay 1429
ORLEANS
Auray 1364
ANJOU
Orléans 1429
DIJON
COUNTY OF BURGUNDY (1477–93)
Blois
BLOIS
BURGUNDY (1477)
Tours
Loire
NEVERS
Bourges
TOURAINE
BERRY
1356
POITOU
BOURBON
Bay of Biscay
La Marche
Poitiers
LA MARCHE
La Rochelle 1372
Limoges
LIMOUSIN
FOREZ
Lyons
ANGOULÊME
Tuchins 1366–7, 1384
VALENTINOIS
Bordeaux (to 1451/3)
Castillon, 1453
DAUPHINÉ (1349)
PÉRIGORD
ALBRET
AGENAIS
Tuchins 1380–1
VENAISSIN
Bayonne (to 1451)
GASCONY (1453)
Avignon
PROVENCE (1481)
ARMAGNAC
LANGUEDOC
Toulouse
Montpellier
BÉARN
BIGORRE
MIREPOIX
Marseilles
FOIX
ROUSSILLON (1463–93)
COMMINGES (1453)
CERDAGNE (1463–93)
Rhine
Rhone

(Left) This mid-15th-century depiction of the highest English criminal court of the period, King's Bench, reveals something of the bureaucratic and legalistic culture of the kingdom. Despite the court's name, the king himself is represented by a panel of judges, while the pressure of business is all too obvious.

(Right) In this early 16th-century illumination, Louis IX of France sits on the famous royal bed of justice ("lit-de-justice") dispensing judgement in person to the poor and sick. He is aided by justice, to the right, and his mother, representing mercy, to the left. The picture captures the personal goodness and sovereign grace the French expected from their ruler.

Nevertheless, the trajectories of the French and English kingdoms have much in common. France too had a kind of domestic politics, and England – or Britain – a politics of territorial expansion. Like the struggles of Richard II's reign and the Wars of the Roses, the conflicts which tore France apart in the 1340s and 50s and 1410s and 20s were, in part, internal quarrels over the quality and legitimacy of government, in which the Plantagenets were involved as French princes (dukes of Gascony) and as claimants to the French throne (after 1328). The great dukes of Brittany and Burgundy, the King of Navarre and the many other nobles and towns participating in conflicts in France were not only interested in their own independence, but also in the quality of government emanating from Paris: how just was it? how consultative? how oppressive fiscally? Their moves to reform that government – echoed (as also in England) in the numerous popular revolts of the later 14th and 15th centuries – tended to have a severe effect on the scope and depth of its authority, as the fluctuating extent of territory under royal direction demonstrates.

At the same time, in Scotland, Wales, Ireland and large areas of France, English rule was expressed, if at all, through a mixture of scattered garrisons and semi-independent vassals whose obedience had to be continually refreshed by injections of cash and reminders of royal power. Impressive as the military and fiscal resources of the Plantagenets were, they could rarely be made to cover more than one theatre and were not enough to secure final victory anywhere apart from Wales. Periods of brief hegemony in Scotland in the first decade of the 1300s and again in the 1330s gave way to periods of slightly lengthier hegemony in western and northern France (1340s–60s, 1410s–40s), and the odd flash in Ireland (1394–45, 1449–50). Overall, however, the tendency of Plantagenet power was a slow withdrawal to the heartland of England and its annexe in Wales. The highly accountable monarchy of the English kings could not fund the conquest of Ireland, or match the huge resources at the disposal of the Valois as they gained control over the vast domains of France; nor could an authority which became ever more obviously English in style prevail against the burgeoning nationalisms of France and Scotland.

Italy and Sicily in the Middle Ages

There were two Italies in the Middle Ages. In the south a wealthy monarchy, founded by the Norman Roger II in 1130, ruled grain-rich lands inhabited by Greeks, Muslims, Latins and Jews, and became involved in the politics of the entire Mediterranean. In the north and centre a galaxy of cities dependent on trade, finance, the cloth and metal industries developed republican governments in which local élites shared power. Only briefly, under Emperor Frederick II (d. 1250), did a single ruler combine rule over north and south, but Frederick learned that it was easier to tame the south, where a tradition of firm government and regular taxation was well established on Byzantine and Arab foundations. In the north factional strife divided city from city and citizen from citizen. Family feuding as described in *Romeo and Juliet* was a reality, and the rivalry of the "Guelfs", loyal to the papacy and the kings of Naples, with the "Ghibellines", loyal to the German Empire, was characteristic of the 13th and 14th centuries.

The Triumphal Arch of Alfonso the Magnanimous, conqueror of southern Italy, in the Castelnuovo, Naples, a magnificent example of Renaissance sculpture.

The Angevin kingdom of Naples was the largest state in Italy, even after its rulers, members of the French royal house, lost the island of Sicily in 1282 to their inveterate rivals the kings of Aragon. This followed a dramatic rebellion in Palermo (the "Sicilian Vespers"), led by Italian settlers who had displaced the old Greek and Muslim majority. The Angevins accepted papal claims to overlordship over Naples; and, since the popes were unable to raise the large armies needed to sustain the Guelf party in northern Italy, the Angevins acted as their agents. But from the death of Robert the Wise (1343) to the seizure of Naples by Alfonso V of Aragon (1442) the Italian south experienced a collapse of royal control. Noble power mushroomed in both southern Italy and the Aragonese kingdom of Sicily – the island kingdom was divided into four competing "vicariates". The two crowns were the object of bitter competition, and the rulers of Naples invaded Sicily several times.

Up north, the republican style of government underwent a subtle transformation; the cities retained their institutions, but effective power fell into the hands of warlords such as the Visconti and Sforza in Milan and the Este in Ferrara, who vowed to end the factionalism that brought republicanism into disrepute. These *signori* (lords) created miniature monarchies throughout northern Italy, spending heavily on the arts; many of the smaller states, such as Urbino, drew income from the employment of their ruler as a mercenary captain or *condottiere* serving greater powers. By the mid-15th century these were five: the regenerated kingdom of Naples (now ruled by the cultured Aragonese monarch Alfonso and his son Ferrante); the papacy; the flourishing Sforza duchy of Milan; and the two major republics that remained, Venice, with its extensive overseas empire, and Florence, in which the Medici family had achieved dominance (though the pretence of republican liberty was stoutly maintained).

The Peace of Lodi in 1454–55 established a balance of power within Italy, accepting the legitimacy of the new rulers of Milan and Naples. Although this peace was easily

1282	1302	1395	1454	1494
Revolt of the Sicilian Vespers	Peace of Caltabellotta brings an end to the war of the Vespers	Giangaleazzo Visconti appointed duke of Milan by the German emperor	Peace of Lodi	French invasion of Italy

ITALY AND SICILY IN THE 13TH AND 14TH CENTURIES

DUCHY OF MILAN

Milan

Turin

Genoa

Savona

Venetian
Padua
Verona
Terraferma
Venice
Capodistria

Mantua

Ferrara

TUSCAN CITY-STATES

Bologna

Ravenna

Rimini

San Marino

Urbino

Ancona

Venetian Dalmatia

Zara

Spalato

Florence

Pisa

Siena

Perugia
Assisi

PAPAL STATES

Dubrovnik-Ragusa

Piombino

Isola d'Elba
(to Pisa, later Piombino)

L'Aquila

Corsica
(to Pisa, later to Genoa)

Rome

Manfredonia

Bonifacio

Gaeta

KINGDOM OF NAPLES

Trani
Bari

Sassari

Naples

Alghero

Salerno

Amalfi

Potenza

Taranto

KINGDOM OF ARBOREA

Sardinia
(to Aragon, 1323)

Oristano

Otranto

Iglesias
Cagliari

Tyrrhenian Sea

Tropea

Catanzaro

upset by quarrels among the five powers, all were agreed on the need to exclude foreign claimants to power, notably the French. This consensus broke down in 1494 when Charles VIII of France, invited by Ludovico il Moro, regent of Milan, conquered Naples with a massive army. The Italian peninsula became the battleground of French and Spanish armies. These wars further stimulated Italian genius, as can be seen in Machiavelli's writings and in the military architecture of Leonardo da Vinci.

Palermo
Cefalù
Messina
Reggio

Trapani

Ionian Sea

KINGDOM OF SICILY OR TRINACRIA
(to Aragon, 1282, 1392)

Catania

Isola Pantelleria
(to Sicily and Tunis jointly)

MALTA
(to Sicily)

Southern Europe and the Balkans, c. 1300–1500

This period witnessed the decline of Mongol influence in south-eastern Europe, the extension of Ottoman political authority throughout the Balkan peninsula and the final collapse of Byzantine successor states in Epiros and the Morea. It also saw the capture of Constantinople in 1453. Ottoman advances were checked to the north and west by Venice and Hungary, who established or retained control of Dalmatia, Croatia, Slavonia and Transylvania.

The final flourishing and fall of the independent realms of Serbia and Bulgaria, under assaults first from the Mongols established to the north, and subsequently and comprehensively by the Ottoman Turks from Anatolia, occurred in the 14th century. Bulgaria's first major setback, however, was at the hands of the Serbs at the battle of Küstendil, where Tsar Michael Shishman (1323–30) was killed. Stefan Dushan Urosh IV (1331–55) promptly acceded to the Serbian throne, and proceeded to expand his realm to embrace Dalmatian and Albanian lands. He was crowned emperor of the Serbs and "Romans" (meaning former Byzantine subjects) in 1346, and in 1354 issued the Zakoknik law code. In the year before his death the Ottoman Turks first entered the Balkans, and in 1361 Sultan Murad I (1359–89) was able to transfer his

capital from Bursa to Adrianople (Edirne). The Ottoman advance was swift, utilising the great land roads across the Balkans. Their success was facilitated by the gradual fragmentation of political authority in the Balkans, and the ruthless efficiency of their armed forces. Concerted Bulgarian and Serbian resistance ended with the deaths of Stefan Urosh V and Ivan Alexander, both in 1371, although the decisive blows were struck notoriously at the Battle of Kosovo Polje in 1389, and with the fall of Vidin in 1396.

Byzantine power was similarly broken by the Ottomans: Thrace was lost in the 1360s, Salonica in 1387 (and again in 1430 after a brief recovery with Venetian assistance). The independent Byzantine Despotates of Epiros and Morea fell in 1430 and 1460 respectively, the latter having briefly annexed the Frankish principality of Achaea. The denouement of the Ottoman advance was the capture of Constantinople in 1453, following a siege by Sultan Mehmed I "the Conqueror" (1451–81), who promptly made it his new capital, Istanbul.

The Venetians were also able to exploit Byzantine weakness, in competition with Hungary, to expand their interests in Dalmatia. Venice had been recognized as suzerain by important maritime cities in the 13th century, including Zadar (Zara, from 1202) and Dubrovnik (Ragusa, from 1232). In 1322, Trogir and Sibenik recognized Venice, followed in 1327 by Split (Spalato) and in 1329 by Nin. The cities continued to manage their own affairs, and accordingly drew up books of statutes, which included outlines of the relative rights of citizens and the Venetian doge or Hungarian king. The Venetians were able also to expand their trading interests across the peninsula to the Black Sea, in competition with Genoa, and to prevent Ottoman advances into Dalmatia.

The Hungarians, besides competing for control of Dalmatia, sought to extend their authority over the

An illustration of the devsirme, the system whereby Christian children aged seven to 14 were removed from their families to be given a military and Muslim religious training with a view to their entering the Janissary corps.

1330	1355	1361	1389	1396	1453	1454	1456
Battle of Küstendil (Velbuzhd)	Death of Stefan Dusan Uros IV	Ottoman capital established at Adrianople (Edirne)	Battle of Kosovo Polje	Fall of Vidin to Ottomans	Fall of Constantinople to Ottomans	Introduction of millet system	Failed Ottoman siege of Belgrade

Southern Europe and the Balkans, 1359–1574

--- Ottoman empire under Murad I, 1359–89

--- Ottoman empire under Bayezid I, 1389–1402

1398 dates of Ottoman control

▨ Venetian territories, 1510

▨ Ottoman empire under Bayezid II, 1481–1512

--- Ottoman empire under Süleyman I, 1574

--- major land routes

Steady expansion into the Balkans from the time of Murad I brought the Ottomans as far as the Danube by the reign of Bayezid II (1481-1512). By the reign of Süleyman I, Ottoman control had reached well into Hungary.

lands bordering the Danube. While competition for control of Wallachia ended with the Ottomans in the ascendant in 1396, an independent Serbia was re-established in 1428 as a buffer state under George Brankovich. The Serbian capital was moved to Smederevo, while Hungary took control of Belgrade. The final Ottoman push against Serbia came in the later 1450s, following their capture of Constantinople. Smederevo fell in 1459, but Hungary was able to retain control of Belgrade, despite a protracted Ottoman siege in 1456, effectively preventing an Ottoman advance into east-central Europe.

Within the conquered Balkan lands, the Ottomans pursued policies that recognized Christians as legitimate but inferior subjects of the Sultan. The *millet* system, introduced in 1454, divided the population according to faith. Each *millet* regulated its own internal affairs, not only in religion, but also in education and law. However, any dispute involving a Muslim was tried under Muslim law. The inferiority of Christians was reinforced by the *devsirme*, whereby every one to five years Christian boys aged seven to fourteen who showed mental or physical ability were taken from their families and educated in Islam and warfare. They were to enter the ranks of the elite Janissary corps.

The Late Medieval Church

Between 1300 and the onset of the Reformation the Catholic church experienced considerable turmoil. The papacy faced extensive and multi-faceted challenges, including alternative theories of ecclesiastical governance with the rise of the cardinals and the emergence of conciliarism, and the growth of national churches increasingly dominated by secular rulers. Lively movements like the Netherlandish *devotio moderna* developed catholic spirituality, but heresies, notably the English Lollards and Bohemian Hussites, raised significant questions.

Elected in 1305, Pope Clement V established his court at Avignon in 1309, ill-health preventing a move to Rome. So, accidentally and tentatively, began the "Avignon papacy". In 1336 Benedict XII began building the massive papal palace, and in 1348 Clement VI purchased the city from Joanna I of Naples. Despite Petrarch's vehement criticisms, these years were arguably the zenith of the medieval "papal monarchy", under notable popes including John XXII (1316–34), Benedict XII (1334–42) and Urban V (1362–70). The papal curia at Avignon – still technically the *curia Romana* – became the hub of Europe, and the church's administrative machinery was at its most efficient.

Yet, as the pope's titular bishopric, Rome beckoned. Initially, turmoil in Italy made return impossible. (Louis IV of Bavaria held Rome in 1328, appointing an antipope to crown him emperor after declaring John XXII deposed.) Between 1353 and 1366 Cardinal Albornoz pacified the papal states, allowing Urban V to return in 1367 – although he retreated to Avignon, to die, in 1370. Gregory XI followed him to Italy in 1376, dying at Rome in March 1378.

Rival papal elections immediately plunged the church into crisis. Urban VI won Rome; Clement VII returned to Avignon. Europe split as realms took sides – often reflecting previous political rivalries, like those of the Hundred Years War. This "Great Schism" raised fundamental questions about the church's constitution, extensively debated in the next 40 years. In 1409 a Council at Pisa, called to unite both obediences, elected Alexander V and split the church three ways. His rivals held their own assemblies (the "Avignonese" Benedict XIII at Perpignan, the "Roman" Gregory XII at Cividale). Another attempted settlement at Constance (1414–18) produced the election of Martin V in 1417, and effective reunification, although the last antipope resigned only in 1430.

Constance was followed by councils at Pavia and Siena (1423–24) and Basle (1431–49). At Basle, pope and conciliarists clashed head-on. The assembly deposed Pope Eugenius IV (whose own Council at Ferrara-Florence in

Begun by Pope Benedict XII in 1336, and extended by his successors throughout the 14th century, the papal palace at Avignon was at the centre of the 14th-century church (left). It provided effective security for the popes (withstanding blockade by French forces in 1398–1403), and a safe permanent base for the church's central government and its records, away from the chaos of contemporary Italy. This 17th-century print clearly shows how the building dominates the surrounding town. The palace continued to be used by papal legates when the papacy returned to Italy in the 15th century.

COUNCILS, 1300-1500

1311–12	1409	1409	1409	1412
Vienne	Pisa (summoned by cardinals): deposed Benedict XIII and Gregory XII; Alexander V elected.	Perpignan (summoned by Benedict XIII)	Cividale (summoned by Gregory XII)	Rome (summoned by John XXIII)

THE RIVAL OBEDIENCES 1379–1409

Following the death of Gregory XI, the church was split with the rival papal elections of Urban VI and Clement VII in 1379. The map shows the competing obediences up to the Council of Pisa in 1409.

Map labels:

NORWAY · SWEDEN · DENMARK

Bergen · Oslo · Aarhus · Copenhagen · Malmö · Roskilde

NORTH SEA

SCOTLAND — Glasgow · Edinburgh

IRELAND — Dublin · Cork

WALES · ENGLAND — York · Chester · Oxford · London · Bristol

Calais · Cherbourg · Brest

Hamburg · Bremen · Stettin · BRANDENBURG · Berlin · Leipzig · Dresden · Breslau · Oder

HOLLAND *to Rome 1379* · Utrecht · *to Avignon 1394* · BRABANT · Cologne · Brussels · SMALL STATES · Hanover · Frankfurt · Prague · BOHEMIA · MORAVIA · Brünn · Elbe

Rouen · Paris · Rheims · Nantes · Tours · Orléans · Dijon · Metz · Strassburg · Nuremberg · Stuttgart · *to Rome 1384* · BAVARIA · Munich · AUSTRIA · Vienna · STYRIA · Graz

FRANCE · Limoges · Basle · Constance · Salzburg · Innsbruck · TYROL *to Rome 1386* · Berne · Geneva · Vienne · Turin · Milan · Venice · Zágráb

Bordeaux · Bayonne · NAVARRE · BEARN · Toulouse · ANDORRA · ARAGON · Barcelona · Valencia · Cartagena

VENAISSIN · ORANGE · Avignon · Marseille · Nizza · REP. OF GENOA · Genoa · Pavia · Ferrara · VENETIAN REPUBLIC · San Marino · PAPAL · *to Avignon 1404* · Florence · Pisa · Siena · Zara · Spalato · STATE · Rome · REPUBLIC OF RAGUSA

Corunna · Oviedo · Bilbao · PORTUGAL · Oporto · Lisbon · Tagus · Douro · CASTILE · Salamanca · Saragossa · Toledo · Cordova · Seville · Cadiz · Malaga · GRANADA muslim · Granada

1380 Avignon;
1381 Roman
1382 Avignon
1385 Roman

Balearics · Corsica · SARDINIA · Cagliari

MEDITERRANEAN SEA

NAPLES · Naples · Bari · Taranto · Palermo · Messina · SICILY (to Aragon) · Catania

Legend:

- areas of Roman obedience, to 1409
- areas of Avignon obedience, to 1409
- areas transferring from Rome to Avignon, with date
- areas transferring from Avignon to Rome, with date
- areas where obedience was contested or tranfered
- neutral states
- The Papal States in the 14th century
- ✝ Church Councils, 1300–1500

The Church Councils:

Vienne 1311–12; Pisa 1409; Rome 1412;
Constance 1414–18; Pavia-Siena 1423–4
Basle 1431–49; Ferrara-Florence-Rome 1438–45
Pisa-Milan 1511–12; Lateran V 1512–17

1414–18	1423–24	1431–49	1438–45	1511–12	1512–17
Constance, (summoned by John XXIII): deposed Benedict XIII and John XXIII; accepted resignation of Gregory XII. Martin V elected 1417.	Pavia-Siena	Basle (at Lausanne from 1447): deposed Eugenius IV 1439; appointed Felix V, as antipope	Ferrara-Florence-Rome (summoned by Eugenius IV)	Pisa-Milan, (summoned by rebellious cardinals)	Lateran V

Once a soul entered Purgatory after death, eventual access to Heaven was assured. The intensely complex ties between the souls in Purgatory and the living on earth, and the numerous memorial practices intended to speed souls to Heaven, were major components of late medieval catholicism. The living were to reduce the sojourn in Purgatory by appropriate actions. This illustration, from a 15th-century English devotional miscellany, demonstrates theory in practice. A priest celebrates commemorative masses; while a layman offers charitable alms on behalf of the dead. Both hasten the release of souls from Purgatory, and their entry into Heaven.

Christ's Passion was the defining feature of late medieval Christianity. Universally re-enacted by priests in each celebration of the Mass, the Passion was no less significant in lay religion. Mental re-enactments were widely encouraged as meditative exercises (for instance in Nicholas Love's Mirror of the Blessed Life of Jesus Christ); a range of devotional practices developed around specific aspects of the Passion, including the Mass of the Five Wounds, and repetitive prayers linked to the reputed numbers of strokes in Christ's scourging, or the number of drops of blood he shed (calculated in one document at 547,500).

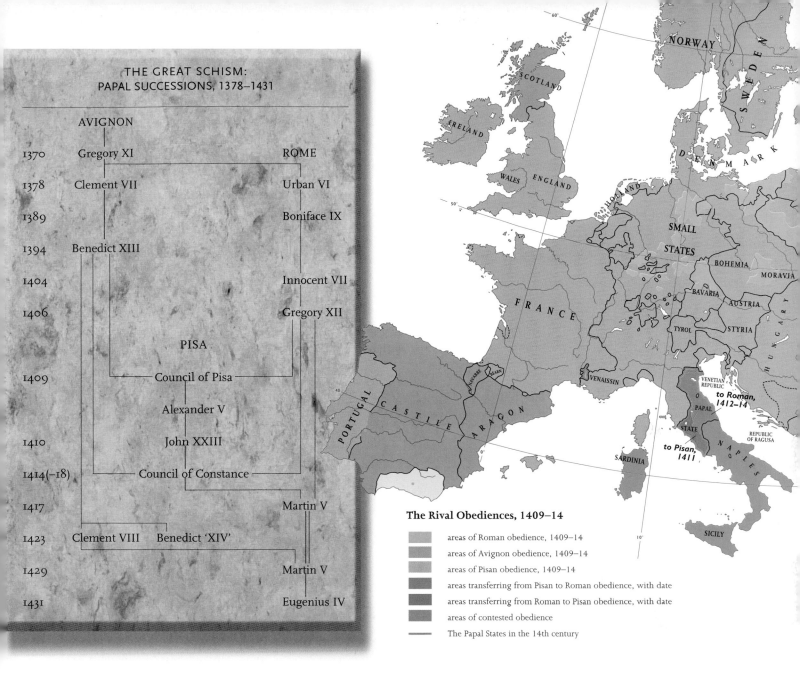

THE GREAT SCHISM: PAPAL SUCCESSIONS, 1378–1431

	AVIGNON	
1370	Gregory XI	ROME
1378	Clement VII	Urban VI
1389		Boniface IX
1394	Benedict XIII	
1404		Innocent VII
1406		Gregory XII
	PISA	
1409	Council of Pisa	
	Alexander V	
1410	John XXIII	
1414(–18)	Council of Constance	
1417		Martin V
1423	Clement VIII Benedict 'XIV'	
1429		Martin V
1431		Eugenius IV

The Rival Obediences, 1409–14

- areas of Roman obedience, 1409–14
- areas of Avignon obedience, 1409–14
- areas of Pisan obedience, 1409–14
- areas transferring from Pisan to Roman obedience, with date
- areas transferring from Roman to Pisan obedience, with date
- areas of contested obedience
- The Papal States in the 14th century

1438–39 nominally re-established union with the Greeks). Basle appointed an antipope, Felix V, but was slowly ground down. Thereafter conciliarism was effectively dead, despite rumblings and another (rebel) Council of Pisa-Milan in 1511–12. A different papacy also emerged, its monarchical powers diminished by the consolidation of national churches overseen by secular rulers, a situation epitomized in French Gallicanism and the Pragmatic Sanction of Bourges (1438). The 15th-century popes became Italian Renaissance princes.

Other aspects of western religion also changed. Crusades continued, but no longer to the Holy Land, and at lower key. This was an age of "flamboyant" religiosity, of shrines, pilgrimages, indulgences, of an almost overpowering concern with Christ's Passion, and with death and Purgatory, all exemplified in the devotional career of Margery Kempe, and the Europe-wide appearance of works

The Council of Pisa, called in 1409 to united church, had the effect of splitting it three ways. The map shows the rival obediences up to the Council of Constance (1414–18), which brought effective reunification.

on the "craft of dying". Spiritual reform movements like the *devotio moderna* sought to channel these energies; heresies sought radical transformation. Wyclif and the English Lollards demanded a more purified, evangelical religion. The Hussites in Bohemia generated a politico-religious revolution; from its tumults emerged a distinct church, grudgingly tolerated within catholicism from 1436.

Nevertheless, the bedrock of catholicism appeared secure. Reform was firmly on the agenda in 1500, as it had been throughout the period; but disruptive Reformation was not being contemplated.

The Almoravids and the Almohads

In the 11th and 12th centuries North Africa and Islamic Spain were overrun by two Berber movements, the Almoravids and the Almohads. Both movements were radical in their reformist aspirations and prized purging of Islam. Under the rule of the Almoravids, parts of North Africa were united and al-Andalus was annexed as a province under the protection of their dynasty. They founded Marrakech as their capital in 1070. The Almohads, under the charismatic spiritual guidance of their Mahdi, Ibn Tumart, created a single state out of North Africa as far west as Ifriqiya and established a firm control over al-Andalus, making Seville the seat of their power in 1170.

The Almoravids, whose name in Arabic, al-Murabitun, means "Those connected to the ribat" (a fortified frontier outpost – in this case that of Wajaj, Son of Zalwi in the Moroccan Sus, the chieftain of the Lamtuna Berbers),

(Right) *The Almoravids were famed throughout the Islamic world for the craftsmanship of their Minbars (wooden pulpits). The Minbar of the Congregational Mosque of Cordoba was especially famous, celebrated for the delicacy of its woodcarving. As a symbol of their overthrow of the Almoravids, the Almohads had this Minbar removed to the Kutubiyya Mosque in Marrakech, the new centre of Islam in the West, before razing the actual Mosque at Cordoba.*

were adherents of the school of law founded in Medina by Malik, Son of Anas (d. 796). This tribe had fallen under the zealous influence of 'Abd Allah Son of Yasin, a jurist who had been trained in Cordoba. The Lamtuna

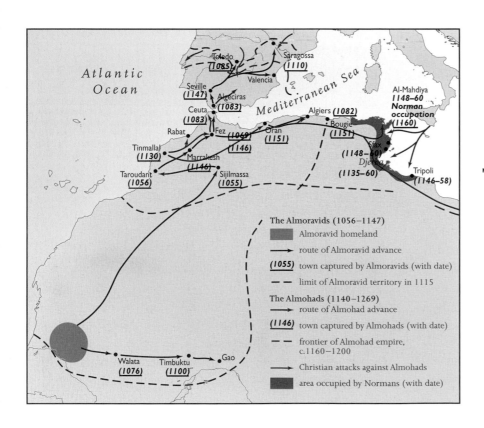

The Almoravids (1056–1147)
- Almoravid homeland
- → route of Almoravid advance
- (1055) town captured by Almoravids (with date)
- – – limit of Almoravid territory in 1115

The Almohads (1140–1269)
- → route of Almohad advance
- (1146) town captured by Almohads (with date)
- – – frontier of Almohad empire, c.1160–1200
- → Christian attacks against Almohads
- area occupied by Normans (with date)

THE ALMORAVIDS AND ALMOHADS c. 1050–c. 1269

The Almoravids and Almohads emerged from the Berber tribes of Morocco in the 11th and 12th centuries to extend their domination over North Africa and Islamic Spain. Under the Almohads, North Africa was united under one rule and Islamic Spain enjoyed a cultural renaissance in the sciences and the arts.

1059	1070	1094	1130	1130–63	1195	1212
Death of 'Abd Allah Son of Yasin, spiritual founder of the Almoravid movement	The Almoravids found Marrakech as their capital	Al-Andalus becomes an Almoravid province	Death of Ibn Tumart, the Mahdi and spiritual leader of the Almohad movement, who had begun his preaching among the Masmuda Berbers in 1123	Caliphate of 'Abd al-Mu'min, with the capture of Marrakech from the Almoravids in 1147 and the conquest of North Africa in 1163	Victory of Almohads over Castile at Alarcos	Defeat of Almohads at Las Navas de Tolosa

Sanhaja Berber group remained the élite clan of the Almoravids during their expansions across North Africa, north into Islamic Spain and south in western Africa, while Malikite jurists exerted a hegemonic influence on the articulation of power and society under them and their successors, the Almohads. With the construction of Marrakech in 1070 as their capital, the Almoravids proceeded to extend their control over North Africa, taking Fez in 1069, Tangiers in 1077, Algiers in 1082 and annexing al-Andalus as an Almoravid province in

1094. In 1086, they had joined forces with the Ta'ifa (factional) Kings of Islamic Spain against Alfonso VI at the battle of Zallaqa, an event chronicled in contemporary poetry, such as the famous ode by Ibn Khafaja (d. 1138/9). In the aftermath of the battle, they set about removing the Ta'ifa Kings from power and exiled them to Morocco in 1094. The Almoravids proved unpopular rulers, incapable of maintaining control over their territories in the face of opposition from Alfonso I of Aragon and Navarre, Muslim unrest in al-Andalus with

ALMORAVID RULERS
(WITH DATES OF ACCESSION)

1. Yusuf Son of Tashufin, 1061
2. 'Ali Son of Yusuf, 1107
3. Tashufin Son of 'Ali, 1143
4. Ibrahim Son of Tashufin, 1145
5. Ishaq Son of 'Ali, 1145

ALMOHAD CALIPHS
(WITH DATES OF ACCESSION)

1. 'Abd al-Mu'min, 1130
2. Abu Ya'qub Yusuf, 1163
3. Ya'qub al-Mansur, 1184
4. Muhammad al-Nasir, 1199
5. Yusuf al-Mustansir, 1213
6. 'Abd al-Wahid, 1224
7. 'Abd Allah al-'Adil, 1224
8. Yahya al-Mu'tasim, 1227
9. Abu l-Ula Idris al-Ma'mun, 1227
10. 'Abd al-Wahid al-Rashid, 1232
11. Abu l-Hasan 'Ali al-Sa'id, 1242
12. Abu Hafs 'Umar al-Murtada, 1248
13. Abu Dabbus al-Wathiq, 1266

The Mosque of Ibn Tumart at Tinmal. It was to this fortress at Tinmal high in the Atlas Mountains of Morocco that Ibn Tumart, the founder of the Almohad movement retreated in 1118 in the face of Almoravid opposition, and it was here that he proclaimed himself Mahdi in 1121.

An Almohad Qur'an in Valencia. The central principle of Almohad belief is the confession of the absolute unicity of Allah. These pages from an Almohad Qur'an dating from the end of the 12th century show the first 23 verses of the Chapter of al-Tur (Mount Sinai). The end of each verse is marked with a gilt circle and the title of the chapter is written in letters of gold.

the re-emergence of the Ta'ifa Kings (in 1144), and the fervent hostility of the Almohads, who defeated them in 1145 and killed the last Almoravid ruler in 1147 in the siege of Marrakech.

The Almohads were born out of a movement created by one man, Ibn Tumart (d. 1130), a preacher and theologian, and native of the Masmuda Berbers from southern Morocco. In 1133 he appointed 'Abd al-Mu'min, the builder of the Almohad empire, as his successor. 'Abd al-Mu'min united the Masmuda, Zanata and Sanhaja Berbers in his onslaught against the Almoravids. The Kutubiyya Mosque was built in Marrakech on the ruins of the Almoravid palace. The remaining Berber states fell in quick succession. In al-Andalus, the Almohads hindered the spread of the Reconquista and under the rule of Abu Ya'qub Yusuf (1163–84) the Almohads sponsored extensively Islamic science and philosophy. Averroes (Ibn Rushd) was personal physician to the Almohads and held the position of Chief Judge of Cordoba.

After the death of Muhammad al-Nasir, the fourth Almohad Caliph, in 1213, the dynasty was effectively at an end. Within 50 years, the Christians had forced the capitulation of Seville (1248) and in 1296 the Marinids emerged as rulers of Morocco. Only the Nasrids of Granada continued as a Muslim kingdom in Spain until its surrender to the forces of Castile in 1492.

The whole Sahara passed under the control of the Almohads, as too did the region beyond it in the country of the Masmuda and the Sus after many wars. Then 'Abd Allah led the people forth to fight the infidel Barghawata ... who fled before him in their mountains and their thickets. The army advanced in pursuit of them. 'Abd Allah Son of Yasin was left alone with a few of his companions. A great host of Barghawata attacked him and he fought them fiercely. He perished as a martyr, Allah's mercy be upon him.

AL-QADI 'IYAD (D. 1149) – DEATH OF 'ABD ALLAH SON OF YASIN, FOUNDER OF THE ALMOHAD MOVEMENT

The Spanish Reconquista (from c.1200)

The term "Spain" was used in the late Middle Ages to mean the Iberian peninsula – even the Portuguese called themselves "Spaniards". It was a geographical and never a political term. The idea of expelling Muslim rule from the entire peninsula developed slowly. A society had been created in which Christians, Muslims and Jews co-existed easily enough and this "living together" (*convivencia*) meant that the three religions accepted one another's existence and even shared events such as marriage celebrations.

By the beginning of the 13th century the war between Christians and Muslims had, however, acquired a holy flavour. The Almohads in the Muslim south expressed a severe, simple form of Islam and had no place for those of different persuasions. Christian knights, benefiting from papal crusade privileges, saw the war in Spain as comparable to that for the recovery of the Holy Land, part of a global struggle between Christendom and Islam. But the most enthusiastic protagonists of that view were often foreign knights who found Spanish co-existence unsettling.

The "heroic age" commenced in 1212 when the combined armies of Castile and Aragon smashed Almohad power at Las Navas de Tolosa. As the Almohad realm fell apart, its provinces were plucked one by one by Christian rulers. The conquest of Majorca by James I of Aragon

(1229) was followed by his seizure of Valencia (1238), while the Castilians and Leonese acquired Cordoba (1236) and Seville (1248). Portugal completed the conquest of the Algarve. Valencia became a major source of income to the kings of Aragon, though rebellions took the shine off their victory; Valencia, like Majorca, was treated as a separate kingdom, and had its own parliaments (*Corts*). After 1250 Muslim Spain mainly consisted of Granada, which became staunchly Muslim within the mainstream Sunni tradition; it received refugees who could not bear to live under Christian rule. The symbol of its Islamic identity was the deliberately archaic palace of the Alhambra, mostly built in the late 14th century for its Nasrid sultans.

Elsewhere the conquerors had to cope with a substantial subject Muslim population (the *mudéjars*), whom they learned to value as artisans and farmers, especially in Valencia where most Muslims were allowed to stay put. Andalusia was settled by Christians and Jews from the north, and the big southern cities lost their Muslim populations; the lack of sufficient settlers was source of worry for the Christian kings in Spain. However, when Granada was the only remaining Muslim state, Aragonese and Portuguese armies, lacking a land frontier with Islam, tended to look across to Africa, where it was assumed the struggle against Islam would continue in order to re-establish Christianity around the entire Mediterranean rim.

The conquest of Granada was delayed by the convenience of receiving occasional tribute payments and of having a land that was available for raids by Christian knights in search of quick profit. It also had good natural defences. Sustained by Genoese and Catalan merchants, Granada was a wealthy kingdom. For much

The siege of Majorca City by the armies of King James I of Aragon, in a fresco from Barcelona.

1212	1229	1238	1248	1492
Almohad armies crushed at Las Navas de Tolosa	Catalan conquest of Majorca	Catalan conquest of Valencia	Castilian conquest of Seville	Granada surrenders to Ferdinand and Isabella

Gijón • • Oviedo Santander • San Sebastián **FRANCE** Montpellier

Santiago
de Compostela • León • **NAVARRE** ROUSSILLON Perpignan

Vigo • Burgos • Pamplona • Jaca • Collioure

Esla Valladolid • Tudela • Huesca • **PRINCIPALITY** Girona
  OF
  Douro Ebro Saragossa **CATALONIA** Lerida

Oporto • Salamanca • **KINGDOM** Barcelona
  CASTILE- Guadalajara • **OF**
Coimbra • **LÉON** Madrid • **ARAGON** Tarragona

Tagus Cuenca • Teruel • Minorca
1231

Cáceres • Toledo • Maò

Mérida • Guadiana Valencia Ciutat de Mallorca
1238 **KINGDOM**
bon Badajoz • **OF VALENCIA** Majorca
1229

Ibiza
1235
Formentera

Alicante •

northern limit of Muslim control, 1180

Crown of Aragon

ANDALUCÍA Guadalquivir Córdoba Cartagena • Crown of Castile
1236

ALGARVE Huelva • **GRANADA** Kingdom of Majorca, 1276–1343

Silves • Seville Granada Almería • *1492* date of Christian reconquest
1248 *1492*

Lagos • Málaga •

El Puerto
de Santa María • Algiers •

Cádiz •

Gibraltar •

Tangier • Ceuta **T L E M C E N**
to Portugal 1415

Oran •
Melilla
MOROCCO **to Castile 1497**
(Marinids) Tlemcen •

THE RECONQUISTA FROM C.1200

*Christian advances in Spain took on new life after the 1220s, with the conquest of Majorca and Valencia by the Aragonese and Catalans and of
Andalusia by the Castilians and Leonese, wars fought under the banner of crusades.*

of the 14th century no serious attempt to overwhelm
Granada was made, and the Nasrid kings of Granada
were adept at playing off Castile, Aragon and Morocco
against one another. Its final suppression in 1492 was a
massive propaganda victory for Ferdinand, king of
Aragon and his wife Isabella, queen of Castile, into

whose territories it was absorbed. The native population
was guaranteed the right to practise Islam, but rebellion
in 1499–1500 led to a change of policy, and Islam was
proscribed throughout Castile in 1502, though it was
permitted in the separate kingdoms of the Crown of
Aragon for another generation.

Civic Assemblies and Representative Institutions

The development of centralized authority in the later Middle Ages was rarely based on despotism, but nearly always on a need for co-operation and consent between rulers and subjects. At the local level, lords of towns and even rural communities often permitted councils and assemblies which could represent their wishes or pass by-laws, and which could quite often be chosen by election. At the state level, representative assemblies, "estates" or parliaments were called into being to enable rulers and subjects to engage in dialogue and bargaining.

Both local and national assemblies reflected contemporary political theory (the just ruler observed legal and moral restraints and consulted at least his leading subjects) and pragmatism (armed forces were usually insufficient to coerce large populations). Local councils generally came first, and were especially important in large towns, where their overlords often allowed considerable delegation of power. From the 11th century "communes" were established in many towns, sworn associations which developed into local governments, but which still depended on external royal or seigneurial authority for their legitimacy. They often gained the right to run their own affairs through elected councils and elected officials, such as consuls and mayors. An extreme case was northern and central Italy, where some 300 towns had become city-states by about 1200. Largely independent of imperial control at the outset, between 1250 and 1400 most except Venice fell under the control of despots (*signorie*) or were

swallowed up into territorial states. Venice and Nuremberg were unusual in being controlled completely by hereditary ("patrician") elites.

Further north, some 100 towns in the Emperor's German lands became "imperial" or "free" cities, and they were more successful in retaining their independence into early modern times. Elsewhere, urban autonomy was limited by the power of monarchs. In England, to take an opposite example to Italy, attempted communes were thwarted by royal power, and although in the 13th century most large towns were allowed elected mayors and councils, kings continued to make clear that they retained ultimate control. The chartered liberties of London were frequently revoked by successive kings down to 1327, and even briefly in 1392. Yet, whether independent or not, most towns of any size had elected councils or assemblies which represented at least the "free" elements of their population, and which might participate in their government. London, for instance, had not only a City council (a mayor and 24 aldermen) but also a Common Council of 150–180 men usually elected from the wards or districts.

They (the Italian city-states) possess neither king nor prince to govern them, but only the judges appointed by themselves.

Benjamin of Tudela, Itinerary, 1159–1173

1188	1215	1258–65	1355–57	1495
First Spanish cortes with apparently representative elements	Magna Carta ("the Great Charter") imposed on King John of England	Revolutionary assemblies in England, including a parliament (1265) with elected county and borough representatives	Revolutionary assemblies in France (estates general)	Regularization of Imperial assembly (Reichstag of Worms)

CIVIC ASSEMBLIES IN EUROPE

Western and Central Europe, with the sites of some of the main assemblies and parliaments
between the 12th and 15th centuries. The political boundaries are those of the 15th century.

Western and Central Europe

Representative assemblies in western and central Europe

●   assemblies with dates of meetings

──   boundary of the Empire

NORWAY
SWEDEN
(Union of Kalmar)
BALTIC SEA
SCOTLAND
IRELAND
ENGLAND
WALES
NORTH SEA
DENMARK
TEUTONIC ORDER
Vistula
Winchester
Westminster *1254 etc*
FLANDERS
BRABANT
Rhine
Cologne 1259
SMALL STATES
Elbe
POLAND
Oder
Paris *1267 etc*
Seine
Mainz 1235
SAXONY
LANDS OF THE BOHEMIAN CROWN
Worms 1269
ATLANTIC OCEAN
Tours *1484*
Loire
Regensburg
Danube
Augsburg *1286*
50°
Bourges *1283*
BURGUNDY
FRANCE
SWISS CONFED.
AUSTRIA
STYRIA
SAVOY
TYROL
Udine *1287*
HUNGARY
Leon *1188*
Benavento *1208*
Carrion *1188*
NAVARRE
BÉARN
Aosta
VENAISSIN
1286 Giaveno
DUCHY OF MILAN
Verona 1244
Venice
Coimbra *1385*
Douro
Medina *1318*
Valladolid *1307, 1542*
Ebro
Avignon
Saluzzo
Turin
Trino *1305*
Cremona
MANTUA
VENETIAN REPUBLIC
Tagus
CASTILE
Madrid *1329, 1562*
Huesca 1162
Murzon *1236*
ANDORRA
Marseille
PROVENCE
FERRARA
MODENA
Ravenna
SAN MARINO
Ancona
OTTOMAN EMPIRE
Toledo *1525, 1559*
Lerida 1301
ARAGON
Barcelona *1192, 1228, 1283*
REP. OF GENOA (to Milan)
LUCCA
1284 Florence
FLORENCE
SIENA
PAPAL STATE
Macerata
Loreto
Recanati
Fermo
HERZEGOVINA
REPUBLIC OF RAGUSA
Seville 1250
Cordova 1510
Valencia 1302
Baleares (Aragon)
Orvieto 1220
Viterbo 1296
NAPLES
Foggia
GRANADA
SARDINIA (to Aragon)
Sassari
Benevento 1443
Naples 1289
Eboli 1290
(Port.)
1421 Cagliari
MEDITERRANEAN SEA
1289 San Martino
Messina 1296
Catania 1397
SICILY (to Aragon)
Syracuse 1398
MARINIDS
ZAYYANIDS
HAFSIDS

Regensburg, on the Danube, became a convenient location for Imperial assemblies. The Alte Reichstag was built for this purpose in the late middle ages, though this Reichsaal (Imperial Hall) was reconstructed in the early modern period: sessions were held here from 1661 to 1806.

On a wider stage, leading inhabitants of provinces and of the developing states came together to act as "communities", especially when they wished to insist on being consulted by their rulers over government, legislation and taxation. In 1215 King John of England had to ratify a long series of concessions demanded by rebels in the name of "the commune of all the land". Even earlier, in 1188, Alfonso IX accepted publicly in a cortes that he shared power with the bishops, nobles and leading townsmen of his kingdom of Leon. That assembly, in the city of Leon, is the first known representative assembly of a whole state, the precursor of many others which came into being in the other Spanish kingdoms as well as in Italy, France, England, the Empire, Bohemia, Poland, Hungary, Sweden, Scotland and elsewhere. By the 14th century they were in existence over most of Europe as channels of communication between rulers and subjects, though not in every case with elective elements representative of the people as a whole.

One special case was the Empire, which was so large and so decentralized after 1250 that it was only during the clash of Louis of Bavaria with the pope in 1338–44 that imperial assemblies were summoned. Otherwise, they were called at the state level (Bavaria and Brandenburg, for example), and only from 1470 onwards was there a representative institution, the Reichstag, for the Empire as a whole. There was no single path of development for European representative assemblies in the Middle Ages, and although many of them declined in the second half of the 15th century, the idea that of them all only the English parliament survived into early modern times is an Anglocentric myth.

Commercial Expansion in the later Middle Ages

Two "Middle Seas" dominated European commercial expansion: the classic Mediterranean, where western Europe met Byzantium and Islam; and the "Mediterranean of the north" consisting of the North Sea and Baltic. The scale of trade on each of these seas differed greatly. By 1200, the Mediterranean was carrying costly pepper, silk and raw cotton. Trade within the north remained more modest: furs and amber from Scandinavia and Russia; wool from England; and rye from the southern Baltic. In both regions the foundations were laid by the carriage of humbler commodities, such as grain, salt, fish, and hides, providing starting capital for the family firms of Venice and Genoa, Bruges and Lübeck. Pisa earned its spurs chasing the Muslims out of Sardinia (1016), where it established extensive agricultural estates; Pisa then extracted the best iron ore in Europe from Elba. Genoa tried to muscle in, leading to a bitter series of wars, which culminated in Genoese victory at Meloria (1284).

By contrast, the northern sea routes were characterised by harmony. Groups of German merchants in Gotland and traders along the Baltic shores began to co-operate in the 12th century, forming a "Hansa" (association) of the significant trading towns of the region, such as Lübeck (recently founded) and Cologne, which conducted much business in England. As German traders penetrated eastwards, they worked alongside crusading

armies, which were colonizing the coasts inhabited by pagan Slavs, Finns and Balts. Much profit came from supplying the Teutonic Knights in their wars, using capacious round ships ("cogs").

A key position in the northern network was occupied by Bruges, which connected the northern network to that of the Mediterranean, via land and river routes across France (passing through the famous Champagne fairs). After 1277, a sea route operated by Genoese and Catalans brought spices and alum (a mineral used in the textile industry) in exchange for English wool and top grade Flemish textiles. Meanwhile, Venice passed its goods across the Alps to German towns such as Nuremberg. However, the Italians and Catalans learned to manufacture their own textiles in the Flemish fashion, and Florence and Barcelona became famous after 1300 for their woollens.

In 1252, Florence introduced the gold florin, marking a return to the minting of gold in western Europe after four and a half centuries. As trade greatly increased it made sense to create high value coins. In addition, banking, in which Florence was also pre-eminent, serviced the needs of long distance trade. Both the wool industry and the Florentine banks peaked before the Black Death (1348).

Within the Mediterranean, bitter rivalries divided Genoese, Venetians and Catalans. All sought a share in the rich spice trade, but Venice, which had penetrated Byzantine markets in the 11th century, achieved predominance in Egypt, while Genoa dominated the trade of Constantinople after 1261, and possessed a major interest in Sicilian wheat. The early crusades had enabled the Italians to bargain for trade privileges in the Latin states, in return for naval aid. The key to success was the weakness of the Byzantine and Islamic fleets. By 1200

(Left) *The soaring columns of the Lonja, or commercial court, Palma de Majorca, designed by Guillem Sagrara in the 15th century.*

1087	1123–24	1281	1394	1494
Pisan and Genoese raid on Mahdia in Tunisia	Venetians receive major trade privileges in the Latin Kingdom of Jerusalem	Genoese and Majorcan ships recorded in London	Francesco Datini, "merchant of Prato", sets up business in Florence	Collapse of Medici Bank

THE COMMERCIAL REVOLUTION
IN THE MIDDLE AGES

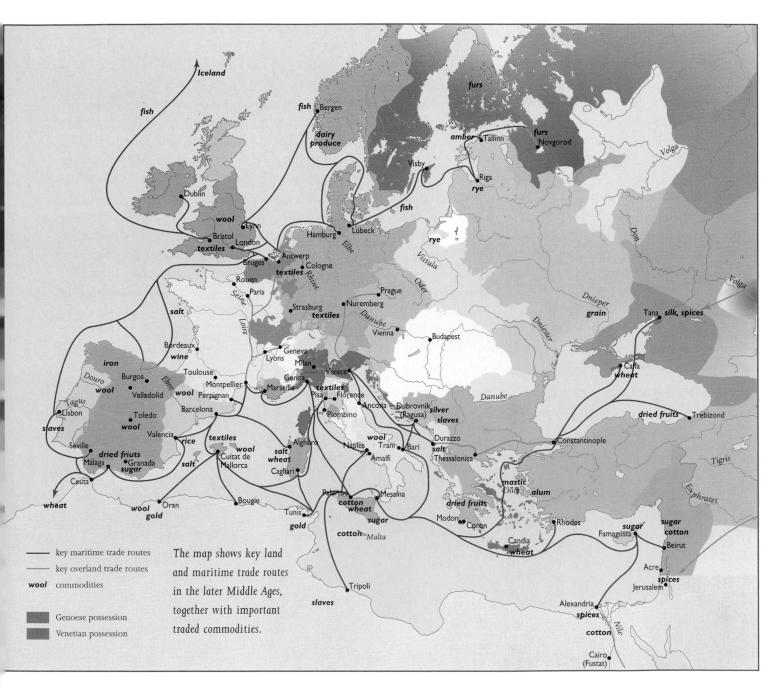

The map shows key land and maritime trade routes in the later Middle Ages, together with important traded commodities.

Legend:
— key maritime trade routes
— key overland trade routes
wool commodities
■ Genoese possession
■ Venetian possession

the Italians had secured mastery over Mediterranean navigation. The acquisition of Crete by Venice in the early 13th century consolidated the Venetian hold on Levantine trade routes.

Although plague greatly reduced the population, demand for luxury goods remained strong, local trade flourished, and in 1500 Venice and Genoa were still dominant. A growing interest in western products such as silk, dried fruits and pottery from Valencia and Granada, alum from the Papal States, and the sugar of Madeira and Sicily, compensated for difficulties in gaining access to products from the Turkish empire, while Genoese businessmen in Seville managed the emerging trade with the New World.

Art and Patronage and the Role of Courts of Rulers

Rulers and their coteries at court were important patrons of art, architecture, literature and music throughout the Middle Ages. "Court" styles often became national styles, and rulers cultural trendsetters. This is particularly noticeable during the 14th and 15th centuries when the value of the arts as a vehicle of personal and dynastic self-promotion was recognized and exploited to the full, not only in Europe, but across the near East and the Orient as well.

On the evidence of the painting, poetry and music it generated, court culture is often characterized as romantic and light-hearted, even frivolous. While this corresponds to an actual courtly ideal, the reality during this competitive and unstable period was substantially different. The artistic culture of any court was bound up with its temporal and spiritual aims. The most pressing of these was maintenance of power and prosperity, and the arts were patronized chiefly to this end. Grand buildings and mausolea constituted physical proof of a dynasty's

wealth, strength and longevity, along with the all-important implication of divine sanction. The size and impeccable planning of Beijing's Forbidden City (*Zijin cheng*), begun by the emperors of the Ming dynasty in 1421, is one expression of this, the sumptuous Ottoman mosques and tombs (*türbes*) constructed at Bursa and (after 1453) Constantinople another. The fortified cities of Delhi undertaken by the Tughluq sultans, the imperial citadel of the Holy Roman Emperors at Prague, and the collegiate and castle buildings initiated and augmented by the Plantagenet and Lancastrian rulers of England all evidence the same desire for local and international recognition. In Europe, ducal courts used art and architecture to compete for recognition alongside royal and imperial ones. The Certosa di Pavia (begun 1396), the Charterhouse of Champmol at Dijon (begun 1383), and the mausoleum complexes of the dukes of Milan and Burgundy, respectively, epitomize the pretensions of their patrons.

Detail from the Apocalypse tapestry cycle woven for Louis I, Duke of Anjou, between 1373 and 1382. This scene represents the appearance of Babylon (personified as a female prostitute) to St John (see Revelation 18:4). The cycle comprises six pieces, each around 23 x 4.5 metres. In 1400, the tapestries were used as the backdrop to the court wedding celebrations of Louis's son, exemplifying the centrality of religious concerns in courtly milieus.

1333	1363	1400	1421	1453
Charles IV, Holy Roman Emperor, begins his great building campaign at Prague	House of Burgundy, collectively one of the greatest patrons of later medieval art, constituted under Philip the Bold	Giovanni di Averardo de' Medici, first of the great Medici art patrons, launches the family on its public career	Forbidden City, Beijng, planned and building commences	Constantinople becomes seat of the Ottoman court, and the Ottoman rebuilding begins

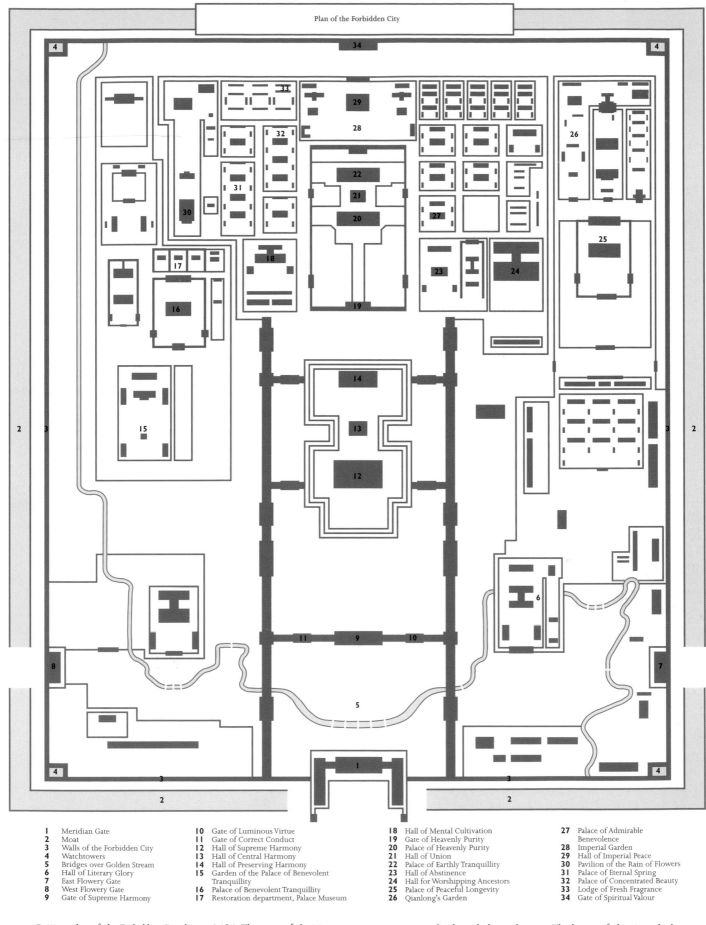

1	Meridian Gate	**10**	Gate of Luminous Virtue	**18** Hall of Mental Cultivation
2	Moat	**11**	Gate of Correct Conduct	**19** Gate of Heavenly Purity
3	Walls of the Forbidden City	**12**	Hall of Supreme Harmony	**20** Palace of Heavenly Purity
4	Watchtowers	**13**	Hall of Central Harmony	**21** Hall of Union
5	Bridges over Golden Stream	**14**	Hall of Preserving Harmony	**22** Palace of Earthly Tranquillity
6	Hall of Literary Glory	**15**	Garden of the Palace of Benevolent	**23** Hall of Abstinence
7	East Flowery Gate		Tranquillity	**24** Hall for Worshipping Ancestors
8	West Flowery Gate	**16**	Palace of Benevolent Tranquillity	**25** Palace of Peaceful Longevity
9	Gate of Supreme Harmony	**17**	Restoration department, Palace Museum	**26** Qianlong's Garden

27	Palace of Admirable Benevolence
28	Imperial Garden
29	Hall of Imperial Peace
30	Pavilion of the Rain of Flowers
31	Palace of Eternal Spring
32	Palace of Concentrated Beauty
33	Lodge of Fresh Fragrance
34	Gate of Spiritual Valour

Beijing, plan of the Forbidden City, begun 1421. The court of the Ming emperors moved from Nanjing to Beijing in 1420/21. The planning and construction of a new imperial city commenced immediately, although it was not completed until the modern era. The layout of the city, which architectural historians consider perfect, symbolizes a harmonic ideal, which the imperial court aspired to but never actually achieved.

241

(Left) *The so-called "Portrait of Tymotheos", painted in 1432 by the Burgundian courtier Jan van Eyck. It supposedly represents either Guillaume Dufay or Gilles Binchois, court musicians to Philip the Good. Above the French inscription "Leal Souvenir" (in faithful memory), "Tum Otheoi" has been added. Tymotheos was Alexander the Great's court musician. Philip the Good adopted the name of the ancient Macedonian ruler for ceremonial purposes, hence the belief that this portrait represents Dufay or Binchois.*

Music and literature commissioned at courts throughout Asia and Europe also contained a mixture of religious and secular content. The secular music of the Ottoman courts and the religious music of Sufi monasticism exerted a strong reciprocal influence upon one another, while the Yuan and Ming dynasty courts encouraged the development of Chinese opera from its roots in traditional drama. So prolific were the dukes of Burgundy in their patronage of music that the period c. 1364–1477 has been dubbed the "Burgundian epoch". The chapel composers they employed, in common with those of other European courts, wrote both liturgical music and secular *chansons* for their patrons. In its variety and opulence, court art and architecture vividly reflects the values, tastes and ambitions of the later medieval world's most powerful patrons.

Court patronage was not purely a matter of political expediency, of course. Aesthetic tastes moulded by education and aristocratic notions of decorum (chivalric values, for example) were influential in determining the nature of court art. Personal commemoration was also important to patrons, and thus much court art has a strong religious element. The illuminated service books made for King Charles V of France (1364–80) and his brother Jean, Duke of Berry (d. 1416), the Apocalypse tapestries woven for Louis I, duke of Anjou, and the paintings commissioned from Jan van Eyck and Rogier van der Weyden by Nicolas Rolin (d. 1462), chancellor to the Duke of Burgundy, exemplify the complex personal concerns of European court patrons north of the Alps. In Italy, members of the Medici court at Florence were patrons of some of the greatest late medieval and early Renaissance artists, including Donatello, Fra Angelico, Fra Filippo Lippi, Ghiberti, Botticcelli and the architect Brunelleschi.

(Left) The choir and sanctuary of King's College chapel, Cambridge. The chapel is one of the most magnificent products of late medieval court patronage in England. Begun in 1446 at the behest of the Lancastrian king Henry VI, it was not completed until 1515, and the sumptuous stained glass and choir stalls postdate 1500. It was originally designed to serve ten priests, six clerks and 16 choristers, and continues to function essentially as its founder intended.

(Above) The mosque complex of Beyazid II (Beyazidiye), Istanbul, built between 1500 and 1505. After the capture of Constantinople by the Ottomans in 1453, successive sultans built a series of great mosques throughout the city. Ottoman courtiers were also enthusiastic patrons of art and architecture, and built many smaller mosques. Each imperial mosque was the centrepiece of a conglomeration of religious and charitable institutions known collectively as a külliye.

Literature and the Vernaculars

The establishment of the European vernaculars as literary languages during the Middle Ages is a cultural development of far-reaching significance, giving rise ultimately to the national and even world literatures we know today. In western Europe, this development is part of a broader sociocultural trend sometimes described as "lay emancipation" from the hegemony of the church and its official language, Latin.

Lay emancipation was actually a two-way process involving interaction between clergy and laity and their respective cultures. Because this interaction occurred in a non-ecclesiastical setting (initially at feudal courts, later also in towns) and did produce a genuinely secular literature articulating the interests of lay elites, the term is nevertheless justified. The birthplace of this literature is early 12th-century France, where an increasingly prosperous aristocracy had the time and money to spend on patronage of the arts, while the employment of clerics to manage the lord's administrative affairs meant the

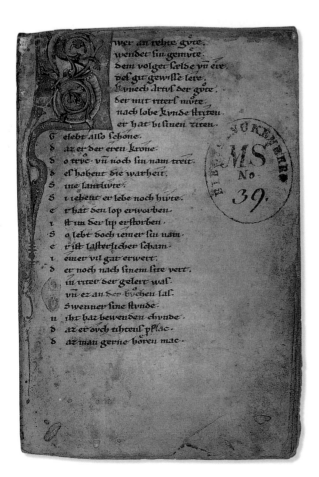

growing presence in seigneurial households of educated men of letters. French court literature (in two languages: French in the north, Occitan in the south) rapidly spread its influence, as its major genres – lyric, epic and romance – were imitated and adapted across western Europe.

With the Angevin accession, England also became an important centre for literature in French; in the German-speaking lands a vernacular literature on the French model emerged c. 1150. In the Iberian peninsula, vernacular literature also got underway in the 12th century, but the influences were from Arabic and Hebrew as well as French. Italian and English were relative latecomers. In Italy, political and dialectal fragmentation assured Latin's continued importance as a *lingua franca*; a continuous vernacular literary tradition began c. 1300. In post-Conquest England the prestige vernacular was French, with English becoming dominant only from c. 1350, as old-established hierarchies disintegrated under the impact of the Black Death.

A special case, because of its isolation from the mainstream, is Iceland. The remarkable literature written down in the 12th and 13th centuries – eddic and skaldic poetry and sagas – was not preoccupied with love and chivalry, but draws on Germanic traditions, as well as Icelandic family history.

The use of the word "literature" in the medieval context is far from self-evident, and must be qualified in several ways. First, "literature" nowadays refers to belles-lettres – works of poetry, drama and prose fiction whose appeal is primarily aesthetic. Many medieval writings easily satisfy this definition (romances, for example, are often avowedly fictional), but the aesthetic aspects frequently coexisted with other – to us – unliterary functions: moral instruction, fostering group identity, ideological legitimation. Some or all of these functions

The Romance of Iwein, adapted from the French by Hartmann von Aue c. 1200. The manuscript format is modest (page size c. 12.4 × 7.5 cm, no illuminations), suggesting a book made for a private individual, perhaps a noblewoman, who might also have read from it to small groups informally. Interestingly, the romance contains a fictional representation of this aurality, in a scene where a young noblewoman reads to her parents in the castle orchard.

(Left) The frontispiece to volume II of the Chroniques de Hainault by Jean Wauquelin shows a kneeling man reading the book to the patron, Philip the Good of Burgundy, and his court; here the setting for recital is formal and hierarchical.

(Below) Frontispiece to Simon de Hesdin's translation of Facta et dicta memorabilia by Valerius Maximus. The picture illustrates the move from Latin to the vernacular: on the left of the pillar, the Roman author reads to the emperor (presumably Tiberius), on the right Simon presents his French translation to Charles V.

may be operative in the same work, or a single manuscript may compile "literary" texts with religious and didactic treatises, suggesting that what mattered to medieval readers was the connections rather than the differences between these genres. Second, "literature" now connotes books that individuals read silently to themselves. Private reading certainly went on in the Middle Ages, but with vernacular literature the typical practice was for written texts to be read aloud by one person to others. Modern scholars call this reception format aurality. Third, the modern concept of the literary "work" – a body of words with an invariant shape determined by the author – does not always obtain with medieval vernaculars. What an author wrote was not necessarily identical with what was recited to a listening public. There is evidence that readers tailored the text to their audience's tastes and reactions. Furthermore, written versions of the "same" work in several manuscripts are rarely identical. This variation, or "mouvance", was the rule rather than the exception. Moreover, because so much of it was motivated, that is, not the outcome of accident or scribal error, it has to be seen as a constitutive feature of a textuality where other people in addition to the author – reciters, scribes, and even the audience – played a part in determining the work's shape.

The Jewish Diaspora in the Middle Ages

The major concentrations of Jewish population in the Middle Ages lay in the Middle East and around the shores of the Mediterranean. Before 400, Babylonia saw the creation of the authoritative text of the Talmudic law code. Babylonia was the seat of religious academies, at Sura and Pumbeditha, and of the Exilarch, a religious and civil leader claiming royal descent. In the late Roman Empire, substantial Jewish communities, including many converts, existed in Spain, Italy, Greece and northern Africa, but the Christianization of the Empire meant that further conversion was forbidden. St Augustine (d. *c.* 605) argued that Jews must be subordinate, but should also be allowed to practise their rites, as a "testimony to the truth" of Christianity. Late Roman legislation against the Jews varied in harshness, and the Visigothic kings of Spain sought to suppress Judaism. Beyond Christendom, the leaders of the Turkic Khazars converted to Judaism in the eighth century.

Under Islam, however, Jews were free to practise their religion subject to a poll tax, and the Exilarch was honoured by the Caliph in Baghdad. Consequently, the Jews of Spain welcomed the Islamic conquest as a liberation and established a flourishing outpost of Babylonian Jewry, open to philosophy and science as well as religious studies. By 950 Cordoba had overtaken Baghdad in scholarship, while Jewish traders from Spain, Sicily and Egypt became active in the spice and silk trade between India and the Mediterranean; their letters still survive. Trade links acted as a stimulus to migration westwards.

The ancient Jewish communities of Italy provided a basis for the expansion of Jewish settlement north of the Alps, dependent on Palestinian rather than Babylonian Judaism. The Rhineland cities had many Jewish inhabitants by 1095, when the First Crusade resulted in violent attacks on the Jews as the enemies of Christ. Until then, their existence had been generally peaceful. Crusades became associated with pogroms, despite the official insistence of the Church that Christians must leave Jews unmolested. Pressure on Jews to convert to Christianity was expressed in acrimonious public debates between theologians of both faiths, such as that in Barcelona in 1263. In northern Europe, the exclusion of Jews from craft guilds meant that Jews were channelled towards moneylending, which

(Left) *Stucco wall decoration from the Transito Synagogue, built c. 1360 for Don Samuel Abulafia, Treasurer to the king of Castile.*

1096	1190	1263	1290	1492
Armies of First Crusade attack Jews in Rhineland	Massacre of Jews in York	Disputation of Barcelona	Expulsion of the Jews from England	Expulsion of the Jews from Spain

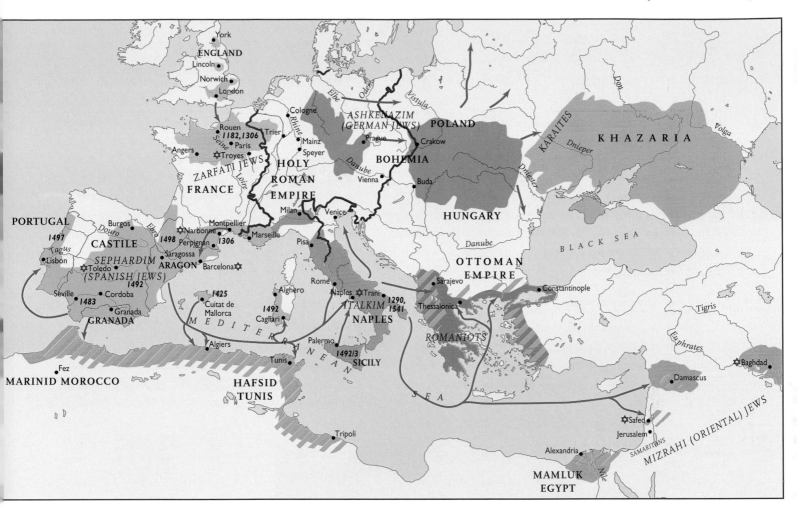

THE JEWISH DIASPORA

Ancient Jewish communities dispersed by expulsions from Germany, Spain and elsewhere penetrated into eastern Europe and the Ottoman Empire, laying the foundations for the two great branches of Judaism, the Sephardim ("Spaniards") and the Ashkenazim ("Germans")

ITALKIM principal Jewish communities

areas of Sephardic settlement post 1492

1492 dates of expulsion

major migrations c.1492

intellectual centres

aroused criticism of their "usury"; in southern Europe they tended to be artisans. But as moneylenders, Jews provided valuable services to kings and peasants alike as far north as York and Lincoln. Credit was essential to economic expansion.

Persecution in Spain by the Almohad Muslims had stimulated migration towards Christian Toledo, which by 1100 had replaced Cordoba as the leading centre of Jewish scholarship, including the mysticism of the kabbalah. At the same time Ashkenazi, or Franco-German, Judaism became famous for its religious devotion; the writings of Rashi, a rabbi from Troyes, revived the study of the Hebrew Bible just as those of the Spaniard Maimonides addressed the role of philosophy in religion.

However, popular hostility to Jews became widespread, and conversion campaigns led by the friars increased tension, notwithstanding many long quiet intervals. Some rulers confined Jews to ghettoes to prevent "contagion'" of Christian society by Jews; others expelled the Jews entirely. Around 1300 there were expulsions from England, France and Naples, while the 1490s saw a new wave of expulsions in Italy, Germany and, most notably, the Iberian peninsula, where the Jewish community had never recovered from pogroms launched in 1391. These pogroms created many forced converts, often practising Judaism in secret, and this phenomenon brought the wrath of the Spanish Inquisition down on the converts. The Spanish Jews or Sephardim headed for Italy and the Ottoman Empire after nearly 1500 years of settlement in Spain.

The Late Byzantine Empire, 1204–1461

After the fall of Constantinople to the Fourth Crusaders in 1204 the Byzantine empire fractured into a variety of competing successor states. In 1261 Constantinople was captured by the "empire" of Nicaea. Byzantium's last two centuries were characterized by fluid military and dynastic relationships with neighbouring states. This was also a period of impressive artistic and architectural production in Constantinople and provincial cities. In the 15th century this complex eastern Mediterranean world was gradually absorbed into the nascent Ottoman empire.

Confusion characterized the immediate aftermath of the Fourth Crusade, as a multitude of interest groups competed to secure Byzantium's richest agricultural land and wealthiest ports. The most significant rivals for the former Byzantine territories were Venice, Bulgaria, the Latin empire of Constantinople, and those three states centred on Nicaea, Trebizond and Epiros which claimed to be the legitimate heirs to Byzantium. For several decades the region was typified by incessant fighting, fragile alliances, and the gradual financial weakening of the Latin empire. By 1239 the Latin emperor Baldwin II (1118–1131) was forced to sell famous relics from Constantinople, including the Crown of Thorns, to Louis IX, King of France, to raise ready cash.

By the mid-13th century the empire of Nicaea had emerged as the most powerful state in the region. Efficient fiscal exploitation of the rich countryside of western Asia Minor enabled the Nicaean emperors to build a palace complex at Nymphaeum, fortify key sites such as Antioch-on-the-Maeander, and rally strong armies. After regaining territory in the Balkans, Emperor

Mosaic portrait of Theodore Metochites located above the entrance to the nave of the Chora Monastery church in Constantinople. Theodore was a scholar, writer, and senior advisor (mesazon and Grand Logothete) to the Emperor Andronicus II. In the early 14th century he rebuilt and decorated the Chora monastery. The church later served as Theodore's mausoleum. It contains the most lavish and sophisticated mosaic and fresco decorations of the Late Byzantine period.

1204	1261	1282	1302	1326	1453
Fall of Constantinople to the Fourth Crusade	Recapture of Constantinople by the "empire" of Nicaea	Outbreak of the Sicilian Vespers prevents Angevin attack	Catalan Company arrives in Constantinople	Ottomans establish capital at Bursa (Prousa) in Asia Minor	Capture of Constantinople by Ottomans

SUCCESSOR STATES TO BYZANTIUM, C. 1218

From that time on with deceit and guile, as is their way, the Byzantines fought battles with the Franks". (From The Chronicle of the Morea). The fall of Constantinople to the Fourth Crusaders in 1204 was followed by the rapid territorial disintegration of Byzantium. A variety of powers competed on the battlefield and in ambuscades for control of the former empire. The Latin empire based in Constantinople enjoyed some initial military success against the Bulgarians, the Seljuk Turks and the three Byzantine successor "empires" (Nicaea, Epirus and Trebizond). But within 30 years the "empire" of Nicaea had emerged as the strongest regional power.

Michael VIII Palaeologus of Nicaea (1259–1282) turned his attention to Constantinople. In 1261, with the assistance of the Genoese, Byzantine forces retook the city. Michael's skilful exploitation of financial, military and diplomatic resources ensured that subsequent threats of a reprisal Crusade from western Europe never came to fruition. In 1282 Byzantine sponsorship of an indigenous rebellion and Aragonese invasion of Sicily diverted the attention of Charles of Anjou, brother of Louis IX, away from an attack on the empire.

Byzantine history in the 14th century is often portrayed as a period of inexorable decline typified by fiscal chaos, civil war, doctrinal discord, bubonic plague,

alienation of crown property to aristocrats, territorial losses to foreign adversaries, abortive attempts at Church Union with Rome, and the inept deployment of mercenaries like the Catalan Company. Yet Byzantine decline should not be overstated. Until the end of the 14th century Byzantium retained the most important cities in the region, Constantinople and Thessalonica, and their fertile hinterlands. The Byzantines also gained new territory in the Peloponnese. Many emperors enjoyed long reigns. Artists flourished in the Byzantine heartlands and neighbouring states regardless of endemic warfare. Humanists, theologians, and historians all found time to write (Emperor John VI Cantacazenus,

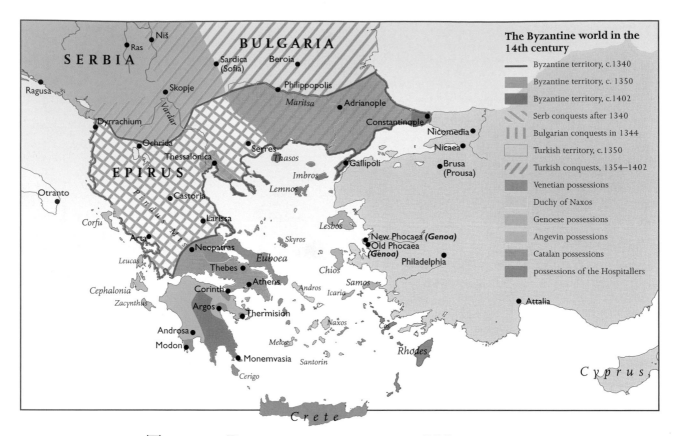

The Byzantine world in the 14th century

- Byzantine territory, c.1340
- Byzantine territory, c. 1350
- Byzantine territory, c.1402
- Serb conquests after 1340
- Bulgarian conquests in 1344
- Turkish territory, c.1350
- Turkish conquests, 1354–1402
- Venetian possessions
- Duchy of Naxos
- Genoese possessions
- Angevin possessions
- Catalan possessions
- possessions of the Hospitallers

THE BYZANTINE WORLD IN THE 14TH CENTURY

"I shall send ... an armed galley to the emperor of Constantinople and shall let him know that I am ready... with as great a company of horse and foot soldiers, all Catalans and Aragonese, as he wishes ... I know he greatly needs these succours, for the Turks have taken land from him...." Roger de Flor, leader of the Catalan Company, outlines his intention to fight for Byzantium in The Chronicle of Muntaner. During the 14th century the Byzantines employed mercenary forces from across the Mediterranean, sometimes to good effect,

for example). Palaces were built in the major Byzantine centres. Byzantium in the 14th century was part of a regional polity that was typified by fluid relationships between different branches of different dynasties rather than by strong imperial, national or ethnic states.

This situation only changed with the penetration of the Ottoman Turks into the Balkans. By the end of the 14th century Byzantine, Serb and Bulgarian princes were all Ottoman clients. Brief respite came in 1402 when the armies of Tamerlane destroyed Ottoman power in Asia Minor. But within 50 years the Ottomans had recovered fully from this setback. Constant pressure by sea and land led to the fall of Constantinople in 1453. By 1461 the last Byzantine outposts in the Peloponnese (Mistra) and Trebizond also succumbed.

"The Crusaders contemplated the grandeur of the city, the palaces, the wealthy monasteries, the rich churches, the astonishing marvels of the town. They were filled with admiration, in particular for St Sophia". Robert of Clari, a participant in the Fourth Crusade, offers a detailed eyewitness description of the urban marvels he encountered in 1204 (From the Conquest of Constantinople). Most detailed descriptions of the topography and monuments of Constantinople during its 1000-year history as capital of the Byzantine empire come from visitors. This drawing of 1535 by Matratici Nasuj shows the medieval city of Constantinople in the first century after its conquest by the Ottomans.

Ottoman Expansion, 1300–1481

From a small principality in north-west Anatolia, the Ottoman state expanded into an empire stretching from Anatolia in the east to Hungary in the west, from the Morea in the south to the Crimea in the north. With its capital at Istanbul, the empire's magnificence, wealth and might inspired both terror and respect among its neighbours. Astute and pragmatic, the early Ottoman rulers exploited their considerable economic potential and developed an efficient centralized state structure.

Under Osman (d. c.1324), Orhan (c.1324–62) and Murad I (1362–89), the small Ottoman principality in north-west Anatolia expanded rapidly westwards against the Byzantines and southwards and eastwards against other small Turkish states. Entering Europe in 1354 with the capture of Gelibolu (Gallipoli), Ottoman forces defeated the Serbian despots of Macedonia, Uglesa and Vlaksin, at the Battle of Çirmen on the Maritsa river in 1371. With the Balkans thus opened before them, they swept into Bulgaria, Macedonia and on into Serbia, defeating and killing the Serbian Prince Lazar at the battle of Kosovo in 1389. Under Bayezid I (1389–1402), the Ottoman advance continued. Crusader forces were defeated at the Battle of Nikopolis (1396) and Bayezid moved into Hungary, taking Vidin. By the end of his reign he controlled lands south of the Danube and Constantinople was under siege. In Anatolia, Ottoman control stretched as far east as Malatya and Sivas.

This considerable military achievement was overturned by the arrival of Timur who defeated the Ottoman army at the battle of Ankara in 1402. The Ottoman state descended into internecine struggle between the sons of Bayezid, from which Mehmed I (1413–21) ultimately emerged to re-establish the position of the empire. Under Murad II (1421–51) the empire expanded. The Ottomans once more gained control of much of Anatolia and advanced again in Europe, defeating John Hunyadi and King Vladislav I of Hungary at the battle of Varna (1444) and finally crushing Hunyadi at the second battle of Kosovo in

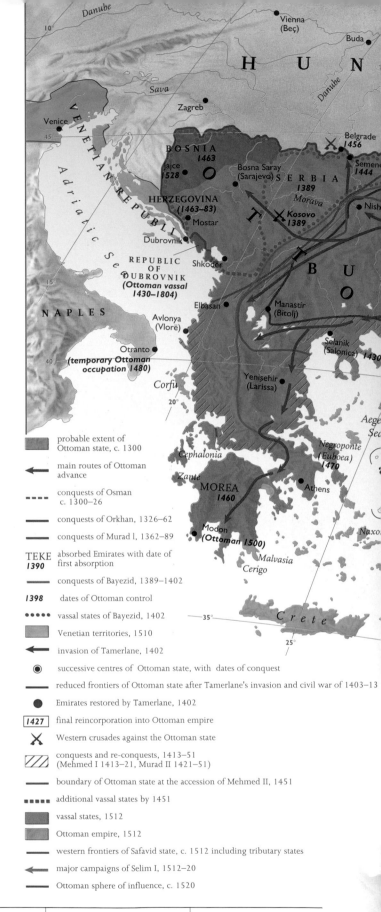

probable extent of Ottoman state, c. 1300

main routes of Ottoman advance

conquests of Osman c. 1300–26

conquests of Orkhan, 1326–62

conquests of Murad l, 1362–89

TEKE 1390 absorbed Emirates with date of first absorption

conquests of Bayezid, 1389–1402

1398 dates of Ottoman control

vassal states of Bayezid, 1402

Venetian territories, 1510

invasion of Tamerlane, 1402

successive centres of Ottoman state, with dates of conquest

reduced frontiers of Ottoman state after Tamerlane's invasion and civil war of 1403–13

Emirates restored by Tamerlane, 1402

1427 final reincorporation into Ottoman empire

X Western crusades against the Ottoman state

conquests and re-conquests, 1413–51 (Mehmed I 1413–21, Murad II 1421–51)

boundary of Ottoman state at the accession of Mehmed II, 1451

additional vassal states by 1451

vassal states, 1512

Ottoman empire, 1512

western frontiers of Safavid state, c. 1512 including tributary states

major campaigns of Selim I, 1512–20

Ottoman sphere of influence, c. 1520

1326	1354	1371	1402	1453
Capture of Bursa	Capture of Gallipoli	Battle of Çirmen	Battle of Ankara	Capture of Constantinople

A R Y

TRANSYLVANIA

BOĞDAN
(MOLDAVIA)
1455

BUJAK

EFLÂK
(WALLACHIA)
1396

Suceava

Yaş (Jassy)

Akkerman
(1484)

Kilia

Danube

Cossack settlements

Dnieper

Dniester

Prut

KHANATE OF THE CRIMEA
(vassal 1475)

Azov

Don

Sea of Azov

Bükres
(Bucharest)

Yergögü
(Giurgiu)

Silistre

Nicopolis
1396

Turnovo

A R I A

Edirne
(Adrianople)
1361

Gelibolu
(Gallipoli)
1354

Dardanelles

Bakhchesaray
(Bahçesaray)

Kefe (Caffa)

Kerç

B l a c k   S e a

ÇERKES
(CIRCASSIA)
1461

Caucasus Mountains

Constantinople
1453

Kastamonu

Sinop

Samsun

Trabzon
(Trebizond)
EMPIRE OF TREBIZON

Tiflis

Bursa
1326

KARASI
1345

Söğüt
1265

Eskişehir
1289

Ankara
1402

A N A T O L I A

ÇANDAR
(KASTAMONU)
1393 1461

Amasya

SARUHAN
1390 1405

GERMIYAN
1380 1428

HAMID
1381–90

MENTEŞE
1390 1426

TEKE
1391 1427

Konya

KARAMAN
1390 1468

E M P I R E

SIVAS
1398

Sivas

Otluk-Beli
1473

KARAKOYUNLU

AKKOYUNLU

Erzurum

Lake Van

Çaldiran
1514

Tabriz
1514

Lake
Urmia

Rhodes

DHU'L-QADR
1398 1515

Taurus   Mts

Adana

Marj Dabiq
1516

Aleppo
1516

Diyarbakir

Raqqa

Mosul

S A F A V I D   E M P I R E
(from 1501)

Cyprus
(Venetian 1489,
Ottoman tributary 1517)

Tripoli

Beirut

Damascus
1516

M A M L U K   E M P I R E

Tigris

Euphrates

40°

45

Alexandria

Jerusalem

Al-Raydaniyya
1517

Cairo
1517

Suez

1517

THE OTTOMAN EMPIRE
c. 1301–1520

From around 1300 the Ottoman state expanded rapidly, stretching by the end of the century across much of
Anatolia and into the Balkans. After Timur's invasion in 1402, the state descended into a decade of civil war,
but by the time of the capture of Constantinople in 1453, the Ottomans were definitively re-established in
Anatolia and southeast Europe.

Three Ottoman coins from the collection in the Fitzwilliam Museum Cambridge span the reigns of the rulers under whom most of Anatolia and the Balkans came under Ottoman sway: Murad I (above left); Murad II (above centre); and Bayezid II (top right).

1448, although having less success against George Kastriote (Scanderbeg) in Albania. Ottoman control extended throughout the Peloponnese.

Two years after the succession of Mehmed II (1451–81), the Byzantine capital Constantinople fell to the Ottomans. By the time of his death, Serbia, Bosnia, and the Peloponnese were all firmly part of the empire and, by the end of the war with Venice (1463–79), the Ottomans also held Euboea (Negroponte). In Anatolia the Ottomans took Trabzon (Trebizond) (1461), defeated the Turcoman leader Uzun Hasan (1473) and conquered their long-time rival Karaman (1474). To the north, the Genoese trading centre of Caffa in the Crimea fell to the Ottomans in 1475 and the whole of the Crimea became an Ottoman vassal state. In 1480 Ottoman forces even occupied Otranto in southern Italy.

Militarily successful, the Ottomans were also aware of their economic power, and cultivated commercial contacts. Indeed, their initial advance was to some extent influenced by their desire to control lucrative trade routes. From an early date, they entered into treaty relations with European states, in particular the City States of Venice and Genoa, concluding a treaty with Genoa in the winter of 1351–52, and a further treaty in 1387. Major export items from Ottoman territories included slaves, grain, alum, cotton and wool, as well as silks and spices traded into Ottoman lands from further east, while they imported metals, wine and cloth.

Diplomatically astute, the Ottomans were soon involved in playing one political faction off against another in Byzantium until they came to dominate internal Byzantine politics. Many foreign diplomatic missions were sent to the Ottoman capital, first at Bursa, then Edirne, and finally Istanbul, and foreigners, particularly Italian merchants, resided at the Ottoman court. Gradually the Ottoman state evolved a highly efficient administrative structure to control its extensive territory and ensure the effective collection of revenue. By 1481 the Ottoman state had become a centralized empire of vast territory, wealth and military might, and was a major economic power.

(Right) A portrait of Bayezid I (1389–1402), Bibliothèque Nationale, Paris. Known as Yildirim ("Thunderbolt"), Bayezid came to the throne in 1389 and attempted to establish a strong centralized state. He conquered large areas of the Balkans and Anatolia; blockaded Constantinople (1391–8); invaded Hungary (1395) and at Nicopolis in 1396 crushed crusading forces sent to repel him. He was defeated by Timur at Ankara in 1402 and died in captivity.

China under the Ming Dynasty

The Ming dynasty (1368–1644) is often understood to have extended earlier Sung dynasty innovations. Literati culture revived, civil examination success remained the aim of most studies, neo-Confucians newly interpreted their classics, merchants developed more towns and long-distance markets, and foreign cavalry preyed at the Great Wall and even Beijing's gates. But, the Ming also saw a more autocratic throne, a more fluid mixture of literati and popular culture, regional merchant groups, and a commercial and industrial life prominent in the maritime world economy. Its humiliating collapse in 1644 set the stage for China's turbulent entry into the modern world.

With the flight of the Mongols north of the Great Wall in 1368, the Ming's founding emperor Zhu Yuanzhang (1368–1398) restored Chinese rule to all of China proper for the first time since the Tang. This highly energetic ruler established the institutions, law code, and practices that would rule China up to this century. But, few of his 15 successors retained his administrative

Chu Yüan-chang (1328–98), founder of the Ming dynasty. In 1368 he proclaimed himself the founder of a new imperial dynasty, taking the title Hung-wu, meaning "mightily martial".

commitment, as most preferred personal pleasures to Confucian rituals and responsibilities. The resulting vacuum of power was commonly, and unofficially, filled by eunuchs, mandarin bosses called Grand Secretaries, and teams of supervisors, all despised by most other officials for replacing and mistreating them. Two activists emperors, however, were Yongle (1403–24), who shifted the capital from Nanjing to Beijing in 1421, led five military campaigns north of the Great Wall, and sent his eunuch commander Zheng He on six voyages as far as the Persian Gulf and east Africa; and Xuande (1426–35), who cooperated with senior officials to stabilize civil rule and border control.

The government in the early 15th century sought to revive the economy of northern China with enforced migrations, state construction projects, tax levies, and military provision policies, largely at the expense of the south. But, sustained economic growth came only after the 1450s and was concentrated mainly in the south. The cultivation and weaving of cotton and silk in the Yangzi delta, prompted by onerous land taxes, obliged many townsmen and some peasants there to consume from c. 1500 regular shipments of rice from faraway Hunan province. Soon, cotton replaced hemp as China's most common cloth. Prime agents in these transactions were Huizhou merchants (from South Anhui province), who dominated long-distance Yangzi Valley trade well into the 19th century. Elsewhere, in Shanxi and in Zhejiang, Fujian, and Guangdong provinces, merchant groups attained similar regional power, partly from trading in Mongolia, Japan, Korea, Okinawa, and Southeast Asia. Their trade in tea, silk, porcelain, and iron was fuelled by the increasingly large imports of Japanese and New World silver. In the view of some recent historians, China was the central production area for the world maritime economy in the 16th and 17th centuries. By then, it was also attracting not just Portuguese, Spanish, Dutch, and English traders but also Jesuit, Franciscan, and Dominican missionaries.

1408	1421	1449	1567	1583	1592–98
Completion of the Yongle Encyclopedia	Capital shifted from Nanjing to Beijing	Emperor captured by victorious Mongol army at Tumu	End of ban on overseas trade by private parties	Jesuit missionary Matteo Ricci settles in Guangdong province	Ming defeat of Japanese invasions of Korea

MING CHINA

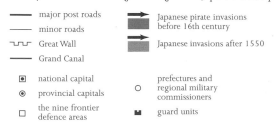

At home, these economic changes stimulated a popular urban culture. Printed books finally replaced manuscript copies for literati in most of southeast China, creating a readership anxious for current news, tales of political scandal, and lively fiction. The outcome was the Chinese novel, a rich compost of faction, fiction and legend, usually written by failed literati. In the countryside, extensive princely estates were set up in the north and southwest. Elsewhere, the hastened pace of commercialized farming led to great disparities in wealth and status, with servile forms of hired labour and tenancy commonly practiced on gentry landholdings by the late 16th century. All social strata complained of a loosening of the old bonds, leading to the social activism of neo-Confucians like Wang Yangming, the iconoclasm of the literatus Li Zhi, and the reformist critiques of the Donglin faction. In fact, eunuch power peaked between 1621 and 1626, distracting official critics from relieving peasant impoverishment in the northwest and army mutinies in the northeast. In 1644, therefore, Li Zicheng's peasant rebels brought down the

The Ming period began with the new regime consolidating its control in China and in the southwest, which the Mongols had incorporated into China for the first time. The first half of the 15th century was one of rapid expansion — sea voyages and invasions of Mongolia and Annam. Thereafter China went onto the defensive, protected by vast armies along the Great Wall. In the following century the Ming were beset by attacks from resurgent Mongols and Japanese-based pirates.

major post roads
minor roads
Great Wall
Grand Canal

Japanese pirate invasions before 16th century
Japanese invasions after 1550

national capital
provincial capitals
the nine frontier defence areas

prefectures and regional military commissioners
guard units

Ming, only to yield Beijing six weeks later to Manchu invaders abetted by Chinese generals. Within a decade their army of less than two million troops would conquer an empire of about two hundred million stunned subjects, now obliged to wear Manchu-style clothing.

257

The Kamakura Shogunate

The Kamakura was the first of the three periods in Japanese history during which some of the functions of government were exercised by those who wielded military power. The period conventionally lasts from 1185, when two rival military groups clashed decisively in western Japan, until 1333, when the remnants of the regime in Kyoto and Kamakura, near modern Tokyo, committed mass suicide. However, this rigid division obscures both the long processes before 1185 which had reduced the effectiveness of civilian government and the continuities with the period that follows.

Japan's medieval age is defined by the advent of the warrior, but this "Japan" was of a different shape from modern Japan, for the northernmost island of Hokkaidô was not considered a part of the empire in that period. It did not form part of the image of Japan for Japanese until the 19th century, when maps first began to include it as an integral part of Japan. The rise of the warrior is intimately connected to the declining effectiveness of provincial government and the accompanying rise of lawlessness in the latter half of the Heian period (794–1185), when government was nominally under the control of the imperial court. Warrior bands were already impinging on the prerogatives of central government in the tenth century, but by the 12th century they were far more powerful and most of them had attached themselves to one or other of two groups, known as the Taira and the Minamoto. The Taira were ascendant in western Japan and the Minamoto in the east, leaving the north to a branch of the once

A scene from the Heike monogatari, or Tale of the Heike, which treats of the clash between the Taira and the Minamoto in the 1180s and the tragic demise of the Taira.

The following extract from *The Tale of the Heike* concerns the battle at Dannoura and the destruction of the Taira forces by the Minamoto. The Taira had with them Emperor Antoku, who was but a child, and when defeat was certain, his mother, known as the Kenreimon'in or the Nun of Second rank, threw herself into the sea with him. He perished, but she was rescued and lived out her days in Kyoto. His fate stood for that of the court as it lay at the mercy of two warring factions who had at their disposal far greater forces than the state could muster.

The Minamoto warriors had already boarded the Taira boats, which were veering out of control because the sailors and helmsmen were lying in the bilges, slain by arrows and swords. The New Middle Counsellor Tomomori went in a small craft to the Emperor's ship.

"We seem to have reached the final extremity," he said. "Jettison everything that might offend the eye." He ran about from stem to stern tidying the ship with his own hands, sweeping, mopping and dusting.

"How is the battle going, Lord Middle Counsellor? How are things going?" the ladies asked.

Tomomori uttered a sarcastic laugh. "You will be getting acquainted with some remarkable eastern warriors [ie, Minamoto]."

"How can you joke at a time like this?" They all began to shriek and scream.

The Nun of Second Rank, who had long ago decided on a course of action, took the [infant] Emperor [Antoku] in her arms. "Although I am only a woman, I will not fall into enemy hands. I will go where His Majesty goes. Follow swiftly, you whose hearts are loyal to him." She walked to the side of the ship.

FROM *THE TALE OF THE HEIKE*

politically dominant Fujiwara clan. The Taira ingratiated themselves with the imperial court in Kyoto and sought to usurp civilian rule, but they were increasingly challenged by the Minamoto, first under Yoshinaka and later under Yoritomo (1147–99). It was the latter who was ultimately victorious in a naval battle at Dannoura in 1185.

Instead of ingratiating himself with the court, Yoritomo established an independent political base for himself and his followers at Kamakura in the east, but his government, known retrospectively as the Bakufu, concerned itself principally with property questions concerning the warrior class and did not at first take over all the functions of the state. Thus the court in Kyoto continued to exercise some governmental and judicial

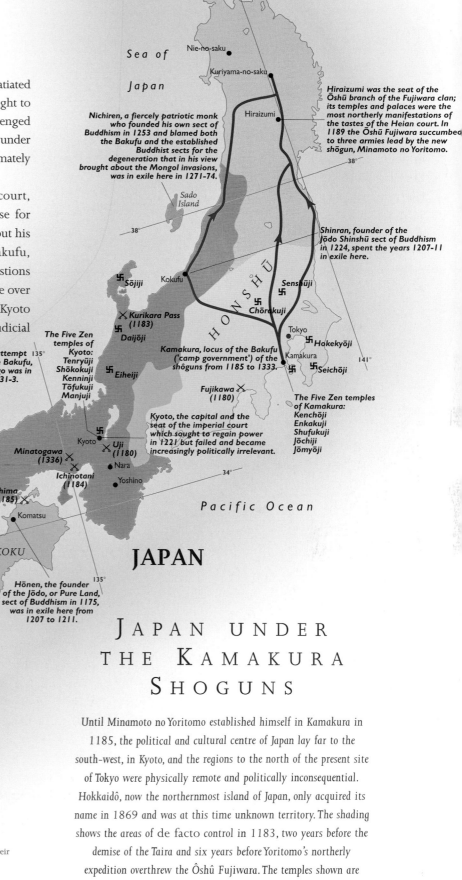

Hiraizumi was the seat of the Ōshū branch of the Fujiwara clan; its temples and palaces were the most northerly manifestations of the tastes of the Heian court. In 1189 the Ōshū Fujiwara succumbed to three armies lead by the new shōgun, Minamoto no Yoritomo.

Nichiren, a fiercely patriotic monk who founded his own sect of Buddhism in 1253 and blamed both the Bakufu and the established Buddhist sects for the degeneration that in his view brought about the Mongol invasions, was in exile here in 1271–74.

Shinran, founder of the Jōdo Shinshū sect of Buddhism in 1224, spent the years 1207–11 in exile here.

The Five Zen temples of Kyoto: Tenryūji Shōkokuji Kenninji Tōfukuji Manjuji

After a failed attempt to overthrow the Bakufu, Emperor Godaigo was in exile here 1331–3.

Kamakura, locus of the Bakufu ('camp government') of the shōguns from 1185 to 1333.

The Five Zen temples of Kamakura: Kenchōji Enkakuji Shufukuji Jōchiji Jōmyōji

Kyoto, the capital and the seat of the imperial court which sought to regain power in 1221 but failed and became increasingly politically irrelevant.

Hōnen, the founder of the Jōdo, or Pure Land, sect of Buddhism in 1175, was in exile here from 1207 to 1211.

At Hakata Bay samurai gathered from all over Japan and engaged the invading Mongol armies in 1274 and 1281; on both occasions storms dispersed and destroyed the invasion fleets. A third invasion was long expected and this necessitated a continuous state of military preparedness, but it never materialised.

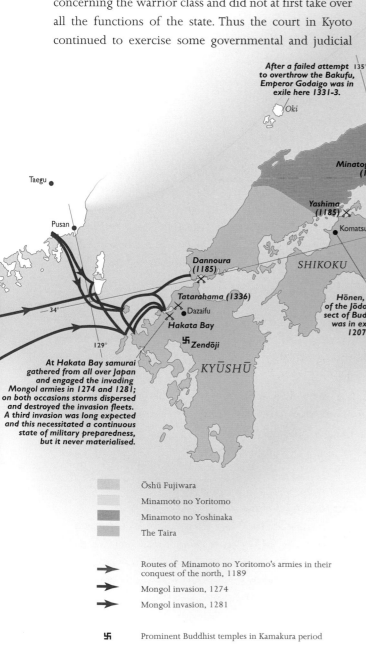

Sea of Japan
Nie-no-saku
Kuriyama-no-saku
Hiraizumi
Sado Island
HONSHŪ
Sōjiji
Kokufu
Kurikara Pass (1183)
Daijōji
Eiheiji
Senshūji
Chōrakuji
Tokyo
Hokekyōji
Kamakura
Seichōji
Fujikawa (1180)
Oki
Kyoto
Uji (1180)
Minatogawa (1336)
Nara
Ichinotani (1184)
Yoshino
Yashima (1185)
Komatsu
Taegu
Pusan
Dannoura (1185)
Tatarahama (1336)
Dazaifu
Hakata Bay
Zendōji
SHIKOKU
KYŪSHŪ

Pacific Ocean

JAPAN

JAPAN UNDER THE KAMAKURA SHOGUNS

Until Minamoto no Yoritomo established himself in Kamakura in 1185, the political and cultural centre of Japan lay far to the south-west, in Kyoto, and the regions to the north of the present site of Tokyo were physically remote and politically inconsequential. Hokkaidô, now the northernmost island of Japan, only acquired its name in 1869 and was at this time unknown territory. The shading shows the areas of de facto control in 1183, two years before the demise of the Taira and six years before Yoritomo's northerly expedition overthrew the Ôshû Fujiwara. The temples shown are some of the newer foundations associated with new currents of Buddhism such as Pure Land and Zen.

Ōshū Fujiwara
Minamoto no Yoritomo
Minamoto no Yoshinaka
The Taira

→ Routes of Minamoto no Yoritomo's armies in their conquest of the north, 1189

→ Mongol invasion, 1274

→ Mongol invasion, 1281

卍 Prominent Buddhist temples in Kamakura period

Japanese warriors, with an attendant on foot, riding to confront the Mongol invaders at the end of the 13th century (right). At this stage the bow and arrow was still of central importance and the sword had yet to achieve the technical perfection which made it the weapon of choice in later centuries. The armour consisted of metal platelets held together by braid.

functions until 1221 when an uprising, which had sought to overthrow the Shogunate, was crushed and the warrior regime in Kamakura took over more, but not all, of the functions of government.

The major challenge to the Kamakura Shogunate came from the Mongol invasions. In 1268 Kublai Khan despatched envoys to Japan inviting submission, but in response the Shogunate executed them in public. The first Mongol invasion was launched in 1274 using ships commandeered from Korea, which had already been overrun, but the invasion fleet foundered during a storm and was forced to withdraw with heavy loss of life. A much larger invasion was launched in 1281 consisting of three fleets, two of which sailed directly from China; this managed to establish a bridgehead in northern Kyushu, but eventually met the same fate as its predecessor. To meet these threats the Bakufu in Kamakura successfully mobilized warriors from most of Japan and employed them to build defensive works in Kyushu as well as to engage the enemy on shore, but because these campaigns, successful though they were, produced no foes who could be dispossessed of their lands, the regime had difficulty meeting its vassals' expectations of reward. The continuing state of military preparedness necessitated by the anticipated third invasion, which never took place, put further strains on Yorimoto's descendants in Kamakura. This unrest emboldened Emperor Godaigo

(1318–1389) to lead a revolt; this was unsuccessful and he was exiled to the island of Oki. Nonetheless, within three years a combination of better-equipped foes had brought down the Kamakura Shogunate by force of arms.

The Kamakura period is characterized by cultural decentralization, (as the court gradually lost its cultural hegemony), by the growth of the arts of the sword and of armour, and by the emergence of literary forms that were oral in origin and martial in content, and thus far from the polite world of Heian literature. Buddhism, too, was transformed from an exacting and elitist creed dependent on Chinese literacy to new forms that were far less dependent upon texts and which either sought to make Buddhism more accessible by raising the importance of the affirmation of faith, such as Pure Land Buddhism, or sought understanding through meditative practices, such as Zen. Zen, in particular, found favour with the warriors, and the powerful Zen temples in Kyoto and Kamakura became the centres of intellectual enquiry in their time.

(Left) A portrait of Minamoto no Yoritomo (1147–99), the founder of the Kamakura shogunate and the first hegemon in Japanese history successfully to translate his military power into political power. He is shown here in formal court attire, although for the most part he eschewed the trappings of court life and jealously preserved the independence of his warrior regime from the court. This particular portrait is said to have come from a Kyoto temple where it hung opposite a portrait of his chief foe, Taira no Kiyomori.

The Muromachi Shogunate

Between the end of the Kamakura shogunate in 1333 and the foundation of the Tokugawa shogunate in 1603 Japan slipped into anarchy and gradually ceased to exist as a unified entity. This is known as the Muromachi period, after the locus of power of the new line of shoguns, but their national political significance diminished in the 15th century and they had no influence over local magnates, who exercised absolute control over their de facto domains.

Out of the confusion that followed the collapse of the Kamakura, a new shogunate, that of the Ashikaga shoguns, emerged. It was based in the Muromachi quarter of Kyoto. The new regime was beset with difficulties from the outset, for switching political allegiances had given rise to two rival lines of succession to the imperial throne. From 1337 there was an alternative court based in Yoshino, in the mountains far to the south of Kyoto, with its own loyal band of supporters. It was not until 1392 that it proved possible to solve the dispute and amalgamate the two lines. In the 15th century the authority of the shogunate entered a terminal decline and after the civil war of the Onin era (1467–77) it could only claim to control the area in the immediate vicinity of Kyoto, where the politically emasculated emperors also resided. From the mid-15th to the end of

The Ginkakuji, or Silver Pavilion, in Kyoto. It was constructed by the shogun Ashikaga Yoshimasa in 1482 and the original intention had been to cover its exterior with silver foil, just as the Kinkakuji on the other side of the city had been covered with gold foil, but he died before his wishes could be carried out.

1392	1467	1543	1575	1592	1600
After more than 50 years of division, the two rival lines of accession finally agree to bury their differences and end a period of divided loyalties	Outbreak of Ônin war in Kyoto between rival warlords, which lasts for 10 years and leads to the political fragmentation of Japan	Arrival off southern coast of Japan of the Portuguese, the first Europeans to reach Japan	Battle of Nagashino in Japan, at which the superiority of firearms is demonstrated for first time	Toyotomi Hideyoshi launches his first invasion of Korea; troops are only finally withdrawn upon his death in 1598	Tokugawa Ieyasu, victorious at Battle of Sekigehara, establishes a new shogunate in Edo and restores a measure of unified administration

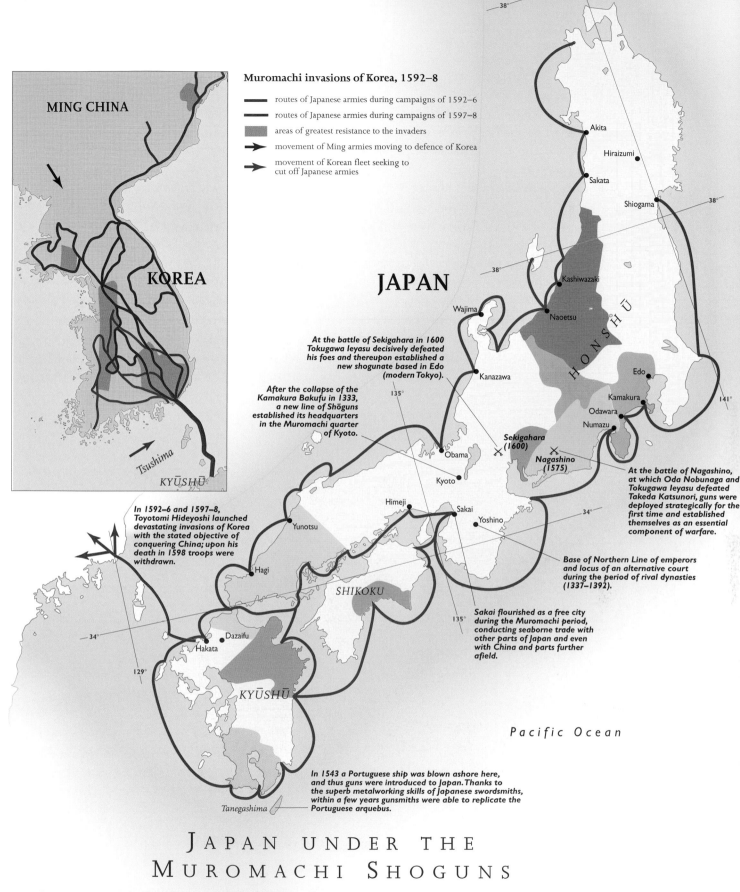

Muromachi invasions of Korea, 1592–8

— routes of Japanese armies during campaigns of 1592–6

— routes of Japanese armies during campaigns of 1597–8

■ areas of greatest resistance to the invaders

→ movement of Ming armies moving to defence of Korea

→ movement of Korean fleet seeking to cut off Japanese armies

MING CHINA

KOREA

Tsushima

KYŪSHŪ

JAPAN

HONSHŪ

At the battle of Sekigahara in 1600 Tokugawa Ieyasu decisively defeated his foes and thereupon established a new shogunate based in Edo (modern Tokyo).

After the collapse of the Kamakura Bakufu in 1333, a new line of Shōguns established its headquarters in the Muromachi quarter of Kyoto.

In 1592–6 and 1597–8, Toyotomi Hideyoshi launched devastating invasions of Korea with the stated objective of conquering China; upon his death in 1598 troops were withdrawn.

At the battle of Nagashino, at which Oda Nobunaga and Tokugawa Ieyasu defeated Takeda Katsunori, guns were deployed strategically for the first time and established themselves as an essential component of warfare.

Base of Northern Line of emperors and locus of an alternative court during the period of rival dynasties (1337–1392).

Sakai flourished as a free city during the Muromachi period, conducting seaborne trade with other parts of Japan and even with China and parts further afield.

In 1543 a Portuguese ship was blown ashore here, and thus guns were introduced to Japan. Thanks to the superb metalworking skills of Japanese swordsmiths, within a few years gunsmiths were able to replicate the Portuguese arquebus.

Sekigahara (1600)

Nagashino (1575)

Pacific Ocean

Akita · Hiraizumi · Sakata · Shiogama · Kashiwazaki · Naoetsu · Wajima · Kanazawa · Edo · Kamakura · Odawara · Numazu · Obama · Kyoto · Himeji · Sakai · Yoshino · Yunotsu · Hagi · Dazaifu · Hakata · Tanegashima

SHIKOKU

KYŪSHŪ

JAPAN UNDER THE MUROMACHI SHOGUNS

From the mid-15th until the late 16th century Japan consisted, in effect, of a fluctuating number of independent states, each controlled by a daimyo. The map shows the location of some of the most powerful daimyo in the early 16th century, while the subsidiary map of the Korean peninsula shows the invasions of Korea launched by Toyotomi Hideyoshi in the last decade of the 16th century. In spite of the political fragmentation there was considerable economic growth during this period and both overland and coastal trade flourished, so the principal coastal routes have also been shown.

the 16th century Japan effectively ceased to exist; rather the Japanese islands were parcelled up among a number of local hegemons known as *daimyo*, who enjoyed complete independence from Kyoto. Territorial boundaries were fluid, and territory often changed hands as daimyo rose and fell. This turbulent period is aptly known as that of the Warring States.

It was at this critical juncture that the first Europeans reached Japan. A Portuguese ship was blown off course and made land on the island of Tanegashima, to the south of Kyushu, in 1543. The Portuguese brought guns, trade and Catholic Christianity, and at first they were well received. Within a remarkably short space of time Japanese gunsmiths, availing themselves of the advanced metalworking skill developed by swordsmiths, were able to reproduce and even improve upon the imported firearms. On account of the small quantities available and a lack of familiarity with the possibilities afforded by firearms, warfare was slow to change, but the strategic deployment of a corps of armed peasants at the battle of Nagashino in 1575 made firearms indispensable thereafter. They were deployed on that occasion by Oda Nobunaga (1534–82), the first to attempt to forge some sort of national unity by force of arms.

Although the missionaries would be expelled and Christianity suppressed in the 17th century, in the 16th

the Jesuits, followed later by Spanish Dominicans, enjoyed considerable success. The number of converts grew rapidly and a number of powerful daimyo embraced Christianity. There were churches in Kyoto as well as in south-west Japan, and a printing press brought in from Macao was used to print books in Latin for Japanese catechumens and even in Japanese for the benefit of Jesuits struggling to learn the language. The European missionaries and traders excited great curiosity and interest, as is evident from the numerous screens and paintings of "southern barbarians", as they were called, extant today. Simultaneously Japanese traders (enjoying freedom from central control)

ventured further afield, even as far as what is now Vietnam and Thailand, where trading stations were established.

After the assassination of Oda Nobunaga in 1582, his mantle was taken up by one of his generals, Toyotomi Hideyoshi (1536-98), who was of peasant origins. At the time of his death, Nobunaga was in *de facto* control of about one third of the country, but Hideyoshi extended his territory both by force of arms and by diplomatic finesse. By 1590 he was the unchallenged master of Japan, albeit with no legitimate office and no credible successor. In the following year he launched an invasion of Korea with the intention of taking over the Ming Chinese empire, but this came to grief and the invasion army was withdrawn in 1598 upon his death. Tokugawa Ieyasu (1542–1616), who had defeated his rivals at the battle of Sekigahara (1600), took Hideyoshi's place. Ieyasu immediately turned his attention to the symbols and machinery of legitimation and continuity, which in the event kept his new shogunate in place until 1868.

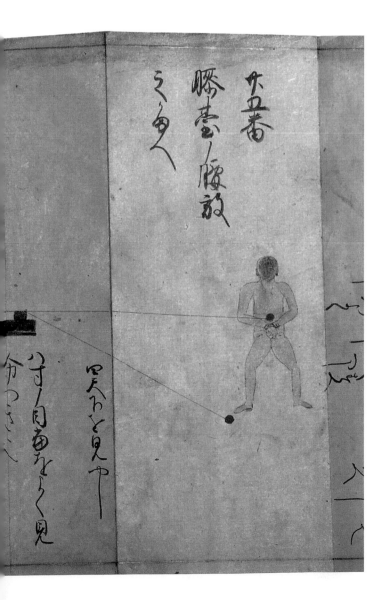

A scene from a 16th-century Japanese gun manual. Guns dramatically changed warfare in Japan by making it possible for peasants to get the better of swordsmen who had spent many years acquiring their proficiency. Oda Nobunaga was the first to appreciate the strategic value of guns at the battle of Nagashino in 1575, when his first 3000 musketeers thinned the ranks of the mounted warriors attacking them. Later, in the 17th century, when peace was restored, swords resumed their status as the weapons of honour and status and gunsmiths found little call for their trade.

Empire and Commerce in Southeast Asia, c.1300–1500

The expanding international connections of medieval Southeast Asia were reflected in the dramatic growth of its maritime trade, in the growing prominence of Chinese and other sojourners, and in the spread of Islam in the archipelago. The principal beneficiary of this after 1400 was the Islamic sultanate of Melaka: it was the last great imperial moment in Southeast Asia before the European conquest.

Both Pagan and Angkor retained a ritual importance long after they collapsed as ritual centres. However, the political unity Pagan had created was broken by the end of the 13th century with the rise of Shan power in central Burma, notably at Ava; the Mons in parts of Lower Burman, based on Pegu, which became an important trading centre; and an independent kingdom in Arakan.

Chinese claims to suzerainty were renewed throughout the region. The integrity of the Dai Viet was retained only after a long struggle against the Chinese power, which culminated in a Chinese re-occupation in 1406. However, the Ming policy of aggressive Sinicization failed. It was challenged by a resistance movement under the leadership of a powerful landholder, Le Loi, who restored the Dai Viet, and who in 1428 founded a new Le dynasty. The dynasty's consolidation of the kingdom can be seen as a definitive moment in Vietnam's national history.

After 1300, three new imperial initiatives dominate Southeast Asian history. A new Tai kingdom of Ayutthaya was founded in 1351 on the lower plain of the Chao Phraya river. Ayutthaya's power rapidly eclipsed Sukothai: key tributaries of Pagan, such as Chiengmai, came within its orbit, and so did much of the Malay Peninsula. Ayutthaya's rulers appropriated not only the administrative legacy of the early Tai kingdoms, but also that of Angkor. Angkor itself was sacked in 1431. The great capital was then abandoned, and Khmer power shifted towards sites closer to the coast. This was a general trend on the mainland: commercial connections, especially the settlement of Chinese traders, were vital to Ayutthaya's success.

In the maritime world, there was a dramatic, if short-lived revival of Javanese power under the kings of Majapahit. Kertarajasa (1293–1309) and his successors dominated much of eastern Java, Bali and Madura, and exercized tributary claims further to the north and west, and into the Straits of Melaka. The period of Majapahit's pre-eminence is most often dated by the career of its dynamic minister, Gaja Mada, who was active from 1330 to his death in 1364. However, geopolitical transformations were also underpinned by economic change.

After 1400, the foundations were laid for what has been termed "an age of commerce" in Southeast Asian history that continued into the 17th century. The region's external connections were strengthened with the relative decline of the overland Asian trade routes, and the growth

The Wat Phra Si Sanphet, built in the 14th century, was the most important temple in the Royal Palace of the ancient Kingdom of Ayutthaya. Its centrepiece was a 16m standing Buddha image with a covering of 179 kg of gold. It was destroyed by the Burmese invasion in 1767. Two large Ceylonese-style Chedis were erected in the 15th century to hold the ashes of two early kings of Ayutthaya. The third was added in the 16th century. All were originally gilded. Since the destruction of the palace in the 18th century, the chedi have become the characteristic feature of the Wat.

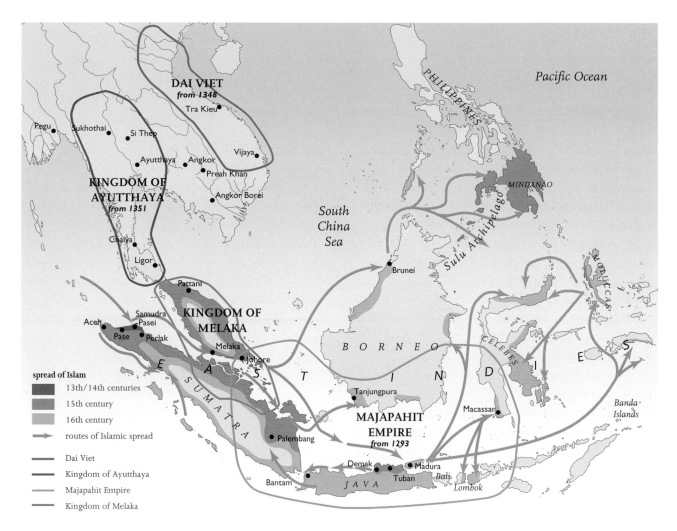

THE RISE OF ISLAM IN MARITIME SOUTH EAST ASIA

The embracing of Islam by Melaka's rulers encouraged the emergence of similar sultanates elsewhere on the Malay Peninsula and farther afield in Jolo and Ternate and Tidore. Islam affirmed a ruler's status and strengthened his trading links in an Indian Ocean world that was fast becoming an Islamic lake. However, there is evidence of conversions to Islam in Sumatra and elsewhere earlier than 1400. A fragment of inscription from the east coast of the Malay Peninsula — the "Trengganu Stone" illustrated here — appears to show a ruler's edict of the primacy of Islamic law, and has been variously dated from between 1302 and 1387. Trade was not the only factor in Islamization. Scholars have also pointed to the role of sufi preachers and teachers; Islam's mystical traditions thrived in many parts of the archipelago. Nor did the coming of Islam necessarily lead to a sharp break with existing cosmologies, particularly in Java; Southeast Asian experiences of Islam were diverse, and continue to be so.

of the maritime trade route, especially after 1368, when the new Ming rulers of China despatched a series of trading expeditions southwards, especially under the eunuch-admiral Zheng He, between 1403 and 1433.

The opportunities this presented were most fully realised in a third imperial initiative. Around 1400, a tributary prince of Majapahit, Paramesvara, established a new kingdom, initially at what is today Singapore, and later at Melaka. Its rulers adopted, but greatly extended, the Srivijayan pattern of Malay maritime power, especially with their proactive policy in attracting the settlement of

foreign trading communities. Melaka thrived because of its links to and protection from China. It had a richly polyglot and plural culture. With a population of more than 100,000, it was the largest city of early Southeast Asia; one of the largest of the medieval world. After adopting Islam, Paramesvara and his successors projected Melaka as the Mecca of the East (see caption)

The Portuguese conquest of Melaka in 1511 by Alfonso de Albuquerque affirmed Southeast Asia's centrality to a new series of global connections that would create the modern world.

Islam and the New States of Africa, c. 1300–1500

The role of Islam within the states of Africa was of great significance in the 14th and 15th centuries. African states prospered through trade with the Muslim world via both land and sea. Travel for religious reasons, pilgrimage and scholarship further enriched the relationship between Africa and the rest of the Muslim world. Thus although some of the states that appeared in this period were new, they were building upon the heritage of Muslim–African contacts (*see* p.192) which stretched back in certain instances to the very early years of Islam.

The era encompassing the 14th and 15th centuries could be defined as the high point of the Islamized states on the continent. The kingdom of Ghana, for instance, one of the earliest states in Africa, was supplanted by the Empire of Mali, which covered an even greater territorial extent. Mali grew from humble beginnings in the 11th to 12th centuries among the Mande peoples on the modern Mali/Guinea border. It was established following epic battles between Sunjata, the ancestor of the Malian royal lineage, and the blacksmith Sumanguru.

Tradition also records that the kings of Mali were converts to Islam in the 12th century, but it was not until the mid-13th century that Islam was more widely practised. Certainly by the time of the fabled pilgrimage of the Malian ruler Mansa Musa to Mecca in 1324, Islam was well established within the domains of Mali.

Yet this highpoint was followed by territorial loss and dynastic infighting, resulting in Mali ultimately being supplanted in the early 15th century by the Songhai empire. Songhai, with its capital at Gao on the Niger Bend, could be described as the greatest of the Islamized West African states. Its rulers (initially the Sonni dynasty and after 1493 that of the Askias) instituted systems of bureaucracy that utilized Arabic for writing and made use of Islamic systems of administration. They also developed extensive trade links, which served to connect Songhai with the wider Muslim world. It was also during this period that Islamic scholarship flourished, especially under the first Songhai Askia ruler, Muhammad (1493–1528). The Sankore Mosque University in Timbuktu, especially, became a primary centre of Muslim learning.

On the opposite side of the continent on the eastern African coast the role of Islam was equally significant. Here, numerous Islamized trade centres, or city states, flourished, centres which are usually referred to as being associated with the Swahili, an African, predominantly Muslim people, formerly thought to be mainly Arab and Persian derived, but now known to have a more complex yet largely African ancestry. Trade centres such as Kilwa in Tanzania grew rich from participation in Indian Ocean trade, directed north to the Red Sea, Arabian Peninsula and Persian Gulf. Utilizing the monsoons, cargoes of mangrove poles, ivory, slaves, and gold were shipped north and finished goods imported in exchange.

(Above) Kilwa (founded c. 800) was a major trade centre at the southern end of the Swahili coast. Trade in gold, copper and ivory from southern Africa generated great riches. Great Zimbabwe appears to have been a major source of gold to Kilwa, as indicated by a Kilwa coin found at the former. In its later phases Kilwa provides an example of the stone town, an architectural tradition that made use of cut coral to build substantial structures, such as the Great Mosque and the Husuni Kubwa palace complex (a structure unique in sub-Saharan Africa with its cliff-top location and octagonal bathing pool).

Early 12th–early 15th century	1324	1394–98	Early 15th century–1590	1487	1590
Empire of Mali in existence	Pilgrimage of Mansa Musa to Mecca	Shift of centre of power of Kanem-Borno from Kanem to Borno	Songhai empire in existence	Bartolomeu Dias rounds Cape of Good Hope	Defeat of Songhai forces by invading Moroccan army at the battle of Tondibi

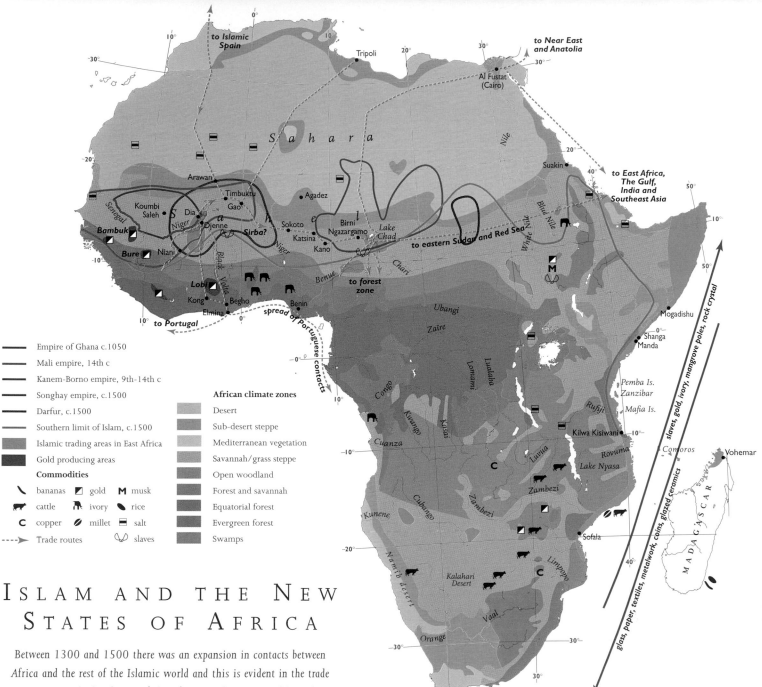

Map legend:

Empire of Ghana c.1050
Mali empire, 14th c
Kanem-Borno empire, 9th–14th c
Songhay empire, c.1500
Darfur, c.1500
Southern limit of Islam, c.1500
Islamic trading areas in East Africa
Gold producing areas

Commodities

\ bananas ▤ gold M musk
🐂 cattle 🐘 ivory ↘ rice
C copper ⬭ millet ▤ salt
--▶ Trade routes ⬭ slaves

African climate zones

Desert
Sub-desert steppe
Mediterranean vegetation
Savannah/grass steppe
Open woodland
Forest and savannah
Equatorial forest
Evergreen forest
Swamps

ISLAM AND THE NEW STATES OF AFRICA

Between 1300 and 1500 there was an expansion in contacts between Africa and the rest of the Islamic world and this is evident in the trade routes maintained. The placing of the African trade centres and/or political capitals is also far from arbitrary. The sites were frequently located at nodal points allowing the collection of goods and commodities from a variety of different environmental zones and at good axes of communication. The arrival of the Portuguese in the first half of the 15th century and their rapid progression down the west African coast is also evident.

Further Islamized states existed in the Central Sudan, where, around Lake Chad, the empire of Kanem-Borno (11th–19th centuries) was situated. Like its contemporaries, it prospered through long distance trade and, through these trade processes, had been gradually Islamized. Within the Nilotic Sudan Muslim kingdoms also developed, sometimes absorbing territory left by the vanished Christian kingdoms. The sultanate of Darfur, in existence from c. 1100 but more fully Islamized from the 16th century, was an example of a territory founded in a previously unoccupied area.

The Islamized states of Africa, though subject to change, proved remarkably durable. Yet towards the end of the period under consideration, a new factor appeared in Africa – Europeans. The first to arrive were the Portuguese who reached Cape Verde in 1444 and the River Congo in 1484. Bartolemeu Dias rounded the Cape of Good Hope in 1487. Ultimately, the arrival of Europeans was to have profound consequences both for Muslim dominated Indian Ocean trade and for the states of Africa.

Science and Humanism

In the Middle Ages teaching and experience were as important for the handing down and development of ideas as books and letters. The strong conviction on the part of the scholars of the Renaissance that the 15th century was a new Golden Age should not obscure their medieval inheritance in terms of ideas and knowledge, both new and passed on from earlier centuries. The diverse intellectual developments of both the Middle Ages and Antiquity provided firm foundations on which scientists and humanists continued to build, both within and without the formal institutions of learning.

The natural sciences were originally perceived as a part of philosophy and the study of God's creation. The practical application of scientific reasoning, and the importance of observation, experiment and mathematical analysis, however, effected many changes in the understanding of the world, both in physics and astronomy as well as medicine, botany and zoology. Many currents of thought articulated by individuals in the later Middle Ages on such matters as anatomy, the circulation of the blood, the relation between the earth and the sun and the replacement of the Ptolemaic with the Copernican perception of the solar system, however, did not achieve precision until the 16th and 17th centuries.

The knowledge and exposition of the natural world by Greek and Roman scholars was transmitted to medieval Europe and the Arabic world both directly in original texts and translations or indirectly via Encyclopaedias of ancient learning such as that compiled by Isidore of Seville. Each generation added its own commentaries and notes. The reception of Aristotle and Greek science in the 13th-century universities thus built on works already known in the spheres of ancient geometry, mathematics and astronomy. Classical works on building and architecture, military engineering and surveying and geometry were essential for the new practical applications of engineering and science. The deductive reasoning taught in the schools was applied to

This Arabic astronomical instrument for determining the time by observation of the altitude of the sun or one of the stars was introduced to the west in the 11th century. It was designed to solve problems of spherical trigonometry and reduce the amount of mathematical calculation required to determine the position of so-called fixed stars in relation to the horizon, and of the sun, moon and stars in relation to the planets. This example was probably intended for London (being a projection for the 52nd degree of latitude) and was made between 1340 and 1400. On the reverse there is a calendar scale with saints' days marked, and a zodiac scale.

natural phenomena as much as to law, doctrine or philosophy. Robert Grosseteste (c. 1170–1253) the theologian had written in the 13th century on the phenomenon of light, mathematics and the *Posterior Analytics* of Aristotle as well as the primacy of experiment or personal experience. Mathematics, long a staple of the seven liberal arts, was linked in the 14th century with natural philosophy by scholars such as William of Ockham (c. 1285–c. 1349) and the Mertonians, i. The medical teachings of Galen and Scribonius were augmented by the new treatises and translations from Salerno and Montpellier.

The humanists and later medieval natural philosophers sought out the ninth-century Carolingian copies of classical texts and made new copies of them in

1045	1134–1150	1175	1215	1250–1284	1283	c. 1470
Hermann of Reichenau's *De mensura astrolabii*	Adelard of Bath, astronomical works	Latin translation of Ptolemy's Almagest from an Arabic version	Robert Grosseteste *De sphaera*	Quadrant described (to find the time of day by observing the height of the sun)	Mechanical clock constructed for Dunstable Priory (the earliest record of a mechanical clock in Europe)	John Doket's commentary on the *Phaedo* introduces Florentine neoplatonism to Cambridge

The text on 34 leaves of Alexander Cortesius' poem De Mathiae Corvini Ungariae regis laudibus bellicis carmen (1487–88) in praise of the Hungarian king, Matthias Corvinus. The poem praises the king in Latin verse for his military prowess. Cortesius (d. 1499) was a humanist scholar and papal secretary and probably wrote the poem in order to win Matthias support for Pope Innocent VIII's military campaign to win back the city of Ancona. The book was written by the scribe Bartolomeo Sanvito (1450–1511) in humanistic cursive minuscule and richly decorated by a Roman or Umbrian master with Matthias represented as a Roman emperor and a battle scene reminiscent of a Roman triumphal arch. Apart from his abilities as a soldier, Matthias was famous for his enlightened learning and his fine library, which reflected the extent to which the new learning had extended north of the Alps. Most of Matthias' library fell into the hands of the Turks after 1526 and his books are now scattered among the great libraries of the world. This copy was acquired by Duke August of Brunswick between 1618 and 1652–53.

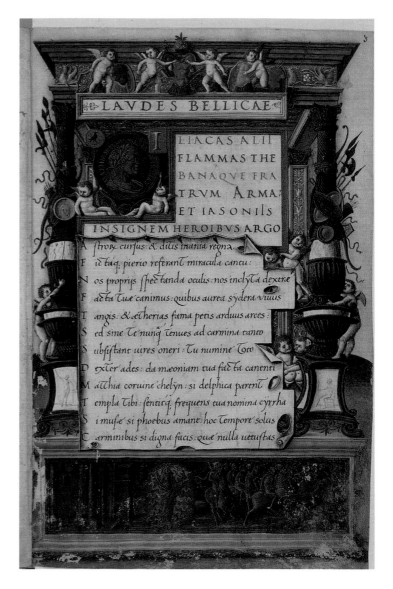

For this century, like a golden age, has restored to light the liberal arts, which were almost extinct: grammar, poetry, rhetoric, painting, sculpture, architecture, music, the ancient singing of songs to the Orphic lyre, and all this in Florence … In you also my dear Paul, this century appears to have perfected astronomy, and in Florence it has recalled the Platonic teaching from darkness to light. In Germany in our times have been invented the instruments for printing books, and those tables in which in a single hour the whole face of the heavens for an entire century is revealed and one may mention also the Florentine machine which shows the daily motions of the heavens.

MARSILIO FICINO, LETTER TO PAUL OF MIDDELBURG, 1492.

a newly-devised script known as humanistic minuscule, based on caroline minuscule. They ensured that Latin and Greek classical texts were among the earliest books to be produced with the new technology of printing from the 15th century onwards and thus promoted their survival as part of the intellectual inheritance of the modern world. They themselves contributed many new works of poetry, treatises on political thought such as those of Niccolo Macchiavelli (1469–1527), legal scholarship, new critical editions of many classical texts and histories such as that by Francesco Guicciardini (1483–1540). The Italian humanists' stress on classical scholarship,

1471	1488	1491–95	1499	1822
The Nürnberg observatory is established by Johann Müller Regiomontanus (translator of Ptolemy); Leonardo da Vinci (1452–1519) foreshadows principle of inertia, light waves, hydro-dynamics and the experimental impossibility of perpetual motion	University of Cambridge establishes public lectureship on "humanity"	Copernicus studies at Cracow university	Erasmus's visit to England	The Papacy sanctions the sun as the centre of the planetary system
			1530	
			Galileo's telescope	

grammar and rhetoric was balanced by the concentration of the humanists north of the Alps on logic, philosophy and theology.

Both humanism and the sciences were nurtured by scholars within universities, in private "academies" and at many European royal courts, and developed directly out of the medieval traditions of knowledge. Many new sites of learning, such as physic gardens, anatomy theatres, libraries, museums and the reformed universities of the German lands, emerged in the course of the 15th and 16th centuries, prompted especially by the practice of mathematics, military and civil engineering and medicine, the enterprise of upwardly mobile artisans, and by new social and political demands.

Laurenziana Library in Florence, one of the major libraries established in the Renaissance, purpose-built for the Medici, reflects the crucial importance of books with ancient, medieval and new texts for Renaissance scholars and their patrons.

George Lichton, a Scottish student who studied Aristotle's Physics at the University of Louvain in the 1460s, drew rough sketches of his lecturer and fellow students (sitting on the floor with their books) in his notebook, now in Aberdeen University Library. The very conservative university curriculum and the increasing loss of autonomy of the universities to secular authorities nevertheless accommodated new subjects, not least Greek and Hebrew, in the course of the 15th century, and stimulated many ingenious minds.

universities
academies and other non-university centres
courts

Uppsala

Aberdeen
Glasgow
St Andrews

North Sea

Copenhagen
Baltic Sea

Rostock

Cambridge
Oxford

Elbe
Oder
Vistula

Leipzig
Frankfurt

Louvain
Kassel
Erfurt

Frankfurt
Mainz
Nuremberg
Prague
Cracow

Seine

Paris

Rhine

Heidelberg

Ingolstadt

Atlantic Ocean

Vienna

Buda

Bay of Biscay

Alps

Milan
Vicenza
Venice

Piacenza
Parma
Padua

Rhône

Montpellier
Avignon
Genoa
Ferrara
Bologna

Pyrenees

Piza
Florence

Douro
Ebro

Lisbon

Rome

Guadalquivir

Naples
Salerno

Mediterranean Sea

PRINCIPAL CENTRES OF HUMANISM AND SCIENCE IN THE 14TH AND 15TH CENTURIES

Printing and the Communication of Knowledge

The advent of printing with movable type in western Europe during the 1450s brought about a revolution in ways that people thought and communicated. Because large numbers of the same book could be shared among people of disparate backgrounds, it affected language as well as the circulation of ideas and knowledge. By the end of the 15th century, religion, politics and exploration had all been irrevocably affected by the ready availability of the printing press.

Printing depends on a number of linked technologies. Paper, much cheaper than vellum as a material, was made in Spain in the mid-12th century. By the mid-15th century paper-mills were widely established across western Europe. Woodblocks were used to print patterns on cloth from at least the 14th century (and had been used in Egypt for short religious texts in Arabic from at least the tenth/eleventh centuries).

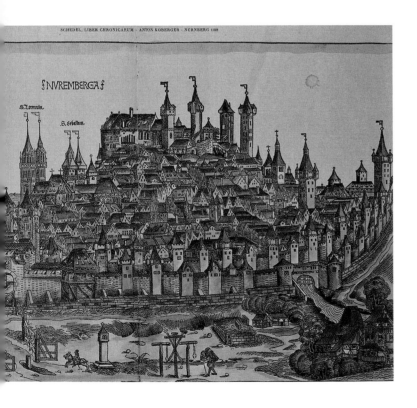

Johann Gutenberg, working at Mainz in the 1440s and 1450s, built partly on what was familiar. Crucially, he also contrived a method of manufacturing letters cast in metal that could be used repeatedly, in different combinations. His invention of what became known as printing type, combined with his adapting the screw press so as to obtain pressure, could not have been fully exploited without adequate supplies of paper.

In some respects Gutenberg was responding to demand, in a period that was becoming increasingly literate. It was, however, some years before his invention was put to widespread use. At first printing with movable type was restricted to the Rhine valley. When Mainz was sacked in 1462, printers dispersed over much of southern Europe, in search of livelihoods; but the real expansion in the number of presses did not take place until after 1470.

Much depended on readers' familiarity with manuscripts; but more depended on money available for investment. Once established, in some towns (such as Cologne, Basel, Paris and Venice) printing became an important part of the local economy. In others (including many small towns in northern Italy), printers moved on after producing just one or two books for local magnates or patrons. In some places, printing was suppressed. An attempt in Cracow to print in Cyrillic type was curtailed because the Roman Catholic Church opposed printing for Orthodox Muscovy. In 1486, in the archdiocese of Mainz, the Church made its first formal attempts to control printing by censorship.

With vastly more copies of books available thanks to printing, trade on an entirely new scale was essential. Although a few books were commissioned, most books

A paper mill, outside the walls of Nuremberg. Such mills depended on plentiful supplies of clean water. From Hartmann Schedel, Liber chronicarum (Nuremberg, 1493). (Trinity College, Cambridge)

c. 1400	1454–55	1465	1466	1467
Johann Gutenberg born into a patrician Mainz family	Completion of printing of the 42-line Bible, also known as the Gutenberg Bible, in Mainz	Greek type used for the first time, by Peter Schoeffer, in Mainz	The Bible printed in German, at Strasbourg	First printing at Rome

THE SPREAD OF PRINTING IN EUROPE TO 1490

- printing established, 1454–69
- printing established, 1470–79
- printing established, 1480–89

North Sea

Baltic Sea

Stockholm

Edinburgh

Dublin

York

Odense

Schleswig

Rostock

Hamburg   Lübeck

Haarlem   Hasselt
Leiden   Zwolle
Oxford   St Albans   Gouda   Deventer
Westminster   London   Delft   Utrecht
St Maartensdijk   Ruilenburg   Nijmegen   Stendal
's Hertogenbosch   Magdeburg
Bruges   Antwerp   Münster
Ghent   Louvain
Audenarde Alost   Merseburg   Leipzig
Abbeville   Brussels   Cologne   Erfurt   Meissen   Breslau

Tréguier   Rouen
Caen   Marienthal   Eltvil   Bamberg   Prague
Lantenac   Mainz   Würzburg   Kuttenberg   Cracow
Bréhant-Loudéac   Rennes   Paris   Nuremberg   Pilsen
Angers   Chartres   Trier   Heidelberg   Brno
Troyes   Metz   Stuttgart   Eichstätt   Ratisbon
Chablis   Hagenau   Esslingen   Ingoldstadt   Winterberg   Vienna
Reutlingen   Blaubeuren   Augsburg
Poitiers   Strassburg   Urach   Schussenried   Passau
Besançon   Basel   Zürich   Memmingen   Munich
Salins   Burgdorf   Beromünster
Promenthoux   Geneva   Rougemont   Budapest
Bordeaux   Lyons   Sion
Vienne   Chambéry   Trent   Cividale
Moutiers   Udine
Embrun   Turin   Milan   Brescia   Vicenza   Treviso
Pavia   Cremona   Verona   Venice
Albi   Piacenza   Mantua   Padua
Toulouse   Genoa   Parma   Ferrara
Savona   Lucca   Bologna
Chaves   Zamora   Burgos   Pisa   Faenza
Valladolid   Siena   Cagli   Iesi
Salamanca   Lérida   Perugia   Foligno
Coria   Segovia   Zaragossa   Trevi   Ascoli Piceno
Toledo   Guadalajara   Hijar   Aquila
Montalban   Huete   Barcelona   Rome   Subiaco
Tarragona
Lisbon   Tortosa
Gaeta
Faro   Valencia   Capua
Cordoba   Valdemusa   Naples
Seville
Murcia

Bay of Biscay

Mediterranean Sea

Cosenza

Palermo   Messina
Regio Calabria

1470	1472	1476	1500
First printing at Paris	Dante, *La divina commedia*, printed for the first time	William Caxton moves from Bruges to Westminster, and prints Chaucer's *Canterbury Tales* (completed 1477)	Italic type used for the first time, by Aldus Manutius in Venice

¶ Mors resecat/mors omne necat quod carne creatur
Magnificos premit ꞇ modicos/cunctis dominatur.

¶ Nob
Tam d

enet imperiū nulli reueretur:
6 q̄z principib⁹ cōmunis habetur.

/nisi terre precio vilis.
2t

were printed speculatively for a market that had to be found. Paper constituted a high proportion of investment in any book, and costs had to be recouped. The short-lived press at Oxford foundered in 1486, probably because there were too few customers. Gutenberg's Bible was sold in Italy and England, as well as in the Rhine valley. In the Low Countries and Germany, humanist works from Italy were easily obtainable. By advertisements, correspondence and word of mouth, the European book trade was drawn together as never before.

The pattern of expansion in printing was irregular, as lessons were learned. The most successful centres tended to be cathedral or university towns. In Venice, initial enthusiasm in 1469–72 gave way to a temporary crisis in 1473 as a result of overproduction. Printing came relatively late to the Low Countries, Spain, and England. For readers, printed books became known much more quickly than the technology by which they were produced. The earliest printed books known to have been imported into England date from the mid-1460s, several years before William Caxton set up his press in Westminster. Books for use specifically in England were also printed in Venice and in Rouen. Books for Spain were printed at Toulouse.

Printing did not displace manuscripts immediately. For some kinds of books (notably Books of Hours, for private devotion) manuscript remained the widely preferred medium. For some of the skills used in making manuscripts, especially for illumination, demand actually increased. In all kinds of activities – politics, religion, law, exploration, domestic life and literature – manuscript and print circulated side by side long after 1500.

The interior of a 15th century printing house and associated bookshop, the printers and bookseller surprised by death. In the printing house, one workman is setting type, holding a composing stick in his left hand and taking type from the case before him with his right; his copy-text is propped up in front. Behind him two others work at the press; the figure at the back is wielding an ink ball, used to ink the type. Note also that the books in the shop are piled flat one on the other.

Exploration and Missionaries

Although Viking navigators had reached America *c.* 1000, this had little impact on geographical thought. The late Middle Ages saw the transformation of a worldview in which Europe, Asia and Africa lay surrounded by the Ocean Sea, to an awareness that Europe was a small part of a much larger world.

Contact with the Mongols in the 13th century revealed the extent of Asia and the location of spices mentioned by Marco Polo in his travel book. The knowledge of the existence of peoples ignorant of Christianity instigated the Franciscan missionaries' travels to Asia. The Avignon popes appointed an archbishop of Peking and the occasional Venetian and Genoan settled at Zaitun (China) in the 14th century.

The appeal of Africa lay more in gold, which was in short supply in Europe around 1400. Trade with northern Africa revealed that gold dust was readily available south of the Sahara; the intrepid Genoese Malfante reached Timbuctu in search of it in 1444. The Portuguese seizure of Ceuta in Morocco (1415) did not secure access to gold: the Muslims refused to trade there after losing the city. Better prospects were offered by navigating the African coast in light, manoeuvrable caravels, a project keenly supported by the Portuguese royal family,

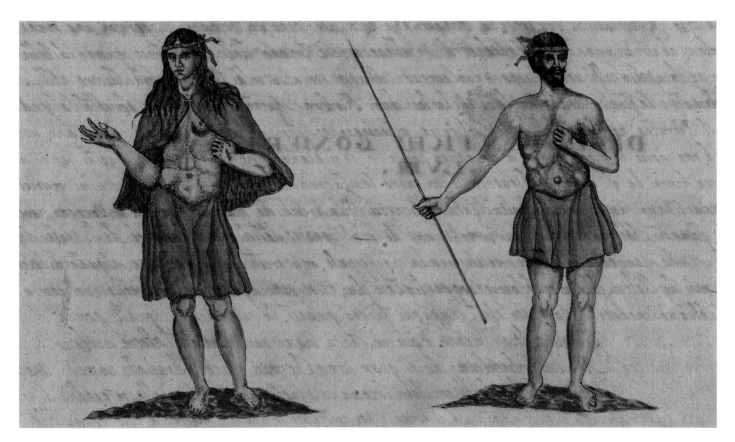

Inhabitants of La Gomera in the Canaries, dressed in animal skins. Their semi-nakedness often surprised western European observers.

1431–2	1415	1471	1492	1497–8	1500
First voyages from Portugal and Majorca to the Canaries	Portuguese seizure of Ceuta	Portuguese establish base at São Jorge da Mina	First voyage of Christopher Columbus	Vasco da Gama reaches India after circumnavigating Africa	Cabral discovers Brazil on the way from Portugal to India

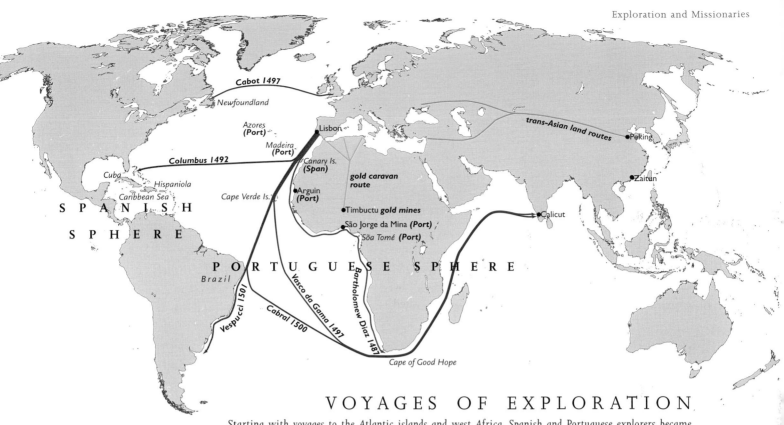

VOYAGES OF EXPLORATION

Starting with voyages to the Atlantic islands and west Africa, Spanish and Portuguese explorers became increasingly keen to open up trade routes linking Europe to Asia, whether around Africa to India, or, more daringly, by jumping across the Atlantic to reach China and Japan.

especially Henry "the Navigator", who combined a chivalric attachment to war against the infidel with a keen eye for profit. The poor, marginal, kingdom of Portugal became an economic powerhouse. Lack of easy access to gold along the African coast stimulated trade in other commodities, notably slaves; trading stations were built at Arguim and São Jorge da Mina, as Portuguese navigators made contact with the peoples of Black Africa, who sought textiles and metal goods.

Out in the Atlantic, the Canaries, for which Castile and Portugal competed until they were assigned to Castile in 1479, had a native population, living in Stone Age conditions. Long the target of Iberian missionaries and slavers, the Islands' conquest was only completed in 1496 by the soldier of fortune Alonso de Lugo. Portugal secured instead the uninhabited islands of the Atlantic: Madeira became a great sugar producer; the Azores offered grain and dairy goods; the Cape Verde islands were a base for slave traders; São Tomé was colonized by forcibly baptized Jewish children. Gradually the idea of rounding Africa to reach the spice islands emerged, culminating in the triumphant Indian voyages of Vasco da Gama (1497–98) and Cabral (1500), who discovered Brazil on his outward journey.

Castile, unable to compete in Portuguese waters, eventually gave its support to the fervent, mystical Genoese seafarer Christopher Columbus, in his plan to reach Japan (Cipangu) across the Atlantic. No one doubted that the world was round, but its size was at issue. Columbus never accepted that the islands he discovered in October 1492 were not part of Asia. This realization is owed to the Florentine publicist and explorer Amerigo Vespucci, who gave his name to the new continents. The northern reaches of the North American continent were revisited when, in an attempt to find a northern route to Asia, the Venetian John Cabot, sailing in English service, rediscovered the areas earlier known to the Vikings (1497).

Columbus expressed disappointment at the limited gold supplies of Cuba and Hispaniola, and at the simple condition of the Taino population. Setting the Tainos to work collecting gold, he (perhaps unwittingly) initiated a tough regime, which caused enormous mortality, compounded by the arrival of western diseases. In Europe, debate raged over the status of the native peoples: were they animals in human shape or rational beings, living in a childlike condition? The debate was old, since the Canary islanders and pagan Lithuanians had aroused similar worries, but the scale of the problem was immeasurably greater.

Music in the Middle Ages

Based on Greco-Roman theory and practice, the western musical tradition first emerged clearly in terms of compositions, musical notation, and theoretical treatises in the ninth century. Musical notation and performance practice thereafter developed rapidly in both ecclesiastical and secular contexts, which undoubtedly cross-fertilized each other. Western music was also receptive to Arab influences, though European music is characterized by polyphony as well as the extraordinary range of liturgical music and the diversity of social and cultural contexts in which music was performed.

Liturgical chant dominates the history of western music in the early Middle Ages. It is documented in manuscripts containing the newly devised musical notation (neumes). The Franks had created a hybrid "Roman" or "Gregorian" chant repertory by combining older, possibly Roman, material with Frankish chant. The extraordinarily creative period of musical composition in the ninth and tenth centuries produced many new syntheses of melody and prose, not least the sequences and tropes. Discussions of music theory by Carolingian and Ottonian musicians were augmented by their successors throughout the Middle Ages and provide important indications of new developments in musical practice. Philippe de Vitry's *Ars nova*, for example, on new principles of musical notation, built on the earlier system of neumes, the development of the stave explained by Guido d'Arezzo in the 11th century and Franconian notation advocated by Franco of Cologne.

Of the diverse musical traditions of the Middle East, India and Asia, only Arab music, not written down before the 13th century, impinged much on European music. Its characteristic microtonal inflection, florid ornamentation and heterophony influenced the music of countries which came under Islamic rule, most notably Muslim Spain and North Africa. Arab music in its turn, however, was influenced by Byzantine musical traditions, as is clear from the treatises written by Arab musicians such as Safi al-Din. Many courts of the Islamic world were famous for their secular music from the Abbasid period onwards.

The famous gift of a Byzantine organ to the Frankish ruler Pippin in 757 added a new sound to the great diversity of musical instruments of the Middle Ages,

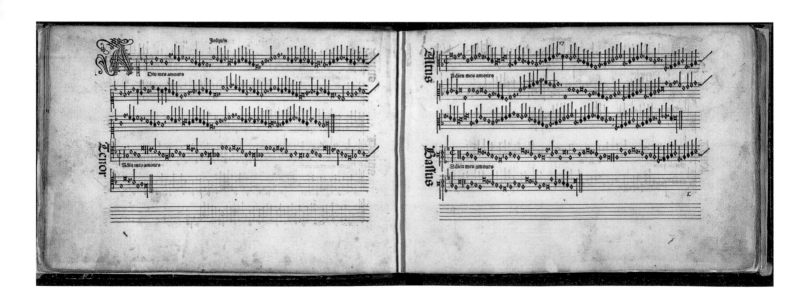

510–524	Mid-ninth century	Before 930	1025–33	1230–94
Boethius, *De Musica*	*Musica enchiriadis*	Hucbald of St Amand, *De institutione Harmonica*	Guido d'Arezzo *Micrologus de Musica* explained the use of the stave	Safi al-Din, music theorist and inventor of instruments *Book of Modes (Kitab al-adwar)*

- **•** important centres of music before the 11th century
- **•** courts and churches as centres of music in 12th and 13th centuries
- **•** ecclesiastical and secular centres of music in 14th and 15th centuries

North Sea

Gotland

Baltic Sea

Edinburgh

Dublin

Vilna

Elbe *Oder*

Vistula

Ely

Glogau

Winchester London
Windsor

Ghent
Cambrai St Amand Cologne
Liège Aachen Limburg Fulda
Caen Rouen Loan Trier
Beauvais Rheims Metz Mainz
Compiègne Inelheim
Chartres Paris
(Notre dame & St Victor)

Prague

Cracow

Rhine

Angers

Nuremberg
Regensburg
Danube Buxheim Munich
Reichenau Lambach Brno
Constance St Gallen Vienna
Einsiedeln Innsbruck

Buda

Bay of Biscay

Poitiers

Dijon

Blaye
Périgueux
Bordeaux

Limoges
(St Marchal)
Clermont

Cluny

Vienne

Rhône

Santiago de
Compostela

León

Le Puy
Rodez
Albi
Toulouse

Gap
Avignon
Montpellier

Turin
Milan Verona
Piacenza Venice
Mantua Padua
Ferrara
Bologna
Rimini
Pesaro
Florence Vallombrosa
Arezzo

Burgos

Douro

Ebro

Narbonne

Madrid

Lérida

Barcelona

Corsica

Tiber

Rome

Guadalquivir

Sardinia

Naples

Mediterranean Sea

Harmonice Musices Odhecaton A, printed by Ottaviano dei Petrucci at Venice (1501) containing the songs of many of the leading composers of the day, including Josquin des Prez and Henricus Isaac. The book is the most important of the early collections of printed music and forms one of Petrucci's many editions of 15th-century music. The book also provides evidence of the movement of musicians throughout Europe. Henricus Isaac, for example, although Flemish served the Medici and the Emperor Maximilian I. Another musician, Guillaume de Machaut, went as far afield as Prague, Poland and Lithuania. (Left)

MUSIC IN THE MIDDLE AGES

Europe and the Middle East showing the principal centres, both ecclesiastical and secular, of music in the middle ages. *As one of the seven liberal arts, music was also studied in the schools and universities as a theoretical discipline closely aligned with mathematics and philosophy.*

1252–84	c. 1275	c. 1320	1320	1325
Cantigas de amore e de Maldizer and *cantigas de Sancta maria* made for Alfonso X of Aragon	*De mensuris et discantu*, anon. English work	*Roman de fauvel* (Paris, Bibliothèque Nationale fr. 146)	Philippe de Vitry, *Ars nova* on the new principles of musical notation	Robertsbridge codex compiled (London, British Library Add. 28550): the earliest known collection of keyboard music

many of them the ancestors of our modern instruments. These included plucked and bowed stringed instruments (including the Arab-influenced lute), pipes, reeds, tuned bells, and brass.

Liturgical drama accompanied by music and chant was elaborated for Passion, Easter, Christmas and Epiphany narratives from the tenth century onwards. Ecclesiastical chant provided the first beginnings of polyphony. In the 12th century, side by side with the famous liturgical organa at Notre Dame in Paris and elsewhere, it is possible to document developments in the secular sphere as well, such as the songs of the goliards (wandering students), the travelling professional musicians such as the jongleurs (in France), Gaukler (in Germany) or skomorokhi (in Russia). There were also the famous French troubadours, such as Bernart de Ventadorn, and the German Minnesänger, such as Walter von der Vogelweide. The troubadours in particular helped to establish the prominence of courts for the performance and encouragement of music by princely patrons.

The ever fruitful interchange between ecclesiastical and secular music bore fruit in the motets of the 13th and 14th centuries, with the superb compositions inserted into the *Roman de Fauvel* by such musicians as Philippe de Vitry (c. 1320). The polyphonic music and masses of Guillaume de Machaut (1300–72), Johanne Ciconia (c. 1335/1370–1412), Guillaume Dufay (1400–74), William Dunstable (d. 1453) and Josquin des Prez (1440–1521) inspired many other musicians, both directly and indirectly. French, Walloon, Italian and English musicians of the later Middle Ages with madrigals, dance and songs, at the courts, in their chapels and in towns all over Europe, created a vibrant and richly creative musical culture which was the basis for the glories of Renaissance music.

The 9th-century St Gallen Psalterium showing King David playing a string instrument, together with musicians with drums.

Gradual from Regensburg, (Right) Third quarter of the 10th century, showing musical notation in the form of neumes. Neumes were developed in western Europe in a great diversity of regional variations. This book uses St Gallen neumes suprascript above the text. The book contains, among other melodies, many of the famous sequences of the musician Notker Balbulus of St Gallen (840–912).

"And in the manner of thunder the iron voice beats upon the ears that they receive no sound beyond only this, the sound so clamours, echoing here and there, that everyone loses the opening of his ears with his hand, totally unable to bear the noise when drawing near, which the various sounds producing in their clamouring. And the melody of the pipes is heard everywhere in the city, and flying fame goes through the whole country."

Wulfstan of Winchester describing the noise made by the vast organ (with 400 pipes) at 10th-century Winchester

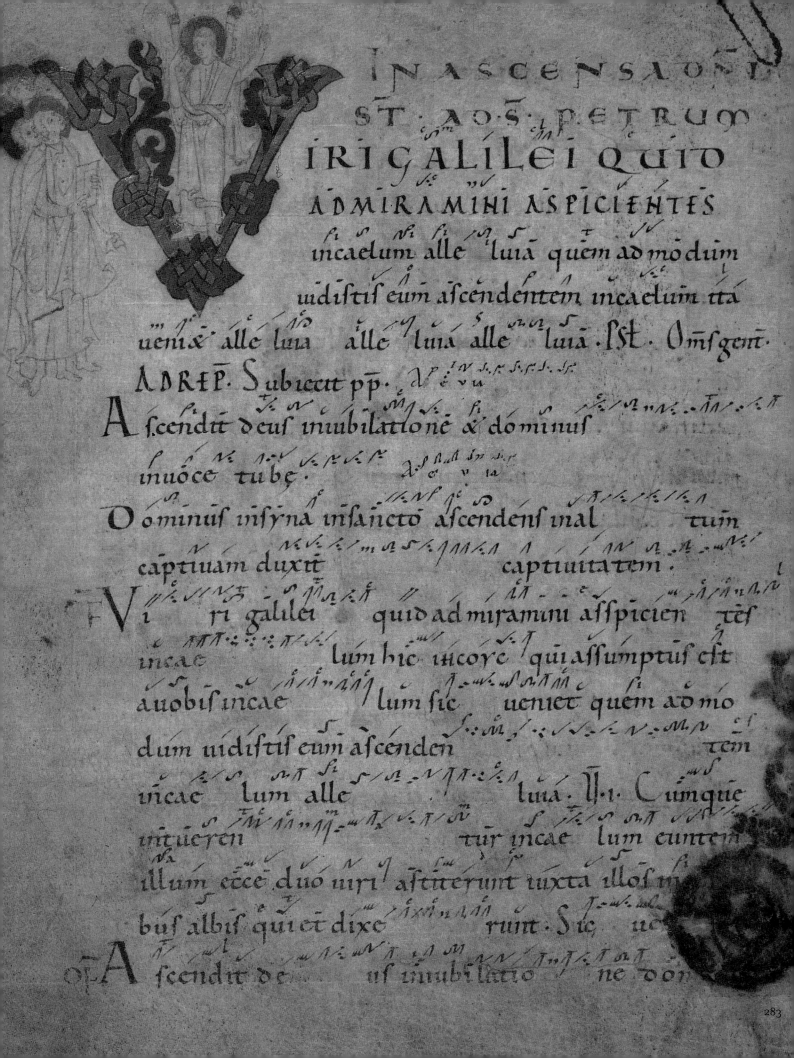

VIRI GALILEI QUID
ADMIRAMINI ASPICIENTES

in caelum alle luia quem ad modum

uidistis eum ascendentem in caelum ita

ueniet alle luia alle luia alle luia · P St · Oms gent

AD REP · Subiecit pp ·

Ascendit deus in iubilatione et dominus

in uoce tube ·

Dominus in syna in sancto ascendens in al   tu in

captiuam duxit   captiuitatem ·

Vi ri galilei   quid ad miramini asspicien tes

in cae   lum hic in core qui assumptus est

a uobis in cae   lum sic   ueniet quem ad mo

dum uidistis eum ascenden   tem

in cae   lum alle   luia · Cumque

intueren   tur in cae lum euntem

illum ecce duo uiri astiterunt iuxta illos in

bus albis qui et dixe   runt · Sic   ue

A scendit de   us in iubilatio   ne dom

The World in 1500

The new maps and world projections of the late 15th and the 16th centuries combined the technical traditions of geometrical measurement and perspective and of empirically based sea charts (portolans) with conceptual *mappae mundi* in the medieval tradition. To these were added attempts to represent knowledge of the world that had been greatly expanded as a consequence of European voyages of exploration, such as the travels of Marco Polo and the Portuguese and Genoese navigators.

Maps embody knowledge and the visualization of the world from many different perspectives. Three dimensions, dramatic physical variety, vast distances, the location of human settlement and wonders are all confined on a small plane within a particular framework and set of conventions. Whether one is considering medieval European maps or their Arabic or Asian contemporaries, the maps are visual aids to understanding man's relation to the terrestrial world. Many maps, such as the Indian Jain charts, provided images of the spiritual dimension as well, and were designed as aids to contemplation. These symbolic maps, although incorporating real geographical elements and knowledge, such as mountains, seas, and continents beyond India, were also religious icons. Japanese Buddhist maps of the 14th century (and later) also incorporated information from the seventh-century account of Hsuang-Tang, *A record of the regions to the west of China*. Maps also helped their users to find places and were particularly valuable to travellers. Their accuracy, however much they also represented subjective interpretations of the world, was of increasing importance. So too was their visual documentation of a shift of perception as a consequence of new knowledge and the dramatic discoveries of the explorers and enterprising merchants, not least the circumnavigation of the world by Magellan. Thus previous knowledge of discrete and disparate regions could now be combined and seen as part of a whole.

In the west, the Ptolemaic template in his *Cosmographia* became known in the course of the 14th century. It was first printed in 1477 and subsequent editions gradually incorporated new geographical information, though its conception of a landlocked ocean was soon discarded. Cartographers in the late 15th and the 16th centuries began to develop maps with special mathematical projections. These incorporated an understanding of scale, perspective and proportional representation on a grid. Allowance began to be made in representations of the world for the decreasing value of the degree of longitude, but all flat representations of the earth's sphere inevitably have a degree of distortion of the size of land masses and an apparently inconstant scale for distances. The major landmark in map making was Gerard Mercator's vast cordiform projection of the world published as a wall map in 21 sheets in 1569. It distinguished between North and South America and posited a large southern continent, though its use for navigation was not clarified until guides

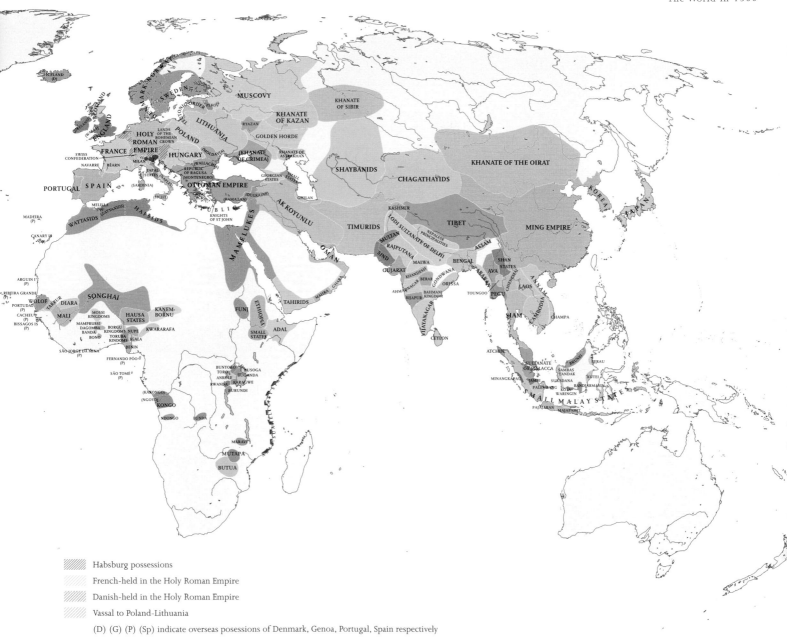

Habsburg possessions

French-held in the Holy Roman Empire

Danish-held in the Holy Roman Empire

Vassal to Poland-Lithuania

(D) (G) (P) (Sp) indicate overseas posessions of Denmark, Genoa, Portugal, Spain respectively

to Mercator's mathematical calculation had been worked out by Edward Wright in 1599.

Mercator's maps were the principal inspiration for the *Theatrum Orbis terrarum* of Abraham Ortelius (1527–98) of Antwerp. This magnificent book, with a collection of 90 maps, 17 times smaller than Mercator's wall map, was produced in a codex format by the Plantin press in 1570. It went through 31 editions, with many new maps being added between 1570 and 1621. It is the ancestor of all subsequent printed Atlases of the world. It was also the first historical Atlas, for Ortelius included original maps (the *Parergon* additions) of many aspects of Antiquity, such as Aeneas' travels and Caesar's conquests, based on his

extensive reading of classical writings. Ortelius drew on many existing maps by over 86 cartographers and other learned discussions for his Atlas. His oval-shaped map of the world, for instance, used Mercator's map of 1569 (with its cordiform projection), Gastaldi's map of the world of 1561 and Guitiérrez and Jerome Cook's map of the Americas of 1562. The oval projection compresses the area of the poles but distortion is less at the centre of the map. Ortelius's contemporary as well as his ancient and medieval sources of information were listed at the beginning of the book. Each map has an accompanying explanatory text. The Atlas thus represents a full account of the state of knowledge by 1570.

Abraham Ortelius, Theatrum orbis terrarum (Antwerp, 1570 and subsequent editions up to 1621 (including special versions in German French and English as well as Latin and all adjusted to take account of new knowledge as it became available. This highly coloured copy is the 1584 edition, now in Cambridge University Library. The distortion of South America was corrected in editions after 1587. The four huge Arctic islands were based on conjecture by Ortelius' friend Gerard Mercator A note is added to New Guinea that it has been represented as an island but that it is uncertain whether or not it was part of the great southern Continent (continens Australis) which here occupies the whole of the bottom of the map. The marking of cities with little buildings is very like some of the medieval mappae mundi. The inland information for the Americas and Africa is mostly conjectural but the precise work of navigators for the coastlines of many regions, not least Africa, India and the East Indies is clearly in evidence. Ortelius managed to leave a personal note on this map, for one of the three cities marked within Europe after Paris and Lyon is Augsburg, his family's home town whence his grandfather had come to Antwerp in the 15th century.

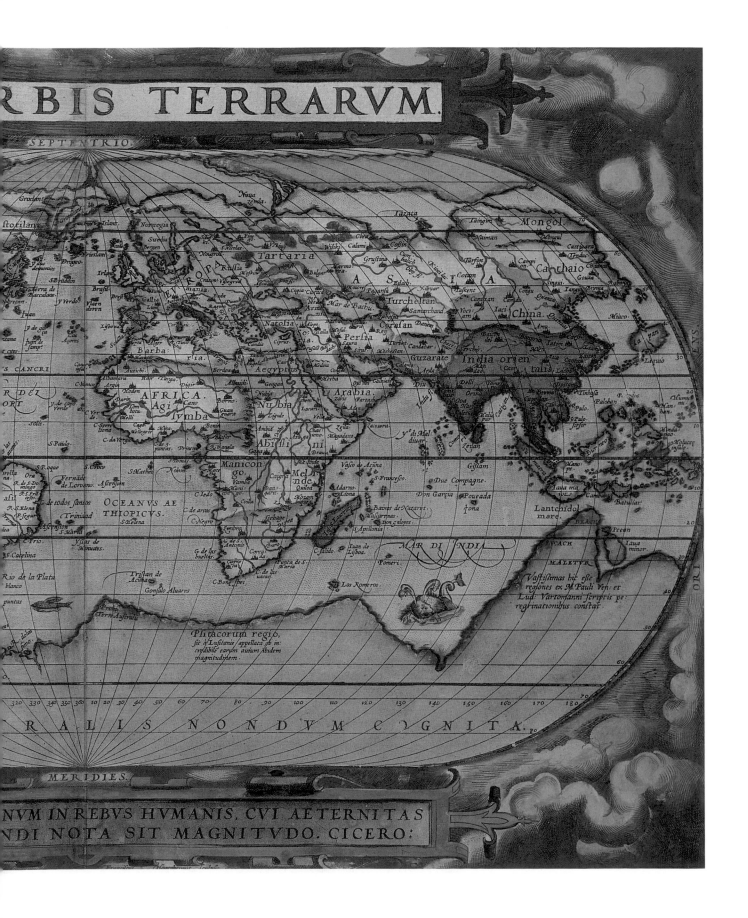

RBIS TERRARVM.

NVM IN REBVS HVMANIS, CVI AETERNITAS
NDI NOTA SIT MAGNITVDO. CICERO:

GLOSSARY

'ABD AL-MALIK (b. c. 646) Islamic caliph who reigned from Damascus between 685 and 705. 'Abd al-Malik began campaigning against the Byzantines whilst still only a teenage boy. His period of rule marked a major period of consolidation within the Islamic empire: civil servants of Roman or Byzantine descent were replaced by Arabs, Arabic became the official language of government and a uniform Islamic coinage was introduced to the caliphate as a whole. 'Abd al-Malik's reign further witnessed a concerted attack on the Christian use of icons or images in worship.

ALBIGENSIAN CRUSADE (1209–29) By the early 13th century Cathars were present in Bulgaria, Bosnia, northern Italy and Languedoc. Seeing themselves as "good Christians" and the Catholic Church as part of the corrupt material world, they replaced Catholic rites by a single sacrament, the *consolamentum*. After failing to pressure Count Raymond VI of Toulouse to act against the Cathars of Languedoc, Pope Innocent III (1198–1216) called a crusade. Religion and politics intermingled and northern French barons turned the Albigensian crusade into a war of conquest. They massacred the Cathars and replaced local lords with northerners.

ARTES The seven liberal arts: grammar, rhetoric and dialectic, arithmetic, geometry, astronomy and music.

ATABEG ("guardian") Turkish title given to a slave officer who governed a province on behalf of a young Seljuq prince.

AURALITY The mixture of literacy and orality involved whenever a written text is read aloud to one or more listeners. Throughout the Middle Ages, aurality was a prevalent reception format for a number of reasons: not all of the public for vernacular literature could read (in the central Middle Ages, literacy was concentrated among clerics, noblewomen, and also town dwellers, who initially acquired "pragmatic" literacy for commercial purposes); manuscripts were expensive to produce and therefore scarce, meaning that only a few privileged readers might own a book or have access to one; finally, and most importantly, the public liked having works of literature read to them. Even in the later Middle Ages, when literacy was rising, recital continued to be popular as a social and sociable occasion.

BASIL II THE BULGAR-SLAYER (976–1025) The longest reigning Byzantine emperor, known generally by the epithet "Bulgar-slayer". This is in recognition of his victories over the Bulgarian ruler, Tsar Samuel, and his annexation of Bulgaria to the empire after 1018. According to contemporary stories, Basil committed atrocities, including the blinding of 99 of every 100 Bulgarian captives taken at the Battle of Kleidion (July 1014); the hundredth was left a single eye to lead his comrades home. However, it is also recorded that Basil was magnanimous in victory, allowing the Bulgarians their own autocephalous archbishop, and to pay taxes in kind. His epithet was applied only in hindsight, as militant emperors sought to galvanize support for wars fought in the Balkans at the end of the 12th century.

BASTIDE A French term for a town foundation, usually fortified.

BHAKTI Literally "devotion", a term whose origins lay in the feudal ideology of Hindu temple kingdoms but which during later medieval times became an ideology which challenged caste hierarchy.

BURGESS, CITIZEN, FREEMAN Terms variously used in different towns for those with full civic rights and responsibilities.

BUYIDS A dynasty from Daylam, in northern Persia on the shore of the Caspian Sea, who were Shi'is. Mu'izz al-Dawlah entered Baghdad in 946 and soon deposed the Caliph, al-Mustakfi, whereupon the latter's son al-Muti' (The Obedient) was installed. In 977 'Adud al-Dawlah took control of Baghdad and initiated the period of the Buyid empire (977–1012). In 1055 they were removed from power when the Seljuks took control of Baghdad. Relations between the Buyids and the Caliphs were complex. It is remarkable, however, that they did not terminate the Sunni office of the Caliphate. During their rule Baghdad enjoyed a period of intellectual and philosophical brilliance.

CASTELLAN The holder or lord of a castle. A hereditary group that emerged in much of Europe in the 11th century. There were wide regional variations in the power and authority of French castellans. In parts of the Île-de-France, Burgundy and Languedoc, the castellans achieved great autonomy from royal or princely authority; their courts replaced other local judicial institutions and their "castellanies", the district under their "ban" or command, became the main local division. In other regions, notably Flanders, Anjou and Normandy, the princes successfully maintained their authority over the castellans.

CHARLES IV (1346–78) Originally called Wenzel, he was the son of John of Luxemburg, king of Bohemia. He grew up at the French royal court, where he received the name Charles. He consolidated his patrimony in Bohemia and Moravia, gaining a strong power-base. In Germany, he distributed royal lands to his followers and contributed to the increasing strength of territorial princes by the Golden Bull. Charles undertook to turn Prague into an imperial capital, with the erection of an archbishopric, the foundation of a university and large-scale building work, including a new cathedral and Charles Bridge. Charles knew five languages (Czech, German, French, Italian and Latin), and wrote an autobiography.

CHRISTOLOGY The debates about the person and nature of Christ as both God and man were a constant preoccupation. Different emphases in terms of Christ's human and divine elements such as Arianism, Monophysitism, Monotheletism, Nestorianism and Adoptionism and many more gained many adherents. The Catholic faith was defined in the Nicene Creed and all variants were regarded as heresies.

COMMUNE A sworn association, especially of townspeople, often headed by a mayor.

CONCILIARISM From the late 1200s, the conciliarist thesis challenged papal monarchy by asserting that the whole church, via a general council, was the ultimate repository of ecclesiastical authority. The idea gained support during the Great Schism (1378–1418) in the search to reunify Catholicism. At the Council of Constance the decree *Haec Sancta* (1415) proclaimed conciliar superiority; another decree, *Frequens*, demanded regular assemblies. Ideas of conciliar and papal supremacy clashed at Basle (1431–49), the radicalized council challenging and deposing Eugenius IV, but eventually being defeated. Pius II's bull *Execrabilis* condemned conciliarism in 1462, but did not end its influence on European ecclesiastical and political thought.

COPERNICAN SYSTEM Expounded by Copernicus, infers that the sun is the centre of the solar system with the earth, planets and their satellites revolving about it and revolving on their own axes.

CORTES A Spanish assembly, often with a representative element.

COUNCILS AND SYNODS The formal meetings of the clergy (and often powerful laity too) to decide on matters of doctrine, religious practice, ecclesiastical organization and Christian social behaviour.

COURT The institution in which a ruling individual or corporation's administrative and financial power was centred. Courts were usually based in a particular location, but might be peripatetic. The term "court" is somewhat ambiguous; understood in the broadest sense it embraces all who served a given ruler, although only a small percentage of these may be understood as "courtiers" proper. Courts of the 14th and 15th centuries might be centred round lay or ecclesiastical dignitaries. Most pertained to rulers beneath the rank of national leaders. The Medici court, for example, developed around an exceptionally successful family of bankers and merchants whose leaders subsequently became dukes of Tuscany.

CRUSADERS People who took part in a crusade. So called because they placed a cross on their clothing when they took the vow to go on crusade: from the Old French *croisé*: "crossed", or wearing a cross.

CUMANS Turkic nomads with animistic-shamanistic beliefs. The Cumans established their power on the Eurasian steppe in the 11th century. They periodically raided, but at other times created alliances with their sedentary neighbours. A group of Cumans fleeing from the advancing Mongols sought entry to Hungary in the mid-13th century. At the time of their arrival, the heir to the throne married the daughter of a Cuman chieftain. Their son, Ladislas IV, ruled over Hungary (1272–90). Despite conflict with the local population, the Cumans gradually settled, were converted to Christianity and integrated.

DEVADANA Literally "gift to god". Usually land granted to temples in medieval India, which allowed temples to enjoy revenue otherwise enjoyed by the state.

DEVOTIO MODERNA A pietistic and quasi-mystical spiritual movement, strongly Christocentric in nature. The *devotio moderna* ("new devotion") originated in the Netherlands in the late 14th century. While often relatively informal, an organized structure was developed – the Brothers and Sisters of the Common Life, for example, with their own houses. Several evolved into fully monastic communities as the church authorities sought to oversee and control the movement. Aiming to revitalize lay religion, works associated with the *devotio moderna* (notably the *Imitation of Christ*, by Thomas a Kempis) were major influences on late medieval devotion, with an impact throughout northern Europe.

DU FU (720–70) Ranked as the premier Chinese poet since at least the 11th century. The powerful emotions, technical mastery, and historical immediacy of his poems like *Spring View* and *Journey North* unforgettably fused his personal tragedies with the trials of his dynasty and country during the An Lushan rebellion. His later poetry's dense imagery, intricate syntax and rich language, as in the two-poem series *Autumn Wilderness* and *Autumn Meditations*, reveal him to be a master poet, capable of using the constraining rules of Regulated Tang Verse (*lushi*) to create works of Shakespearean intensity and complexity.

ELECTORS In theory, the princes elected the king of the Romans; in practice no election happened in the presence of all the eligible princes. In the mid-13th century (1257, 1273) the college of seven electors emerged, formalized in the Golden Bull of 1356. The electors were the archbishops of Mainz, Cologne and Trier, the king of Bohemia, the count-palatine of the Rhine, the duke of Saxony and the margrave of Brandenburg. This excluded many powerful lay and ecclesiastical princes.

FRANKS Western Europeans involved in the crusades to the Middle East. So called because they came from areas inhabited by the Frankish peoples: the Rhineland and what is now modern France. Also used for the people of Gaul and the Rhineland in the early Middle Ages.

GALLICANISM The particularly strident French manifestation of the late medieval trend towards national churches, resisting papal interference at local level. Important in disputes between King Philip IV (1285–1314) and Pope Boniface VIII (1295–1303), it reappeared in the Great Schism (1378–1418) and persisted throughout the 15th century. The Pragmatic Sanction of Bourges (1438) epitomized its claims for French ecclesiastical autonomy. Gallican sentiment was exploited by France's rulers: posturing as defenders of French liberties against papal encroachment, the kings entered into ambiguous concordats with the papacy, like that of 1472, to extend and entrench their authority over the French church.

GELD A land tax originally levied in Anglo-Saxon and Anglo-Norman England in the 990s to pay off Danish raiders (the tax was known as "Danegeld"), and recorded prominently in the Domesday Book (1086). In the 12th century it was abandoned in favour of less cumbersome taxes.

GERBERT (940–1003) Archbishop of Rheims (991–97), Archbishop of Ravenna (998), Pope Sylvester II (999–1003). He studied mathematics and astronomy in Spain and introduced the use of the Arabic abacus into his teaching of mathematics when master at the school of Rheims. There he also taught the logical works of Aristotle and Boethius.

GOTHIC The general term applied to the artistic and architectural styles that predominated in most parts of Europe between c. 1200 and c. 1550. For the cultural élite of Renaissance Italy, the style was barbaric, hence the appellation "Gothic". Large Gothic churches are characterized by pointed arches, diaphanous walls perforated by large windows with stone tracery, and high, ribbed vaults of stone, supported externally by flying buttresses. Like Romanesque, however, Gothic is an umbrella term covering a great variety of buildings. Figural arts in the Gothic style are typically more naturalistic than in Romanesque. Pose and gesture are mannered, with bodies often exhibiting a pronounced curve, and draperies and facial features are treated in a softer, less linear fashion. Foliage carving may be remarkably natural in appearance.

GREGORIAN REFORM Gregory VII (1073–85) claimed that papal power was above any temporal rule, and popes could depose Emperors. He ignited a debate over the relations between spiritual and temporal power, but also laid the foundations of the growth of papal power within the Church. The "Gregorian reform" in fact started prior to the pontificate of Gregory VII and continued after him. Monastic reform movements were followed by a wider ecclesiastical reform, demanding the purity of the clergy. Reformers focused on clerical celibacy and the fight against simony (buying ecclesiastical office). Papal reform led to the reinterpretation of the "liberty" of the Church as complete independence from lay involvement.

GAZI AND JIHAD These terms are usually translated as "warrior of the faith" and "holy war" respectively. Views as to their importance in the early Ottoman state differ, it being traditionally argued that *jihad* was the driving force behind the early Ottoman advance and that, as recently stated, the "gazi ethos" was central to the Ottoman world before 1453, while being a *gazi* was a central component of the early Ottoman ruler's multiple identity. Both these interpretations are, however, by no means universally accepted. Others argue that in fact jihad was merely one amongst various factors accounting for the initial success of the Ottoman state and that, while the concept of gazi was undoubtedly important later, it was not of major significance in the very early period. Colin Imber pointed out that the term gazi probably did not enter everyday Turkish speech in western Anatolia until sometime after the middle of the 14th century, when it meant merely "hero" or "warrior".

HANSE Originally an association of travelling merchants, and later an association of trading towns. Used especially of the German Hanse, described more familiarly but misleadingly in English literature as the Hanseatic League.

HEIKE MONOGATARI Or The Tale of the Heike The most important of the "war tales" of the Kamakura and Muromachi periods, it covers the struggle between the Minamoto and the Taira in the second half of the 12th century. It had its origin in ballads sung or chanted by itinerant priests to the Japanese lute (biwa), and seems to have begun its transformation from an oral tradition into a text early in the 13th century. It contains many striking scenes of conflict and accounts of the brave doings of warriors, but it is imbued with Buddhist melancholy and a sense of the unavoidably ephemeral nature of earthly life and ambitions. It has long enjoyed the status of a classic and was used as a source of Nô plays and other literary forms.

HUMANISM A literary movement focusing on grammatical and rhetorical studies and the Latin and Greek writings of classical antiquity which provided a new ideology of education. Humanists emphasized the importance of education and classical learning as a qualification for membership of a social and political élite.

HUSSITES Moderates, who demanded ecclesiastical reform, and radicals, such as the community of Tabor, who wished to lead an apostolic life based on an egalitarian vision, holding property in common, and strict morality. Radicals rejected existing social and political institutions and awaited the imminent advent of Christ. The four articles formulated the demands of the moderates: communion in both kinds (consecrated bread and wine) to the laity; free preaching; limits to the property and secular lordship of priests; and purgation of public sins. The moderates defeated the radicals and finally accepted Sigismund as king. Hussitism introduced the use of the Czech language in government and worship.

HUSSITISM Mixing aspirations for ecclesiastical reform with Czech anti-German nationalism, Hussitism coalesced following the burning of Jan Hus at the Council of Constance in 1415. From 1419 it was a revolutionary movement in Bohemia, both politically and ecclesiastically. Its identifying tenet was Utraquism, offering laypeople both bread and wine in the mass; its unifying symbol was the chalice. The Hussites repelled repeated crusades, but internal tensions caused violent divisions, the moderates defeating the radicals. From 1436, after negotiations with the Council of Basle, the Bohemian Utraquist Hussite church was a reluctantly tolerated variety of Catholicism, surviving until the 17th century.

IBN BATTUTA (c. 1304–69) A North African traveller who composed a travelogue in which he claims to have journeyed across the Abode of Islam for nigh-on three decades. Leaving Tangiers in 1325 and travelling to Egypt and Syria, he performed the pilgrimage to Mecca in 1326, whence he proceeded to Iraq and Iran. He also visited the Muslim community of the Volga Bulgars and Transoxania. A protracted visit to India in 1333 led to a visit to China. In 1349 he returned to Fez and Spain. He made a second journey in 1352–53 to sub-Saharan Africa.

IBN RUSHD (1126–98) Known to the West as Averroes. He is particularly prized as a commentator on Aristotle, and the translations of his commentaries from Arabic to Latin in the 12th and 13th centuries restored to Europe much of classical and late antique thought that had been lost. Ibn Rushd was also a renowned physician in his own day, as well as a practised astronomer and the author of many works on Islamic jurisprudence. He held the position of Chief Judge of Cordoba under the second Almohad caliph Abu Ya'qub Yusuf (1163–84).

IBN SINA Known to the West as Avicenna, Ibn Sina was the most important Islamic philosopher of the Middle Ages. Born near Bukhara, the then Samanid capital, Ibn Sina was exposed by his father to Fatimid Isma'ili doctrines, which were of a preponderantly Neo-Platonic stamp. In 1014, in the city of al-Rayy, he first entered into Buyid service and in 1023 he was granted the patronage of 'Ala' al-Dawla (d. 1041/2), the ruler of Isfahan, who remained his patron until Ibn Sina's death in 1037. Ibn Sina was a famed physician as well as an influential metaphysician, whose psychology exerted much influence of contemporary and subsequent theories of the soul.

IBN TUMART (d. 1130) A preacher and theologian, and native of the Masmuda Berbers from southern Morocco. Theologically opposed to what he considered to be the anthropomorphic tendencies of the Almoravid conception of Allah, he preached the doctrine of Tawhid, the absolute unicity of Allah, whence his followers were known as the Almohads, i.e. al-Muwahhidun, those who confess the unicity of Allah. Back in Morocco, after a visit to the religious centres of the East, he proclaimed himself the Mahdi, the figure who was blessed with divine guidance and whose mission it was to restore Islam from its decadent wickedness and debauchery. He is buried in the mountain stronghold of Tinmal in the Atlas Mountains.

INVESTITURE CONTROVERSY This began when Emperor Henry IV refused to abandon his customary rights to appoint the archbishop of Milan. For the "liberty of the Church", the pope soon completely prohibited lay investiture, that is, rulers giving clerics the symbols of their office. After Pope Gregory VII (1073–85) excommunicated the Emperor (1077), Henry gained absolution, but the conflict continued, with Gregory claiming that the pope could depose the emperor and Henry calling for the deposition of the pope. Henry invaded Rome and although Gregory was freed by his Norman allies, he died soon afterwards. The controversy was only resolved in the 1122 *Concordat of Worms*, with the division of the temporal and spiritual aspects of clerical office. The Emperor renounced investiture with the ring and crosier, symbols of spiritual power.

ISMA'ILIYYA Name used by opponents for the branch of the Shi'a to which the Isma'ilis adhered. By tracing the Imamate though the son (Isma'il) of the Imam Ja'far al-Sadiq ("the True"; d. 765), it diverged from the branch of the Shi'a known as Twelver Shi'ites. A revolutionary mission against the Abbasids had been organized by the Isma'ilis by the middle of the ninth century, though they split in 899 into the Isma'ilis and the Qarmatian splinter group, based in Bahrayn. In 909 the Isma'ilis founded a state in North Africa which subsequently became the Fatimid Imam-Caliphate of Egypt, where they founded Cairo as their capital. There are many Isma'ili communities spread across the world today.

IVORY-TOWER Intellectual training for its own sake.

JOHN VI CANTACUZENUS (c. 1292–1383) An aristocrat and soldier. For many years he served as *Grand Domesticus*, head of the Byzantine army. He fought in the civil wars that characterized Byzantine politics in the mid-14th century, declaring himself emperor in 1347. After seven years of civil and international warfare that saw him ally, to little effect, with both the Serbs and the Ottomans, Cantacuzenus abdicated and became a monk. He sought to remain in the public sphere through writing. His literary compositions include theological treatises and a major historical work, the *Historiae*. His account of the period 1320–1356 is a polemic of self-justification. Nonetheless, it also contains much original eyewitness and documentary evidence.

KANEM-BORNO A large empire situated in the central Sudan. Its origins are obscure. Arabic historical sources refer to Kanem from the ninth century and Islamic influences within the region would appear to date from this time. By the mid-11th century the ruler had converted to Islam. Following dynastic upheaval between 1394–1448 the centre of the empire was moved from Kanem (east of Lake Chad) to Borno (west of the lake). A new capital, Birni Gazargamo, was subsequently built during the reign of Ali Dunamami (1472–1504).

KASTRA In late antiquity the cities of the empire were known by the Greek term of *poleis*. The much-reduced cities of the Byzantine empire from the seventh century onwards became known instead as *kastra*, from the Latin term for military camps. These cities were now in effect military citadels and bases from which resistance to further Arab expansion was organized under the command of the local *strategos* or general. Only as military conditions stabilized within the empire from the ninth century onwards did these settlements begin to take on a more civilian aspect.

KOUMBI SALEH It has been suggested that Koumbi Saleh in southern Mauritania was a Muslim merchant town attached to the capital of the kingdom of Ghana. Archaeological excavation uncovered the remains of a regularly planned town made up of multi-storey houses and containing a large mosque. Whether this was one of the towns described by Al-Bakri is unclear as no trace of the royal town has yet been found and until this is achieved any identification will remain insecure.

LOLLARDY England's only native medieval heretical movement. Lollardy originated around John Wycliffe (d. 1384) at Oxford. The academic element soon faded, and the ideas became increasingly nebulous. Whether Lollardy was really a movement is debated; yet reformist and anticlerical ideas were common in late medieval England. Two of Lollardy's main features were denial of transubstantiation at mass and advocacy of an English Bible. Heresy trials recurred throughout the 15th and early 16th century; from 1415, after a failed revolt, Lollardy was tinged with treason and was a statute crime. Lingering despite persecution, it eventually fed into the English Reformation.

MACEDONIAN RENAISSANCE From the late ninth century onwards the Byzantine empire entered into a period of artistic and cultural efflorescence occasioned partly by the demise of iconoclasm, and partly by the improvement in the empire's military and economic situation. This phenomenon is known as the "Macedonian Renaissance", after the figure of Basil I "the Macedonian". Basil ascended the imperial throne in 867, having murdered his friend and associate, the Emperor Michael III. In spite of this inauspicious start to his reign, Basil proved himself to be a generous patron of the arts, as too did a number of his imperial descendants such as the Emperors Leo VI (886–912) and Constantine (913–59).

MAMLUK A term meaning "owned", it is especially used in the sense of "slave soldier". Mamluks were generally of Turkic origin and formed an integral part initially of the soldiery, and then of the bureaucracy of many Muslim states. The use of Turkic ghulams, an earlier term for mamluk, was established on a significant scale by al-Mu'tasim, Abbasid Caliph (833–42), and his precedent was followed by dynasties such as the Ayyubids, founded by Saladdin. The apogee of the institution is the Mamluk Sultanate of Egypt and Syria (1250–1517).

MAMLUK SULTANATE In 1250 the ruling Ayyubid dynasty in Egypt was overthrown by one of its Mamluk or slave regiments. The last Ayyubid ruler was replaced by a Mamluk officer, Aybeg. The Mamluk era, which lasted until 1517, was renowned for its military system based on slave soldiers raised and trained as property of the state. The effectiveness of the Mamluk military was well attested in Nubia where in 1276 Christian Nubian forces were defeated at Dongola and 10,000 Nubians were killed or taken prisoner.

MANSA MUSA The greatest of the rulers of the Empire of Mali. He extended the borders of the state but also left a lasting impression beyond Africa following his pilgrimage to Mecca begun in 1324. His *hajj* caravan was extensive as he was accompanied by numerous followers including 500 slaves, each of whom reputedly carried a staff of gold. This gold supply was further supplemented by another 80 to 100 camel loads each weighing 300 pounds. Gold was spent so prodigiously by Mansa Musa and his entourage that when the Arab writer Al-Umari was in Cairo 12 years later, the inhabitants were still singing the praises of Mansa Musa. However, such profligate spending meant that gold was also devalued in Egypt.

MAYOR The chief magistrate or official of a town, especially in France and England.

MISTRA A fortress was first constructed at Mistra near Sparta by the Latin lords of the Morea. From 1262 onwards the site became the centre of Byzantine authority in the Peloponnese. A thriving urban settlement developed beneath the fortified hilltop. Mistra is remarkable for its large number of late medieval palaces and churches. The town was not only a political centre but also home to scholars, including the Platonist philosopher Gemistheus Plethon. The best preserved of all the late Byzantine sites, Mistra was occupied by the Ottomans in 1460, six years after the fall of Constantinople.

MOUVANCE A term used by contemporary scholars to describe the mobility and fluidity of the literary work in a manuscript culture. The texts of the same work transmitted in different manuscripts are rarely absolutely identical; where these variations are not the result of accident or scribal error, they suggest that a work existed only in variant realizations, each with its individual characteristics and rationale. At the limits, a particular realization can be so divergent from the others that it becomes difficult to say whether it is still a version of the "same" work, or constitutes a new work in its own right.

NEACASTRA During the 12th century many sites across the Byzantine empire were fortified. Sometimes fortifications were built from scratch and at other times existing sites were refurbished. The nature of such fortifications varied considerably. Some forts were located in elevated positions, others in low-lying areas. Some were places of permanent habitation; others temporary refuge spots. One of the most heavily fortified regions was the theme (province) of Neacastra in western Asia Minor where rural populations, previously living in open villages, were moved to hilltop sites to protect them from neighbouring Turcoman nomads.

NICHIREN (1222–1282) One of the major figures in the emergence of new forms of Buddhism in the Kamakura period and the founder of what became known as the Nichiren or Lotus sect. In his youth he studied various sects of Buddhism eclectically but with a growing devotion to the Lotus Sûtra. In 1253 he began to make a reputation for himself as a turbulent priest by preaching against the Pure Land and Zen sects and declaring that a declaration of faith in the Lotus Sûtra was alone sufficient for salvation. In 1260 he wrote a polemic entitled *Risshô ankokuron* (On establishing orthodoxy and bringing peace to the nation), in which he urged suppression of Pure Land Buddhism and warned of the likelihood of a foreign invasion if this were not achieved, and presented this to the Bakufu. He was attacked and exiled, but the arrival of Kublai Khan's envoys in 1268 seemed to confirm his prediction and his denunciations became bolder. He was only narrowly saved from execution and went into exile on the remote island of Sado. He was released from exile in 1274 but the failure of the two Mongol invasions in that year and in 1281 disappointed his expectation of imminent punishment of the Japanese population for what he saw as their religious failings. Unlike Pure Land and Zen Buddhism, his version of Buddhism was homegrown, but he was not so much the precursor of ultranationalism that he has sometimes been taken to be, but a Buddhist leader who was unusually intolerant of other varieties of Buddhism.

NIZAM AL-MULK (1018–92) Chief Vizier of the Seljuq Sultans Alp-Arslan and Malik Shah. He accompanied Alp-Arslan on all his military campaigns, although he was not present at the Battle of Manzikert against the Byzantines in 1071. He continued as Chief Minister after Alp-Arslan's death in 1072, serving the Sultan Malik Shah as the *de facto* ruler of the Seljuq Sultanate. In 1091 he composed his celebrated Siyasat-nama (Treatise on Statecraft). His fame is also associated with the foundation of numerous madrasas, schools for religious instruction, the most renowned being the Nizamiyya in Baghdad, for a while under the directorship of the Sunni theologian, al-Ghazzali (d. 1111).

NUR AL-DIN MAHMUD (1146–74) Son of Zangi Zangid Sultan of Aleppo who died in 1146, and the prime mover in the Muslim resistance against the Crusaders. He captured Damascus in 1154, using an army that comprised Turkish Mamluks and Kurdish warriors, of whom Ayyub and his son Saladin are the most famous examples. This army was not a standing army but was mustered for seasonal campaigns. The capture of Damascus meant that Muslim Syria was united under one ruler. His notion of the Jihad, the Holy Struggle, involved the promotion of his own image as the Muslim leader *par excellence*, an extensive programme of architecture and the foundation of madrasas, schools for the study and teaching of religious learning.

ORDER OF THE GOLDEN FLEECE An order of knighthood founded by Philip III the Good of Burgundy in 1430. Subscribing to principles of chivalry, a highly select number of members committed themselves to defend the duchy and the Christian religion.

PATRONAGE The financial support or purchase, in part or in whole, of works of art. Thus, single works might have multiple patrons (group portraits, for example). A patron did not necessarily commission or oversee the completion of a work. However, in practice this often happened, particularly before the development of the open art market. Where the courts of rulers are concerned, the practice of patronage is to be understood in more than simply financial terms. It was a process of self-aggrandizement, motivated by the desire to appear powerful, wealthy, learned and pious.

POPE INNOCENT III (1198–1216) Elected pope at the age of 37, he asserted papal authority to an unprecedented degree in pastoral care,

reform and politics. According to Innocent, the pope, vicar of Christ, head of Christendom, was responsible for the spiritual welfare of all Christians. At the Fourth Lateran Council, attended by over 1,200 churchmen and representatives of lay powers, Innocent implemented wide-ranging reforms including yearly confession for the laity and changes in marriage law. He launched a crusade against heretics and approved new religious movements. He even intervened in a controversial German royal election, claiming that the pope could examine the suitability of the candidates.

PREDESTINATION The idea in which the elect are sure of eternal salvation. The Carolingian theologian Gottschalk advocated double predestination, with eternal damnation certain for the others. His views were condemned but Calvin revived them during the Reformation.

PREMYSL OTAKAR II (1253–78) The interregnum in the Empire and political divisions in Poland facilitated the rise of Otakar, King of Bohemia and Duke of Austria. Called king of "iron and gold" due to his military victories and riches, he wanted to become German emperor. Building an alliance with the Teutonic Knights and Béla IV, King of Hungary, his power frightened the German princes. Although one of the electors, he was not invited to vote in 1273 and refused to accept Rudolf of Habsburg's election. He was defeated and killed in the battle of Dürnkrut. Dante praised Otakar's worthiness in his *Divine Comedy*.

PTOLEMAIC SYSTEM Conceived the earth as the fixed centre of the universe, in which the apparent motions of sun, moon and stars as seen from the earth were understood to be real, and the heavens were understood to move about an axis passing through the centre of the earth through the North and South Poles. All the planets, and the sun and the moon, were thought to be carried around the earth on transparent and concentric globes known as the celestial spheres whose speed increased with distance from the earth.

PTOLEMY'S MAP OF THE WORLD No world map survives from antiquity; reconstructions and visual interpretations of Ptolemy, only certainly known in Byzantium from the 13th century, were not produced until the 15th century in Europe. In any case, 15th-century reconstructions of Ptolemy's world may have been more influenced by contemporary projections than is at present acknowledged.

PURGATORY After lengthy evolution, by 1300 Purgatory was identified as a place between Heaven and Hell, although its formal doctrinal affirmation was delayed until 1439. Following an immediate personal judgement after death, admission to Purgatory allowed those destined for Heaven who died without making full satisfaction for their earthly sins to undergo torments to complete the cleansing process there. Awareness of Purgatory, and the desire to curtail its torments, stimulated many spiritual practices of late medieval Catholicism, especially the acquisition of indulgences, and the explosion in post-mortem commemorative masses and prayers frequently associated with religious houses, chantry foundations and fraternities.

QAGHAN ("emperor" in Turkish) The term used of the Mongol sovereigns who succeeded Chinggis Khan.

QU 'RAN The compilation of revelations received by the Prophet Mohammed from the Archangel Gabriel. According to Islamic tradition, Mohammed wrote down these revelations in the form of verses inscribed on animal bones and suchlike. These revelations were then organized into a collection on the basis not of their chronology, but rather according to the length of each verse. The compilation is said to have found its canonical form in the reign of the Caliph 'Uthman (644–56), although the earliest evidence for its existence dates only from the end of the seventh century.

RAJPUT Term applied to Hindu aristocratic clans centred in northern and western India from the time of the Gurjara-Pratiharas. They bore the brunt of early Turkish invasions in India and were partially incorporated into late Sultanate and Mughal political structures.

REGALIAN RIGHTS Powers which had been wielded by the Carolingian kings, notably authority over fortifications, coinage, taxation, forests and other natural resources, and the most serious crimes (known by the 13th century as "high justice").

RELICS OF SAINTS In the form of bones, dust from their tombs or other material, mementoes were revered as holy objects and a lively traffic in relics, particularly across the Alps, was established in the eighth and ninth centuries. As new saints were added, so new relics, usually whole bodies, became an important factor in the setting up of new churches.

ROMANESQUE The general stylistic term applied to European architecture and art from c. 1000 to c. 1150, and later in many countries. Some argue that the term is also applicable to architecture of the seventh to the tenth centuries. Romanesque buildings are typically of weighty construction, with round arcade and window arches as in Roman architecture (hence the term Romanesque). Besides churches, Romanesque domestic and military buildings survive throughout Europe. In the figural arts, the style is characterized by expressive and highly contrived gesture, a lack of naturalism relative to Gothic art, and in book painting, the frequent use of vivid colours.

SAAMI Northern Scandinavia and adjacent parts of Finland with the Kola peninsula was known broadly as Lapland. It was inhabited by the nomadic Saami who lived by hunting, mostly reindeer, and fishing. They are ethnically distinct from the rest of the peoples of Scandinavia, but they adopted a Finnish language at a very early stage. Their lands stretched as far south as Dalarne in Sweden; Ottar, a Norwegian chieftain who in the ninth century described these parts, says that his own wealth depended heavily on taxes extorted from the Saami. Throughout the Middle Ages, when there were no fixed borders between Norwegian, Swedish, Finnish and Russian Lapland, the Saami were haunted by competing Norwegian, Swedish and Russian tax collectors.

SAINTS AS PATRONS Holy men and women of the early Christian church, including the Apostles and Christ's disciples, the early Christian martyrs, early popes, bishops and founders of monasteries, were honoured as saints. Churches and monasteries were dedicated to their memory and saints were regarded as intercessors in prayers offered by the faithful to God.

SAKAI A Japanese town which owed its commercial prominence to its possession of a fine natural harbour at the eastern end of the Inland Sea. As the reach of the Muromachi shogunate shrank in the 14th and 15th centuries, especially after the Ônin Wars of 1576–77, the merchants of Sakai gradually translated their economic power (derived from their connections to the wealthy temples of Nara) into political independence. Sakai merchants thereafter took part in the officially sanctioned so-called "tally" trade with Ming China and the city became an *entrepôt* port for trade with Korea, the Ryûkyû kingdom (now the Japanese prefecture of Okinawa) and various locations in Southeast Asia. In the second half of the 16th century Portuguese traders were also to be found there. By then it had a population of around 30,000 and was self-governing under a

council composed of leading merchants. Many took an interest in the development of the tea ceremony, some had already sponsored some secular printing, and after the introduction of firearms Sakai became a major production centre for guns. The city was protected by a moat and other defences, but it could not withstand the assault of Oda Nobunaga, who, in his drive to reunify Japan, took Sakai in 1569. The contraction of foreign trade after the 1630s, when the freedom to trade overseas was severely limited, spelt the end of Sakai's commercial dominance.

SAMANIDS An Iranian dynasty of Emirs (originally local Sassanid dihqans, land-owning élites) who ruled Khurasan and Transoxania from 819–1005, establishing their capital first in Samarqand and then in Bukhara. Although they enjoyed *de facto* independence, they remained loyal to the Caliphate, preaching in the Caliph's name and initially issuing coinage also in his name. Their success originated from their capable management of the trade routes from the east and the north and of the rich silver mines located in their territories: Chinese pottery has been found in their territories and silver dirhams minted by them have been found in northern Russia and Scandinavia. They were fabled patrons of the arts and the sciences.

SKÅNE MARKET At the southwestern tip of Skåne, the "ear" of Skåne, a great annual market developed, based on the herring fisheries in the autumn. Several Hanseatic towns had their own areas with booths to which they returned each year and where their own law applied. Valdemar IV of Denmark, having recovered Skåne from Sweden in 1360 and conquered Gotland in 1361, tried to restrict the privileges of the Germans at the Skåne market, provoking a war that he lost in 1370. He was forced to renew the privileges of the Hanseatic towns and even pay compensation. However, internal divisions weakened the towns and their attempts to exclude foreigners from the Skåne market led the English and Dutch to find other sources of fish, such as Iceland.

STEFAN DURAN UROS IV (1331–55) Duran distinguished himself at the Battle of Küstendil (Velbuzhd, 1330), and was able to depose his father the following year. He expanded his realm to embrace formerly Byzantine lands south of Serbia, seizing Ohrid, Prilep and the Strymon region (in the modern Republic of Macedonia), and securing tacit Bulgarian support by marrying Helena, sister of Tsar Ivan Alexander. Duran interfered in the Byzantine civil war of 1341–47, backing first John VI Kantakuzenos, and later John V Palaeologos. In 1346 he had himself crowned Emperor of the Serbs and Romans by the man he had proclaimed Serbian patriarch, and his son Stefan Uros V became junior king. Duran's regime embraced tenets of Byzantine administration, and translated Byzantine law texts, which were used as the basis for a new Serbian legal code, the *Zakoknik*, issued in 1354.

STEFAN UROSH II MILUTIN King of Serbia (1282–1321). The second son of Stefan Urosh I, grandson of Stefan the First-Crowned, Stefan Urosh II enjoyed the epithet Milutin, "child of grace". He took an anti-Byzantine position from the beginning of his reign, in 1282, capturing both Skopje and Dyrrachium (modern Durrës). Milutin also replied to an assault by the Bulgarian Shishman of Vidin, and appeased his overlord, the Mongol Khan Nogay. In 1298, Milutin took as his fourth wife, the daughter of the Byzantine emperor Andronicus II. Henceforth, he looked to Constantinople for support within and beyond Serbia, including securing the exile of his rebellious son to the imperial capital in 1314. Milutin died in Kosovo, 29 October 1321.

STUDIUM GENERALE An institution of higher education founded on or recognized by an authority of a universal nature such as the pope or an emperor. Its members enjoyed rights which transcended all local divisions concerning the personal status of masters and students, which enabled members to enjoy revenues from ecclesiastical benefices without living in them. The titles awarded by the universities were universally valid. Licences to teach conferred by the degrees were licences to teach throughout Christendom. The title of master or doctor was valid everywhere.

SU SHI (1037–1101) A master of virtually all Chinese literary and artistic forms, this poet-painter-calligrapher-official-gourmand exemplified literati tradition at its best. His writing is technically refined yet continually spontaneous, sometimes socially committed yet often personally detached, fond of mundane pleasures yet consistently witty and sophisticated. His criticism of Wang Anshi's reforms, however, won this cultural hero 30 years of distant provincial postings relieved by only a few court appointments.

SUFISM Term denoting Islamic mystical movements which in the Indian context facilitated the spread of Islamic ways of life among non-Muslims.

SULTAN Literally: "supreme power". A title first conferred on the Seljuq leader by the Caliph, and subsequently adopted by the heads of other Islamic dynasties.

SYMEON, KHAN OF THE BULGARIANS (c. 894–927) Bulgaria reached its apogee in the reign of Khan Symeon, who engraved the title "emperor of the Bulgarians and the Romans" on his seals. Distancing himself from the Bulgars' pagan capital, Pliska, Symeon expanded the stone walls of his fortress at Preslav and constructed within a palace complex surrounded by churches and stone residences for his nobles arranged along limestone-paved roads. The new capital "richly decorated with stone, wood, and colours", was celebrated by John the Exarch. The "colours" were provided by polychrome wall and floor tiles, produced at nearby monasteries. Inscribed boundary stones show that Bulgaria reached to within 20km of Thessalonica.

SYNODS see councils

TAGSATZUNG A diet made up of delegates from member republics of the Swiss Confederation.

THEMATA The Persian and Arab raids of the seventh century and the consequent militarization of Byzantine society led to the dismantling of the provincial administrative system on the basis of which the empire had hitherto been governed. Instead, from the seventh century onwards, the empire was divided up into themata or "themes", districts primarily administered by the local *strategos* or general and his entourage. With each theme, there existed military landholdings on which soldiers and their families were settled, cultivating the soil in return for providing military service to the empire. The precise date of this administrative reorganization is unknown.

VALDÈS OR VAUDÈS (d. c. 1205–07), a rich merchant from Lyons, converted to religious life in the 1170s. He distributed his riches, had passages of the Bible translated and started to preach the Gospels. His followers, the Poor of Lyons, lay men and women, imitated his example. In 1180, Valdès and his followers made a "Profession of Faith", attesting their orthodoxy, and were permitted to live a life of poverty and begging; they could preach if the local priest gave his permission. When the newly elected archbishop of Lyons prohibited preaching, Valdès refused to obey, referring to the biblical message. This led to excommunication, and the Waldensians eventually developed their own organization and belief-system, different from Catholic ones.

VENICE Relations between Byzantium and Venice had long been close. Venetian Doges often held Byzantine titles while the city's merchants benefited from trading concessions. In 1082 Byzantium extended Venice's commercial privileges considerably in return for naval support against the Normans in the Adriatic. Subsequent relations between the two powers fluctuated, deteriorating rapidly after 1171 when Venetian merchants were expelled from Constantinople. The contemporary Byzantine historian Nicetas Choniates believed that the Fourth Crusade (1202–04) was organized by Doge Enrico Dandolo to avenge those who "nursed an implacable hatred against the Romans" and "looked with an avaricious eye on their goods". (From Choniates, O City of Byzantium).

WANG ANSHI (1024–85) Reform official whose seven years as Prime Minister aroused fierce controversy. To revive the Sung dynasty's revenues and military fortune, he largely replaced a mercenary army with a peasant militia, introduced government loans to peasants, delegated considerable power to clerks in provincial offices, and imposed his own Confucian commentaries on examination students. His legacy, however, was less organizational reform than decades of intense factionalism. Eventually, in the eyes of his critics, his followers were responsible for the loss of north China to Jurchen invaders.

WANG YANGMING (1472–1528) The most influential Ming thinker. In stressing the importance of a man's innate knowledge of morality over formal bookish learning, he essentially argued that any person could become a Confucian sage. His stress on the need for a clear mind, sincere will and the interiorization of Confucian values, however, was only to prepare a man for the successful application of this moral knowledge to the complicated realm of action, so that knowledge and action could become one. A respected official, successful general, critic of eunuch rule, and inspiring lecturer, he had more direct disciples than any other pre-modern Chinese thinker.

WRIT A letter bearing a terse executive order: developed under the late Anglo-Saxon kings, and later introduced by the Norman and Angevin kings of England into their French possessions.

WU, EMPRESS (728–805) The sole female sovereign in Chinese history. Born into a locally eminent clan in north central China, she entered the harem of one emperor, only to become a Buddhist nun at his death. His son, upon visiting her temple, became besotted with her, and made her his secondary concubine and then his principal wife. Soon, she was attending court audiences and controlling his decisions. At his death in 683 she retained considerable power over the two sons who in turn succeeded him. In 690 she declared herself Emperor of her own short-lived dynasty. Reviled by traditional historians, she proved an effective, if ruthless, administrator whose promotion of examination graduands reduced rival aristocrats' influence.

ZHU YUANZHANG (1344–98) Founding emperor of the Ming Dynasty and the first peasant-born emperor in China for over 1,500 years. His rise from dire poverty to the Dragon Throne saw him drive the Mongols from China and establish autocratic practices and institutions that were central to imperial rule right up to 1911. A glutton for work, he reportedly ruled on 1,660 memorials discussing 3,391 issues in one eight-day stretch. His inveterate distrust of southerners, especially scholar-officials, led to many arbitrary decisions and three extensive purges of his court from 1380 onward, just as his xenophobia prompted him to bar all Chinese from trading with foreigners.

Bibliography

Part 1

The Age of Charles Martel, P. Fouracre, London 2000
The Anglo-Saxon Missionaries in Germany, ed. and trans. C. Talbot, London 1954
The Aristocratic Families of Early Imperial China: A Case Study of the Po-ling Ts'ui Family, Patricia B. Ebrey, Cambridge University Press 1978
The Birth of Vietnam, K.W. Taylor, Berkeley 1983
Britain in the First Millennium, E. James, London 2001
Buddhism in Chinese Society: An Economic History from the Fifth to the Tenth Centuries, Jacques Gernet (trans. F. Verellen), New York: Columbia University Press 1995
Byzantine Architecture – an Introduction, C. Mango, Cambridge 1994
The Byzantine Commonwealth. Eastern Europe 500–1453, D. Obolensky, London, 1971
Byzantium: The Empire of the New Rome, C. Mango, London 1983
The Cambridge History of China, vol. 3, Sui and T'ang China, 589–906, Part I, ed. Denis C. Twitchett, Cambridge University Press 1982
The Cambridge History of Southeast Asia. Vol. I: From Early Times to c. 1800, Nicholas Tarling (ed.), Cambridge 1992
Charles the Bald, Janet L. Nelson, London 1992
Christianizing the Roman Empire, A.D. 100–400, R. MacMullen, New Haven 1994
Chronicles of the Vikings. Records, memorials and myths, R.I. Page, London 1995
Constantine VII Porphyrogenitus, De administrando imperio, ed. and trans.G. Moravcsik and R.J.H. Jenkins, Washington D.C. 1967
The Conversion of Europe. From paganism to Christianity 371–1386 AD, Richard Fletcher, London 1997
Dicuil, Liber de mensura orbis terrae, ed. and trans. J.J. Tierney, Dublin 1967
Early Christian and Byzantine Art, J. Lowden, London 1997
The early medieval Balkans. A critical survey from the sixth to the late twelfth century, J. V. A. Fine, Jr., Ann Arbor 1983
Early Medieval Ireland 400–1200, D Ó Cróinín, London 1995
Early Medieval Italy. Central power and local society, 400–1000, C. Wickham, London 1982
Early Medieval Italy, C. Wickham, London 1983
Early Medieval Spain, (2nd edn.), Roger Collins, London 1995
"The earth is our book". Geographical knowledge in the Latin West c. 400–1000, N. Lozovsky, Michigan UP 2000
Encyclopaedia of the Viking Age, John Haywood, London 2000
England and the Continent in the eighth century, W. Levison, Oxford 1946
The First Bulgarian Empire, S. Runciman, London 1930
The Fourth Book of the Chronicle of Fredegar and its continuations, J.M. Wallace-Hadrill, London 1960
France in the Making, 843–1180, (2nd edn), J. Dunbabin, Oxford 2000
The Frankish Church and the Carolingian Reforms, R. McKitterick, London 1977
Frankish Institutions under Charlemagne, F.L. Ganshof, Providence, Rhode Island 1968
The Frankish kingdoms under the Carolingians, 751–987, R. McKitterick, London 1983
Fredegar. The fourth book of the Chronicle of Fredegar and its Continuations, ed. and trans, J.M. Wallace-Hadrill, London 1962
From Durrow to Kells. The insular Gospel-books, 650–800, G. Henderson, London 1987
From Muslim Fortress to Christian Castle, T.F. Glick, Manchester UP 1995
The Germanic invasions, L. Musset, London 1975
Germany in the early middle ages, 800–1056, Timothy Reuter, London 1991
Gifts of Power: Lordship in an Early Indian State, Heitzman, James, Delhi: Oxford UP, 1997.
The Golden Peaches of Samarkand: A Study of Tang Exotics, Edward Schafer, University of California Press 1963
Greek Thought, Arabic Culture. The Graeco-Arabic Translation Movement in Baghdad and Early 'Abbasid Society (2nd–4th/8th–10th Centuries), Dimitri Gutas, London: Routledge 1998
Hagarism: The Making of the Islamic World, M. Cook and P. Crone, Cambridge 1977
History, Culture, and Region in Southeast Asian Perspectives (Rev. Edn.), O.W. Wolters, Singapore 1999
The History of Cartography I Cartography in prehistoric, ancient, and medieval Europe and the Mediterranean, J.B. Harley and David Woodward, Chicago 1987
A History of India 1, Thapar, Romila, Harmondsworth: Penguin 1965
A History of Islamic Spain, W.M. Watt, Edinburgh UP 1965
A History of South-East Asia (4th Ed.), D.G.E. Hall, London 1981
A History of the Byzantine State and Society, W. Treadgold, Stanford 1997
The Hungarians and early medieval Europe. An introduction to early medieval Hungarian history, András Róna-Tas, Budapest 1999
Indian Feudalism: c. 300–1300, R.S. Sharma, University of Calcutta Press 1965
The Indianised States of Southeast Asia, G. Goedès, Honolulu 1968
Ireland before the Normans, D Ó Corrín, Dublin 1972
Islam, F. Rahman, University of Chicago Press 1979
Islamic Art and Architecture, R. Hillenbrand, London 1999)
Islamic History: A Framework for Inquiry, R. Stephen Humphreys, New York: I.B. Tauris 1991
Kings and kingship in early Scotland, M.O. Anderson, Edinburgh 1973
Late Antiquity. A Guide to the post-classical world, eds. G.W. Bowersock, Peter Brown and Oleg Grabar, Cambridge, Mass. and London 1999
Late Merovingian France. History and Hagiography, 640–720, P. Fouracre and R. Gerberding, Manchester 1996
The Making of Early Medieval India, B. D. Chattopadhyaya, Oxford University Press 1994
The Making of Orthodox Byzantium, M. Whittow, London 1996
Mapping Time and Space. How medieval Mapmakers viewed their world, Evelyn Edson, London 1997
Maritime Trade and State Development in Early Southeast Asia, K.F. Hall, Honolulu 1985
Medieval Scandinavia, Birgit and Peter Sawyer, Madison, Wisconsin 1993
The Merovingian kingdoms, 450–751, I.N. Wood, London 1994
The Missionary Life. Saints and the evangelisation of Europe 400–1050, Ian Wood, Harlow 2001
Moorish Spain, R. Fletcher, London 1992
The Mountains and the City. The Tuscan Appennines in the early middle ages, C. Wickham, Oxford 1988
Muslims. Their Religious beliefs and Practices (2 volumes), A. Rippin, Routledge 1991
Muslim Kingship, Aziz al-Azmeh, London 1997
Muslim Spain and Portugal, H. Kennedy, Longman 1996
The New Cambridge Medieval History II c. 700–c.900, ed. R. McKitterick, Cambridge 1995
The New Cambridge Medieval History III c. 900–c.1024, ed. T. Reuter, Cambridge 1999
The New Islamic Dynasties: A Chronological and Genealogical Manual, Clifford Edmund Bosworth, Edinburgh UP 1996
The Origins of France, E. James, London 1982
The Oxford Dictionary of the Christian Church, 3rd edn, E. Livingstone, Oxford 1997
The Oxford illustrated history of the Vikings, ed. P. Sawyer, Oxford 1998
Pagans and Christians in late Antiquity. A sourcebook, A.D. Lee, London 2000
Patterns of Power in early Wales, Wendy Davies, Oxford 1990
The Plan of St Gall, W. Horn and E. Born, Berkeley, Los Angeles and London 1979
The Prophet and the Age of the Caliphates, H. Kennedy, London 1986
The Republic of St Peter. The birth of the papal state, 680–825, T.F.-X. Noble, Philadelphia 1984
The Rise of Cities in North-west Europe, A. Verhulst, Cambridge 1999
Rome. Profile of a City, 312–1308, (2nd edn), R. Krautheimer, Princeton 2000
Rule of Benedict, trans. Justin McCann, 1954
Scandinavian Scotland, Barbara Crawford, Leicester 1987
Scotland: the making of the kingdom, A.A.M. Duncan, Edinburgh 1975
The Shaping of 'Abbasid Rule, Jacob Lassner, Princeton University Press 1980
The Short Oxford History of Europe: the early Middle Ages, ed. Rosamond Mckitterick, Oxford 2001
Soldiers of Christ, Saints and Saints' Lives from late antiquity and the early middle ages, eds. and trans.T.F.X. Noble and T. Head, Pennsylvania 1995
State and society in the early middle ages. The middle Rhine valley, 400–1000, Matthew Innes, Cambridge 2000
The struggle for power in medieval Italy, G. Tabacco, Cambridge 1989
Studies in Medieval Islamic Art, ed. O. Grabar, Aldershot: Variorum 1976
Three Christian capitals. Topography and politics. Rome, Constantinople and Milan, Richard Krautheimer, Berkeley 1983
Towns and trade in the age of Charlemagne, R. Hodges, London 2000
The Vikings (2nd edn), E. Roesdahl, London 1998
Viking Age Iceland, Jesse Byock, London 2001
The Viking-Age rune-stones. Custom and commemoration in early medieval Scandinavia, Birgit Sawyer, Oxford 2000
The Viking World, James Graham-Campbell, London 1980
Wales in the early Middle Ages, Wendy Davies, Leicester 1982
Warlords and holy men: Scotland AD 80–1000, A.P. Smyth, London 1984

Part II

A History of Illuminated Manuscripts, C. de Hamel, Oxford: Phaidon 1986
African Civilisations (2nd edn), G. Connah, Cambridge UP 2001
Al Hind: The Making of the Indo-Islamic World, Volume 2:
Sufis of Bijapur 1300–1700 Social Roles of Sufis in Medieval India, R. Eaton, Princeton University Press 1978
Alexios I Komnenos, M. Mullett and D. Smyth, Belfast 1996
Ancient Ethiopia, D. Phillipson, London: British Museum Press 1998
Ancient Ghana and Mali, N. Levtzion, London:Methuen 1973
Arab Historians of the Crusades, trans. Francesco Gabrieli, London: Routledge and Kegan Paul 1978
"Archaeological evidence for the development of urbanization of Kiev from the eighth to the fourteenth centuries", O.M. Ioannisyan, in D. Austin and L. Alcock (eds), *From the Baltic to the Black Sea: Studies in medieval archaeology*, London 1990, pp. 285-312.
Ars Sacra 800–1200 (2nd edn), P. Lasko, New Haven and London: Yale UP 1994
The Byzantine Empire, 1025–1204, M.Angold, London and New York 1997
Byzantium and Bulgaria, R. Browning, London 1975
Byzantium and the Crusader States, R.-J. Lilie, Oxford 1993
Byzantium's Balkan Frontier. A political study of the northern Balkans, 900–1204, P. Stephenson, Cambridge 2000
The Cambridge Economic History of Europe I (2nd edn), ed. M.M. Postan, Cambridge 1966
The Cambridge Economic History of Europe II (2nd edn), eds. M.M. Postan and E. Miller, Cambridge 1987
The Cambridge Economic History of Europe III, eds. M.M. Postan, E.E. Rich and E. Miller, Cambridge 1963
The Cambridge History of Early Inner Asia, ed. D. Sinor, Cambridge University Press 1990
The Cambridge History of Egypt. Volume 1, Islamic Egypt, 640–1517, ed. Carl Petry, Cambridge University Press 1998
The Cambridge History of Iran, V. The Saljuq and Mongol Periods, ed. J.A. Boyle, Cambridge University Press 1968
The Cambridge History of Iran, VI. The Timurid and Safavid Periods, eds. P. Jackson and L. Lockhart, Cambridge University Press 1986
Capetian France, 987–1328 (2nd edn), E.M. Hallam and J. Everard, London 2001
Cathedrals of Europe, A. Prache, Ithaca and London, Cornell University Press 1999
The coming of the friars, R.B. Brooke, 1975
Commerce and Society in Sung China, Shiba, Yoshinobu, Center for Chinese Studies, University of Michigan 1970
The Commercial Revolution of the Middle Ages 950–1350, R.S. Lopez, London 1971
The common legal past of Europe 1000–1800, M. Bellomo, trans. Lydia Cochrane, Washington 1995
Culture and Conquest in Mongol Eurasia, Thomas T. Allsen, Cambridge UP 2001
Daily Life in China on the Eve of the Mongol Invasion, Gernet, Jacques, Stanford UP 1970
The Delhi Sultanate: A Political and Military History, Peter Jackson, Cambridge UP 1999
East Central Europe in the Middle Ages, 1000–1500, J. W. Sedlar 1994
The emergence of Rus, 750-1200, Jonathan Shepard and Simon Franklin, London 1966
The Empire of Manuel I Komnenos, 1143–1180, P. Magdalino, Cambridge 1993
The Empire of the Mahdi. The Rise of the Fatimids, Heinz Halm, trans. Michael Bonner, Leiden: E.J. Brill 1996
England under the Norman and Angevin Kings, 1075–1225, R. Bartlett, Oxford 2000
Anglo-Norman England 1066–1166, M. Chibnall, Oxford: Blackwells 1986
The entry of the Slavs into Christendom: an introduction to the medieval history of the Slavs, A.P. Vlasto, Cambridge, 1970
"European Russia, c. 500–c. 1050", T. Noonan, in T. Reuter (ed.), *The New Cambridge Medieval History, c. 900–c. 1050*, Cambridge 2000, pp. 487-513.
The Fall of Srivijaya in Malay History, O.W. Wolters, Ithaca 1970
The Feudal Transformation 900–1200, J.-P. Poly and E. Bournazel, trans. C. Higgitt, New York and London 1991
The first European revolution c. 970–1215, R.I. Moore, Blackwells 2000
Four Studies on the History of Central Asia, vol. I, W. Barthold, trans. V. and T. Minorsky, Leiden: Brill 1956–62
Four Studies on the History of Central Asia, W. Barthold, trans. V. and T. Minorsky, Leiden: Brill 1956–62
France in the Making 843–1180 (2nd edn), J. Dunbabin, Oxford 2000
Geography, technology, and war. Studies in the maritime history of the Mediterranean 649–1571, John H. Pryor, Cambridge 1988
Germany in the High Middle Ages c. 1050–1200, H. Fuhrmann, Cambridge 1995
The Growth of the Medieval City, D. Nicholas, London 1997
The History of English Law, F. Maitland, London 1898
History of Poland (2nd ed), A. Gieysztor et al., 1979
The History of the Mongol Conquests, J.J. Saunders, Routledge and Kegan Paul 1971
Holy Land pilgrimage in the later Roman Empire, A.D. 312–460, E.D. Hunt, Oxford 1982
Illuminating the Law. Legal manuscripts in Cambridge Collections, Cambridge, Fitzwilliam Museum, 3rd November–16th December, 2001, S. L'Engle and R. Gibbs, London: Harvey Miller 2001
The Illustrated Beatus. A corpus of the illustrations of the Commentary on the apocalypse, vols I, II and III, John Williams, London 1994 and 1998
The Italian city-republics, D. Waley, Harlow 1988
The Italian City-State, P. Jones, Oxford 1997
Jerusalem pilgrimages before the Crusades, J. Wilkinson, Warminster 1977
The Khmers, Ian Mabbett and David Chandler, Oxford 1995
Pagan: the Origins of Modern Burma, Michael Aung-Thwin, Honolulu 1985
La production du livre universitaire au moyen age. Exemplar et pecia, L. Bataillon, B.G. Guyot and R.H. Rouse, Paris 1988
The Late Medieval Balkans. A critical survey from the late twelfth century to the Ottoman conquest, J. V. A. Fine, Jr, Ann Arbor 1987

The Making of Gratian's Decretum, A. Winroth, Cambridge 2000

The Making of the Slavs, Florin Curta, Cambridge 2002

The Mamluks in Egyptian Politics and Society, eds. Thomas Phillip and Ulrich Haarmann, Cambridge University Press 1998

Mapping Time and Space. How medieval Mapmakers viewed their world, Evelyn Edison, London 1997

Mediaeval Isma'ili History and Thought, ed. Farhad Daftary, Cambridge University Press 1996

Medieval Art. Painting. Sculpture. Architecture. 4th–14th Century, J. Snyder, New York, Harry N. Abrams, Inc. 1989

Medieval Canon Law, James A. Brundage, London and New York 1995

Medieval Germany 1056–1273 (2nd ed.), A. Haverkamp 1994

Medieval Germany, 500–1300. A political interpretation, B. Arnold 1997

Medieval Heresy. Popular movements from Bogomil to Hus (2nd edn), M.D. Lambert 1992

Medieval monasticism, forms of religious life in Western Europe in the Middle Ages (2nd edn), C.H. Lawrence, London 1989

Medieval Persia 1040–1797, D.O. Morgan, Longman 1988

The Medieval Town, E. Ennen, Amsterdam 1979

The Middle East in the Middle Ages: The Early Mamluk Sultanate 1250–1382, Robert Irwin, London: Croom Helm 1986

Money and its Use in Medieval Europe, P. Spufford, Cambridge 1988

The Mongols, David Morgan, Oxford: Blackwell 1986

New Towns of the Middle Ages, M. Beresford, London 1967

The papacy 1073–1198, I.S. Robinson, Oxford 1990

Papal Envoys to the Great Khans, Igor De Rachewiltz, Faber 1971

The papal monarchy, C. Morris 1989

Parisian scholars in the early 14th century. A social portrait, W.J. Courtenay, Cambridge 1999

The Pictorial Arts of the West 800–1200, C.R. Dodwell, New Haven and London, Yale 1993

The Pilgrim's guide to Santiago de Compostela, Annie Shaver-Crandell and Paula Gerson, London 1995

The Political Development of the British Isles 1100–1400, R. Frame, Oxford 1990

Pre-Ottoman Turkey, Claude Cahen, London: Sidgwick and Jackson 1968

Realm of St Stephen: a history of medieval Hungary, 895–1526, P. Engel and A. Ayton, 2001

The Rise and Rule of Tamerlane, B.F. Manz, Cambridge University Press 1989

The rise of Christian Russia, A. Poppe, London 1982

Roman Law in Europan History, Peter Stein, Cambridge 1999

Roman roads, Raymond Chevalier, London 1989

Rural Economy and Country Life in the Medieval West, G. Duby, London 1962

"Rus", Simon Franklin, in D. Abulafia (ed.), *The New Cambridge Medieval History V* 1198-1300, Cambridge 1999, pp. 796-808.

Saladin. The Politics of the Holy War, Malcolm Cameron Lyons and D.E.P. Jackson, Cambridge University Press 1995

Scholastic humanism and the unification of Europe. 1 Foundations. 2. The heroic age, R. Southern, Oxford 1995

Sermons and rhetoric of Kievan Rus, Simon Franklin (trans), London 1991

The seven liberal arts in the Middle ages, eds. R. Southern and D.L. Wagner, Bloomington, Indiana 1984

The Slave Kings and the Islamic Conquest, 11th–13th centuries, André Wink, Leiden: E.J. Brill 1990

Southeast Asia in the 9th to 14th centuries, David Marr & A.C. Milner (eds.), Singapore 1986

Statesmen and Gentlemen: The Elite of Fu-chou, Chiang-hsi, in Northern and Southern Sung, Robert Hyam, Cambridge 1986

The Thorny Gates of Learning in Sung China: A Social History of Examinations, Chafee, John, Cambridge 1985

Universities in the Middle Ages, A History of the University in Europe 1, ed. H. Ridder-Symoens, Cambridge 1992

War-horse and Elephant in the Delhi Sutlanate, Simon Digby, Oxford University Press 1971

Where Kings and Gods Meet: The Royal Centre of Vijayanagara, India, John Fritz, George Michell and Nagaraja Rao, University of Arizona Press 1984

Writing, society and culture in early Rus c. 950–1300, Simon Franklin, Cambridge 2002

Part III

1587, A Year of No Significance, Huang, Ray, Newhaven 1981

A Byzantine Government in Exile: Government and Society under the Laskarids of Nicaea, 1204–1261, M. Angold, Oxford 1975

A Comparative Study of Thirty City-State Cultures, ed. M.H. Hansen, Copenhagen 2000

A history of the Hussite revolution, H. Kaminsky, 1967

A Ming Society, in the Fourteenth to Seventeenth Centuries, Dardess, John W., Los Angeles 1996

A Short History of Switzerland, E. Bonjour, H.S. Offler and G.R. Potter, Westport: Greenwood 1985

Abraham Ortelius and the first Atlas, eds. M.P.R. van den Broek, P. van der Krogt and P. Meurer, Houten 1999

African Civilisations (2nd edn), G. Connah, Cambridge University Press 2001

The Archaeology of Islam, T. Insoll, Oxford: Blackwells 1999

Ars Nova and the Renaissance, New Oxford History of Europe, 1300–1540, eds. Dom Anselm Hughes and Gerald Abraham, Oxford 1960 and 1998

The Art and Architecture of China, L. Sickman and A. Soper, Harmondsworth 1956

The Art and Architecture of Islam 1250–1800, S.S. Blair and J.M. Bloom, New Haven and London: Yale University Press 1994

"Astronomy in Christian Latin Europe, c. 500–c.1150", Bruce Eastwood, Journal for the History of Astronomy 28, 1997: pp. 235–58.

Barcelona and its rulers, 1096–1291, S. Bensch, Cambridge 1995

Before Columbus, F. Fernández-Armesto, Macmillan 1987

The Berbers and the Islamic State. The Marinid Experience in pre-Protectorate Morocco, Maya Shatzmiller, Princeton: Markus Wiener Publishers 2000

Black Death Transformed, Samuel Cohn Jr., Arnold: London 2002

The Black Death, trans. and ed. Rosemary Horrox, Manchester Medieval Sources Series, Manchester 1994

The Burgundian Netherlands, W. Prevenier and W. Blockmans, Cambridge 1986

"Carolingian Musicæ", Susan Rankin, in *Carolingian Culture: emulation and innovation*, ed. R. McKitterick, Cambridge, 1994, pp. 274–316.

Celestial treasury. From the music of the spheres to the conquest of space, Marc Lachièze-Rey and Jean-Pierre Luminet, trans. Joe Laredo, Cambridge 2001

Christians and Jews in the twelfth-century Renaissance, A.S. Abulafia, Routledge 1995

The commercial revolution in the Middle Ages, R.S. Lopez, Englewood Cliffs, NJ 1971

Commercio e navigazione nel Medioevo, M. Tangheroni, Rome-Bari 1996

The Confusions of Pleasure, Commerce and Culture in Ming China, Brook, Timothy, Los Angeles 1998

The Court of Burgundy: Studies in the History of Civilization, Otto Cartellieri, New York: Haskell 1970

The early Middle ages to 1300, New Oxford history of Music 2 (new edn), eds. Richard Crocker and David Hiley, Oxford and New York 1990

The Early Palaeologan Renaissance (1261–1360), E.Fryde, Leiden 2000

Emperor Michael Palaeologus and the West, 1258–1282, D.J. Geanakoplos, Cambridge (Mass.) 1959

England's Jewish solution, R Mundill, CUP 1998

Frederick II, a medieval emperor (3rd ed.), D. Abulafia, Pimlico 2002

The formation of Muscovy, 1304–1613, R.O. Crummey, Boston 1987

The fur trade and its significance for medieval Russia, J. Martin, Cambridge 1986

Genoa and the Genoese, S.A. Epstein, Chapel Hill UNC Press 1996

Germany in the late middle ages, J. Leuschner, 1980

Germany in the later middle ages, F.R.H. Du Boulay, 1983

Greek Thought. Arabic culture, The Graeco-Arabic translation movement in Baghdad and early Abbasid society, D. Gutas, London 1998

The growth of the law in medieval Russia, D.H. Kaiser, 1980

A History of modern Indonesia since 1200 (3rd edn.), M.C. Ricklefs, Houndmills 2001

The growth of the law in medieval Russia, D.H. Kaiser, 1980

The Image of the World. 20 centuries of World Maps, Peter Whitfield, London 1994

Imperial China, 900–1800, Mote, F.W., Cambridge, Mass. 1999

Islamic Spain, 1250-1500, LP Harvey, U of Chicago 1991

The Italian City-State, P.J. Jones, Oxford 1997

The Italian City Republics (3rd ed.), D.P. Waley, Harlow 1988

Italy in the age of Dante and Petrarch, J. Larner, Harlow 1980

The Jews of Europe after the Black Death, A. Foa, Berkeley, U. of California Press 2000

The Jews of Spain, J Gerber, Free Press, NY 1991

Kingdoms and Communities in Western Europe 900–1300 (2nd ed.), S. Reynolds, Oxford 1997

Kinship and politics: the making of the Muscovite political system, 1345–1547, N.S. Kollmann

The last centuries of Byzantium, 1261–1453 (2nd edn), D. Nicol, Cambridge 1993

The late medieval Balkans. A critical survey from the late twelfth century to the Ottoman conquest, J.V.A. Fine, Jr, Ann Arbor 1987

Later Medieval France: the Polity, P. S. Lewis, London 1968

The Legacy of Muslim Spain, ed. Salma Khadra Jayyusi, Leiden: E.J. Brill 1992

Levant trade in the later Middle Ages, E. Ashtor, Princeton, NJ 1983

A Mediterranean Emporium: the Catalan kingdom of Majorca, D. Abulafia, Cambridge 1994

A Mediterranean Society, vol. 1, economic foundations, SD Goitein, Berkeley, U. of California Press 1967

Mapmakers of the 16th century, Robert W. Karrow, Chicago 1993

The mapping of the World, R.W. Shirley, London 1983

Medicine for the Soul: the Life, Death and Resurrection of an English Medieval Hospital: St. Gile's, Norwich, c. 1249–1550, Carole Rawcliffe, Sutton: Stroud 1999

The medieval expansion of Europe (2nd ed.), J.R.S. Phillips, Oxford 1998

Medieval listening and reading: the primary reception of German literature 800–1300, D.H. Green, Cambridge 1994

Medieval Parliaments: a Comparative Study, A. Marongiu, London 1968

Medieval Russia 980–1584, J. Martin, Cambridge, 1995

Medieval Scandinavia : From Conversion to Reformation, circa 800–1500, Birgit and Peter Sawyer, London: University of Minnesota Press 1993

Mehmed the Conqueror and his Time, Franz Babinger, Princeton University Press 1978

Music at the Court of Burgundy 1364–1419: A Documentary History, C. Wright, Henryville: Institute of Medieval Music 1979

Muslim Spain and Portugal. A Political History of al-Andalus, Hugh Kennedy, London: Longman 1996

The New Cambridge Medieval History V, ed. David Abulafia, Cambridge University Press 1999

The New Cambridge Medieval History VI, ed. Michael Jones, Cambridge University Press 2000

The New Cambridge Medieval History VII, c. 1415–c. 1500, ed. C. Allmand, Cambridge 1998

The Northern Crusade: The Baltic and the Catholic Frontier 1100–1525 (2nd edn), Eric Christiansen, Harmondsworth 1997

Northern Renaissance Art. Painting, Sculpture, the Graphic Arts from 1350 to 1575, J. Snyder, New York, Harry N. Abrams Inc. 1985

The organ in western culture, 750–1250, Peter Williams, Cambridge 1993

Les Origines et la formation de la littérature courtoise en Occident (500–1200), Reto R. Bezzola, Paris 1944–63

Roger II of Sicily, H Houben, CUP 2002

Ortelius' Atlas maps: an illustrated guide, M.P.R. van den Broek, Houten 1996

The Ottoman Empire 1300-1481, Colin Imber, Istanbul, The Isis Press 1990

The Ottoman Empire. The classical age, 1300–1600, H. Inalcik, London 1973

Piety and Charity in Late Medieval Florence, John Henderson, Chicago University Press 1997

The Political Development of the British Isles, 1100–1400, R. Frame, Oxford 1990

Political Life in Medieval England, 1300–1450, W.M. Ormrod, Basingstoke 1995

Popes and Princes, 1417–1517: Politics and Piety in the Late Medieval Church, J.A.F. Thomson, London, Boston, and Sydney 1980

The Popes at Avignon, 1305–1378, G. Mollat, London 1963

Prince Henry "the Navigator", P. Russell, Newhaven 2000

"The principalities of Rus' in the fourteenth century", N.S. Kollmann, in M. Jones (ed.), *The New Cambridge Medieval History VI 1300–1415* Cambridge 2000

The problem of a Catalan Mediterranean Empire (English Historical Review, suppl. No.8), J. Hillgarth, Harlow 1976

Public reading and the reading public in late medieval England and France, Joyce Coleman, Cambridge 1996

The realm of St. Stephen. A history of medieval Hungary, 895–1526, P. Engel, London 2001

Religion and Devotion in Europe, c.1215–c.1515, R.N. Swanson, Cambridge 1995

Religious violence between Christians and Jews, ed. A.S. Abulafia, Palgrave 2002

The Rise of the Fiscal State in Europe 1200–1815, ed. R. Bonney, Oxford 1999

Rome reborn: the Vatican Library and Renaissance Culture, ed. Anthony Grafton, New Haven 1993

Rulers and nobles in fifteenth century Muscovy, G. Alef, London, 1983

"Russia", N.S. Kollmann, in C. Allmand (ed.), *The New Cambridge Medieval History VII 1415–1500*, Cambridge, 1998

Science and thought in the 15th century, Lynn Thorndike, New York 1929

The Sicilian Vespers, S. Runciman, Cambridge 1958

Southeast Asia in the Age of Commerce, 1450-1680 (2 Vols.), Anthony Reid, New Haven 1988 & 1993

Spain in the Middle Ages, A Mackay, London 1977

The Spanish Kingdoms, 1250-1517 (2 vols), J. Hillgarth, Oxford 1976–8

The Swahili, M. Horton and J. Middleton, Oxford: Blackwells 2000

Time in history, G.J. Whitrow, Oxford 1989

Thailand: A Short History, D.K. Wyatt, New Haven 1984

Trade and Empire in the Atlantic, 1400-1600, D. Birmingham, Routledge 2000

'Trade and Islam on the River Niger', T. Insoll, Archaeology, Nov/Dec 2000: pp. 48–52.

Trade and traders in Muslim Spain, O.R. Constable, Cambridge 1994

Venice: a maritime republic, F.C. Lane, Baltimore, MD 1973

The Two Italies, D. Abulafia, Cambridge 1977

War, Justice and Public Order: England and France in the Later Middle Ages, R. W. Kaeuper, Oxford 1988

The Western Church in the Later Middle Ages, F. Oakley, Ithaca and London 1979

Western plainchant. A handbook, David Hiley, Oxford 1993

Index

Picture Credits

All reasonable efforts have been made by the Publisher to trace the copyright holders of the photographs contained in this publication. In the event that a copyright holder of a photograph has not been traced, but comes forward after the publication of this edition, the Publishers will endeavour to rectify the position at the earliest opportunity.

AA&Acollection = Ancient Art and Architecture Collection Ltd, London
l = left; r = right; t = top; b = below

2 by permission of the Syndics of Cambridge University Library; **6 (from top to bottom)** Museo del Duomo, Cividale del Friuli, Italy/Roger-Viollet, Paris/Bridgeman Art Library; Church of San Ambrogio; akg-images; Topkapı Palace Museum; Germanisches Nationalmuseum, Nuremberg; **7 (from top to bottom)** Michael Holford; Hirmer Fotoarchiv Munich; National Palace Museum, Taipei, Taiwan, Republic of China; Hutchison Library; Werner Forman Archive/Beijing Museum, Beijing; **8 (from top to bottom)** 1990, Photo Scala, Florence; akg-images/Erich Lessing; Bildarchiv Steffens/Henri Stierlin; The British Museum; Staatsbibliothek Bamberg, Msc.Lit.6, fol. 48v; **10** akg-images; **12** Domkapitel Aachen, photo by Pit Siebigs; **13** akg-images; **14** akg-images/Jean-Louis Nou; **17** Biblioteca Medicea Laurenziana, Florence, ms. S. Marco 190, c.74r (with permission of Ministero per i Beni e le Attività Culturali); **18** akg-images; **19** The Bodleian Library, University of Oxford, MS Pococke 375 fols. 3v-4r; **20–21** 1990, Photo Scala, Florence; **22** akg-images/Erich Lessing; **24** Cathedral Treasury, Monza; **27** Museo Arqueologico, Madrid; **29** Bildarchiv Steffens/Abdelaziz Frikha; **30** AA&Acollection; **32** Biblioteca Apostolica Vaticana (Vatican), Vat. Reg. Lat. 316; **34** Museo del Duomo, Cividale del Friuli, Italy/Roger-Viollet, Paris/Bridgeman Art Library; **40** Bayerishche Staatsbiblothek, Munich; **43** Rijksarchief te Gent, photo by Noel van Cleven; **44** Universiteitsbibliotheek Utrecht; **45** akg-images/Erich Lessing; **47** Church of San Ambrogio; **49** Schatzkammer der Residenz, Munich; **53** Cliché Bibliothèque nationale de France, Paris; **54** akg-images/Jean-Louis Nou; **56** The British Museum; **59** The British Library; **60** The Trustees of the National Museums of Scotland; **63** The Board of Trinity College Dublin; **64** e.t. archive; **66** Robert Harding Picture Library; **70** Kunsthistorisches Museum, Wien oder KHM, Wien; **72** AA&Acollection/Chris Hellier; **74** 2003, Photo Scala, Florence/HIP; **75** AA&Acollection/R. Sheridan; **76** akg-images; **77** Diözesanmuseum Limburg; **78** 1990, Photo Scala, Florence; **84** Bildarchiv Steffens/Ladislav Janicek, Mainz; **85 (l)** Sonia Halliday Photographs **(r)** Topkapı Palace Museum; **86** Daud Ali; **89** Philip Parker; **90** AA&Acollection/A.Eaton; **92** Werner Forman Archive, Christian Deydier, London; **94** Photo J. Nober, Ruhrlandmuseum Essen; **95 (t)** akg-images **(b)** Bayersiche Staatsbibliothek, Munich; **98** Fitzwilliam Museum, Cambridge; **100** Germanisches Nationalmuseum, Nuremberg; **101** Domkapitel Aachen, photo by Ann Münchow; **102–103** akg-images/Dirk Radzinski; **106–107** e.t. archive; **109** akg-images; **110** Cliché Bibliothèque nationale de France, Paris; **111** by permission of the Masters and Fellows of Sidney Sussex College, Cambridge; **112** Staatsbibliothek Bamberg; **113** by permission of the Syndics of Cambridge University Library; **116** The Master and Fellows of Trinity College Cambridge; **118** Robert Harding Picture Library; **120** The Viking Ship Museum, Denmark, photo by Werner Karrasch; **122** akg-images/Jean-Paul Dumontier; **124** The Master and Fellows of Trinity College Cambridge; **126** Biblioteca Apostolica Vaticana (Vatican); **128** akg-images; **129** The British Museum; **130** Cliché Bibliothèque nationale de France, Paris; **132** akg-images; **133** Tour Ferrande – Pernes les Fontaines (France), photo by F. Vachet; **134** 1990, Photo Scala, Florence; **136** Országos Széchényi Könyvtár; **137** FOTO STUDIO H, Czech Republic; **140** Biblioteca Apostolica Vaticana (Vatican); **141** The British Library; **142–143** Staatliche Museen zu Berlin – Preussischer Kulturbesitz, Museum für Islamische Kunst; **146** Robin Constable/Hutchison Picture Library; **147** Hutchison Picture Library; **148** akg-images; **150** akg-images/British Library; **154 (t)** Staatliche Museen zu Berlin – Preussischer Kulturbesitz (Jörg P. Anders)/bpk 2003 **(b)** with the permission of the Master and Fellows of Trinity Hall, Cambridge; **155** Cliché Bibliothèque nationale de France, Paris; **156** R. Sheridan/AA&Acollection; **157** 1990, Photo Scala, Florence; **158** Hirmer Fotoarchiv Munich; **159** akg-images; **162 (l)** akg-images/Erich Lessing **(r)** akg-images/Rabatti-Dominigie; **163** akg-images/Jean-Francois Amelot; **164** 1990, Photo Scala, Florence; **165** The British Library; **167** AA&Acollection/Kadakawa; **168** Werner Forman Archive/Biblioteca Nazionale, Venice; **169** Icon Gallery, Ohrid; **170** The British Museum; **172–173** National Palace Museum, Taipei, Taiwan, Republic of China; **179** F. Jack Jackson; **181** AA&Acollection/Kadokawa; **183** The Conway Library, Courtauld Institute of Art, photo by Robert Byron; **184** Hutchison Library; **187** J. Worker/AA&Acollection; **189** D. Matherly/AA&Acollection; **190** Werner Forman Archive/Beijing Museum, Beijing; **192** Robert Aberman/Hutchison Picture Library; **194–195** Château-Musée, Ville de Saumur, photo by Christophe Petiteau – Montévidéo; **197 (t)** R. Ashworth/AA&A Collection **(b)** akg-images; **198** akg-images; **201** Library of The National Museum, Prague; **204–205** akg-images/Claudia Quaukies; **206** akg-images; **208** AA&A Collection; **211** Diebold-Schilling-Chronik 1513 ZHB Luzern (Eigentum Korporation); **212–213** 1990, Photo Scala, Florence; **214** 1990, Photo Scala, Florence; **218** the Masters of the Bench of the Inner Temple, London; **219** The British Library; **220** 1993, Photo Scala, Florence; **222** Austrian National Library; **224** Print Collection, Miriam and Ira D. Wallach, Division of Art, Prints and Photographs, The New York Public Library; **226 (t)** The British Library **(b)** Rheinisches Bildarchiv Köln: Stadt Köln; **229** akg-images/Erich Lessing; **230–231** Oronoz fotógrafos; **232** Bildarchiv Steffens/Henri Stierlin; **235** Bristol Record Office; **237** Fremdenverkehrsamt Regensburg; **238** Oronoz fotógrafos; **240** Sonia Halliday Photographs; **242 (t)** National Gallery London **(b)** by kind permission of the Provost and Scholars of King's College, Cambridge, photo by Tim Rawle; **243** J. Lynch/AA&Acollection; **244** Universitätsbibliothek Giessen; **245 (t)** Brussels, Royal Library of Belgium, 9243 (vol. II), f.1 **(b)** Cliché Bibliothèque nationale de France, Paris; **246** Bildarchiv Steffens/Henri Stierlin; **248** Werner Forman Archive; **251** R. Sheridan/AA&Acollection; **254** Fitzwilliam Museum, Cambridge; **255** Oronoz fotógrafos; **256** National Palace Museum Taiwan; **258** Formerly the property of University of Bristol; **260** The British Museum; **261** by permission of the Syndics of Cambridge University Library; **262** M. Jones/AA&Acollection; **264** Spencer Collection, The New York Public Library; **266** Robert D. Fiala; **268** Werner Forman Archive; **270** Whipple Museum of the History of Science, Cambridge University; **271** Herzog August Bibliothek Wolfenbüttel, Cod. Guelf. 85.1., 1 Aug. 2°, 3 recto; **272 (l)** University of Aberdeen **(r)** Sonia Halliday Photographs, photo by Jane Taylor; **274** akg-images; **276–277** The British Library; **278** Biblioteca Geral da Universidade de Coimbra, Portugal, Ms. 314; **280** Civico Museo Bibliografico Musicale; **282** Lebrecht Music Collection; **283** Staatsbibliothek Bamberg, Msc.Lit.6, fol. 48v; **286–287** by permission of the Syndics of Cambridge University Library